SOCIAL JUSTICE FEMINISTS

in the United States and Germany

Social Justice Feminists

in the United States and Germany

A Dialogue in Documents, 1885–1933

Edited by Kathryn Kish Sklar,

Anja Schüler, and Susan Strasser

CORNELL UNIVERSITY PRESS

ITHACA AND LONDON

Financial support for this book was provided by the
German Historical Institute, Washington, D.C.

First published 1998 by Cornell University Press
First printing, Cornell Paperbacks, 1998

Printed in the United States of America

Library of Congress Cataloging-in-Publication Data

Social justice feminists in the United States and Germany : a dialogue in documents,
1885–1933 / edited by Kathryn Kish Sklar, Anja Schüler, Susan Strasser.
p. cm.
Includes bibliographical references and index.
ISBN 0-8014-8469-3 (pbk. : alk. paper)
1. Women social reformers—United States—History. 2. Women social reformers—
Germany—History. 3. Middle class women—United States—History. 4. Middle class
women—Germany—History. 5. Political culture—United States—History.
6. Political culture—Germany—History. I. Sklar, Kathryn Kish. II Schüler, Anja.
III. Strasser, Susan.
HQ1419.S65   1998
305.42'0973—dc21   98-16972

Paperback printing   10 9 8 7 6 5 4 3 2 1

*To the memory of the women who
sustained this transatlantic dialogue*

Contents

Illustrations

Acknowledgments

We are grateful for the multiple sources of funding that supported our work on this book over several years. After meeting in Berlin in 1991, Kitty Sklar and Anja Schüler conceived the book in Washington, D.C., in 1992, where Anja was working on her dissertation with support from the German Academic Exchange Service, and Kitty was a Fellow at the Woodrow Wilson International Center for Scholars. They interested Susan Strasser in the project when she was a Fellow at the German Historical Institute in Washington, D.C. Kitty worked on the book during a memorable year at the National Humanities Center, Research Triangle Park, North Carolina, in 1995–96.

The assistance of the German Historical Institute in Washington, D.C., was central to the making of this book. The endorsement and support of two directors, Hartmut Lehmann and Detlef Junker, made the project possible; Daniel Mattern and Manfred Boemeke facilitated the Institute's participation. Luzie Nahr and Iris Golumbeck helped us track down sources and valuable bibliographical information.

Sally Robertson and Tammy Huck provided expert translation support; Corinna Hörst and Beate Popkin contributed to the translation of many other documents. Transcription help came from Pamela Abraham, Rolf Ahrens, Unsal Cahit Basar, Julia Bruggemann, Rick Doyle, and Dorothea Germer.

Eileen Boris, Christiane Harzig, Nancy Reagin, Ruth Rosen, and Barbara Sicherman read versions of the manuscript and provided us with invaluable advice. Gisela Brinker-Gabler read the manuscript more than once, furnishing inspiration as well as much helpful guidance.

Victoria Brown provided information on Mary Rozet Smith. Leila Rupp helped us identify many European women mentioned in the dialogue. Sophie de Schaepdrijver helped with information on Belgian, Dutch, and other European women. Adriane Feustel supplied a photograph of Alice Salomon. Mary Beth Norton helped with the Cauer article. Suzanne Sinke gave us biographical information on Dutch women. Peter Agree of Cornell University Press encouraged the book's development as well as its progress to publication. Andrew Lewis provided astute copyediting. Michelle Mioff and Kari Wimbish aided mightily with copyediting and page proofreading. Kathleen Babbitt created an excellent index.

The staffs of the Swarthmore College Peace Collection, the Social Welfare History Archives at the University of Minnesota, the archives at the University of Colorado at Boulder, and the Leo Baeck Institute in New York City helped with many requests.

Manfred Berg generously shared his knowledge of German history. Tom Dublin cooked for us. Bob Guldin helped with the title.

Our greatest thanks go to each other. This has been a collaboration forged by hard work, laughter, and good meals; it has seen us each through major events in other parts of our lives. Our friendship and our respect for each other's talents, skills, and knowledge have ripened as our book has developed.

K. K. S.
A. S.
S. S.

Editorial Note

We have silently changed punctuation and paragraph breaks to make the documents more readable. Misspellings have been retained and noted, except in the case of Florence Kelley's name, which was so often misspelled that we have decided to correct it. German spellings of place names have been translated into English.

All proper names have been annotated. Where we have been unable to obtain biographical information, this has been noted. In document footnotes, we have provided short biographical notations about people mentioned but not central to the ongoing discussions between German and American women reformers. Biographies of the central figures appear in the Biographical Notes; in the index, these names are highlighted in bold type. Further biographical information on most of the Americans can be found in *Notable American Women*. Unfortunately, there is no German equivalent.

We have limited the citation of scholarly works to the Introduction. Full citations will be found in the bibliography. Acronyms have been supplied for organizations that used them.

Wherever possible, we have tried to find the English originals of quotations that were translated into German. Names of German organizations and institutions are translated and explained in the glossary.

Social Justice Feminists

in the United States and Germany

Introduction: A Transatlantic Dialogue

Between 1885 and 1933 middle-class women social reformers in the United States and Germany conducted a transatlantic dialogue that explored each other's political cultures. Each group was drawn into the dialogue in the belief that it could be empowered by its contact with the other. In both countries industrial development was taking place in the context of the emergence of the nation-state as a new political force. Demands for social justice for working people were mobilizing support for progressive political and social agendas within these nation-states. This mixture of economic, political, and social transformation involved the energies of women in both countries on an unprecedented scale. Especially significant in this context were middle-class women reformers who pursued social justice goals through middle-class institutional means. Remarkably and surprisingly, important aspects of their efforts were shaped by the dialogue they maintained with one another across national boundaries.

This book depicts their dialogue through documents in which they communicated with or about one another. The dialogue began in the 1880s when each nation was emerging as a new economic and political force in the world. It flourished during the three decades between 1885 and 1915, when robust women's organizations developed in both countries. The outbreak of World War I in 1914 and the turbulent decade after the war dramatically altered the dialogue, changing both its participants and its content. The dialogue's tragic conclusion in 1933 marked the end of an era of cooperation between women reformers in Germany and the United States. Yet for nearly half a century between 1885 and 1933, this dialogue constituted a singular and powerful force in the lives of innovative women reformers. Through it we can see fundamental aspects of civil society and state formation within each country: the relative importance of voluntary

1

groups; of class conflict; of national, regional, and municipal institutions; of democratic access to state power; and above all, the relationship of women to the state.

We hope this book will contribute to three aspects of comparative historical inquiry: the still burgeoning international discussion among scholars of women and the welfare state, the newer work on women's international organizations, and the effort to internationalize U.S. history.[1] We hope to add to the first discussion less by evaluating comparative welfare state regimes than by highlighting one of the international dialogues that helped shape their construction. Thus we are looking more at origins than at outcomes, more at the position women activists occupied within their larger political cultures than at their achievements. Our documents present a wide variety of welfare state initiatives, including protective labor legislation for women and mothers' pensions, but our attention remains focused on the dialogue between American and German women reformers about these measures rather than on the measures themselves. Similarly, we hope to add to the discussion of women's international organizations by seeing them in terms of this American-German dialogue rather than by analyzing them as organizations. We hope this cross-national dialogue can serve as a model for other efforts to internationalize U.S. history.

This collection highlights one transatlantic dialogue. Other cross-national dialogues were conducted by other groups of women devoted to other forms of social activism. In Germany and the United States, suffragists, labor organizers, socialists, birth controllers and eugenicists, and women social scientists communicated and cooperated with their counter-

---

[1] Too large to review here, the welfare state historiography is perhaps best illustrated by the new (1994) journal, *Social Politics: International Studies in Gender, State and Society*, edited by Barbara M. Hobson, Sonya Michel, and Ann Shola Orloff. See especially the special issue "Gender and Rationalization in Comparative Historical Perspective—Germany and the United States," *Social Politics* 4 (Spring 1997). Examples of work in this area include Seth Koven and Sonya Michel, eds., *Mothers of a New World*; Eileen Boris, *Home to Work*; Kathryn Kish Sklar, *Florence Kelley and the Nation's Work*; and Ulla Wikander, Alice Kessler-Harris, and Jane Lewis, *Protecting Women*. For the thorny topic of protective labor legislation for women in Germany and the United States, see Sabine Schmitt, " 'All These Forms of Women's Work Which Endanger Public Health and Public Welfare': Protective Labor Legislation for Women in Germany, 1878–1914," and Alice Kessler-Harris, "The Paradox of Motherhood: Night Work Restrictions in the United States," both in Wikander, Harris, and Lewis, *Protecting Women*; Kathleen Canning, "Social Policy, Body Politics"; Kathryn Kish Sklar, "Two Political Cultures in the Progressive Era"; and Boris, *Home to Work*, pp. 348–55 and passim.

For overviews of women's international organizations, see Leila Rupp, *Worlds of Women;* Rupp, "Constructing Internationalism," and Francesca Miller, "The International Relations of Women of the Americas." For an interpretation of internationalism in the suffrage movement that also includes women in the Second International, see Ellen Carol DuBois, "Woman Suffrage Around the World: Three Phases of Suffragist Internationalism," in Daley and Nolan, *Suffrage and Beyond*, pp. 252–76. For an example of the internationalization of U.S. history, see Carl Guarneri, ed., *America Compared*.

parts. Both German and American women maintained dialogues with women in other countries. All these dialogues deserve to be explored.[2] Here we focus on the trajectory of contact between middle-class women in Germany and the United States who, between 1880 and 1933, participated in nation-building through social welfare and social justice activism. We explore their communication and the context that shaped it. These documents are not definitive; we expect that others will emerge as scholars further investigate this and other cross-national and transnational dialogues that sustained women's activism in these decades.

Who took part in this dialogue? The women whose writings are collected in this book came from middle-class families, had access to the best education available to women in their respective countries, and resided in major urban centers. Participants in both countries were affiliated with national and international suffrage movements that, inspiring new levels of women's activism, brought woman suffrage to Germany in 1919 and to the United States in 1920. Active within the radical wing of the bourgeois women's movement in both countries, these reformers sought to bring some of the energy of those movements to bear on the abundant social problems in their societies. Although some—Florence Kelley on the American and Anna Lindemann on the German side—were socialists, all (including Kelley and Lindemann) derived most of their support from middle-class networks and institutions. They were overwhelmingly Protestant, with a few Jews on each side.

Jane Addams and Florence Kelley were the dialogue's leading participants in the United States. During the decades between 1885 and 1933

[2] For a dialogue between Americans and Germans on birth control, see Atina Grossman, *Reforming Sex,* especially pp. 37–45 and 51–57. For a business dialogue between Germany and the United States, see Mary Nolan, *Visions of Modernity.* For suffrage and labor dialogues between the United States and Great Britain, see Patricia Greenwood Harrison, "Interaction between the British and American Woman Suffrage Movements," and Jane Marcus, "Transatlantic Sisterhood." Little has been written on the international dialogue of women socialists. For the contacts between socialist women, see Richard Evans, *Comrades and Sisters,* pp. 133–35. For a comparison of the suffrage movements in Germany and the United States (although it does not consider the dialogue between the two movements), see Nancy F. Cott, "Early-Twentieth-Century Feminism in Political Context: A Comparative Look at Germany and the United States," in Caroline Daley and Melanie Nolan, eds., *Suffrage and Beyond,* pp. 234–51.

For international dialogues on protective labor legislation for women, see Ulla Wikander, "Some 'Kept the Flag of Feminist Demands Waving': Debates at International Congresses on Protecting Women Workers," in Wikander, Harris, and Lewis, *Protecting Women,* pp. 29–62. Wikander also provides a list of women's international congresses, 1878–1914, pp. 54–56. See also "International Women's Congresses, 1878–1914: The Controversy over Equality and Special Labour Legislation," in Maud L. Edwards et al., eds., *Rethinking Change,* pp. 11–36.

For contacts between German and American women sociologists, see Theresa Wobbe, *Wahlverwandtschaften,* and a useful sourcebook, Claudia Honegger and Theresa Wobbe, eds., *Klassikerinnen des Soziologischen Denkens.*

they and many of their associates developed close relationships with women reformers in Germany. For them Germany was not just another country. Deeply involved in nation-building and in reshaping democracy in the United States, these women learned a great deal from what they saw in Germany. Constrained by their own traditions of limited government, they were fascinated by the powerful state structures of German government. Accustomed to universal white male suffrage, they sympathized with the struggle to extend democracy in Germany.

In Germany, Alice Salomon and other politically active women, such as Minna Cauer and Marie Elisabeth Lüders, formed the dialogue's core. For them, women's middle-class political culture in the United States offered a model of feminist nation-building that they sought to emulate. German women, coming as they did from a polity committed to the power of the state, were fascinated by the empowerment of women within American public life. They marveled at the integration of women's activism within the larger purposes of American nationhood and its democratic ethos.

This dialogue invites three levels of comparison. At the macro-level we see the effects of democratic compared to monarchical institutions. At the middle level we view the complex play of two constantly changing and internally contested political cultures. At the micro-level we observe the evolution of specific programs designed by dialogue participants. Each level gives us a valuable perspective on this transatlantic dialogue; together they help us understand how rich and rewarding it became, and why it persisted so long. At a time when formal diplomatic relations between the two countries were not particularly friendly, these women built substantial cultural bridges.[3]

The cross-cultural context of these documents challenged the editors to create terms capable of embracing the dialogue's participants on both sides of the Atlantic. We needed to distinguish among socialist, feminist, suffragist, and reform strategies for improving society and the lives of women, and we needed to do so in terms that would apply to similar groups of women in quite different political cultures.[4] For example, we could not call them "social democratic," for although this term fit the Americans well enough, in Germany it connoted membership in the Social Democratic Party, and most German participants in this dialogue were not SPD members. We tried using the term "social feminists," which worked in Germany, where, due to laws that limited women's agitation for political causes, only a minority of women social activists supported woman suf-

[3] For diplomatic relations, see Hans-Jürgen Schröder, *Confrontation and Cooperation.*
[4] For an astute analysis of the difficulties of comparative work, see "Pitfalls of Comparative Labour History: How Comrades Are Compared," in Stefan Berger, *The British Labour Party and the German Social Democrats,* pp. 1–18. Berger's book also has a chapter on the relationship between the two labor parties.

4

frage. But in the United States where most women activists supported woman suffrage, the term was too broad, embracing virtually all women's public activities and failing to express the innovative place that dialogue participants held in their political cultures.[5] "Maternalist" did not work because it characterized dialogue opponents better than dialogue participants. And maternalist derivatives, such as "progressive maternalist" or "feminist maternalist" failed to embrace the social justice goals that motivated most dialogue participants.

One term—social justice feminists—fit most dialogue participants on both sides of the Atlantic. "Social justice" and "feminist" were terms they themselves used. In a letter to Jane Addams in 1911, Alice Salomon referred to their shared "belief in social justice."[6] Between the time that the term "feminism" came into use in the United States around 1910 and was preempted by others around 1920, participants in the dialogue applied it to their own efforts.[7] Certainly dialogue participants met Linda Gordon's definition of feminism as "a critique of male supremacy, formed and offered in the light of a will to change it, which in turn assumes a conviction that it is changeable."[8]

Thus we believe that "social justice feminism" best describes the activism that sustained this dialogue between American and German women for almost five decades. It matches the left-of-center position that they occupied in their respective political cultures, while it also reflects their commitment to improve the status of women.

Social justice is a term that arose within Christian socialism during the last three decades of the nineteenth century. Whereas Marx constructed scientific arguments about the exploitation of labor by capital, Christian socialists drew on moral arguments and spoke of social justice. In both Germany and the United States this moral discourse could appeal to middle-class constituencies who feared the revolutionary rhetoric of Marxian socialism. "Social justice"—"soziale Gerechtigkeit"—was related to the "social gospel," the importance of the "social question," and what the "social

---

[5] For a critique of the ungainly breadth of "social feminism," see Nancy F. Cott, "What's in a Name?"

[6] Alice Salomon to Jane Addams, December 11, 1911, reprinted here in Part II, document 7.

[7] According to Alice Thatcher Post, at the Second International Congress of Women at Zurich in 1919, three committees were formed to examine all resolutions and report to the Executive Committee: a "political" committee, a "feminist" committee, and an "educational & general" committee. Serving on the "feminist" committee were Chrystal Macmillan, Aletta Jacobs, and Jeanette Rankin. Alice Thatcher Post, "Journal of the Second International Congress of Women, 9 April–18 May 1919," Mercedes Randall Collection, Rare Book and Manuscript Library, Butler Library, Columbia University.

[8] Linda Gordon, "What's New in Women's History," p. 29. For overviews of definitions of European feminism, see Richard Evans, "The Concept of Feminism," and Karen Offen, "Reflections on National Specificities in Continental European Feminisms."

classes" owed each other. In a time threatened by class war and marked by violent conflicts between labor and capital, the need for social justice was often explicitly linked to the need for "industrial peace."[9]

By 1890 "social justice" discourse had entered the vocabulary of a wide range of social activists, including middle-class women reformers. It was a plastic term that could embrace diverse social goals, and applied particularly well to public policies, such as protective labor legislation or widows' pensions. The term gained in ascendancy throughout the decades before World War I because it offered an alternative to charity as the justification for public policies that intervened in the relationship between capital and labor, and signified a redistribution of resources based on fairness rather than pity or fear.

Other politically active women participated in the transatlantic dialogue between German and American reformers, but social justice feminists did most to shape the dialogue's contours over time. The authors of most of the documents in this book had two goals: to create a more just society generally, and to create a more just society for women in particular. On both sides of the Atlantic they believed in an expanded view of women's citizenship: that although women were denied full civil or political rights, they themselves could do much to shape their societies' responses to the effects of the industrial revolution, to the development of their respective nation-states, and to the strengthening of democracy within their national boundaries.[10] Alice Salomon, the leading figure on the German side of the dialogue, called Jane Addams, the leading figure on the American side, a "social politician."[11] This phrase expressed their common belief that middle-class women could use their position in civil society to promote social change.

On both sides of the Atlantic these women were responding to "the social question." Large investments of capital in industrial enterprise had generated a powerful and seemingly uncontrollable force in modern life—industrial capitalism. The reorganization of work, especially manufacturing, in large-scale power-driven factories that employed large numbers of workers, had prompted a massive migration from the countryside to cities. Workers often faced widespread unemployment and social dislo-

[9] For "social justice" origins in the United States, see Ronald White et al., *The Social Gospel.* For Germany, see E. I. Kouri, *Der deutsche Protestantismus und die Soziale Frage.* For the link between social justice and industrial peace, see Carl Mote, *Industrial Arbitration: A World-Wide Survey of Natural and Political Agencies for Social Justice and Industrial Peace* (Indianapolis: Bobbs Merrill, 1916).

[10] For a discussion of women's "social citizenship," see Wendy Sarvasy, "From Man and Philanthropic Service to Feminist Social Citizenship."

[11] See Salomon, *Twenty Years of Women's Social Work in Chicago,* reprinted here in Part II, document 7.

cation. A widening gulf between rich and poor threatened the social fabric. Working-class slums multiplied in both countries. These problematic changes were summarized as "the social question"—"die soziale Frage."

As it became more urgent in both countries to resolve the "social question," middle-class women articulated a variety of responses within a wide range of voluntary associations. Some women, located primarily in progressive associations, responded with social justice strategies designed to alter the socioeconomic system, not simply to alleviate its pain. In the United States, for example, women in the National Consumers' League (NCL) campaigned for the establishment of a legal minimum wage to prevent the downward spiraling of wages in poorly paid occupations, particularly the garment industry. German social justice feminists also advocated a minimum wage for industrial homeworkers, as well as their inclusion in the compulsory insurance system.[12] These strategies differed from women's traditional charitable activity in two ways. First, they recognized the injustice of contemporary conditions. Second, they sought structural changes in the social, political, or economic status quo, particularly by intervening in marketplace or familial relationships to establish new standards of fairness.

Working within organizations dominated by middle-class women, social justice feminists spearheaded the construction of coalitions to support state action on behalf of what they viewed as answers to the "social question." Nation-building for them meant improving the quality of life of working people. Theirs was a struggle for "others" in which their own middle-class perspective inevitably shaped their social activism. Yet while their shared class perspective created many similarities between these American and German women, profound differences in the political cultures and institutions of the two nations positioned them differently within each national polity. This book focuses on those differences, using it to illuminate their larger political cultures and clarify the opportunities and constraints of middle-class women's activism within each country.

In the United States, where social justice feminists were carried forward both by the mainstream of the women's movement and the mainstream of progressive reform, their coalitions were relatively extensive and effective. The social breadth and depth of the suffrage movement in their country combined with a wave of reform that crested around 1910. This combination placed a great deal of power in the hands of social justice feminists. They used it to expand the state's responsibility for human welfare and the

[12] Boris, *Home to Work*, chaps. 2 and 3; Robyn Dasey, "Women's Work and the Family," in Alice Salomon et al., eds., *Heimarbeit and Lohnfrage*; Sabine Schmitt, *Der Arbeiterinnenschutz im deutschen Kaiserreich*.

state's ability to intervene in market relationships on behalf of exploited working people.[13]

In Germany, social justice feminists were more vulnerable. Situated between an insurgent socialism and a threatened bourgeoisie, they struggled to create a middle way. Based on a much smaller and more fragmented suffrage movement and a more conflicted political culture—in which the forces creating the nation-state and even those creating social welfare were often at odds with the forces promoting political democracy—their coalitions were smaller or shorter-lived. Nevertheless, they also acquired significant power in public life, through which they promoted more democratic solutions to social problems.[14]

Situated differently in their own national polities, American and German women responded to different opportunities. Because American social justice feminists were able to draw on the grassroots activism of a sizable suffrage movement, they more easily mobilized support for their legislative goals. Lacking such options and located in a state with strong administrative capabilities, German social justice feminists focused instead on the development of democratic trends within social work and on filling appointive positions within the regulatory state. This tended to push them to the political center, especially when compared to their American counterparts.

Neither group put an end to the abuses of industrial capitalism; their methods and goals were not revolutionary. Nevertheless, they did a great deal to recast the social contract in both countries at a time when fundamental economic changes mandated commensurate social and political changes.

In the United States, social justice feminists could be found in a wide range of women's organizations. The largest of these was also the earliest—the Woman's Christian Temperance Union (WCTU). Founded in 1874, the WCTU became by the 1890s the largest American women's organization before or since. It endorsed woman suffrage in 1882, and in the 1890s reversed its earlier belief that excessive drinking caused poverty, concluding instead that poverty caused drinking. Since the WCTU and other women's organizations were organized around "departments," which per-

---

[13] For an overview of the American coalitions, see Kathryn Kish Sklar, "The Historical Foundations of Women's Power in the Creation of the American Welfare State, 1830–1930," in Koven and Michel, *Mothers of a New World*, pp. 43–93.

[14] For German coalitions, see Barbara Greven-Aschoff, *Die bürgerliche Frauenbewegung in Deutschland*, and Richard Evans, *The Feminist Movement in Germany, 1892–1933*. For the effectiveness of German women's social work generally, see Karen Hagemann, "Rationalizing Family Work." For the conflicted qualities of German political culture, see David Blackbourn and Geoff Eley, *The Peculiarities of German History*, pp. 144–55. For an analysis of the relative power of the Prussian civil service and the weakness of the Prussian parliament before Bismarck, see Hermann Beck, *The Origins of the Authoritarian Welfare State in Prussia*, esp. p. 218.

mitted members to select the social issues on which they preferred to work, the power of large women's organizations was often brought to bear on social issues that only a minority of their members actually pursued. In this way social justice feminists exercised an influence disproportionate to their numbers. By far the largest generator of social justice feminism after 1890 was the social settlement movement. Beginning with the founding of Hull House in 1889, and continuing throughout the period embraced by this book, the settlement movement drew a steady stream of college-trained women into brief postgraduate training in urban slums and subsequently guided their club work in social justice directions. The organization that best promoted social justice feminism was the National Consumers' League, founded in 1898. The NCL generated an aggressive agenda of hour, wage, and other legislation affecting the working conditions of women and children. The Women's Trade Union League (WTUL), created in 1903, was the NCL's closest ally, but the NCL promoted its agenda by drawing on much larger organizations, especially the General Federation of Women's Clubs (GFWC), established in 1890. For example, in 1901 the NCL's executive director became chair of the GFWC's Committee on the Industrial Problem as It Affects Women and Children. After 1900 even the National American Woman Suffrage Association (NAWSA), founded in 1890 from the merger of the National Woman Suffrage Association and the American Woman Suffrage Association (both created in 1869), also became a vehicle for social justice feminism as suffragists increasingly referred to the positive social changes that women would institute when they gained the right to vote.[15]

In Germany social justice feminists first emerged in the progressive wing of the League of German Women's Associations (Bund deutscher Frauenvereine, BDF), founded in 1894, and the Association of Progressive Women's Clubs (Verband Fortschrittlicher Frauenvereine), formed in 1899. Social justice feminists could also be found in the radical wing of the German Association for Woman Suffrage (Deutscher Verein für Frauenstimmrecht), founded in 1902, and the Society for Woman's Welfare (Verein Frauenwohl), founded in 1888, which agitated for political and social rights for women and which at the local level often affiliated with the League for the Protection of Motherhood and Sexual Reform (Bund für Mutterschutz und Sexualreform), formed in 1905. Social justice feminists also helped shape the local coalitions that opposed state-regulated prostitution. Although those coalitions were dominated by conservatives who,

[15]   This interpretation of the importance of social justice feminism within women's organizations and the suffrage movement is our own, but support can be found in Sklar, *Florence Kelley and the Nation's Work*; Anne Firor Scott, *Natural Allies*; Nancy F. Cott, *The Grounding of Modern Feminism*; and J. Stanley Lemons, *The Woman Citizen*.

unlike their counterparts in the United States between 1830 and 1860 and in England in the 1870s, did not sympathize with prostitutes, they generated new approaches to women's issues in Germany between 1904 and 1914.[16]

In both Germany and the United States women justified their entrance into public life with biologically based arguments about "woman's nature"—to clean up cities as they cleaned up homes, to care about the needy as they nurtured their own children, to support peace because they gave birth to life. These arguments—called essentialist today—were designed to counteract other essentialist arguments that mandated women's absence from public life—women's retiring nature, their capacity to supply men with a retreat from commercial activity, their identification with values other than the economic marketplace, their childlike dependency. By affiliating with some values traditionally associated with women, women activists defended themselves against the inevitable accusations that their actions were illegitimate because they fell outside the approved range of women's endeavors. To be effective in public life they had to claim public life as an appropriate arena for women. Such claims were especially important for social justice feminists, who had to contend with conservative critics of their social initiatives as well as with opponents of women's public activism generally.

On both sides of the Atlantic during these decades, women did much to shift provisions for social welfare away from traditional poor law considerations based on the ability to work (supporting those who could not work and forcing others to work) to more organic views of social health as the basis of economic health. In both countries the child, the family, pregnant women, mothers, and the body generally became sites of public responsibility. For the women represented in this book, those sites also became important measures of social justice.[17]

These organic views of social welfare were especially visible in Germany and the United States, where their origins were also particularly clear. In-

[16]   Our interpretation of German women's political cultures builds on Nancy R. Reagin, *A German Women's Movement*; Jean H. Quataert, *Reluctant Feminists in German Social Democracy*; Ute Gerhard, *Unerhört*; Evans, *Feminist Movement in Germany*; and Evans, *Comrades and Sisters*. See also Ute Frevert, *Women in German History*; Bärbel Clemens, *Menschenrechte haben kein Geschlecht*; Theresa Wobbe, *Gleichheit und Differenz*; and Ann Taylor Allen, *Feminism and Motherhood in Germany*. Two valuable collections of documents are *Frauen gegen den Krieg* and *Frauenarbeit und Beruf*, both edited by Gisela Brinker-Gabler.

[17]   For overviews of this shift, see Michael B. Katz, *In the Shadow of the Poorhouse*, and George Steinmetz, *Regulating the Social*. While this emphasis on the body created a foundation for eugenic solutions to social problems, such solutions, which emerged primarily in the 1920s, should not be conflated with the reform strategies of social justice feminists. For a warning against conflating eugenicists and birth controllers, see Grossman, *Reforming Sex*, pp. v–vi. See also Renate Bridenthal, Atina Grossman, and Marion Kaplan, eds., *When Biology Became Destiny*.

tellectually, new attitudes toward social welfare began with Darwin's depiction of the life of the human species as first and foremost a biological process. Ideas about organic growth had been strong in Germany for a generation before Darwin. For example, in both Germany and the United States, German theologians had led the way in refuting literal biblical interpretations of creation. In the United States Darwin fit well with the culture's commitment to progress and change. While social darwinist ideologies in both countries preached the doctrine of the survival of the fittest, both nations also generated reform darwinist beliefs that measured social progress in terms of the progress experienced by working people.

Economically, these new reform darwinist attitudes toward social welfare were sparked by rapid industrialization, which in addition to creating new kinds of work, spawned a new and seemingly uncontrollable phenomenon—unemployment. Through no fault of their own, workers became unemployed and their families were thrown into poverty. Socially, new attitudes toward social welfare were promoted by new notions of what the dominant classes owed to subordinate groups, particularly since working people were demonstrating new powers of combination, and, thanks to the benefits of industrial productivity, the dominant classes were enjoying unprecedented improvements in their standard of living.

Politically, women joined with men in implementing these new attitudes toward social welfare—in Germany through administrative channels, in the United States through legislation. In both countries the nation-state became the crucible in which these intellectual, economic, social, and political changes were tested and contested. In both countries social justice feminists were important agents in that process.

The dialogue ended differently for women in the two countries. In the early 1930s, as the New Deal began to incorporate many social measures forged by social justice feminists, most of their German peers were forced into exile. These documents tell that story. They also depict the larger context within which social justice feminists worked in each country.

Promoting a Dialogue: American Women
Forge Ties with German Activism, 1885–1908

In addition to the colossal flow of immigration and return migration between Europe and North America in the decades around 1900, transatlantic contacts were sustained by a vital international culture that drew on both elite and oppositional sources. Young people from privileged backgrounds frequently studied in countries not their own, and their families often took lengthy trips abroad. Equally significant were the oppositional communities of political exiles, refugees, and intellectuals, who stimulated the flow of new ideas and values across national boundaries. The two largest oppositional forces, the socialist and woman suffrage movements, provided institutional resources that linked local groups with international activities. Despite the relative difficulty of international travel in that era compared to our own, for some groups transatlantic contacts were not unusual.

Three leading American participants in the dialogue—Jane Addams, Mary Church Terrell, and Florence Kelley—exemplified the access of elite young women to European travel and study in the 1880s.[18] Germany was an essential stop on the European tour that many upper-middle-class American women took upon the completion of their formal education. The "grand tour" immersed them in European culture, added polish to their schooling, and enhanced their competitiveness in the marriage market. For some members of the generation born between 1859 and 1869, however, travel and study in Germany led to different results. In their early twenties Addams, Church, and Kelley each began to question received authority. Their experiences in Germany helped shape their developing social consciences and served as a basis for their later dialogue with German women.

Traveling with her stepmother on a "grand tour" of Europe, Jane Addams spent the winter of 1883–84 in Dresden and its environs. Her conscience was "stung into action" one morning by a scene outside the window of her hotel room in Saxe-Coburg. "A single file of women with semicircular heavy wooden tanks fastened upon their backs" was crossing and recrossing the town square. "They were carrying in this primitive fashion to a remote cooling room these tanks filled with a hot brew incident to one stage of beer making. . . . Their faces and hands, reddened in the cold morning air, showed clearly the white scars where they had previously been scalded by the hot stuff which splashed if they stumbled ever so little on their way." Jarred into concern, Addams pressed the innkeeper into service as an interpreter and interviewed "the phlegmatic owner of the brewery." He received the young American "with exasperating indifference." She returned to a breakfast for which she had lost her appetite.[19] Five years later in Chicago Addams finally found an effective way to counteract human suffering.

[18]   More than ten thousand Americans studied at German universities in the nineteenth century, the great majority of whom were men, among them the presidents of Harvard, Cornell, and the University of Michigan as well as the founder and many of the first faculty members of Johns Hopkins University, the "Göttingen in Baltimore." Steven Muller, "Nach dreihundert Jahren." Thus many prominent leaders of the Progressive Era were able first hand to observe the German state system forcefully address problems posed by industrialization and urbanization. German universities became models for American graduate study, but transferring ideas about positive government proved more difficult.
[19]   Jane Addams, *Twenty Years at Hull House,* pp. 74–75.

Mary Church studied in Berlin in 1889. As an African-American seeking to escape from American racism, she encountered the best and the worst of German attitudes toward race. A light-skinned mulatto, an Oberlin graduate, and the daughter of a wealthy Memphis real estate investor, she knew she enjoyed opportunities not open to most African-Americans, especially European travel and study. Living alone in a *pension,* she often passed for white and reveled in the absence of racial obstacles in her movements through German society. Once, however, two male students from the American South identified her as a Negro who would be "socially ostracized" in the United States, and she had to change her lodgings. To one landlady whose anti-Semitism "irritated and annoyed" her, she explained: "The people who see little or no good in my racial group delight in telling the world about its vices and defects just as you have enjoyed regaling me with those you claim are characteristic of Jews."[20] Liberated from one form of racism, but encountering another, Mary Church's visit to Germany taught her to challenge all social prejudice.

Travels in Germany permitted Addams, Church, and Kelley to build real fluency on the foundations they had established in college language courses. Addams continued with German lessons after her return to the United States. Church became so proficient (she kept a diary in German during her stay) that when she returned to speak at the 1904 congress of the International Council of Women (ICW), she delivered her address in German. Kelley retained her language skills by reading German social democratic periodicals. None of these three became bilingual, but all had an understanding of German culture based on linguistic fluency.

Part I of this book focuses on Florence Kelley, who more energetically than any other member of her generation, explored the possibilities for cooperation between German and American reform movements. Florence Kelley's sojourn in German political culture lasted longer than that of Addams or Church and generated a deeper dynamic of personal and political growth. Unlike most of her contemporaries, Kelley plunged into German political culture, joining the Social Democratic Party and writing about it for American suffrage publications.[21] She exemplified the attraction of socialism to women engaged in social justice reform, and her writings about the intersection of women and social justice illuminate that attraction.

Kelley's capacity to see the relationship between German and American political cultures gives us a clearer view of their similarities and differences at the moment when women social reformers in each political culture were

---

[20] Mary Church Terrell, *A Colored Woman in a White World,* p. 90.
[21] Founded in 1875 as the Sozialistische Arbeiterpartei Deutschlands (German Socialist Workers' Party), the name by which Kelley knew it, in 1890 the party adopted the name by which it is known today, Sozialdemokratische Partei Deutschlands (SPD). To avoid confusion we are using only the party's post-1890 name.

beginning to speak to one another in the 1880s. Her experience on both sides of the Atlantic offers a revealing example of the process by which women social reformers transcended national boundaries in their search for wider social understanding.

Between 1885 and 1898, at the same time that she became a leading voice among American women social justice reformers, Kelley also served as a bridge of communication between women's political culture in the United States and the social democratic movement in Germany.[22] In 1885, she wrote from her residence in Heidelberg to woman suffrage periodicals in the United States urging women activists to adopt strategies that she associated with the German Social Democratic Party. Then, between 1894 and 1898, she reported on the accomplishments of American women reformers to the readers of two major German social reform periodicals.

In both instances her writings reached across boundaries of class, gender, and nationality. Writing from Germany for an American audience and from the United States for a German one, her vision embraced both national perspectives. First addressing a female audience about male-dominated political activism, and later readers of both sexes about predominantly female activism, her outlook encompassed both women and men. Corresponding first to a middle-class audience about working-class politics, and then to a class-bridging readership about class-bridging activism, her concerns reached beyond the limits of her own class identity.

When, from Heidelberg in 1885, Kelley wrote a series of letters to American woman suffrage periodicals, she was in the process of reconstructing her own political identity—discarding the politics of her upbringing and adopting those of German socialism. Heretofore her political outlook had been shaped by her Radical Republican father, William Darrah Kelley, congressman from Philadelphia between 1860 and 1890, and by her great aunt, Sarah Pugh, abolitionist leader and woman suffrage advocate.

After graduating from Cornell University in 1882, Florence Kelley expected more of herself than her society seemed to tolerate in a woman. Rejected for graduate study at the University of Pennsylvania because she was a woman, she entered the University of Zurich, one of a few European institutions awarding degrees to women.[23] Courses on contemporary social questions and the history of popular social movements informed her understanding of German politics. These courses brought her into contact with students from Germany and Russia whose socialist beliefs had forced them into exile. Zurich was the center of the Social Democratic Party

[22] By "women's political culture" or "women's public culture" we mean women's participation in public culture and the separate institutions that women built to facilitate their participation. See the passages indexed under "women's political culture" in Sklar, *Florence Kelley and the Nation's Work*.

[23] Ibid., chaps. 1–4. See also Gabi Einsele, "Kein Vaterland."

(SPD) of Germany, which was banned in Germany by antisocialist laws from 1878 to 1890, so, unbeknownst to her, by choosing to attend this Swiss university she had come to reside in one of the most politically volatile cities in Europe.[24]

In Zurich, Kelley escaped her gendered destiny of philanthropic work and adopted a new persona by converting to socialism. The social justice themes of the SPD meetings resonated with those of her childhood. "This might well have been a Quaker meeting," she later wrote about her first socialist meeting. "Here was the Golden Rule! Here was Grandaunt Sarah!"[25]

Kelley's commitment to European socialism was reinforced by her marriage, in October 1884, to Lazare Wischnewetsky, a Russian Jewish medical student, with whom she had three children during the next three years. Living in Heidelberg, Germany, in 1885, and expecting the birth of her first child, she translated a major work by Frederick Engels, *The Condition of the Working Class in England in 1844*, and began to cut her ties with her elite Philadelphia family. She was twenty-six years old.[26]

Florence Kelley's dramatic effort to change her political identity by changing her personal identity echoed that of Clara Zetkin, who after 1889 became the chief leader of and theoretician about women within the Social Democratic Party. Despite middle-class origins, Clara Zetkin relocated herself relatively easily within the emerging German socialist movement.[27] Florence Kelley had a different problem. No equivalent American socialist movement existed to welcome her into its ranks. After returning to the United States in 1886 she tried and failed to find a place for herself within the German-speaking Socialist Labor Party, but that attempt ended in her expulsion from the party for her too-energetic insistence on the importance of the writings of Marx and Engels.

Even before that clash, while still in Germany, Kelley had turned to what would become a more fruitful constituency for her views, the public culture of middle-class American women. In letters to the *Woman's Tribune* and *The New Era*, two newly founded suffrage periodicals, she sought to influence the direction of the suffrage movement by invoking German exam-

[24]   For the SPD in 1885, see W. L. Guttsman, *The German Social Democratic Party*, pp. 42–71; Vernon L. Lidtke, *The Outlawed Party*, pp. 176–213; and Steinmetz, *Regulating the Social*, pp. 194–97.
[25]   Florence Kelley, *The Autobiography of Florence Kelley*, pp. 73–74.
[26]   Sklar, *Florence Kelley and the Nation's Work*, chap. 5. The full German title of Engels's book was *Die Lage der arbeitenden Klasse in England, Nach Eigener Anschauung und authentischen Quellen* (The condition of the working class in England, From personal observation and authentic sources). Kelley's translation was published as *The Condition of the Working Class in England in 1844* (New York: John W. Lovell, 1887). Hers is still the preferred scholarly translation.
[27]   See Karen Honeycutt, "Clara Zetkin," pp. 96–166; Richard J. Evans, "Theory and Practice in German Social Democracy"; and Sklar, *Florence Kelley and the Nation's Work*, p. 116.

ples.[28] Comparing the public culture of German socialist women with that of American middle-class suffragists, she wove together strands of class and gender in the two cultures to create a striking, if not entirely convincing, design for the adoption of German ideas in the United States.

In contrast to her more recent dealings with the Social Democratic Party, Florence Kelley's knowledge of the American woman suffrage movement began in her childhood. Her father's congressional support for the movement since 1860 meant that she had grown up hearing stories about his conversations with Susan B. Anthony, whom he called the "Major." Even before her graduation from Cornell, Florence Kelley had cofounded the Century Working Women's Guild in Philadelphia, a school for self-supporting women. As an undergraduate at Cornell, she had decided to focus her life work on reforms related to working women, and the success of this early class-bridging experiment heightened her resolve. When Susan Anthony wrote to her in Zurich urging that she become more active in the suffrage movement, she declined, replying: "When my student life is over, I shall give myself to work for the best interests of the workingwomen of America."[29] So her commitments were clear. But a formidable problem confronted her: in the mid-1880s few other middle-class women shared her interest in working women. In her 1885 letters, therefore, she tried to use her position within German political culture to generate concern for working women within the American suffrage movement.

All of Kelley's 1885 letters to American suffrage periodicals argued that the movement should adopt the gender-specific aspects of class-based German movements. Just as German social democrats championed the interests of German working women, she argued, so too could the American suffrage movement promote the well-being of American working women. Knowingly or not, Kelley exaggerated the extent to which the Social Democratic Party championed women's interests. In trying to use women's issues to promote a larger agenda, she made the most of the party's rather limited gestures toward gender equality.[30] Since no response was printed in reaction to Kelley's letters, we do not know how they were received.

[28] Florence Kelley, "Letters from the People," "Correspondence from Heidelberg," and "Movement Among German Working Women," reprinted here in Part I, documents 1, 2, and 3. While she was mailing letters to woman suffrage publications in 1885, Kelley was also interpreting German politics to an American audience in a series of letters to the *Times-Philadelphia* titled "Bismarck's Tariff," "Socialism in Germany: Bismarck's Exceptional Laws," and "German Workwomen: Taking Part in Politics." See Sklar, *Florence Kelley and the Nation's Work*, pp. 83, 409. For more on the *Tribune*, see Linda C. Steiner, "The Women's Suffrage Press," pp. 262–64.
[29] Florence Kelley to Susan B. Anthony, [Zurich], January 21, 1884, quoted in Sklar, *Florence Kelley and the Nation's Work*, p. 85.
[30] Kelley's characterization of the weakness of the German middle-class women's movement and the strength of the socialist women's movement anticipated by a decade Clara Zetkin's 1895 claim that because the German bourgeoisie was "among the most backward and narrow-minded of all bourgeoisies . . . the task of solving the question of female emancipation in the

Kelley's effort to graft elements of German social democracy onto the American woman suffrage movement in the 1880s did not bear fruit. She returned to the United States with Lazare and took up residence in New York City in 1886 and by 1888 had given birth to two more children. But after Lazare grew mentally unstable and violent she fled with the children to Chicago in December 1891 and at Hull House discovered a social movement capable of mixing class and gender along the lines that she had advocated in 1885.[31]

Founded by Jane Addams in 1889, Hull House marked a new departure in women's reform activism by providing a site where unmarried women reformers could reside and combine their talents. The settlement movement sought to build community spirit and social cohesion in the turbulent neighborhoods of recently arrived immigrants. As Jane Addams put it, "The original residents came to Hull-House with a conviction that social intercourse could best express the growing sense of the economic unity of society. They wished the social spirit to be the undercurrent of the life of Hull-House, whatever direction the stream might take."[32] As a women's settlement, Hull House sought to enhance the power of working-class women and girls in a variety of ways, including the organization of trade unions, the establishment of a cooperative boarding house for self-supporting women, and a nursery and kindergarten for the children of wage-earning mothers.

Sustained by her colleagues at Hull House, Kelley became a potent force for change in the social laboratory of Chicago. In 1893 she was appointed Chief Factory Inspector of the State of Illinois, a position that put her in charge of the enforcement of state legislation regulating manufacturing in an area almost half the size of Prussia.[33] No woman in Germany came close to wielding such power. This office brought her to the attention of German Social Democrats, for whom she wrote a series of penetrating articles about social reform in the United States.

Leading Social Democrats already knew Kelley as the author of an article published just before her departure from Zurich in 1886. The article, "Social Democracy and the Question of Women's Work," had appeared in *Der Sozialdemokrat,* the official newspaper of the Social Democratic Party, which was banned in Germany and printed in Zurich. Kelley's essay argued against the party's platform, adopted in 1875, of "prohibiting all women's labor which is detrimental to health and morality." She argued that the party's position sought to eliminate unfair competition with male workers rather than to protect female workers. Instead she proposed "protective

---

bourgeois sense has also fallen to the working class." Clara Zetkin, *Die Gleichheit,* January 9, 1895, p. 1, quoted in Evans, "Theory and Practice," p. 298.

[31] Sklar, *Florence Kelley and the Nation's Work,* chaps. 6–8.

[32] Addams, *Twenty Years at Hull House,* pp. 207–8.

[33] In 1911 Prussia embraced 134,622 and Illinois 56,665 square miles.

measures, which aim to preserve the working class in general, namely by reducing working hours, prohibition of Sunday and night labor, application of hygienic measures at work to protect the health of women and men workers, as well as special measures before, during, and after confinement."[34] This article as well as her translation of Engels's *Condition of the Working Class* (published in New York in 1887) brought her into contact with prominent party members. She met Engels in London in 1886 and maintained a lively correspondence with him until his death in 1895. In 1889 her stirring account of child labor in the United States, first published as a pamphlet by the Women's Temperance Publication Association, was translated and published in the SPD's chief theoretical journal, *Neue Zeit*.[35]

After Kelley's appointment as Chief Factory Inspector of Illinois, Heinrich Braun solicited her writings for his journals, *Sozialpolitisches Centralblatt* (Central Newsletter for Social Politics) and *Archiv für Soziale Gesetzgebung und Statistik* (Archive for Social Legislation and Statistics). Braun had founded *Sozialpolitisches Centralblatt* in 1892 as a more popular equivalent to the *Archiv*, which he launched in 1888. Both sought to provide a forum for the "investigation of social conditions in all lands."[36]

Through his journals Braun believed he was counteracting a tendency within the party to believe that economic forces alone would create a new social order. Instead, he urged independent investigation, free of ideological or theoretical constraint. Like other contemporary periodicals and institutions, Braun's two journals provided a forum for the interaction of German trade unionists, academic social scientists, government bureaucrats, journalists, factory owners, and other professionals, particularly physicians. As such, they sustained the growth of "Kathedersozialist" approaches to social problems that cooperated with the Bismarckian Reich and were independent of the Social Democratic Party.[37] No exact equivalent existed in the United States at the time, although publications by the National Civic Federation (founded in 1900) and the American Association for Labor Legislation (founded in 1906) were to address comparable issues.[38]

---

[34] [Florence Kelley], "Die Sozialdemokratie und die Frage der Frauenarbeit," n.p.

[35] Florence Kelley, *Our Toiling Children*.

[36] The phrase "investigation of social conditions in all lands" is the subtitle of the *Archiv für Soziale Gesetzgebung und Statistik*, quoted in Stanley Pierson, *Marxist Intellectuals and the Working-Class Mentality in Germany*, p. 73. In 1895 Heinrich Braun married Lily Gizycki (born von Kretschman), who struggled throughout her life to blend the often-disparate causes of socialism and feminism. See Alfred G. Meyer, *The Feminism and Socialism of Lily Braun*.

[37] "Kathedersozialist" has often been translated as "armchair socialist," though its literal meaning is "podium socialist," which invokes its other meaning—"academic socialist."

[38] S. Pierson, *Marxist Intellectuals*, p. 73. Those journals were the *National Civic Federation Review* (est. 1903), and the *American Labor Legislation Review* (est. 1911). For more on these two organizations, see Marguerite Green, *The National Civic Federation and the American Labor Move-*

Had Kelley remained in Germany, she might have become a strong voice on women's issues within the Social Democratic Party. Instead, she became a strong voice on women's issues within American social reform. Rather than urge German reform strategies on Americans as she had in the 1880s, in the 1890s she reported to Germans on state-of-the-art reform strategies undertaken by American women. In articles written for German reform periodicals between 1894 and 1898, she remained acutely conscious of the differences between German and American political contexts and acknowledged the continuing backwardness of her native land. Few American states had compulsory education laws, for example, and child labor was rampant. Yet women reformers were making a significant difference, and her articles depicted their successful struggles to pass and enforce legislation against child labor, tenement workshops, and the exploitation of women workers. Although she still viewed German political culture as the more advanced and sophisticated, she nevertheless depicted class-bridging coalitions of American women as taking advantage of opportunities that she knew her readers would realize were unavailable to German women.

Florence Kelley wrote about a dozen articles for Heinrich Braun's two periodicals in the 1890s. The three reprinted here trace the trajectory of her experience in Chicago, first as a zealous chief factory inspector; second as a chronicler of the history of women factory inspectors; and finally, as an advocate of consumer leagues as the best antidote to sweatshops.[39]

Taken together, these articles underscore the strength of women's public activism in the United States. Although her article on her work as factory inspector did not say so, Kelley owed her powerful position to the network of middle- and working-class women who, operating out of their headquarters at Hull House, mobilized public opinion against sweatshops. As the German-born governor who appointed her put it, "The sweatshop agitation was done by women."[40]

There was a demand in American public culture for the activism generated by women's public mobilization. One important ingredient in that demand was the relative weakness of organized labor. The American Federation of Labor (AFL), the nation's strongest labor organization, shunned political activism, especially activism undertaken on behalf of unskilled workers. Samuel Gompers turned the AFL away from political solu-

ment, p. 84, and Sklar, "Two Political Cultures." For the *Verein für Sozialpolitik,* see Irmela Gorges, "The Social Survey in Germany before 1933," in Martin Bulmer, Kevin Bales, and Kathryn Kish Sklar, eds., *The Social Survey in Historical Perspective,* pp. 316–39. For more on *Archiv,* see David Lindenfeld, *The Practical Imagination,* pp. 287–88.

[39] Florence Kelley, "The Factory Laws in Illinois," "Women Factory Inspectors in the United States," and "The Sweating System in the United States," reprinted here in Part I, documents 4, 5, and 6. For a complete list of Florence Kelley's German writings, see Sklar, *Florence Kelley and the Nation's Work,* pp. 409–11. For the history of home work, see Boris, *Home to Work.*

[40] John Peter Altgeld, in *Inter Ocean,* August 1, 1893, quoted in Sklar, *Florence Kelley and the Nation's Work,* p. 236.

tions for labor problems because, in his words, "the power of the courts to pass upon the constitutionality of the law so complicates reform by legislation as to seriously restrict the effectiveness of that method."[41] The strength of the judiciary within American political institutions offered a channel by which capital often shaped political outcomes. Therefore, Gompers and the AFL turned to "pure and simple unionism," which emphasized direct negotiation between workers and employers and limited the AFL's mission to skilled workers who could mount effective strikes because they could not easily be replaced. As a result, industrial unionism, or the organization of workers through whole industries (such as railroad workers or garment workers), rather than by craft (such as train engineers or button-hole makers), developed later in the United States than in most Western democracies. While this state of affairs led to violence that often erupted into open class warfare and made the American workplace the least regulated and most hazardous among industrial nations, it also created opportunities for middle-class women reformers. Focusing their attention on women wage-earners, the great majority of whom were young and unskilled and therefore ignored by organized labor, reformers sought to use gender issues pertaining to these workers as a lever for addressing class issues bearing on unskilled workers.

Women reformers in the United States stepped into other public opportunities that did not exist in Germany. In the 1890s one of the best examples was women's employment as factory inspectors. In Germany factory inspection was too well established and dominated by men for women to make contributions on the scale that Chicago women enjoyed, thanks to cross-class coalitions of women activists.[42] But by 1910 that difference between the two countries was reduced, as inspectors' jobs became absorbed into patronage politics in the United States and as women were appointed to more civil service positions in Germany. When Florence Kelley wrote her 1897 article on women factory inspectors, she was standing on the brink of this reversal. She hoped that as women's organizations shifted their attention away from factory inspection, civil service laws would bring more public officials under civil service regulation, thereby giving women factory inspectors a chance to compete in a system based on merit rather than within the male-biased system of patronage politics. But civil service reform remained notoriously incomplete throughout Kelley's lifetime. Although a weak civil service had initially presented opportunities for women, it eventually accounted for the lack of women's opportunities.[43]

[41] Samuel Gompers, *Seventy Years of Life and Labor*, 1:194. See also Sklar, "Historical Foundations," in Koven and Michel, *Mothers of a New World*, pp. 43–93.
[42] For German factory inspectors, see Jean Quataert, "A Source Analysis in German Women's History."
[43] For the effect of the weakness of American civil service laws on women factory inspectors, see Helena Bergman, "That Noble Band?"

Kelley lost her position as chief factory inspector in 1897 when a new governor replaced her with a man whose main loyalties were to his political party. Unemployed and with three children to support, she took a part-time library job. When Heinrich Braun heard of her plight, he made her an offer she could not refuse: fifty dollars a month as long as she regularly supplied the *Archiv* with reports on "the social course of events in the States," critical reviews of "all remarkable social laws," together with their texts, and the activities of factory inspectors, bureaus of labor statistics, and strikes. Thus Kelley's dialogue with German political culture paid off literally—supplying the school fees for her youngest child. Her work also rewarded her intellectually. "I send my German check to the school, every month, as soon as it comes," she wrote her mother. "Although I have only eight [articles] a year, I find that I keep my eyes open and my ears sharpened for ideas much more acutely than I used to do; so the employment is really a healthful one."[44] In 1897 Florence Kelley found German Social Democrats more responsive to her writings than any audience in the United States.

Nevertheless, a use for Florence Kelley's talents soon emerged within her own political culture. The failure of civil service reform in the United States reflected a general administrative weakness of state and federal governments, especially compared to Germany. Consisting primarily of parties and courts, and lacking in administrative muscle, American governments were relatively underdeveloped.[45] Yet that weakness created new opportunities for women's voluntary organizations. As Florence Kelley's account of Chicago's anti-sweatshop campaign shows, class-bridging coalitions of women led the way, rather than health officers or other city or state officials.

Women's anti-sweatshop campaigns in several states combined in 1898 to form the National Consumers' League, and Kelley became its national secretary in 1899, a position she held until her death in 1932. In that position she advanced gender-specific legislation as a surrogate for class-specific legislation. For example, the NCL successfully championed before the U.S. Supreme Court in 1908 the constitutionality of a ten-hour working day for women, and in 1917 used the same strategies successfully to defend the constitutionality of ten-hours laws for men in nonhazardous occupations.[46]

[44] Heinrich Braun to Florence Kelley, Berlin, March 24, 1897, and July 24, 1897; and Florence Kelley to Caroline B. Kelley, Chicago, September 15, 1898, and August 9, 1898; quoted in Sklar, *Florence Kelley and the Nation's Work,* p. 297.
[45] For an analysis of the American state as consisting primarily of courts and parties, see Stephen Skowronek, *Building a New American State.* For the civil service movement, see Ari Hoogenboom, *Outlawing the Spoils.* For a comparison with the more successful British movement, see Noel Annan, "The Intellectual Aristocracy."
[46] See Sklar, "Historical Foundations," in Koven and Michel, *Mothers of a New World,* pp. 73–74.

The NCL did much to fulfill Florence Kelley's 1885 vision of middle-class women's organizations taking responsibility for the welfare of wage-earning women. With sixty-four powerful locals by 1904, the NCL shaped social and labor legislation in the United States to a degree unknown by any women's organization in Germany. In part the NCL's power was due to the weakness of class and the strength of gender as vehicles for political mobilization in the United States. In any case, it was informed by the class-based vision of social justice for women that Florence Kelley witnessed in Germany in the mid-1880s.

Florence Kelley was part of a much larger exchange of ideas in which American and German people valued what they found in one another's political cultures. Looking at German political culture allowed her to see her own more clearly, especially its possibilities for change. On both sides of the Atlantic, Florence Kelley's dialogue with German political culture created a new and expansive space for her reform career, one that sharpened her insight and liberated her imagination. In this way she exemplified the benefits derived from the transatlantic dialogue that increasing numbers of her peers in Germany and the United States joined after 1890.

Mary Church Terrell and Jane Addams were two of the many of Kelley's contemporaries whose social reform work also carried them into dialogue with German women reformers. In her address to the delegates assembled at the 1904 congress of the International Council of Women at Berlin, "The Progress of Colored Women," Terrell emphasized the affinity between the voluntary community work of black women, particularly the ten thousand members of the National Association of Colored Women (NACW), and the efforts of the international gathering at Berlin. In 1908, Jane Addams told American audiences about the superiority of German labor legislation. Speaking in terms that closely resembled Kelley's 1885 arguments, she demonstrated the continuing importance of the German model for progressive American feminists who believed that their state should be doing more to advance social justice.

German Reformers Consider the American Example, 1891–1914

German women had many opportunities to learn about American women's political activism, but from the beginning they realized that fundamental differences in the political cultures of their two nations limited the applicability of American patterns in Germany. As one observer of the founding of the ICW commented, "In Germany we have to work with great tact and by conservative methods. . . . The difference between our position and that of our American sisters is largely due to the fact that you live in a republic, we in a monarchy."[47] This formal difference in political organization symbolized other more substantive political dissimilarities that made it difficult for women in the two nations to borrow from each other's movements. Nevertheless, selectively and cautiously, many German women looked to the United States for strategies that they might adopt. Their efforts tell us a great deal about women's movements and nation-building in the two countries.

German women learned about American women's activism through printed sources, travel to conferences in the United States, and personal relationships with American women. Books like Lina Morgenstern's *Die Frauen des neunzehnten Jahrhunderts* (Women of the Nineteenth Century, 1888–1891) chronicled the lives of a number of American reformers, among them Lucretia Mott, Margaret Fuller, Elizabeth Cady Stanton, and Harriet Beecher Stowe. One of the most widely read German women's magazines, the quasi-political *Die Frau* (Woman, 1893–1944), reported on virtually every aspect of the American women's movement. It featured articles on coeducation, women's access to professions, suffrage, and social reform efforts sponsored by women, and it reviewed important American books like Charlotte Perkins Gilman's *Women and Economics* (1898). Social welfare periodicals also reported on American women's activism. Thus German readers learned almost instantly about the formation in 1890 of the New York Consumers' League, an organization that sought to regulate working conditions in department stores and to end sweatshop labor.[48] Both male and female reformers who traveled to the United States from Germany published quite substantial reports about social welfare measures initiated by women, such as the founding of settlement houses or the establishment of juvenile courts.[49]

Admiration for the American model of women's activism was most fully stated in Minna Cauer's 1893 essay "Women in the United States of America." Cauer, herself a feminist as well as a pioneer in German social welfare reform, sought to legitimate the American combination of feminism with social welfare reform. She did this by emphasizing the nation-building process that had shaped the American women's movement: "The nature of the American women's movement is rooted in that country itself," she argued.[50] A strong women's rights movement emerged out of the struggle

[47] International Council of Women, *Report of the International Council of Women*, p. 219.
[48] See R. S., "American Women Act to Solve the Social Question," reprinted here in Part II, document 1. For an analysis of attitudes toward consumption around the time when a consumers' league was founded in Berlin in 1907, see Warren Breckman, "Disciplining Consumption."
[49] See Emil Münsterberg, *Das amerikanische Armenwesen*, and Elsa von Liszt, *Soziale Fürsorgetätigkeit in den Vereinigten Staaten*.
[50] Minna Cauer, "Women in the United States of America," reprinted here in Part II, document 2.

to end slavery, for example, and its consolidation occurred after the Civil War.

Assuming that German readers were sympathetic with their own nation's unification in the 1870s, which tardily brought the German people into modern nationhood, Cauer built on this sympathy by emphasizing the ways that "women in the United States identified with their country and never lost sight of how they could contribute to its general welfare." For Cauer and for other German women in the 1890s, the American pattern presented a challenge because it combined the respectable goal of social welfare service with feminist notions, especially woman suffrage, that most middle-class Germans identified with socialism and other forms of what was generally considered unacceptable political activity. By characterizing the advancement of women's interests as nation-building, Cauer resolved that challenge and forged a respectable basis for the advancement of women's participation in public life. German women, she concluded, "are not permitted to participate in important higher education; the government does not make it easy for them to follow the way to their ideals and goals." Nevertheless, they were enhancing their nation by supporting one another. "Only the consciousness of giving something noble and encouraging to their own sex, and therefore also to their fatherland, supports the women, steels their courage, and inspires their endurance."[51] Cauer's emphasis on women's part in nation-building strongly contrasts with most conservative and even radical feminist German female social welfare activists, who tended to frame women's public activism as "balancing" the masculine influence in public life with feminine values and influence.[52]

German writers often expressed admiration for the American model of women's activism while simultaneously distancing themselves from it by pointing to its inherently American qualities. *Volkswohl*'s sketch of the founding of the New York Consumers' League noted the participation of German women in the league.[53] But Käthe Schirmacher's report on the women's congresses at the Chicago World's Fair in 1893, highlighted American women "who are unusual by German criteria," including women ministers, women lawyers, women doctors, suffragists, and temperance advocates. "Think what you will," Schirmacher emphasized, "the fact is that these women exist in America, that they are organized, and that they appeared forcefully at the congress."[54] Helene Lange, who became the lead-

---

[51] Ibid.

[52] For example, this "balance" informed the activities of the Bund für Mutterschutz. See Ann Taylor Allen, "Mothers of a New Generation."

[53] R.S., "American Women Act to Solve the Social Question," reprinted here in Part II, document 1. See also Louis L. Athey, "From Social Conscience to Social Action."

[54] Käthe Schirmacher, "The International Women's Congress in Chicago," reprinted here in Part II, document 3.

ing German feminist between 1890 and 1914, and who, more than any other single individual held together the coalition of conservative and progressive women activists during the first decade of the twentieth century, began her 1899 review of Elizabeth Cady Stanton's autobiography by noting, "No where else but in the United States of North America could this book have been written, this life lived."[55] Yet, however exotic, the American movement offered Cauer, Schirmacher, and Lange a robust example of "free women citizens in a free state" that they implicitly recommended to their readers.[56]

American women had less access to information about their German counterparts. Although an occasional publication, such as Theodore Stanton's *The Woman Question in Europe* (1884), brought contemporary accounts of European women's movements to the United States, there was no American equivalent of *Die Frau* consistently providing reports on the women's movement in Germany.[57] American suffrage periodicals and *Life and Labor,* the WTUL publication, occasionally ran articles on the German women's movement, but this coverage was infrequent. In 1915 the author of a study of feminism in Germany and Scandinavia tried to correct the belief "even in enlightened suffrage circles, that the German women are a leaderless and hopelessly domesticated group and are content to remain so."[58] The dialogue between German and American social justice feminists was an important antidote to ignorance.

Although the majority of German women had to learn about American women from printed sources, a few gained firsthand experience. German women travelers to the United States did not mirror their American equivalents' search for European culture or education. Instead, confident in the superiority of their own culture, they traveled to attend specific events, such as world's fairs. At least one German reformer, Anna Schepeler-Lette, visited the Centennial Exhibition in Philadelphia in 1876.[59]

German and American women reformers first met in an institutionalized

---

[55] Helene Lange, "An American Leader of the Women's Movement," reprinted here in Part II, document 4.

[56] Cauer, "Women in the United States," reprinted here in Part II, document 2.

[57] In 1881 Theodore Stanton, the son of Elizabeth Cady Stanton, married Marguerite Berry, daughter of a freethinking French Protestant family. The German contributors to Stanton's *The Woman Question in Europe* were Marie Calm, Jenny Hirsch, and Amalie (Anna) Schepeler-Lette. Calm (1832–1887) was a German teacher and writer whose nonfiction concerned the position of women teachers and women's higher education. Hirsch (1829–1902), raised in an orthodox Jewish family, in 1869 translated John Stuart Mill's *The Subjection of Women* into German; she edited *Der Frauen-Anwalt* (Woman's Advocate) and coedited the *Deutsche Hausfrauenzeitung* (The German Housewife's Paper). Schepeler-Lette (1827–1897) was an educational reformer and cofounder of the League of German Women's Associations (Bund Deutscher Frauenvereine, BDF).

[58] Katherine Anthony, *Feminism in Germany and Scandinavia,* p. iv.

[59] See note 57.

context at the women's congresses held as part of the Columbian Exposition in Chicago in 1893. The German delegation consisted of nine women, among them Hanna Bieber-Böhm, Auguste Förster, Anna Simson, Käthe Schirmacher, Annette Hamminck Schepel, and Marie Fischer Lette. Dazzled by the power of American women's organizations that they saw at the Chicago World's Fair in 1893, early in 1894 German women created within months after their return the League of German Women's Associations (Bund Deutscher Frauenvereine, BDF), an umbrella organization for non-socialist women's clubs explicitly modeled on the National Council of Women (NCW).[60]

Regardless of its attractions, travel across the Atlantic around the turn of the century could be wearisome and expensive, even after new steamships cut travel time to ten or twelve days. Transatlantic travel was more affordable for the typical American clubwoman than for her German counterpart. Whereas girls from upper-middle-class American families might first view Europe on a "finishing tour" after college, German women reformers typically visited the United States at a later age, usually to attend a women's conference. The trip to the fourth meeting of the International Council of Women in Toronto in 1909, for example, was advertised to members of the Berlin Girls' and Women's Groups for Social Assistance Work (Mädchen und Frauengruppen für soziale Hilfsarbeit) for $103 or 413 marks,

[60] May Wright Sewall, ed., *The World's Congress of Representative Women*, p. xxiv. For the German delegation in Chicago, see pp. 67–84. These delegates represented movements for moral reform, higher education, and vocational training. Wilhelm Adolf Lette (1799–1868) established vocational classes for middle-class women in 1866. His daughter Anna (see note 57), president of the Lette Association after 1872, was a supporter of women's higher education and professional training and became one of the prominent leaders in the German women's movement. It is not clear how Annette Hamminck Schepel and Marie Fischer Lette were related to her. The German delegates represented a wide range of women's clubs. Hanna Bieber-Böhm was president of a club for juvenile protection in Berlin. Auguste Förster represented the General German Women's Association (Allgemeiner Deutscher Frauenverein, ADF). Anna Simson was a delegate of an educational club (Frauenbildungsverein) in Breslau. Annette Hamminck Schepel and Marie Fischer Lette represented the Pestalozzi-Fröbel Haus, a school for kindergarten teachers, and the Lette Association in Berlin. No detailed biographical information is available on Simson, Hamminck Schepel, Fischer Lette, or Förster.

The BDF created the first nationwide German women's organization that united all non-socialist women's associations who chose to join and hold regular conferences. The much smaller General German Women's Association was active primarily in Leipzig. For the founding of the BDF, see Gerhard, *Unerhört*, pp. 166–67. For the National Council of Women (NCW) as a model for the BDF, see Agnes von Zahn-Harnack, *Die Frauenbewegung*, p. 19. For earlier contacts between the American women's movement and Europe, see Barbara Schnetzler, *Die frühe amerikanische Frauenbewegung und ihre Kontakte mit Europa*. The founding of the BDF made German women eligible to join the International Council of Women (ICW), the first major international women's organization, conceived along with the NCW in Washington, D.C., in 1888 at a meeting of the National Woman Suffrage Association (NWSA) that celebrated the fortieth anniversary of the first women's rights convention, held in Seneca Falls, New York.

originating from London. An ensuing trip to the West Coast could be made for an additional $80 (320 marks). Together these constituted more than two months' salary for a female teacher in Germany.[61] Alice Salomon, then corresponding secretary of the ICW, was able to attend the Toronto congress only because, beginning in 1906, the ICW provided travel grants for all its leaders. Likewise, the Women's International League for Peace and Freedom (WILPF), founded in 1919, sometimes paid travel expenses for members who would otherwise have been excluded from its meetings.[62]

For Americans participating in the dialogue at the turn of the century, the trip across the Atlantic was more routine. ICW president May Wright Sewall spent three months in France, Belgium, and Germany to prepare for the 1893 meeting. The Executive Council of the ICW met almost exclusively in Europe in the years before World War I, since very few Europeans could afford a transatlantic crossing every year.

Before World War I, international women's organizations also provided a venue at which German and American women could meet. Formally launched at the "World's Congress of Representative Women" during the Columbian Exposition, the ICW held general conferences in London (1899), Berlin (1904), Toronto (1909), and Rome (1914). The ICW offered a capacious tent that attracted social justice feminists and suffragists, although the organization excluded discussion of all controversial political and religious questions, and only passed vague resolutions on woman suffrage. This restriction created a need for and led to the founding of the International Woman Suffrage Alliance (IWSA) between 1899 and 1902, and its formal emergence at the 1904 ICW meeting in Berlin. The IWSA provided suffragists with a forum to exchange ideas and plot strategy. Like the ICW, it refused to get entangled in controversial national debates on woman suffrage and supported votes for women on the same terms that applied to the male franchise. The IWSA publicized its cause at congresses in Copenhagen (1906), Amsterdam (1908), London (1909), Stockholm (1911), and Budapest (1913). Meetings of the ICW and IWSA made their participants aware of women's activism in other parts of the world and publicized women's activism in host countries. The ICW rapidly grew from three national member organizations in 1897 to twenty-three in 1913, claiming to represent 6 million women, chiefly in Europe and North America. Its proceedings, published in English, French, and German, were widely distributed among the member associations of the German and American women's councils.[63]

---

61 *Monatsprogramme der "Mädchen- und Frauengruppen für soziale Hilfsarbeit,"* 1909, Fachhochschule Alice Salomon, Berlin, Archives.
62 Rupp, "Constructing Internationalism," p. 1577.
63 International Council of Women, *Women in a Changing World*, p. 39. For the founding of the International Woman Suffrage Alliance (IWSA), see Mineke Bosch with Annemarie

Personal acquaintances first established at women's international congresses often continued over many years through correspondence and repeated visits. Alice Salomon, for example, first met Jane Addams at the ICW congress in Toronto in 1909. Two years later, Salomon arranged for the German translation of Addams's autobiography, which also served as a textbook in Salomon's Women's School for Social Work. Addams renewed the personal acquaintance when she visited Europe during and after World War I, and Salomon visited Hull House again during her travels in the United States in 1923 and 1924.

In their encounters in print and at conferences, many similarities in the political cultures of German and American women drew them together. On both sides of the Atlantic women's public activism was buttressed by lifelong, intimate partnerships between women. Jane Addams and Mary Rozet Smith exemplified what was called a "Boston marriage" in the United States. Although Smith did not accompany Addams to international conferences, or on her semiofficial trips to Germany, the two did travel widely together, and Smith's money often funded Addams's international travel.[64] In Germany, Lida Gustava Heymann and Anita Augspurg maintained a similar relationship. Other leading participants in the transatlantic dialogue were unmarried or divorced, among them Gertrud Baer, Gertrud Bäumer, Alice Hamilton, Elisabet von Harnack, Florence Kelley, Helene Lange, Marie Elisabeth Lüders, and Alice Salomon. For most (though not all) women, lives of public leadership were incompatible with heterosexual marriage.[65]

Women's organizations in Germany and in the United States each contained a conspicuous cultural minority. Jewish women in Germany and African-American women in the United States brought diversity to women's organizations at the local and national levels, but they also posed a challenge to the dominant culture's capacity to tolerate difference. In 1904 at the ICW congress in Berlin, Alice Salomon's status as one of the organizers and Mary Church Terrell's address seemed to symbolize the ability of both national groups to embrace diversity. Yet Terrell and Salomon's subsequent struggles with the leadership of their national organizations revealed the persistence of racism within each political culture.

Kloosterman, *Politics and Friendship*, pp. 1–20, and Edith Hurwitz, "The International Sisterhood."

[64] Smith also funded Alice Hamilton's travels with Addams. See Alice Hamilton to Louise deKoven Bowen, Amsterdam, May 16, [1915], in Barbara Sicherman, *Alice Hamilton*, p. 192.

[65] Historical analysis of Boston marriages among Progressive women activists is still fragmentary. The most complete survey is Trisha Franzen, *Spinsters and Lesbians*. For Addams, see Sklar, *Florence Kelley and the Nation's Work*, pp. 192, 373–74. For the German context, see Reagin, *German Women's Movement*, p. 129. For the international context, see Leila Rupp, "Sexuality and Politics."

Jewish women participated in German women's organizations and in social welfare work in a much larger proportion than their numbers in the population as a whole would have predicted. At the same time that they maintained robust separate organizations, large numbers of Jewish women also entered the mainstream of middle-class women's public culture in Germany, especially in urban areas.[66] Alice Salomon, whose Women's School for Social Work (Soziale Frauenschule) attracted a predominantly Christian student body, exemplified the assimilationist thrust that motivated many German Jews. Just after the outbreak of World War I, at the age of forty-two, Salomon converted to Christianity. She later remembered that "many liberal Jews believed in assimilation and had their children brought up as Christians, following the official State policy and the counsel of historians, both maintaining that unity within a nation cannot be complete without oneness of creed."[67] Yet the Nazis ignored conversions, and driven from her home in 1937, Salomon emigrated to the United States.

Differences between white and black women in the United States also proved problematic. Partly because white women's organizations discouraged their participation or excluded them from membership, partly because their own communities relied heavily on the work of their separate associations, most African-American women gave their organizational energies to black women's clubs. Still, those who chose to work within predominantly white groups played an important role of educating white women about the needs of black Americans. Mary Church Terrell exemplified that educational work through her participation in the NAWSA, the ICW, and the WILPF. As a delegate to the third quinquennial congress of the ICW in Berlin in 1904, she educated her audience about the progress and problems of African-American women. As she demonstrated in her defense of black troops as part of the French occupation of the Rhineland after World War I, and as the ensuing debate in the WILPF showed, prejudice against black people was an international as well as a national problem.

The attempted integration of cultural minorities into the dominant society was part of the larger process of nation-building then under way in each country. Both had recently forged a new national unity from a looser federation of states. In 1871 Prussia, under the leadership of Otto von Bismarck, created the German Reich by uniting with a group of German states that included Bavaria, Baden, Saxony, and the Rhineland. A corre-

[66] Marion A. Kaplan, *The Jewish Feminist Movement in Germany,* and Marion A. Kaplan, *The Making of the Jewish Middle Class,* pp. 192–227, esp. 218.
[67] Alice Salomon, "Character is Destiny: An Autobiography," typescript, Salomon Papers, Memoir Collection, Leo Baeck Institute, New York, pp. 122–23; published in German as Alice Salomon, *Charakter ist Schicksal.* Also available in the library of the Fachhochschule Alice Salomon, Berlin.

sponding process of state formation in the United States accompanied the American Civil War and Reconstruction, with the admission of eleven new states to the Union between 1861 and 1890.

In both countries political integration facilitated the process of industrial development. The triumph of free labor in the United States accelerated the settlement of the remaining frontier and set the stage for rapid industrialization. In Germany the centralized government promoted industrial development and checked the power of landed interests. The rapidity of industrialization in each country was especially visible in dramatic increases in steel production. German steel production rose twenty-fold between 1880 and 1914, from 690,000 to almost 14 million tons. American steel production increased seven-fold, rising from the much larger base of 3 million tons in 1880 to more than 25 million in 1914. Population growth in both countries was also phenomenal. In Germany the population increased by 70 percent between 1880 and 1925, from 45 to 63 million; while the U.S. population more than doubled over the same period, rising from 50 to 106 million between 1880 and 1920.[68]

German immigration to the United States contributed to that population increase and constituted an indirect basis for women's transatlantic dialogue. The vast majority of Germans who left the "fatherland" went to North America. Following the emigration of about 100,000 Germans to the British-American colonies in the eighteenth century, approximately five and a half million Germans settled in the United States in the nineteenth century, by far the largest group of European immigrants. The majority, usually originating from the lower-middle and the lower classes, came in search of better economic and social conditions. Among them were farmers and artisans as well as some teachers, academics, and political refugees. Later, these groups were joined by skilled and unskilled industrial workers and servants. In some centers of German immigration like Chicago, German-Americans and their children made up almost a third of the population before immigration peaked in 1890.[69]

By many measures, however, differences between the two emerging nations seemed to outweigh their similarities. For participants in the transatlantic dialogue, one of the most striking differences was the access American women enjoyed to higher education. That access was fueled by

[68]   *Historical Statistics of the United States, Colonial Times to 1970*, part 1 (Washington, D.C.: U.S. Government Printing Office, 1975), pp. 9, 693; Brian R. Mitchell, *European Historical Statistics, 1750–1975* (New York: Macmillan, 1980), pp. 30, 420.
[69]   For German immigration to the United States, see Kathleen Conzen, "Germans"; Günther Moltmann, "Charakteristische Züge der deutschen Amerika-Auswanderung im 19. Jahrhundert," in Frank Trommler, ed., *Amerika und die Deutschen*, pp. 40–49; and Linda Pickle, *Contented among Strangers.* For German-American women in Chicago, see Christiane Harzig, *Familie, Arbeit und weibliche Öffentlichkeit in einer Einwanderungsstadt.*

the feminization of the teaching profession between 1830 and 1860, which itself was a response to the vast expansion of the common school system during the settlement of the North American continent in the nineteenth century. The contemporaneous ideology of Republican motherhood, which during the early years of universal white male suffrage emphasized the capacity of mothers to train responsible citizens, also promoted women's education. After 1860 these trends bore fruit in two types of institutions: land-grant state universities and elite women's colleges. State universities, founded through the Morrill Act of 1862, were "open to all," including women. Vassar, Smith, and Wellesley began accepting students between 1865 and 1875. By 1880 one of every three students enrolled in an institution of higher learning in the United States was a woman. This produced a generation of college-educated women who sought work commensurate with their talents. Many found that work in various aspects of social reform.[70]

While American women were often excluded from graduate study in their own country, German women who sought any university degree had to study abroad. Demands for higher education for German women were first articulated during the revolution of 1848. Thereafter, like Americans, German women justified their demand for higher education on the grounds that they needed to be better educated as mothers and wives. Throughout much of the nineteenth century, the education of middle- and upper-class women beyond elementary school was limited to private girls' schools, with a curriculum that stressed languages, needlework, drawing, and music. As the documents in this book show, some women succeeded in making the most out of these very limited educational opportunities. Language classes and occasional stays in England and France enabled them to conduct the transatlantic dialogue in English, follow conference proceedings, and function as interpreters in English or French at international women's congresses.

After massive petitioning by the bourgeois women's movement throughout the 1880s, especially by the General Association of German Women Teachers (Allgemeiner Deutscher Lehrerinnenverein, ADLV), the core of the German movement in that decade, the options for women's higher education widened in the 1890s. Minimally, female pupils could attend the "Lyzeum" featuring "women's education," which did not prepare them for any specific work. Or they could opt for three years of quasi-academic work and a year in a teacher's seminary, which qualified them to teach at

---

[70] Public universities accepting women by 1870 were Iowa (in 1855); Wisconsin (in 1867); Kansas, Indiana, and Minnesota (in 1869); and Missouri, Michigan, and California (in 1870). See Barbara Miller Solomon, *In the Company of Educated Women.* See also Sklar, *Florence Kelley and the Nation's Work*, pp. 50–68.

elementary and girls' schools, one of the few acceptable professions for middle-class women. A few students chose the newly established "Mädchengymnasium" (secondary education classes for girls), required for university admission. Public secondary education for women was established in 1893, but not institutionalized until 1908.[71]

Graduation from a Mädchengymnasium did not, however, guarantee access to a university. Women were generally excluded from regular enrollment; until 1896 women could not even audit a class in a Prussian university without the permission of the Ministry of Education. Other German states were more liberal: the University of Heidelberg opened its medical school to women in 1900, and all departments in 1901. Alice Salomon took up her study of economics at the University of Berlin in 1902 with special permission of some progressive faculty members and received her doctorate in 1906. Only in 1908 did the Prussian government agree to general admission of women to its universities. By then women had gained access to universities in many other European countries, and even in other German states.[72]

Even more salient than these educational differences were the different state systems that German and American women encountered. In Germany the central state system was quite strong, whereas in the United States it was relatively weak. Elections for the national legislature or Reichstag were based on universal male suffrage, but because the German Reich was a monarchy, the kaiser and his ministers held far greater power than the Reichstag. Moreover, participation in municipal and regional elections in Prussia, the largest of the German states, was limited to property holders. As a result, the electorate split along class lines with the Social Democratic Party in the Reichstag representing most working-class voters and a range of centrist and rightist parties representing most middle-class voters in the Reichstag and in local and regional elections.[73]

Such class splits did not occur in the United States. Class-oriented voting was avoided, partly because white male suffrage was established before the industrial revolution, and the emergence of modern political parties and popular voting before 1830 organized the polity along lines that did

[71] On women's higher education in Germany, see Frevert, *Women in German History*, pp. 120–25; Gerhard, *Unerhört*, pp. 138–67; and James C. Albisetti, *Schooling German Girls and Women*. On female university students in the Weimar Republic, see Gitta Benker and Senta Störmer, *Grenzüberschreitungen*.

[72] Switzerland first admitted women to university classes (though not to degree-granting programs) in the 1840s, France in 1863, the Scandinavian countries in 1870, the Netherlands in 1878, and Belgium in 1883. See Gerhard, *Unerhört*, p. 140.

[73] The chief exception to such class-based voting in Germany were confessional divisions; the Catholic Center Party received most of the votes of Catholics from all classes. In the United States, by contrast, ethnicity and class divided Catholic voters into different parties. For the SPD, see Carl Schorske, *German Social Democracy*.

not conform to what later emerged as an industrial working class and a middle class of owners and managers. Thus class became a strong vehicle for political mobilization in Germany, but a weak one in the United States.

On both sides of the Atlantic, middle-class women understood the importance of the state in their efforts to gain new public power. This made them aware of the differences in their two political traditions. For example, German advocates of woman suffrage commented on Susan B. Anthony sending NAWSA envelopes through the U.S. mails bearing the motto, "No just government can be formed without the consent of the governed." When she tried to use the envelopes during a trip to Germany, her letters were returned with the explanation that "such sentiments are not allowed to pass through the post office."[74] German women thought that American women had greater access to the power of the state because they had participated to a greater degree in the process of nation-building. In many ways they were right, the chief problem being that the state they had helped build was itself relatively weak.

Perhaps the single most dramatic difference in the political cultures of middle-class women in Germany and the United States during the crucial decades between 1850 and 1908 were the laws that regional German governments enacted to prohibit women from participating in political activities. Passed in the wake of the failed 1848 revolution, these laws (the *Vereinsgesetze*) barred women from attending political meetings or joining political organizations.[75]

Emily Balch encountered these laws in the mid-1890s when she attended a mass meeting addressed by Wilhelm Liebknecht, leader of the Social Democratic Party and Reichstag member. "This form of meeting was a device for getting around the law forbidding apprentices or women to attend meetings of a political organization," she remembered. "Police sat on a table on the platform with their spiked helmets in their hands. If their helmets were put on, the meeting was thereby closed."[76] Although the laws

---

[74] Lange, "An American Leader," reprinted here in Part II, document 4. The quotation is from Elizabeth Cady Stanton, *Eighty Years and More: Reminiscences, 1815–1897* (1898; reprint, New York: Fisher Unwin, 1971), p. 176.

[75] Antisocialist laws (1878–90) banned "associations with the purpose of overthrowing the existing state and social order by working for social democratic, socialist or communist ideas." Michael Schneider, *A Brief History of the German Trade Unions*, p. 51. Since members of the Reichstag enjoyed immunity, however, the Social Democratic Party (SPD) continued to grow even though its meetings and literature were banned. For women in the SPD, see Heinz Niggemann, *Emanzipation zwischen Sozialismus und Feminismus*, and Sabine Richebächer, *Uns fehlt nur eine Kleinigkeit*. Evans, *Feminist Movement in Germany*, pp. 72–73, 87, 93, argues that these laws made the German women's movement more conservative. Women's organizations could be disbanded for sending delegates to Socialist Party conventions. For another example of the laws' operation, see Mary Nolan, *Social Democracy and Society*, p. 123. See also Ute Gerhard, *Verhältnisse und Verhinderungen*.

[76] Quoted in Mercedes M. Randall, *Improper Bostonian*, pp. 93–94.

were unevenly enforced and working-class socialist women felt their effects far more harshly than did middle-class reformers, these statutes prevented women from engaging individually and collectively in the political life of their communities or their nation. Nominally, at least, their actions had to be "above" politics.

Although bans against socialist groups were lifted in the 1890s, those against women remained in force until 1908, when they were repealed because their enforcement among powerful social groups had become too difficult. For example, the government took no action when after 1900 "the wives" were admitted to the annual meetings of the Federation of Farmers (Bund der Landwirte), even though political talk prevailed. When liberal journalists publicized police tolerance of the "squires' wives," the minister of the interior ruled that women might be admitted to political meetings if they listened in a "section" (*Frauenabteilung*) apart from the men. At about the same time, the Society for Social Reform (Gesellschaft für soziale Reform), a progressive group of men who sought the cooperation of women experts on labor legislation, decided to test the law. They invited Helene Simon, one of the first women economists, to address their annual meeting. Her lecture was entitled "The Reduction of Working Hours for Women and the Protection of Adolescents in Factories." The police responded with an order stating that she was not to be admitted to the hall. After some negotiation, her lecture was delivered by a one of the men, while she listened from the "women's section" with instructions "neither to show signs of approval or disapproval" of her own lecture. Such incidents made the laws' enforcement comical.[77]

Still, the *Vereinsgesetze* had many enduring consequences besides the obvious effect of excluding women from participation in political activities. First and perhaps most important, they restrained women's organizations in many German states from pursuing the goal of woman suffrage.[78] The earliest German woman suffrage association was formed in 1902, a generation later than its equivalent in the United States, and suffrage never became the *raison d'être* of the mainstream of the German women's movement as it did in the United States. Just when the bans on women's attendance at political meetings were lifted, the German Protestant Women's Federation (Deutsch-Evangelischer Frauenbund, DEF) was becoming a powerful conservative force in women's political culture. Although the DEF supported municipal and church suffrage before the war, it opposed national woman suffrage. In 1908 the DEF joined the League of

[77] Salomon, "Character is Destiny," pp. 91–92.
[78] Hamburg and a few other jurisdictions tolerated the existence of women's suffrage organizations, however.

German Women's Associations explicitly to strengthen conservatives in a debate over reform of abortion laws.[79]

The DEF differed from anti-suffrage groups in the United States in two revealing ways: it was much larger, and its primary loyalty lay with the struggle against socialism. After it joined the BDF in 1908, the DEF shaped much of the mainstream of the German women's movement by participating extensively in social welfare programs, which they fostered in explicit opposition to socialism.[80] Successful in its antiabortion effort, the DEF left the BDF in 1918 over the BDF's support of national woman suffrage. After the enactment of national woman suffrage by the revolutionary government in November 1918 and its incorporation in the Weimar constitution in 1919, the DEF mobilized women's votes for conservative parties, and several of its members ran for national office.

No equivalent antisuffrage, antisocialist, pro–social welfare organization existed in the United States. Although leaders of some American anti-suffrage groups tried to discredit the woman suffrage movement by associating it with socialism, their exhortations seemed wildly improbable. Mrs. Gilbert E. Jones, founder of the National League for the Civic Education of Women, wrote in 1909 that if women had studied the principles of government "woman suffrage could not have gained the headway that it has and many of them would very clearly see how the movement is strongly allied with Socialism."[81] But Mrs. Jones, a non-entity in American political culture, did not complicate the lives or actions of pre–World War I American social justice feminists. In Germany, on the other hand, the opinions of the leaders of the Deutsch-Evangelischer Frauenbund had to be taken very seriously indeed, since they not only commanded the power of their extensive membership but also drew upon a larger conservative network of men who held public office. This difference in the mainstream of the women's movements in Germany and the United States did much to shape the destinies of social justice feminists in both countries. In Germany after 1910 much of the mainstream of the women's movement was not readily available for common cause with social justice feminists. In the United States, common cause with the mainstream of the women's movement brought social justice feminists unprecedented power.

In addition to deterring the development of a strong suffrage movement

[79]   Gerhard, *Unerhört*, pp. 203–5; Doris Kaufmann, *Frauen zwischen Aufbruch und Reaktion*, pp. 47–60.
[80]   Evans, *Comrades and Sisters*, pp. 194–96; Reagin, *German Women's Movement*, p. 46.
[81]   Mrs. Gilbert E. Jones, "Some Impediments to Woman Suffrage," *North American Review*, August 1909; quoted in Jane Jerome Camhi, *Women Against Women*, p. 96. For a discussion of social welfare activities among American anti-suffragists, see Thomas J. Jablonsky, *The Home, Heaven, and Mother Party*, pp. 58–63.

in Germany, the *Vereinsgesetze* discouraged women's organizations from conducting their own internal political debates. This denied their individual members the political skills that might have developed through such debates and undermined the strengthening of their collective will that such debates might have engendered.[82] Another profound effect of the laws was to deepen the wedge between working-class and middle-class women's activism. Police tended to overlook the presence of women at middle-class political meetings but had a legal excuse to disrupt any socialist meeting with women in attendance.

This class distinction in the enforcement of the law widened the already ample gulf between the public activism of working-class and middle-class women. For example, antagonisms on both sides prevented socialist women's groups from joining the BDF. At the BDF's founding congress in 1894, participants invited "working women's organizations" to join, but explicitly excluded those with "clear political tendencies"—that is, all socialist women's groups. Although a group of social justice feminists, including Minna Cauer, Lina Morgenstern, and Salomon's mentor, Jeanette Schwerin, publicly protested against the exclusion, this split within the BDF prompted Clara Zetkin, nominal leader of women within the SPD, to declare a "clean separation" ("reinliche Scheidung") between the two women's movements. And so they remained for decades to come.[83]

In sum, the *Vereinsgesetze* inhibited the development of social justice feminism in Germany. Lacking the ability to discuss political issues freely at public meetings, German women could not readily pursue the four-stage process that characterized groups of American women reformers: investigate, educate, legislate, enforce. Although they did investigate, educate, and lobby, their efforts were muted compared to their American counterparts and focused primarily on issues related to education rather than the industrial workplace.

By contrast, as early as the 1880s in the United States the Woman's Christian Temperance Union's motto, "Do Everything," encouraged political activism on behalf of a wide range of social legislation. In many northern states women began to vote in school board elections in the 1870s; by the 1890s these were often hotly contested around issues related to child

---

[82] See Reagin, *German Women's Movement*, pp. 17, 25, 184; Evans, *Feminist Movement in Germany*, p. 11.

[83] See Gerhard, *Unerhört*, pp. 178–80; Richard J. Evans, "Bourgeois Feminists and Women Socialists in Germany"; Karen Honeycutt, "Socialism and Feminism in Imperial Germany"; and Clara Zetkin, "Proletarische und Bürgerliche Frauenbewegung," *Die Gleichheit*, November 21, 1900, p. 186. In *Reluctant Feminists*, Jean Quataert discusses the conflict between Zetkin and Lily Braun over the extent to which Social Democratic women should cooperate with bourgeois feminists, pp. 107–36.

labor or the inadequacy of schools in working-class districts.[84] Facing no obstacles to their activism, by 1900 American social justice feminists emerged as vibrant, class-bridging agents within the American women's movement. Then, during the ensuing two decades, social justice feminist leaders became major players in American public life. Crucial to their power was the political and financial autonomy of their institutions, particularly social settlements and women's organizations like the NCL.[85] For example, between 1909 and 1919 the NCL and its sixty-four locals campaigned for the passage of state minimum wage laws for women successfully in fourteen states.

Social justice feminists in Germany had quite a different history. Just as men's political culture in Germany divided sharply along class lines, so too did women's. While cross-class activities enhanced the position of American social justice feminists, the rigidity of class politics undercut their equivalents in Germany.

Both American and German women sought state funding for the social services they offered, but in Germany such funding was much more widespread, partly because it was seen as an effective way to counteract the growth of socialism. Funds for women's social work in Hanover, for example, came to women's organizations with the proviso that they oppose the "unpatriotic forces" associated with the Social Democratic Party.[86] Thus while the mainstream of the middle-class women's movement in the United States developed an independent relationship with a relatively weak state, the mainstream of German middle-class women cooperated with a relatively strong state. The strength of the American mainstream lay in its ability to build an autonomous partisan political presence; the strength of the German mainstream lay in its ability to tap into the resources of the state while remaining nominally nonpartisan.

Social justice feminists who joined these mainstreams faced different challenges. In the United States they sought to channel the mainstream women's movement to support their legislative goals; in Germany they struggled against being absorbed into the class and state imperatives of the mainstream. American social justice feminists faced the challenge of forging a state system capable of implementing their goals. German social jus-

[84] See Sklar, "Historical Foundations," in Koven and Michel, *Mothers of a New World*, pp. 43–93. Frances Willard, president of the WCTU between 1879 and her death in 1898, set a strong example for later social justice feminists, although most did not know of her support for socialism in her later years. She wrote in her diary on August 17, 1893: "The International Socialistic Congress in Zurich holds my thoughts." Carolyn De Swarte Gifford, ed., *Writing Out My Heart*, p. 379.
[85] For settlements, see Sklar, *Florence Kelley and the Nation's Work*, pp. 171–205, and Mina Carson, *Settlement Folk*. For the National Consumers' League, see Sklar, "Two Political Cultures."
[86] Reagin, *German Women's Movement*, p. 58.

tice feminists faced the challenge of forming coalitions capable of sustaining their goals.

Conservative social initiatives became even more important in Germany with the end of the antisocialist laws. In the 1890s the SPD emerged as the largest political party in Germany, but its power was substantially curbed by the undemocratic structures of German political institutions and the power of the civil service, which insulated administrative officials from the effects of popular protest votes. Women's provision of social welfare services buttressed the power of conservative municipal governments and integrated the activism of the conservative mainstream of the German women's movement into a larger conservative agenda. This, in turn, undercut their pursuit of expanded rights for women and seriously compromised their ability to act independently of state mandates.

After the bans against women's political activity ended in 1908, neither suffragists, social justice feminists, nor conservative social welfare activists sought to expand their independent political base. Rather, they worked even more closely with mainstream political parties. Most social justice feminists supported the Progressive Liberal Party, which combined a commitment to universal suffrage with a belief in social justice.[87]

Progressive German feminists were not actively courted by the Progressive Liberal or other centrist parties, but they did feel attracted to the SPD, many of whose leaders (both women and men) were themselves middle class. Alice Salomon described this struggle in her autobiography: "Labor loomed high on my social-work horizon. The socialist movement grew strong after it had been freed of restrictive laws. I knew that I must decide where I stood. For women twenty years older than I, this had been no problem. They were, rather, liberal; socialism had not yet affected the bourgeoisie and the intellectuals."[88]

Salomon knew that "some women of the leisure class" were helping to organize women's trade unions in England and in the United States, "but in Germany the class-war theory had too firm a hold on the minds of organized labor." Unless she became a "party-socialist, such an attempt would be impossible."[89] While social justice feminists like Salomon might personally identify with labor, they were forced to choose between joining a movement that sought the destruction of the German state as it was presently constituted and courting the centrists who controlled municipal institutions.

Salomon said that she remained politically independent by joining

---

[87] Ibid., p. 184; Gerhard, *Unerhört*, pp. 280–91. See also James C. Hunt, "The Bourgeois Middle in German Politics."

[88] Salomon, "Character is Destiny," p. 49.

[89] Ibid.

women reformers "who knew that there is no wealth but life and that life must be valued and protected."[90] Hedged in on the left by an insurgent socialism and on the right by the conservatism of state-dominated social welfare, women like Alice Salomon walked a fine line—especially compared to their freer-wheeling American counterparts.

By comparison, Jane Addams confidently brushed off socialists. "During the first decade of Hull-House," she wrote in 1910, "it was felt by propagandists of diverse social theories that the new Settlement would be a fine coin of vantage from which to propagate social faiths, and that a mere preliminary step would be the conversion of the founders. . . . The early socialists used every method of attack,—a favorite one being the statement, doubtless sometimes honestly made, that I was a socialist, but 'too much of a coward to say so.' "[91] Unlike her German peers, Addams did not feel compelled to clarify her relationship with organized socialism.

The closer grappling of German social justice feminists with socialism did not mean that all German middle-class women were more conservative than their American counterparts. The contrary was sometimes the case. One women's organization far too radical for American tastes was the League for the Protection of Motherhood and Sexual Reform (Bund für Mutterschutz und Sexualreform), created by Helene Stöcker in 1905. Claiming about 3800 members at its height around 1910, the League drew on the efforts of male sexual reformers and radicals within the bourgeois women's movement. It advocated sexual ideas that could never have gained a hearing in the mainstream of the American suffrage movement, supporting women's right to abortion, contraception, and extramarital sexuality. The League's influence was greatest soon after its founding, but a bitter conflict between its two founders in 1910 led by 1914 to the disintegration of its loose coalition of male professionals and feminists.[92]

After 1908 the woman suffrage movement grew even more fragmented in Germany. In 1902, Anita Augspurg, Lida Gustava Heymann, Minna Cauer, and Käthe Schirmacher organized the first bourgeois German woman suffrage organization, the German Association for Woman Suffrage (Deutscher Verein für Frauenstimmrecht), in Hamburg. Later Anna Lindemann emerged as an important leader in that group. A rival organization emerged in 1911 to defend property-based suffrage—the German Federation for Woman Suffrage (Deutsche Vereinigung für Frauenstimmrecht), and in 1913 the progressives around Augspurg, Heymann, and Cauer seceded from the Association to form yet a third group, the German

---

[90]   Ibid., p. 53.
[91]   Addams, *Twenty Years at Hull House,* p. 57.
[92]   Allen, "Mothers of a New Generation"; Grossman, *Reforming Sex,* pp. 16–17; Evans, *Feminist Movement in Germany,* pp. 120–39.

Union for Woman Suffrage (Deutscher Bund für Frauenstimmrecht). The 1902 Association sought equality with male voters; the 1911 Federation pursued "equal citizenship"—leaving room for current suffrage differences based on class; and the 1913 Union demanded a radical reform of the German electoral system.[93]

Meanwhile, however, progressive women's groups in Germany were swamped numerically and politically by more conservative organizations. Before 1914 these included the DEF, founded in 1899, and the German Catholic German Women's Federation (Katholischer Deutscher Frauenbund, KDFB), founded in 1903. After 1914, conservative women's organizations increased in size and challenged the primacy of the older and more liberal member associations of the BDF.[94]

After 1908, when the split between conservatives and progressives deepened within German bourgeois feminism, dialogue with Americans was undertaken primarily by the progressives. American social justice feminists were reaching the apogee of their national influence, and German progressives, conscious of the deepening conflicts in their domestic environment between progressives and conservatives, Protestants and Catholics, liberals and socialists, drew professional and personal strength from the American example. Professionally, when they compared their own positions within their political culture to those of their American equivalents, they discovered assets as well as liabilities. Personally, they drew inspiration from the intense spiritual commitment to their work that they shared with their American peers.

No one better exemplified that commitment than Alice Salomon, who came to be called "the German Jane Addams." Salomon was born in Berlin to a Jewish family in 1872. As a young woman, she joined the Girls and Women's Groups for Social Assistance Work, founded in 1893 by Berlin philanthropists, among them Minna Cauer. In many respects this work emulated early activities in American settlements, but Salomon and other German women reformers never considered actually living in working-class neighborhoods. Convincing middle-class parents to permit them to work in a kindergarten or engage in "friendly visiting" twice a week was difficult enough. To transcend the geographical boundaries of class proved impossible. Furthermore, German women, even German women whose fathers

---

93 Gerhard, *Unerhört,* pp. 216–25, 280–92. See also Amy Hackett, "Feminism and Liberalism in Wilhelmine Germany."
94 These conservative organizations included the Red Cross women's auxiliary (Vaterländischer Frauenverein), founded in 1866; the German Women's League (Deutscher Frauenbund), founded in 1907; the Women's Federation of the German Colonial Society (Frauenbund der deutschen Kolonialgesellschaft), founded in 1907; and the Union of German Protestant Women's Leagues (Vereinigung Evangelischer Frauenverbände Deutschlands), founded in 1918. For their activities, see Roger Chickering, " 'Casting Their Gaze More Broadly.' "

were deceased, rarely controlled their own financial resources and had no equivalent to the American financial support network supplied by women's colleges.

Salomon's entry into women's organizations was mentored by Jeannette Schwerin (1852–99), whom she succeeded as president of the "Groups" in 1899. Schwerin, a prominent social reformer and a progressive leader in the bourgeois women's movement, introduced Salomon to the BDF in Hamburg in 1898, and to the third congress of the ICW in London in 1899. At the 1904 Berlin congress, Salomon chaired sessions on women's employment, protective labor legislation, and the professions.

In 1908 in Berlin Salomon founded the Women's School for Social Work. Financially self-supporting because salaries were modest and the students many, Germany's first secular institution for social work training was enormously successful. Salomon recruited her faculty from the leading women in public life associated with poor law administration and charity organization societies. Other schools of its type quickly emerged, usually supported by municipal funds. Their raids on her staff required her to recruit new faculty constantly. In 1914 the school moved into its own building. Salomon's school created an opportunity for German women to pursue "the social question." In a context that offered girls only "polishing" schools or private tutoring beyond the tenth grade, she brought them into contact with contemporary social problems.[95]

After 1910, Salomon's combined positions as a leading social welfare professional and a prominent figure in the ICW made her the chief German participant in the dialogue with progressive women reformers in the United States. In 1911 she penned a deeply personal letter to Addams after reading her autobiography, *Twenty Years at Hull House,* in which she spoke of the similarity of their personal commitment to social reform— their view of their work as a calling rather than a profession.[96]

Salomon's views of social work were strongly influenced by her 1909 tour of American social settlements, when she concluded that American social endeavors "do not start so much with the needs of the individual— the needy one—but with the society, the nation." She thought that American social provision was highly gendered, "Everything that concerns caring for human life, for body, mind, and soul, has to be done by women."[97] Salomon returned to Germany with a firm commitment to turn these qualities into a profession.

[95] Salomon, "Character is Destiny," pp. 93–102.
[96] Salomon to Addams, 11 Dec. 1911, reprinted here in Part II, document 7.
[97] Salomon, "Social Work in America," reprinted here in Part II, document 6; and Salomon, "Der Internationale Frauenbund in Kanada," *Die Frau* 16 (1908/9): 713.

The Dialogue Changes during World War I

The outbreak of World War I permanently altered the dialogue between progressive women reformers in Germany and the United States. On both sides of the Atlantic social justice feminists faced the choice of supporting the war effort or working for international cooperation. As the limitations of nation-building and nationhood became more apparent, they embraced international cooperation, changing their dialogue from a cross-national to a transnational one.

Germany's declaration of war against Russia and France, Germany's invasion of Belgium, and England's declaration of war against Germany in August 1914 launched four years of unprecedented loss of life. The battle of the Somme, in July 1916, produced nearly a million casualties among British, German, and French soldiers; nineteen thousand British soldiers died in one day. Since the United States entered the war rather late—April 1917—American losses and hence the power of American leaders to influence the terms of the peace treaty were far less than those of their British and French allies. An armistice was finally declared on November 11, 1918, followed by a vengeful peace treaty. Reverberations of the carnage of World War I continued until 1945.[98]

Their nations' wartime commitments put women social reformers on opposing sides of a great cataclysm. Even before the United States entered the war, pro-British and anti-German sentiment in the United States made it clear on which side the Americans would fight. Nevertheless, publicists for Germany tried to tilt the opinion of American women in a more favorable direction with articles in American suffrage magazines about the arduous support German women were giving to their nation's war effort, and the heroic sacrifices women were making.[99] Now women's efforts at nation-building only aided the war effort and enlarged the gulf between their two peoples. Yet even though pro-war sentiments in both countries left little room for dissent on the home front, a small group of progressive feminists in Germany and the United States began almost immediately to wage peace instead. War severely limited but did not stop the dialogue between them. Some who had maintained the transatlantic dialogue since the 1890s, joined now by new recruits, shifted the terms of the dialogue from social peace to international peace. In so doing they reshaped

[98] For the Battle of the Somme, see John Keegan, *The Face of Battle,* p. 280, and Craig Mair, *Britain at War,* pp. 50–51. For the weak military basis of the American negotiating position at the peace talks, see David Trask, *The American Expeditionary Force and Coalition Warmaking.*

[99] See Mabel Harding, "German Women and the War," reprinted here in Part III, document 1. For the general effort to influence American public opinion, see Reinhard Doerries, "Promoting *Kaiser* and *Reich*," in Schröder, *Confrontation and Cooperation,* pp. 135–66. See also Regina Schulte, "The Sick Warrior's Sister."

women's peace activism, recast social justice feminism, and redefined the imperatives of nation-building. They joined a movement of men and women that had begun at the Hague Conference of 1899, where twenty-six governments agreed to establish a Permanent Court of Arbitration and sought to reduce global conflict through international cooperation.[100]

In 1914, international women's organizations like the ICW or the IWSA passed vague resolutions about peace, but they did nothing to foster reconciliation among their members. Some women did more. American and German women social reformers and pacifists met with women from other nations at conferences held at The Hague in 1915, at Zurich in 1919, and at Vienna in 1921. Gathering first to call for an end to the war, and then to shape the peace, women from warring and neutral nations launched a new era of feminist international cooperation. Since both the ICW and the IWSA opposed the 1915 meeting, a new international women's organization evolved during the war, one based on woman suffrage, social justice feminism, and peace.

Women who attended these congresses faced severe censure from their compatriots for undercutting their nations' war efforts. In Germany the board of the BDF declared the gathering at The Hague "incompatible with the patriotic sentiments and national duties of the German women's movement."[101] Its president, Gertrud Bäumer, threatened any who attended with ostracism, a threat that kept some liberal and internationally oriented members like Alice Salomon at home. For Salomon, this board decision posed a particular dilemma: participation in the congress would have deprived her of any chance for the presidency of the BDF—a position to which she aspired. Salomon later remembered that "progressive women before the war, now seemed reactionary to me."[102]

Yet another factor helps explain Salomon's absence from The Hague: the close integration of German social welfare activism within the imperatives of the state. Salomon spent the last years of the war as the head of the women's department of the War Office for her home province. This job meant, in her words, "actual service in the war machine." She recruited German women to work in noncombat positions in Poland, Russia, and

---

[100] The Hague conference of 1899 was the occasion for the first international peace gathering of women, organized by Margarethe Selenka, a member of the Munich Peace Society. She and Austrian Berta von Suttner presented to the conference president a list of 565 women's peace rallies in eighteen countries. Berta von Suttner (1843–1914), whose 1889 novel, *Die Waffen nieder!* (Lay Down your Arms!), made her a leader of the international peace movement, received the Nobel Peace Prize in 1905 and toured widely in the United States in 1904 and 1912.

[101] See Bäumer, "The League of German Women's Associations and the Women's Congress at the Hague," reprinted here in Part III, document 3.

[102] Salomon, "Character is Destiny," p. 127. Salomon was probably referring to Gertrud Bäumer and Helene Lange.

Ukraine and organized the work, the working conditions, and the living conditions of women and children in Prussia. Later she claimed to have "not a grain of nationalistic enthusiasm in me" and explained her wartime work as a surrender "to the argument that everyone who refused to serve weakened the ranks of our soldiers and increased the danger of defeat, and because I would probably soon be conscripted, anyway; but also because the war seemed easier to bear if I drowned myself in work."[103] Nevertheless, when Jane Addams traveled to Berlin to present the resolutions of the Women's Peace Congress at The Hague, Alice Salomon saw her and helped arrange her interview with the German chancellor.

Addams herself endured scorching criticism upon her return to the United States in 1915. When her description of visits to battlefields emphasized the unsavory side of the war, her aura as a secular saint evaporated, to be restored only gradually and partially several years later. The words that undid her popularity were spoken at a large public meeting in Carnegie Hall where she said that soldiers at the front believed "it was an old man's war" and that those who had grown up with modern ideals "had to be inflamed to do the brutal work of the bayonet." In practically every country, she said, "We heard a certain type of young soldier say that it had been difficult for him to make the bayonet charge unless he had been stimulated; that the English soldiers had been given rum before such a charge, the Germans ether and that the French were said to use absinthe."[104]

Addams's remarks were distorted and ridiculed in the *New York Times* by Richard Harding Davis, war correspondent and popular writer on masculine themes, who claimed she had called the soldiers cowards. Thereafter she was denounced, she later wrote, "from one end of the country to the other."[105]

Such determined opposition to their international endeavors also required the small group of German and American women who persisted in their contact with one another to leave the mainstream of their suffrage movements. Pronouncements by the leadership of the BDF guaranteed that in Germany. Although censure was less overt in the United States, Carrie Chapman Catt, president of the NAWSA, distanced herself from the peace movement in a letter to Jane Addams in November 1915, believing her efforts "to further suffrage activities will be not a little impaired if I ally myself too much with the peace activities." Catt reminded Addams that the

---

103   Ibid., pp. 138–39. For an American equivalent, see Barbara J. Steinson, "Sisters and Soldiers." See also Jürgen Kocka, *Facing Total War.*
104   Jane Addams, *Peace and Bread in Time of War,* p. 136.
105   Ibid. See also Michael A. Lutzker, "Jane Addams: Peacetime Heroine, Wartime Heretic." Battlefield testimony in support of Addams's remarks can be found in Keegan, *Face of Battle,* p. 277. For Richard Harding Davis's masculinist view of the war, see his book, *With the Allies* (New York: Scribner's, 1914).

International Woman Suffrage Alliance had voted against holding a peace congress and that "the majority who voted against it have been very much nettled by [the] fact" that a minority had nevertheless organized a conference at The Hague.[106]

Catt was right. When war made it impossible for the IWSA to meet in its chosen location of Berlin in 1915, suffragists in neutral Holland had proposed their own country as an alternative, but the twenty-six national affiliates voted against meeting. The Dutch organizers, particularly Aletta Jacobs, then decided to bypass the suffrage alliance and appeal directly to "prominent women" in each country.[107] Those who responded reconfigured women's international gatherings.

Although European socialist parties had for half a century opposed war as a capitalist tactic, support for the war by the German and French socialist parties in 1914 eliminated this historical antiwar bloc and made the peace initiatives of social justice feminists even more important.[108] Socialist women opposed to the war met as the third International Conference of Socialist Women in Bern in March, 1915, and sent greetings to the women assembled later that spring at The Hague. Earlier socialist women's conferences had taken place at Stuttgart in 1907 and Copenhagen in 1910. No American women attended these conferences, and they did not continue during the war.[109]

At The Hague in 1915 the new group's collective identity was not yet clear, but its institutional break with the IWSA was obvious. War made peace the only topic of what remained of the transatlantic dialogue between German and American social justice feminists. At the Women's Peace Congress in 1915, delegates formed a Women's Committee for a Permanent Peace with branches in their respective nations. At Zurich in 1919 the group renamed itself the Women's International League for Peace and Freedom.

Merely by meeting, these women achieved what other groups could not. As Emily Balch, an American delegate to The Hague, put it, "In this world

---

[106]   Carrie Chapman Catt to Jane Addams, New York City, November 12, 1915, Carrie Chapman Catt Papers, Library of Congress, reel 2. Also in Mary Lynn McCree Bryan, ed., *The Jane Addams Papers, 1860–1960* (Ann Arbor: University Microfilms International, 1984) (hereafter *JAP*).

[107]   See Aletta Jacobs, *Memories*, pp. 82–83.

[108]   Although Marx and Engels declared in *The Communist Manifesto* that "the worker has no fatherland," the SPD was gradually integrated into the German nation-state, and hence into support for the war. On the party's internal split over that support, see Schorske, *German Social Democracy*, and Roland N. Stromberg, "La patrie en danger." On opposition to the war by leading women in the SPD, see Brinker-Gabler, *Frauen gegen den Krieg*. For the imperialist roots of the war, see John Lowe, *The Great Powers*.

[109]   For the 1907 and 1910 meetings, see Gisela Brinker-Gabler, "The Women's Movement in the German Empire," p. 69. For the 1915 meetings, see Leila Rupp, *Worlds of Women*, p. 35, and Brinker-Gabler, *Frauen gegen den Krieg*, pp. 165–80.

upheaval the links that bind the peoples have been strained and snapped on every side. Of all the international gatherings that help to draw the nations together . . . practically none have been convened. Science, medicine, reform, labor, religion—not one of these causes has been able as yet to gather its followers from across the dividing frontiers."[110]

Balch might have added "woman suffrage." This odd assortment of suffragists, social justice feminists, and pacifists owed a great deal to the suffrage movement. The organizers of the Hague congress required all delegates to agree to two principles in order to attend the conference: support for woman suffrage and support for the peaceful resolution of international conflicts. The dialogue between German and American women social justice reformers was rooted in the suffrage movement. This new, more radical group affirmed its loyalty to that movement at the same time that they reached beyond it.[111]

Although they did not achieve their immediate goals, women at the Hague and Zurich conferences left a vivid testimony of opposition to the disastrous course of male-dominated politics that had produced war. Many decades later, under the auspices of the United Nations, women in Mexico City in 1975, Nairobi in 1985, and Beijing in 1995 brought their collective voices powerfully to bear on women's issues and women's rights. Yet on the still-urgent issues of war and peace women's voices have been more muted, especially compared to those of women activists between 1915 and 1919.

In 1915 the mood was optimistic on board the *Noordam* when the large American peace delegation of forty-two progressive feminists and pacifists embarked for Holland.[112] "A white flag bearing in letters of blue the word 'Peace' floated from our masthead," Madeleine Doty later wrote, "This made our ship the center of all eyes."[113]

[110] Emily G. Balch, "Journey and Impressions of the Congress," in Jane Addams, Emily G. Balch, and Alice Hamilton, *Women at The Hague*, p. 2.
[111] For the American branch of WILPF, see Louise Degen, *The History of the Woman's Peace Party*; Carrie A. Foster-Hayes, "The Women and the Warriors"; and Anne Marie Pois, "The Politics and Process of Organizing for Peace."
[112] These American women were in the process of transforming the American peace movement from an effort dominated by elite men and dedicated to the principle of nonviolence to a more democratic movement, dominated by women and dedicated to the principle of international arbitration. For that transition, see C. Roland Marchand, *The American Peace Movement and Social Reform*; Harriet Hyman Alonso, *The Women's Peace Union and the Outlawry of War*; Harriet Hyman Alonso, *Peace as a Women's Issue*; Harriet Alonso and Melanie Gustafson, "Bibliography on the History of U.S. Women in Movements for Peace"; and Harriet Hyman Alonso, "Nobel Peace Laureates, Jane Addams and Emily Greene Balch."
Social justice feminists in the American delegation to The Hague included Jane Addams, Alice Hamilton, Grace Abbott (1878–1939, later head of the Federal Children's Bureau), Leonora O'Reilly (1870–1927, labor activist representing the Women's Trade Union League), Emily Greene Balch, Sophonisba Breckinridge (1872–1920, University of Chicago sociologist and Hull House resident), and Madeleine Doty.
[113] Madeleine Zabriskie Doty, *Short Rations*, p. 4.

The American delegates used their time at sea to prepare themselves for the upcoming discussions. "Sunny weather and a boat steadied by a heavy load of grain" aided their deliberations, Emily Balch remembered. First, the secretary of the Chicago Peace Society gave a brief course of lectures on peace questions. Then the group considered the preliminary program drafted by the British, Dutch, and German planning committee in Amsterdam in February. "Some days we met morning, afternoon, and evening and we added largely to the contents of the programme as sent to us," Balch said.[114] This preconference consolidation of their position was to make the American delegates a formidable force at the congress.

Although shipboard meetings had their heady moments, Jane Addams and Alice Hamilton shunned romantic interpretations of their endeavors. Hamilton wrote Mary Smith: "We have long passed the stage of poems and impassioned appeals and 'messages from womankind,' and willingness to die in the cause, and now we are discussing whether it is more dangerous to insist on democratic control of diplomacy than it is to insist on the neutralization of the seas."[115]

Shipboard evenings "were devoted to personal reminiscences," Doty recalled. "Like the Canterbury Pilgrims of old, each told his tale." This process uncovered hidden talents among the quieter personalities. One of these, Doty said, was Annie Molloy, who had helped organize a union of telephone operators that by 1915 numbered ten thousand members: "In the early days the union won a fight for better conditions by arbitration. Out of that success sprang the powerful organization of to-day. If they could arbitrate, the telephone girls reasoned, Europe ought also to be able to arbitrate, so they sent forth their cherished leader. She they felt might bring peace to earth." Each member of Molloy's union had taxed herself sixty cents monthly to pay for the trip.[116]

At twenty-eight delegates, the German group at The Hague congress was also large. Prominent social justice feminist delegates included Anita Augspurg, Lida Gustava Heymann, and Helene Stöcker. Gertrud Baer, Elisabeth Rotten, and Constanze Hallgarten, who became leading figures in the German pacifist movement of the 1920s, also attended.[117] Since most French women boycotted the congress, and British women were pre-

[114] Addams, Balch, and Hamilton, *Women at The Hague,* p. 3.
[115] Alice Hamilton to Mary Rozet Smith, [*S.S. Noordam*], April 22, [1915], in Sicherman, *Alice Hamilton,* p. 186.
[116] Doty, *Short Rations,* p. 6; for Molloy and the Telephone Operators' Department of the International Brotherhood of Electrical Workers, see Stephen H. Norwood, *Labor's Flaming Youth,* p. 140.
[117] On German women pacifists and the different positions of different women's organizations toward the war, see Brinker-Gabler, *Frauen gegen den Krieg.* For short biographies of these German women pacifists, see Helmut Donat and Karl Holl, eds., *Die Friedensbewegung.* For SPD women who opposed the war, many of whom were imprisoned, see Ursula Herrmann, "Social

vented by their government from attending, the strong American and German delegations meant that it was above all a forum for their meeting.[118]

Mary Chamberlain, a staff member of the reform magazine *Survey*, reported on the conferences at The Hague in 1915 and Zurich in 1919.[119] Paul Kellogg, the magazine's editor, said she brought "liveliness and affection" into their offices.[120] To her description of the congresses she brought insight and compassion. Other accounts sustained Chamberlain's view of the organizational challenges she observed. Emily Balch, who participated in all three women's peace congresses and taught economics and sociology at Wellesley College between 1896 and 1919, wrote that "there were vigorous differences of opinion over details, and some energetic misunderstandings, for which the necessity of translating each speech into two other languages supplied many openings, besides the difficulties arising from different parliamentary usages. One's every faculty was on the stretch hour after hour, and we wondered afterwards why we felt so exhausted."[121] Jane Addams's steady leadership was crucial to the effectiveness of the Hague congress, administratively and morally. Alice Hamilton wrote to Mary Smith, "J.A. was simply wonderful as president. She could not have been better. And Grace Abbott and Miss Breckinridge helped her as nobody else could have."[122]

Addams's commitment to peace arose partly from her experience in an immigrant neighborhood. She told women at The Hague and elsewhere of watching five hundred bright Italian boys marching past Hull House to entrain for the war, followed by an equal number of young Bulgarians on the same errand, friends and brothers of the settlement, soon to fall before one another's fire in a war for which they were in no way responsible and for reasons which they could not understand.[123] Addams's multiethnic

Democratic Women in Germany and the Struggle for Peace Before and During the First World War," in Ruth Roach Pierson, ed., *Women and Peace,* pp. 90–101.

[118] For the absence of most British delegates, see Lida Gustava Heymann and Anita Augspurg, "Women's Work for International Reconciliation and Job Creation," reprinted here in Part III, document 2. Judith Wishnia refers to a Mathilde Duchène as an exception in 1915, in "Feminism and Pacifism: The French Connection," in R. Pierson, *Women and Peace,* pp. 103–13. See also Leila B. Costin, "Feminism, Pacifism, Internationalism and the 1915 International Congress of Women."

[119] Mary Chamberlain, "The Women at The Hague" and "The Women at Zurich," reprinted here in Part III, documents 4 and 8.

[120] Paul Kellogg, "Mary Chamberlain, 1909." Although Chamberlain was a staff writer for *Survey,* she published very little there under her own name. An exception was Mary Chamberlain, "Women and War Work," *Survey,* May 19, 1917, pp. 153–54.

[121] Balch, "Journey and Impressions," in Addams, Balch, and Hamilton, *Women at The Hague,* pp. 16–17.

[122] Alice Hamilton to Mary Rozet Smith, Den Haag, May 5, [1915], in Sicherman, *Alice Hamilton,* p. 189.

[123] Mrs. Philip [Ethel] Snowden, *A Political Pilgrim in Europe,* p. 78.

experience was more familiar to Americans than to Germans, but social workers throughout Europe could understand the war's toll on wage-earning families.

Delegates heard draining testimony about the war. "Day by day, as we sat side by side, we had learned of the suffering in war-ridden lands," Madeleine Doty remembered. "Black-clad wives had made speeches. Sorrowing mothers had shown their agony. The battle-field became a reality, covered with dead and dying sons and husbands. These glimpses of tragedy wrung our hearts. We ceased to be enemies or friends. We were just women."[124]

Drawn together on the basis of their sex, these women used commonplace beliefs about women to justify their nonconformist behavior and evoked nurturant values to defend their actions. Jane Addams articulated this theme in 1915:

> The belief that a woman is against war simply because she is a woman and not a man cannot of course be substantiated. In every country there are women who believe that war is inevitable and righteous; the majority of women as well as men in the nations at war doubtless hold that conviction.

On the other hand, she continued,

> Quite as an artist in an artillery corps commanded to fire upon a beautiful building like the *duomo* at Florence would be deterred by a compunction unknown to the man who had never given himself to creating beauty and did not know the intimate cost of it, so women, who have brought men into the world and nurtured them until they reach the age for fighting, must experience a peculiar revulsion when they see them destroyed, irrespective of the country in which these men may have been born.

Lida Gustava Heymann expressed similar sentiments in 1915 when she said that women at the Hague conference wished "to do their duty as wives and mothers, to protect life" as well as "to further justice."[125]

These women sought justice for themselves as well as for others. Resolutions passed at The Hague repeatedly called for women's "political enfranchisement," declaring that "women should be granted equal political rights with men," and "that women should share all civil and political rights

124 Doty, *Short Rations*, p. 23.
125 Addams, Balch, and Hamilton, *Women at The Hague*, pp. 127, 145. For discussions of essentialism in the women's peace movement, see Linda Gordon, "The Peaceful Sex?"; Jo Vellacott, "A Place for Pacifism and Transnationalism in Feminist Theory"; Kathryn Kish Sklar, "Jane Addams's Peace Activism"; and Margaret Hobbs, "The Perils of 'Unbridled Masculinity': Pacifist Elements in the Feminist and Socialist Thought of Charlotte Perkins Gilman," in R. Pierson, *Women and Peace*, pp. 149–69.

and responsibilities on the same terms as men." At The Hague and subsequently in Zurich and Vienna, delegates to women's peace congresses struggled to find language that would express their commitment to justice for women and at the same time represent their pursuit of social justice.[126]

Peace was a complex issue in 1915, and the new dialogue was anything but easy. As Catt wrote Addams, "Peace has come to mean the close of the war with dishonor to some of the participants."[127] If "peace" meant the acceptance of German territorial expansion into Belgium and France, then it was clearly pro-German. The absence of French delegates to the Hague conference reflected that concern, as did the size of the Belgian delegation—only five.[128] Yet this did not mean that the German women at the conference were supported by their government. Local and national police viewed Lida Gustava Heymann and Anita Augspurg, progressive feminists from Munich, with deep suspicion. Frida Perlen of Stuttgart was denied permission to leave Germany, perhaps because she had been active in the organizing committee for the conference. German women who worked for peace through organizations like the Women's Committee for a Permanent Peace or the New Fatherland League (Bund Neues Vaterland), of which Minna Cauer and Helene Stöcker were members, had to face surveillance, harassment, and censorship. Alice Hamilton described how German censorship effectively hindered pacifists from contacting each other and how formerly cosmopolitan people had difficulty receiving any information about the war beyond the official government version. German pacifists had very limited means for publicizing their cause. Their mail and telephone conversations were monitored and their apartments were searched; any information had to be disseminated in small meetings that soon were infiltrated by spies. Nonetheless, by 1917 the German Women's Committee for a Permanent Peace had branches in twenty-nine cities. German women pacifists established "peace libraries" that made pacifist literature available, to which the American Women's Peace Party contributed material.[129]

[126] Addams, Balch, and Hamilton, *Women at The Hague,* p. 152. For an analysis of women's peace and social justice language, see Jo Vellacott, "Women, Peace and Internationalism, 1914–1920."

[127] Catt to Addams, November 12, 1915.

[128] For pro- and anti-German propaganda seeking to sway American public opinion at this time, see James Morgan Read, *Atrocity Propaganda,* and Reinhard R. Doerries, "Promoting *Kaiser* and *Reich.*" For overviews of the diplomatic relationship between German and the still-neutral United States, see John W. Coogan, *The End of Neutrality,* and Robert David Johnson, *The Peace Progressives and American Foreign Relations.* For background on French and Belgian women, see Wishnia, "Feminism and Pacifism," in R. Pierson, *Women and Peace,* pp. 103–11; Nadine Lubelski-Bernard, "The Participation of Women in the Belgian Peace Movement, 1830–1914," ibid., pp. 76–89; and Sandi E. Cooper, "Women's Participation in European Peace Movements: The Struggle to Prevent World War I," ibid., pp. 51–75.

[129] Alice Hamilton, "At the War Capitals," *Survey,* August 7, 1915, p. 420; Frevert, *Women in German History,* p. 163; Hermine Schützinger to Jane Addams, Berlin, June 15, 1916 (filed

The new women's peace movement made history primarily through the resolutions drafted by the planning committee of Dutch, German, and English women at Amsterdam, refined on the *Noordam,* endorsed at The Hague, and adopted by Woodrow Wilson as the centerpiece of his Fourteen Points. Resolutions adopted at The Hague are reprinted here in a form similar to that in which they were distributed by members of the national Women's Committees for a Permanent Peace in their respective countries.[130] The first German edition of the resolutions was printed in Holland and mailed to Germany. A second edition could only be printed in Germany with great difficulty. Heymann and Augspurg's determination to print and distribute The Hague resolutions brought them to the attention of the members of state legislatures and the Reichstag, which they petitioned throughout the war. Their action also alerted the military authorities.

The Hague resolutions became the basis for President Woodrow Wilson's Fourteen Points, announced in a speech to Congress on January 8, 1918. After her return to the United States in 1915, Addams consulted with President Wilson about the implementation of The Hague resolutions. "He was very much interested in them," she remembered, "and when I saw him three months later, he drew out the papers I had given him, and they seemed to have been much handled and read. 'You see I have studied these resolutions,' he said."[131] Although neither the women's congress nor Wilson succeeded in affecting the punitive peace terms that British and French leaders were determined to impose, the Hague congress offered an alternative model based on internationalist rather than nationalist principles.

Six of Wilson's Fourteen Points echoed resolutions passed at the women's congress in 1915. His first, "Open covenants of peace, openly arrived at," reflected the Hague delegates' call for "democratic control of foreign policy." His second, "Absolute freedom of navigation upon the seas," resembled their notion "that the seas shall be free and the trade routes open on equal terms to the shipping of all nations." His third, "The removal, so far as possible, of all economic barriers and the establishment of an equality of trade conditions among all the nations," was a muted expression of their more direct statement on trade: "Inasmuch as the investment by capitalists of one country in the resources of another and the claims

with Eleanor Daggett Kasten to John Necom, Chicago, June 1, 1916), Women's Peace Party Correspondence, WILPF Papers, Swarthmore College Peace Collection (SCPC) (and *JAP,* reel 9). For the German peace movement, see Roger Chickering, *Imperial Germany and a World without War,* and Brinker-Gabler, *Frauen gegen den Krieg.* See also Heymann and Augspurg, *Erlebtes, Erschautes,* pp. 115–54.
[130] "Resolutions adopted by the International Congress of Women," reprinted here in Part III, document 5.
[131] *Report of the International Congress of Women, Zurich, May 12 to 17, 1919,* p. 196.

arising therefrom are a fertile source of international complications, this International Congress of Women urges the widest possible acceptance of the principle that such investments shall be made at the risk of the investor, without claim to the official protection of his government."

Similarly, his fourth point, "that national armaments will be reduced to the lowest point consistent with domestic safety," modified their call to eliminate profit in arms making: "That all countries should . . . take over the manufacture of arms and munitions of war and should control all international traffic in the same." His fifth point, "A free, open-minded, and absolutely impartial adjustment of all colonial claims, based upon . . . the principle that . . . the interests of the population concerned must have equal weight with the equitable claims of the government whose title is to be determined," was a watered-down version of their insistence that "no territory should be transferred without the consent of the men and women in it, and that the right of conquest should not be recognized." His fourteenth point, "A general association of nations must be formed," borrowed their call for "the organization of the Society of Nations," with "a permanent International Court of Justice," a "permanent International Conference," and a "permanent Council of Conciliation and Investigation." Wilson's other eight points, numbers six through thirteen, mentioned specific territorial disputes, which he resolved to settle on terms that recognized national sovereignty and rejected conquest. The women's congress did not address specific territorial issues.[132]

In one respect, however, Wilson's Fourteen Points differed significantly from the Hague resolutions. The Hague resolutions systematically called for the inclusion of women in all foreign policy decisions and declared that "it can only recognize as democratic a system which includes the equal representation of men and women." His Fourteen Points did not mention women.

When Wilson announced the Fourteen Points in 1918, he was hailed as a hero. In 1915 women had been ridiculed for advocating the same points, but by 1918 their ideas had taken root in American public life. Yet by failing to credit an international congress of women with the origin of his ideas, and by failing to recognize their call for the inclusion of women in the formation of foreign policy, Wilson cut himself off from the power and vitality of a new expression of women's political culture. At a time when he needed all the help he could get, he ignored the aid that they could offer.[133]

[132] "Address of the President of the United States, January 8, 1918," printed in John Whiteclay Chambers II, *The Eagle and the Dove*, and in Addams, Balch, and Hamilton, *Women at The Hague,* appendix 3, pp. 152–54.
[133] For more on Wilson's context at Versailles, see Harold Nicolson, *Peacemaking 1919*. For Wilson's domestic context, see Thomas J. Knock, *To End All Wars.*

The most deeply felt resolution emerged just as the congress was about to end. "As the days came for departure, a restlessness grew visible," Madeleine Doty recalled. "The suffering of war had laid its hold on the delegates. They wanted something more than mere resolutions—they wanted immediate action. To go quietly home had become impossible." [134] Therefore the delegates resolved "to carry the message expressed in the Congress Resolutions to the rulers of the belligerent and neutral nations of Europe and to the President of the United States." [135] Two groups of delegates were selected, each containing representatives from neutral and belligerent nations. No German women were chosen, possibly because the women's peace movement was accused of being pro-German, but Americans were represented in each group. One group, consisting of Jane Addams, Alice Hamilton, and two Dutch women, Aletta Jacobs and Frederika Palthe, carried the resolutions to prime ministers and foreign ministers in Holland, England, Germany, Austria, Hungary, Switzerland, Italy, France, the Belgian government in exile at Le Havre, and the United States. Another group—Emily Balch of the United States, Chrystal Macmillan of Great Britain, Rosika Schwimmer of Hungary, and Cornelia Ramondt-Hirschmann of Holland—visited Denmark, Russia, and Sweden.[136]

Addams initially considered the plan to present the resolutions of the congress to the heads of warring and neutral nations as "hopelessly melodramatic and absurd." She wrote to Mary Smith, "There is only one chance in 10 thousand that it will succeed." [137] Still, Addams agreed to travel to the capitals of the warring European countries with Aletta Jacobs, accompanied by Hamilton and Jacobs's friend Frau van Wulfften-Palthe. In Berlin the women secured an audience with the German chancellor, Theobald von Bethman Hollweg. The German women's movement, however, remained true to its resolution regarding all pacifist work as "unpatriotic." Gertrud Bäumer invited Addams to speak at the Lyceumclub, with the restriction that she talk only about her prewar settlement work. Alice Salomon invited her to speak at Berlin's social settlement. The bourgeois German women's movement denied that the topics of their dialogue with American reformers had shifted dramatically with the outbreak of the war, while the Social Democratic paper, *Der Vorwärts,* assessed the situation clearly: "To ignore Jane Addams won't do because of the prominent position she has in the international women's movement, and apparently the League of German Women's Associations does not want to loose all its ties. So the Berlin ladies had the brilliant idea to celebrate Jane Addams as an

[134] Doty, *Short Rations*, p. 24.
[135] Addams, Balch, and Hamilton, *Women at The Hague,* appendix 3, p. 159.
[136] Ibid., pp. 22, 99.
[137] Jane Addams to Mary Rozet Smith, The Hague, May 9, 1915, SCPC (and *JAP,* reel 8).

outstanding social politician. . . . To talk about [the Hague congress] was of course not permitted." [138]

One of Addams's traveling companions described her as subdued during her Berlin visit.[139] Nevertheless, this unprecedented series of consultations between women peace advocates and government officials expressed the new level of equality that this group of social reformers were claiming for themselves in international affairs.

Delegates at The Hague decided to reconvene to "frame the terms of the peace settlement after the war." The ensuing meeting took place in Zurich in May 1919, while the Allied leaders were hammering out peace terms in Paris.

The previous year had been stirring but perilous for German social justice feminists. After the Russian Revolution of 1917, Germany had negotiated a separate peace to keep the Bolsheviks from fomenting revolution among German troops along the Eastern front. Madeleine Doty, visiting Russia and Germany that year, described the revolutionary potential evident in German cities.[140] The collapse of German armies in the Western front in the autumn of 1918 led to the proclamation of a republic by Social Democratic Party leader Philipp Scheidemann, on November 9, 1918. His announcement came a day after Kurt Eisner, a radical Independent Socialist, declared a separate republic in Bavaria. Even before the formal abdication of Kaiser Wilhelm II, who fled to Holland in late November, the political struggle in Germany shifted from one between socialists and monarchists to one between liberal and radical socialists. In Berlin, insurrections promoted by Rosa Luxemburg and Karl Liebknecht, founders of the German Communist Party and leaders of the Spartakus movement, led to their assassination in January 1919. Anita Augspurg and Lida Gustava Heymann supported the Eisner government, a step that led to their political isolation after Eisner was assassinated in February 1919. During these revolutionary days, many German WILPF members tried to negotiate between the warring parties and suffered arrest, imprisonment, exile, and even death. With Luxemburg, Liebknecht, and Eisner dead, the Social Democratic Party consolidated its control over the former empire. A coalition of liberal and socialist parties met in Weimar in February 1919 to draft a constitution for the new republic, which was completed in August.[141]

---

[138] *Vorwärts,* Berlin, May 27, 1915; emphasis in the original.

[139] Diary of Lola Maverick Lloyd, May 1915, Lola Maverick Lloyd Papers, Schwimmer-Lloyd Collection, New York Public Library, quoted in Melanie Gustafson, "Lola Maverick Lloyd," p. 68.

[140] Madeleine Z. Doty, *Behind the Battle Line* and *Short Rations.*

[141] Bussey and Tims, *Pioneers for Peace,* p. 40. For more on the Munich Revolution, see "Kurt Eisner," in Harold Josephson, ed., *Biographical Dictionary of Modern Peace Leaders*; Martin H. Geyer, "Munich in Turmoil"; and Anton Kaes, Martin Jay, and Edward Dimendberg, eds., *The*

Partly because of this dramatic background to the German women's participation, the meeting at Zurich that spring was, in Alice Hamilton's words, "a very deep and moving experience"—"much deeper than 1915." She wrote home: "These women, some of them, have been through repeated revolution, those from Munich especially, and as pacifists opposed to all violence they have been in danger from revolutionists as well as from militarists. . . . But most dreadful of all are the tales of starvation."[142]

This deeper affinity was all the more remarkable for the four years of war that had isolated the delegates within their own nations. Helena Swanwick, who in 1915 had chaired the committee that planned the Hague congress and who was elected vice president of WILPF in 1919, remarked,

> What was surprising . . . was that we, who had not met since the spring of 1915, who had had to work without any direct communication and over whose heads four years of such tragic and embittered folly had passed, came together to find ourselves in accord, not only as to the war, but as to the peace: what we wanted it to be and how we would work for it.[143]

At both The Hague and Zurich, resolutions related to the war's origin or to the conduct of soldiers were ruled "outside the scope of the Congress" by its organizers, but war-related tensions surfaced nonetheless.[144] Complicating their attempts at transnational solidarity, some delegates at Zurich in 1919 believed that German women owed them an apology for their nation's responsibility in launching and pursuing so brutal a war. Perhaps in response to this feelings, Lida Gustava Heymann addressed French and Belgian women: "[We] stretch out our hands to you and implore you to forget the crimes that German men and soldiers have committed in your country—remember that there are still women in Germany who love you, who have suffered with you through all these years in which war was passing over the earth." Mary Chamberlain found these sentiments inadequate. Although Heymann "shouldered in part the blame," Chamberlain thought a more forceful statement would have been more appropriate.[145]

Nevertheless, the long-standing mutual respect of social justice feminists in the United States and Germany helped forge this larger international network of women reformers. Alice Hamilton characterized the German delegates at The Hague as "an unusually fine lot of women, so able and so

Weimar Republic Sourcebook, pp. 35–59. See also Hans Mommsen, *The Rise and Fall of Weimar Democracy*, and Mommsen, *Imperial Germany*, pp. 233–54.
142   Alice Hamilton to Norah Hamilton, Zurich, May 14, [1919]; Alice Hamilton to Jessie Hamilton, Zurich, May 15, [1919], in Sicherman, *Alice Hamilton*, pp. 222, 225.
143   Quoted in Anne Wiltsher, *Most Dangerous Women*, p. 204.
144   Addams, Balch, and Hamilton, *Women at The Hague*, p. 147.
145   Chamberlain, "The Women at Zurich," reprinted here in Part III, document 8. See also Alice Hamilton to Mary Rozet Smith, Zurich, May 19, [1919], in Sicherman, *Alice Hamilton*, pp. 230–31.

fair and so full of warmth and generosity."[146] The importance of that American-German connection within the 1915 and 1919 gatherings was visible at The Hague in resolutions that endorsed a lasting rather than a punitive peace, and at Zurich in resolutions that called for an end to the blockade of Germany.

Delegates at Zurich directed a great deal of their attention to the British blockade, which was designed to force Germany's acceptance of the punitive peace terms. The effects of the blockade were evident on women the Americans considered friends. Jane Addams had difficulty recognizing Leopoldine Kulka, an Austrian delegate she knew from the Hague congress, when they met in Zurich. "My first reaction was one of overwhelming pity and alarm as I suddenly discovered my friend standing at the very gate of death," she later wrote.[147] The congress called for the immediate lifting of the blockade, and "that all resources of the world, food, raw materials, finance, transport, shall be organized immediately for the relief of the peoples from famine and pestilence." Despite their appeal, however, Herbert Hoover and other Allied officials continued to withhold food until the new German government paid for it with the amount of gold stipulated by recent treaty agreements.[148]

The assembled delegates responded with dismay when the peace terms were announced, and resolved that the terms would "create all over Europe discords and animosities which can only lead to future wars. . . . [That] by the financial and economic proposals a hundred million people of this generation in the heart of Europe are condemned to poverty, disease and despair, which must result in the spread of hatred and anarchy within each nation." They "strongly [urged] the Allied and Associated Governments to accept such amendments of the terms as shall bring the peace into harmony with those principles first enumerated by President Wilson."[149]

This solidarity among women whose governments were still technically at war was strengthened by their belief that they were creating what men could not. Helena Swanwick described the stirring moment on the last morning of the congress when Jeanne Mélin of France arrived from her

[146] Hamilton to Smith, May 5, [1915].
[147] Addams, *Peace and Bread*, p. 159. For German perspectives on the blockade, see Anne Roerkohl, *Hungerblockade und Heimatfront*; Belinda Davis, "Food Scarcity and the Empowerment of the Female Consumer in World War I Germany"; and John Williams, *The Other Battleground*. See also Charles Paul Vincent, *The Politics of Hunger*.
[148] *Report of the International Congress of Women, Zurich*, p. 68. For Hoover's negotiations, see Herbert Hoover to Norman H. Davis, New York City, March 17, 1920, "An Accounting to the Treasury Department for the Handling of the German Gold," box 61, "German Gold," American Relief Association Papers, Hoover Institution on War, Revolution, and Peace, Stanford University.
[149] *Report of the International Congress of Women, Zurich*, pp. 18, 60.

shattered region in the Ardennes. Lida Gustava Heymann, who had just been speaking, "leapt to her feet, with outstretched hands, her gaunt figure tense, her eyes and face burning with passion." Clasping Mélin's hand, she said, "A German woman gives her hand to a French woman, and says in the name of the German delegation, that we hope we women can build a bridge from Germany to France and from France to Germany, and that in the future we may be able to make good the wrong-doing of men." Mélin replied with a stirring speech against the male politicians at Versailles and urged women everywhere to be "les forces de demain" and to struggle for a just and peaceful society.[150]

This exchange prompted Emily Balch to rise and cry out, "I dedicate my life to the cause of Peace!" Then all the delegates rose and a great shout went out in several different languages: "We dedicate our lives to Peace!" Helena Swanwick had "never witnessed or imagined so remarkable an affirmation." Such scenes could be staged, of course, "but only intense feeling can cause them to occur spontaneously, as this did."[151]

Like many of their German counterparts, American leaders of the women's peace movement also suffered the consequences of their activism. At Zurich, Balch learned that the president of Wellesley, seeking to distance the institution from her pacifism, had fired her; she celebrated the news by performing the radical act of smoking a cigarette.[152] Addams's peace advocacy cost her dearly, in cash as well as prestige. Her average annual income in the ten years before 1915 was almost four thousand dollars a year. During the next fifteen years, although she was at the peak of her intellectual power, it fell to less than fifteen hundred dollars a year. In five of those fifteen years, she earned less than one thousand dollars a year. This was less than the annual wages of many young working women who attended Hull House events. Addams later commented: "It almost seems as if an internationally minded person should be defined as a friend of every country except his own."[153]

By the end of the war, German and American women had established a new dialogue, one that centered around peace and the prevention of future wars. Women from both countries continued the dialogue, traveling through war-torn Europe at great personal risk, imperiling their reputations at home, but finding fresh fellowship in a new international organiza-

[150] Wiltsher, *Most Dangerous Women*, p. 211. For more on Mélin, pacifist and radical suffragist, see Steven C. Hause and Anne R. Kenney, *Women's Suffrage and Social Politics in the French Third Republic*, pp. 172, 210, 213.
[151] Helena Swanwick, *I Have Been Young*, p. 318.
[152] "A Case of Academic Freedom—1918," in Mercedes M. Randall, ed., *Beyond Nationalism*, pp. 102–8.
[153] James Weber Linn, *Jane Addams: A Biography*, pp. 356, 393. See also Lutzker, "Jane Addams." Addams's loyal and wealthy supporters, Mary Rozet Smith and Louise De Koven Bowen, protected her and Hull House from financial distress.

tion that still exists today. In both countries these women represented a minority at a time when the mainstream women's movements prepared to claim their rewards for supporting the war effort. During the next decade these rifts would remain.

The Limitations of Nationhood in the 1920s

The immediate postwar crisis in Germany, marked by famine and political revolution, made the relationship between American and German social justice feminists even more urgently important. American women publicized the brutal effects of the British blockade of Germany; German women desperately appealed to them for financial aid.

Jane Addams was central to the effort to relieve suffering in Germany, which was administered by American and British Quakers and supervised by Herbert Hoover, director of the American Relief Administration from 1919 to the mid-1920s. Although fighting had ceased with an armistice signed on November 11, 1918, a British blockade of German ports remained in force for another eight months, designed to coerce Germany's agreement to punitive peace terms. Madeleine Doty and other Americans in England at the time were astonished at the tolerance British police showed toward Trafalgar Square demonstrations by socialist and women's organizations demanding the lifting of the blockade.[154] Beginning in March 1919, however, in anticipation of the new German government's signing of the peace treaty, Herbert Hoover had been implementing terms negotiated at Brussels that called for German reparations in the form of ships and gold in exchange for food.[155] By March, political conditions were calmer in Germany, but officials in the new government were fully aware that the German susceptibility to bolshevism was a trump card in their effort to end the blockade and obtain American food aid.[156] Indeed, during

[154]   Madeleine Zabriskie Doty, "A Tap on the Shoulder," unpublished autobiography, chapter 12, Sophia Smith Collection, Smith College.
[155]   Arthur Walworth, *Wilson and His Peacemakers*, pp. 429–31. For Hoover's implementation of the Brussels terms, see box 61, "German Gold," March 1919–May 1920, American Relief Assistance Papers, Hoover Institution on War, Revolution, and Peace, Stanford University.
[156]   Klaus Schwabe, "Die USA, Deutschland und der Ausgang des Ersten Weltkrieges," pp. 23–26; and Klaus Schwabe, *Woodrow Wilson, Revolutionary Germany, and Peacemaking*, p. 209. See also "The Council of Foreign Ministers Discusses the Special Revictualing of Bavaria to Counteract Bolshevism," in Suda Lorena Bane and Ralph Haswell Lutz, eds., *The Blockade of Germany after the Armistice*, pp. 305–10. For food scarcity as a cause of German defeat, see Ralph Haswell Lutz, *The Causes of the German Collapse in 1918*, pp. 180–87. For the absence of a substantial communist threat in Weimar Germany, see Niall Ferguson, *Paper and Iron*, p. 438. For women's lives during the war, see Ute Daniel, "Der Krieg der Frauen 1914–1918" and *Arbeiterfrauen in der Kriegsgesellschaft*. For women's lives immediately after the war, see Karen Hagemann, "Men's Demonstrations and Women's Protest."

the preceding year Herbert Hoover received almost daily reports of the progress of bolshevism in Germany, some coming indirectly to him from members of the conservative wing of the Social Democratic Party.[157] Gold payments began early in May 1919, and later that month Hoover began releasing shipments of food to the German government. Hoover again withheld food when the Germans fell behind in their payments that summer, but after approximately 170 million dollars in gold had been paid, food began to flow more freely in early July. Jane Addams and Alice Hamilton entered Germany at that moment, bearing Hoover's request to locate reliable persons to supervise the food distribution. Alice Salomon was prominent among those they recommended.

Emily Hobhouse, a prominent English Quaker and a member of the Amsterdam committee that had planned the Zurich women's conference, later wrote Addams: "We agreed that 1st only Americans could do it; 2nd only Jane Addams could induce Americans to do it; 3rd you probably could induce Mr. Hoover to give us supplies at the lowest possible rate." At risk here were not only women and children, but as Addams and Hamilton put it in their 1919 *Survey* article, "the shipwreck of a nation."[158]

The political reconstruction of the devastated nation began in August 1919 with the establishment of a German republic through the Weimar constitution, which called for "universal, equal, direct, and secret suffrage of all German citizens, both men and women."[159] An impressive number of women were elected to the Reichstag during the Weimar Republic, with forty-one serving as late as 1930, about 7 percent of the total, while before 1929 only one percent of the U.S. Congress consisted of women.[160]

German progressive women reformers welcomed the adoption of woman suffrage, which in 1917 had for the first time been jointly promoted by a coalition of bourgeois and social democrat suffragists. Yet the enactment of woman suffrage did not dissolve the differences between conservative and progressive women. On the contrary. The Weimar Republic, born while parts of Germany were occupied by foreign troops, itself

---

[157]   See, for example, Cable Message from the American minister, Stockholm, December 2, 6 p.m., no. 3258, box 62, "Germany," October 30, 1918–December 18, 1918, American Relief Assistance Papers, Hoover Institution on War, Revolution, and Peace, Stanford University.
[158]   Emily Hobhouse to Jane Addams, [Berne, Switzerland], November 23, 1919, Jane Addams Papers, SCPC (and *JAP*, reel 12); Jane Addams and Alice Hamilton, "After the Lean Years," reprinted here in Part IV, document 1. See also John V. Crangle and Joseph O. Baylen, "Emily Hobhouse's Peace Mission, 1916."
[159]   Article 17, "The Constitution of the German Republic," in Kaes, Jay, and Dimendberg, *Weimar Republic Sourcebook*, p. 47.
[160]   Helen L. Boak, "Women in Weimar Germany"; Gabriele Sandmann-Bremme, *Die politische Rolle der Frau in Deutschland*, p. 124, cited in Frevert, *Women in German History*, pp. 171–72; appendix, "Women in Congress," in L. Sandy Maisel, ed., *Political Parties and Elections in the United States*, pp. 1257–58.

burdened with the payment of punitive reparations, and its government called traitors by right-wing nationalists, lent a leftist coloring to woman suffrage. The origins of woman suffrage in the Weimar Republic actually deepened the divisions between conservative and progressive women, including many of those engaged in social welfare work.[161]

Those divisions were also evident at the international level of women's organizations, which now were split along peace and social justice rather than suffrage lines. At Vienna, the first conference to convene under the new name adopted at Zurich—the Women's International League for Peace and Freedom—delegates voted "to initiate and support laws looking to the gradual abolition of property privileges . . . and to awaken and strengthen among members of the possessing classes the earnest will to transform the economic system in the direction of social justice." The revolutionary moment through which they were passing consolidated the delegates' commitment to social justice. In the debate over the resolution on "the gradual abolition of property privileges," for example, a vaguer substitute motion proposed by Jeanne Mélin of France, which supported the goal of the transformation of the economic system, was defeated in favor of the original resolution.[162] With this and other resolutions, WILPF decisively embraced issues of economic and social justice as well as those of suffrage and peace.

Florence Kelley's *Survey* article on the Vienna congress conveyed that gathering's mixture of great optimism and forlorn desperation, as hopes for the future competed for attention with the threat of starvation that still haunted central Europe. She repeated the convention's resolution on "property privileges" verbatim and said its support was "well-nigh universal."[163] This must have been a very gratifying moment for Kelley. At the age of sixty-two she had lived to see some of her fondest hopes ratified by a forceful new international organization. Her own commitment to social justice goals were shaped by her experience in Germany as well as the United States, and now the commitment of others to those goals arose from a melding of European and American women.

Germans and Americans at Vienna were both aware of the eruption of race as an issue within the League in 1921. During the year preceding the conference, German propagandists had invoked racist stereotypes to claim

---

[161] Reagin, *German Women's Movement*, p. 204; Frevert, *Women in German History*, pp. 169–70; and Renate Bridenthal and Claudia Koonz, "Beyond Kinder, Küche, Kirche: Weimar Women at Work," in Bridenthal, Grossmann, and Kaplan., *When Biology Became Destiny*, pp. 33–65.

[162] *Report of the Third International Congress of Women*, pp. 101–2.

[163] Florence Kelley, "The Women's Congress at Vienna," reprinted here in Part IV, document 5. See also "Co-operation toward ending Social Injustice," in *Report of the Third International Congress of Women*, p. 261; "How can the Privileged Classes co-operate to end Social Injustice?" in ibid., pp. 99, 102–3.

60

INTRODUCTION

that French African colonial troops were raping white women in the occupied Rhineland and had appealed to white American women for help.[164] Responding to this appeal and based on their opposition to militarism, Jane Addams and other members of the Executive Committee of the American branch of WILPF signed a petition seeking the removal of the colonial troops. Mary Church Terrell set her straight. Terrell, who had spoken out against discrimination against black American troops during World War I, recognized the prejudice behind the petition. Her letter to Addams presented a cogent argument and convincing evidence against the petition, including the testimony of German women politicians.[165]

Mary Church Terrell's perspective informed a resolution passed four months later at Vienna entitled "The Military Use of Native Populations of Colonies." That resolution, presented by Emily Balch, argued that the use of colonial troops was a new form of slavery, an extension of imperialism, and a way of evading the growing opposition to militarism among European men. Yet the resolution "avoided other questions involved in the use of coloured troops in occupied districts . . . because these questions are of quite a different order and complicate the issue."[166] Appended to the resolution was a statement from Helen Curtis, whose husband had represented the United States in Liberia and who expressed a sympathetic view of African troops away from home.

Yet despite these social justice gains at Vienna, all was not well with their coalitions at home. The transatlantic dialogue in the 1920s between German and American social justice feminists took place against a backdrop of minimal gains won by its German participants and steady losses incurred by the Americans.

In German cities, the political changes of the Weimar era gradually became apparent in the early twenties. While those effects differed depending on local political configurations, national patterns began to emerge—patterns that did not bode well for social justice feminists. For despite the substantial support that they gained from a national government that legitimized women's participation in public life, and despite the enormous need for social welfare services throughout Germany, social justice feminists were almost as constricted in their coalition-building options as they had been before the war.

Women to their right and their left were clearly empowered by the re-

[164] On this campaign, see Gisela Lebzelter, "Die 'Schwarze Schmach,' " p. 42; Reagin, *German Women's Movement*, pp. 223–24.

[165] Mary Church Terrell to Jane Addams, Washington, D.C., March 18, 1921, reprinted here in Part IV, document 7. For more on the context of Terrell's protest, see William J. Breen, "Black Women and the Great War."

[166] "Military Use of Native Populations of Colonies," reprinted here in Part IV, document 8; Kelley, "Women's Congress at Vienna," reprinted here in Part IV, document 5.

cent changes, but for women in the progressive middle the new era was more ambiguous. The entrance of conservative women into public life dramatically accelerated, quickened by the advent of woman suffrage and wartime legitimizing of women's initiatives. Conservative challenges to the left-liberal government were amplified now by women's voices. Municipalities still relied on volunteers to provide social welfare services, but some cities controlled by the SPD required that half of these volunteers come from the working class. Combined, these changes deepened the tensions between bourgeois and socialist women. In these circumstances, progressive middle-class women reformers remained politically engaged, but conditions were not propitious for the expansion of coalitions influenced by their leadership.[167] A series of articles that Alice Salomon wrote for the *Survey* in the early twenties, and the letters reprinted here in Part IV, illustrate yet another problem that German social justice feminists faced after the war. How could they implement the social welfare principles embedded in the Weimar constitution when a succession of fiscal crises deprived them of the means?[168]

In the United States the postwar era was even less friendly to social justice feminists. Initially, Kelley, Addams, and their colleagues continued to exercise tremendous power. In 1921 their coalitions reached the height of their power with the passage of the Sheppard-Towner Maternity and Infancy Protection Act, which for the first time made federal funding available for maternal and infant health. Providing funds for states that wished to participate in the program, the act was administered by the U.S. Children's Bureau. Nowhere else did women exercise equivalent control of a major national program. Florence Kelley was a central player in the Women's Joint Congressional Committee (WJCC), which coordinated the efforts of women's organizations in support of the act. That year the WJCC was called "the most powerful lobby in Washington."[169]

Almost immediately, however, this coalition began to dissolve. The first challenge to its authority was also the most profound. That challenge came from a group of former suffragists, who in 1916 had formed the National Woman's Party (NWP) to promote radical tactics in support of the passage

[167] Reagin, *German Women's Movement*, pp. 208–12. For an analysis of how women in the SPD were absorbed into male-dominated agendas, see Karen Hageman, "Men's Demonstrations and Women's Protests." For new cultural patterns in which women of the popular classes turned away from politics, see Katarina von Ankum, *Women in the Metropolis*. For the influence of American mass culture on German women, see Kate Lacey, *Feminine Frequencies*.

[168] Alice Salomon, "Social Service in Germany Today," *Survey*, September 1, 1920, pp. 664–67; "Childcare in Germany," *Survey* 48 (1922): 603; "Pensions and the Mark," *Survey*, December 15, 1923, p. 390; "Health and the Mark," *Survey*, April 15, 1923, p. 87.

[169] Charles Selden, "The Most Powerful Lobby in Washington," *The Ladies' Home Journal*, April 1922, pp. 5, 93–96, quoted in Cott, *Grounding of Modern Feminism*, p. 98.

of the suffrage amendment. Some social justice feminists initially supported the party. After the passage of the suffrage amendment, however, when the NWP decided in 1921 to advance a new amendment dedicated to equal rights between the sexes, many social justice feminists feared that this strategy would overturn decades of gender-specific legislation that they had established despite the hostility of American courts to state regulations of working conditions or state provisions for the working poor.[170]

The NWP represented a small minority within the suffrage movement clustered around the charismatic leadership of Alice Paul and funded almost entirely by Alva Belmont. Despite the absence of extensive grassroots support, the NWP attracted sufficient numbers of suffragists and reformers to mount a significant challenge to social justice feminism in the 1920s. The NWP's call for "equal rights" echoed the sea change that had occurred within American feminism as nineteenth-century beliefs in the differences between the sexes, the spiritual superiority of women, and the importance of motherhood gave way to twentieth-century beliefs in the similarity of the sexes. Intimate relations between women were pathologized, and heterosexuality rather than motherhood defined women's chief personal relationships. Redoubtable leaders like Kelley and Addams began to seem old as well as old-fashioned.[171]

Social justice feminists lost a major battle in 1923, when the U.S. Supreme Court ruled the District of Columbia's minimum wage law for women unconstitutional. Having succeeded in using hours laws for women as an entering wedge to achieve hours laws for men, Kelley and the NCL had achieved the passage of minimum wage laws for women in several states with an eye toward the same goal. This ruling stopped their momentum. The injury stung especially sharply because the ruling heralded the passage of the suffrage amendment as the arrival of equal rights for women. If minimum wages for men were unconstitutional, so too were minimum wages for women.[172]

Just at this moment another new opposing force emerged—right-wing nationalists who attacked Kelley, Addams, and their colleagues as socialists. In the United States the most ferocious attacks on progressive women activists came from the U.S. Department of War. In the aftermath of World War I, the extraordinary strength of the women's peace movement challenged militarist goals. Aided by right-wing patriotic women's groups, military leaders did what they could to discredit the entire women's

---

[170] See Kathryn Kish Sklar, "Why Did Most Politically Active Women Oppose the ERA in the 1920s?"
[171] For Paul and Belmont, see *Notable American Women*. For the changes in American feminism in the 1920s, see Cott, *Grounding of American Feminism*.
[172] See Sybil Lipschultz, "Social Feminism and Legal Discourse."

movement.[173] In 1923, the chemical division of the Department of War published and began to distribute a chart that depicted the influence of WILPF on almost every other American women's organization, including the League of Women Voters, the GFWC, the WCTU, the National Congress of Mothers and Parent Teachers Associations, the National Women's Trade Union League, the American Home Economics Association, the NCL, the National Association of University Women, the National Council of Jewish Women, the Girls' Friendly Society, Young Women's Christian Associations, and the National Federation of Business and Professional Women. In a veritable declaration of war, the chart depicted these groups as part of what they called the Socialist-Pacifist Movement in America, and declared them to be "an Absolutely Fundamental and Integral Part of International Socialism."[174] Bolshevism, it seemed, could threaten American as well as German nationhood.

One of the first tangible effects of these attacks on social justice feminism came in 1924, when the NCW was planning for the 1925 meeting of the ICW in Washington. At the insistence of the Daughters of the American Revolution, leaders in the NCW pressured the American branch of WILPF to resign from the NCW, thereby preventing WILPF members from participating in the ICW meeting. Although Jane Addams urged WILPF leaders to resist this capitulation, they complied in the fall of 1924.[175]

The resignation of the American branch of WILPF occurred after WILPF's own international meeting in Washington during the summer of 1924. In connection with that meeting Jane Addams and Madeleine Doty arranged to defray the expenses of German delegates by scheduling speaking engagements for them in the United States. For Salomon and German WILPF delegates, American lecture tours in these years generated substantial income. The Americans cast a protective cloak over German friends like Lida Gustava Heymann and Gertrud Baer who might be vulnerable to accusations of bolshevism.

Indeed, in 1922, Gertrud Baer, a friend of Anita Augspurg and Lida Heymann in Munich, who had served as head of the women's division in the ministry for social welfare of the short-lived Bavarian Republic in 1919,

[173] See Cott, *Grounding of Modern Feminism,* pp. 247–53. For the onset of right-wing attacks on progressives, see H. C. Peterson and Gilbert C. Fite, *Opponents of War.*

[174] The chart is reproduced in Cott, *Grounding of Modern Feminism,* p. 242. See also Joan M. Jensen, "All Pink Sisters." The attack on presumed socialists began during the war. Because immigrants felt it first, settlement residents observed its effects early. See Alice Hamilton, *Exploring the Dangerous Trades,* pp. 265–66; Peterson and Fite, *Opponents of War,* pp. 43–60; and Kathleen Kennedy, "Declaring War on War."

[175] Carrie A. Foster, *The Women and the Warriors,* pp. 53–55.

had been detained by the Department of Justice when she arrived in the United States. Although she was eventually released, Baer's confinement taught her American friends to expect official American hostility to German WILPF members. In 1924 they knew that they and they alone would be responsible for the protection of German WILPF members in the United States. Sure enough, when WILPF members took the "Pax Special" train from Washington to Chicago and stopped in towns along the way, they were accused of "subversion" and spying by the Daughters of the American Revolution and the American Legion. The incidents caused some local committees to cancel meetings, but the group also received support from civic, university, church, and labor groups.[176] Hull House, which Salomon had considered Chicago's greatest attraction in 1909, still remained such in the 1920s, both for German WILPF members and social reformers like Salomon and Elisabet von Harnack, who reported on the position of women in American culture and on social reform programs.[177] For Gertrud Baer, a visit to Hull House had an almost spiritual quality: "I try to take a little of the Hull House atmosphere with me into the old shaken world," she wrote Addams after she returned home in 1924.[178] But the meaning of Hull House within American public life had subtly shifted. It too had been shaken.

WILPF members were absent from the ICW meeting in May 1925; so also was their view of racial justice. Mary Church Terrell's autobiography noted that one of the most serious frictions that "ever occurred between white and colored club women was caused by the segregation of the race in the Washington Auditorium when the Quinquennial of the International Council of Women met." Mary McLeod Bethune, then president of the National Association of Colored Women (NACW), asked Terrell to arrange music for the ICW program. Terrell complied, and two hundred African-American singers from Richmond, the Hampton Institute, and Howard University were scheduled to sing. "But the night on which the colored musicians were to appear colored people who went to the auditorium discovered" that they were segregated "in the most undesirable section of the building." The singers refused to appear. Terrell remembered, "Practically all the officers in the National Association as well as thoughtful people in the group felt that the drastic action had been forced upon them by those who subjected the race to the humiliation of segregation in the National Capital, adding insult to injury by doing so when a large number of foreign

---

[176] Bussey and Tims, *Pioneers for Peace*, pp. 48–49. See also Beth Wenger, "Radical Politics in a Reactionary Age."
[177] For male observers of American society in the 1920s, see Nolan, *Visions of Modernity*.
[178] Gertrud Baer to Jane Addams, New York City, June 4, 1924, SCPC (and *JAP*, reel 15).

women were present to witness it." Members of the choirs said that they were too depressed to sing.[179]

Alice Salomon experienced similar unhappiness with the discriminatory policies of her own national organizations. In 1919 she had been passed over for the presidency of the BDF because of her Jewish heritage. "My colleagues informed me that the members hesitated to make anyone of Jewish name and ancestry President, since the attitude of the population was no longer reliable in this respect." She initially accepted this policy, but after the BDF also vetoed her summer visit to a Norwegian friend in 1920 when she hoped to resume informal German relations with the ICW, she resigned from its board and immersed herself in the international women's movement.[180]

Although they observed it first hand, German participants in the transatlantic dialogue did not publicly comment on the declining power of their American friends. Perhaps they hoped to maintain for their own purposes the prewar reputation the American women's movement had enjoyed in Germany. In exchange, American reformers celebrated Weimar Germany and hoped for the best from its strong affirmation of democratic principles. The *Survey* devoted a whole issue to the Weimar Republic on the occasion of its tenth anniversary. Marie Elisabeth Lüders, a prominent legislator and social reformer, portrayed contemporary German women. World War I had fostered a social revolution for women, she insisted, and "henceforth woman stands and will stand, both in professional and in personal life, no longer behind, but beside the man."[181] Yet her frustration with the limitations of contemporary political parties revealed another gap between the ideal hopes and the practical realities of Weimar Germany.

Despite such gains German social justice feminists continued to admire the achievements of their American peers. Elisabet von Harnack's report on the "truly preventive and constructive" work of American social workers suggested that the Weimar welfare state could benefit from the example of programs pioneered on the other side of the Atlantic.[182] While the United States lagged behind in instituting such pillars of the European welfare state as old-age pensions and health insurance, American state mothers' pensions programs were among the most progressive in the world. Except for New Zealand, no other government provided cash payments for destitute mothers that helped them to bring up their children at home—a sys-

[179] Terrell, *Colored Woman*, pp. 370–71.
[180] Salomon, "Character is Destiny," p. 172A. For the resumption of German participation in the ICW, see Ute Gerhard, " 'National oder International?' "
[181] Marie Elisabeth Lüders, "The German Woman's Place," reprinted here in Part IV, document 14.
[182] Elizabet von Harnack, "Pensions for Single Mothers," reprinted here in Part IV, document 13.

tem that von Harnack and other German social justice feminists applauded. American mothers' pensions programs earned the admiration of German women who expected a great deal from their government.[183]

One of Alice Salomon's last contributions to *Die Frau* was a tribute to Jane Addams upon her receipt of the Nobel Peace Prize in 1932. Still the figurehead of American social reform, Addams actually spent much of the 1920s outside the United States. As the acknowledged leader of the international women's peace movement, she remained honorary president of WILPF until 1929. She also sustained WILPF's financial existence for many years, contributing $500 monthly, raised from American members and her own personal funds until the U.S. branch assumed this obligation in 1930.[184] She also donated her prize money to WILPF in 1932. When Addams received the award she was celebrated by her friends and coworkers on both sides of the Atlantic. Before her death in 1935, Addams composed her own epitaph, which did not mention the Nobel Prize, but simply stated: "Jane Addams of Hull House and the Women's International League for Peace and Freedom."[185]

As coalitions sustaining progressive women's social welfare activism declined in power in the United States, German social justice feminists found themselves squeezed even more than they had been in the past by the strength of political groups on their right and left. The transatlantic dialogue between women activists in the two countries remained strong, but it no longer spoke for the mainstream of the women's movement in either country. In many ways the dialogue had become more important to its participants than it had been in the early years of their encounter before 1900. Then it served as a tool for the advancement of each national group within their native political cultures. During and after World War I, it became a expression of personal and professional loyalties that transcended national allegiances.

The Dialogue Destroyed

When Jane Addams received the Nobel Peace Prize, social justice feminists and pacifists on both sides of the Atlantic celebrated her achievements. At the same time, women activists in Germany and the United States had to contend with the repercussions of a severe worldwide economic crisis that was deepening daily. Neither Germany's politically developed but finan-

---

[183] Salomon had long been a proponent of mothers' pensions in Germany. See Salomon, "Das Problem der Witwen- und Waisenversorgung," *Die Frau* 14 (1906/7): 330–42. For the U.S. context, see Molly Ladd-Taylor, *Mother-Work*, chap. 5.
[184] Bussey and Tims, *Pioneers for Peace*, pp. 77–78.
[185] Jane Addams's tombstone in the Cedarville Cemetery, Cedarville, Illinois.

cially impoverished welfare state nor the American reliance on the forces of capitalism seemed equal to the challenge of alleviating the suffering of millions of families who had lost their livelihoods.

The programs of the New Deal might have renewed the exchange of ideas between social justice feminists on both sides of the Atlantic. But instead, beginning early in 1933, the transatlantic dialogue was dominated by anxious inquiries about the personal safety of old friends under Nazi rule and their pleas for help. The three documents in the Epilogue reveal both a public and a private view of a changed and terrorized Germany only six weeks after the Nazis came to power.

In 1933, Alice Hamilton and Jane Addams received from the Oberlaender Trust, an endowed branch of the Carl Schurz Memorial Foundation, traveling fellowships designed to enable distinguished Americans "to become better acquainted with the achievements of the German people in their respective fields." When illness prevented Addams from accepting her award, Hamilton recruited Clara Landsberg, Hamilton's former Hull House roommate who had taught German, to take Addams's place. Landsberg was Jewish. The two women traveled extensively for nine weeks, crossing Germany from east to west and from north to south, subjected to Nazi censorship and propaganda. Their trip filled them with anguish. "Our hearts are just torn to pieces," Hamilton wrote her cousin from Berlin.[186]

When Hamilton and Landsberg arrived in Germany, the National Socialists had already brutally consolidated their power, despite the predictions of the conservative parties that they would be contained in a coalition government. The two American women came to a country where dissident political leaders had been jailed or exiled, books had been burned, and the press was censored.[187] On the pretext that communists had set the fire that destroyed the Reichstag building on February 27, the Nazis began relentlessly to destroy their political opponents, arresting not only members of the Communist Party, but also Social Democrats and pacifists. The "Decree of the Reich President for the Protection of People and the State" (Verordnung des Reichspräsidenten zum Schutz von Volk und Staat), passed the day after the Reichstag fire, suspended vital constitutional safeguards of the Weimar Republic. Even so, the National Socialists did not score a significant electoral victory in early March, gaining only a slim majority in coalition with the ultranationalist German National People's Party. On March 24, the "Enabling Act" (Ermächtigungsgesetz), passed by all parties still represented in the Reichstag with the exception of the SPD, gave Hitler's gov-

---

[186] Alice Hamilton to Agnes Hamilton, Berlin, April 18, 1933, reprinted in Sicherman, *Alice Hamilton*, p. 339.
[187] For the Nazi rise to power, see Conan Fischer, *The Rise of the Nazis*; Karl Dietrich Bracher, *The German Dictatorship*; and Martin Broszat, *The Hitler State*.

ernment legislative powers. With the Communists outlawed since March, the bourgeois parties dissolved under Nazi pressure during June and early July. The SPD was outlawed on June 22. Its leaders were either arrested or driven into exile, a choice that many radical feminists now also faced.

At the end of March 1933, every organization in Germany was subjected to "Gleichschaltung," a "forced and voluntary coordination" of political and professional organizations that characterized the first months of Nazi rule.[188] Socialist, communist, pacifist, and feminist associations were outlawed outright, including WILPF and Helene Stöcker's League for the Protection of Motherhood and Sexual Reform. More mainstream organizations were given a chance to cooperate with the government under a set of strict guidelines. On May 10, Nazi leader Robert Ley announced the establishment of a "German Women's Front" (Deutsches Frauenwerk), a new umbrella organization integrating all civic and religious women's organizations that remained after Gleichschaltung. Organizations that chose to submit to nazification had to pledge loyalty to the political goals of the National Socialists, expel members with Jewish ancestors, submit their agendas and financial records for party approval, and elect only Nazi women to leadership positions. Their other choices were to dissolve voluntarily or to face destruction.[189] The party auxiliary, the Nazi Women's Organization (Nationalsozialistische Frauenschaft), founded in 1931, became the most important women's organization in the Third Reich, with about 2.3 million members in 1939. By 1941, about one of five German women was a member of a Nazi women's organization.[190]

German women's organizations that were still alive responded quickly. The ultraconservative organizations of urban and rural housewives (which had already left the BDF in 1932 over the BDF's support of a disarmament initiative) joined the Women's Front. So did large patriotic women's organizations and the German Protestant Women's Federation. On May 9, the Jewish Women's League (Jüdischer Frauenbund) left the BDF to spare the organization from expelling its Jewish members. Nevertheless, the BDF dissolved itself on May 15, as did the General Association of German Women Teachers.[191]

Years before the National Socialists seized power, progressive bourgeois and Social Democratic women had warned that a Nazi regime would annul all gains women had made during the 1920s and reduce women to "ser-

[188]   The term "forced and voluntary coordination" is from Michael Kater, *Doctors under Hitler,* p. 19.
[189]   Claudia Koonz, *Mothers in the Fatherland,* p. 143. See also Jill Stephenson, *Women in Nazi Society.*
[190]   Ute Benz, ed., *Frauen im Nationalsozialismus,* p. 14.
[191]   Koonz, *Mothers in the Fatherland,* pp. 143–44; Frevert, *Women in German History,* p. 209 Gerhard, *Unerhört,* pp. 377–78.

vants of men" and "childbearing machines." They found it hard to understand how such an outspokenly antifeminist party got a substantial part of the female vote, even if women only rarely represented the majority of Nazi voters. Apparently the Nazi promise of "Woman's Emancipation from Women's Emancipation" appealed to more than just ultraconservative women.[192] Indeed, the women's movement had been under attack from the right as bourgeois-liberal, dominated by Jewish women, internationalist, and pacifist even before the Nazis came to power. Now the lives of Jewish, pacifist, and socialist women were in danger, and all politically active women were ostracized.

Although women could join the party, Nazi ideology banned them from leadership positions, except in women's organizations, the German Labor Front (Deutsche Arbeitsfront), and the National Socialist Welfare Organization (Nationalsozialistische Volkswohlfahrt), where their political influence remained extremely limited. The party never nominated a female Reichstag deputy. In 1933, all seventy-four women in appointed political positions lost their jobs, as did 19,000 women officeholders at the regional and local levels.[193] Gertrud Bäumer, who held the highest of those positions—*Ministerialrat*, "senior councilor," in the Interior Ministry—moved to Silesia with a small pension. She continued to edit *Die Frau,* which after 1945 produced much controversy about her involvement with the regime, and she wrote a number of historical novels. Under Nazi rule, career opportunities for women in the public service, legal, and academic professions were systematically closed. The number of women teachers dropped by 15 percent.[194] What remained of women's social activism was channeled into National Socialist women's and welfare organizations or went underground into illegal activities, which, when discovered, led to lengthy sentences or execution.[195]

In the *Volksgemeinschaft,* the "German national and ethnic community," which became the fullest statement of the Nazi vision of society, women were relegated to hearth and home and to what the new regime held to be their most important duty—raising healthy children. In 1934, a systematic education for mothers and mothers-to-be was introduced, and until 1941 about three million German women attended "Mother Schools," which taught frugal household economics and authoritarian childrearing principles. A Women's Aid Service *(Frauenhilfsdienst),* founded in 1936 and count-

---

[192] Frevert, *Women in German History,* p. 209.
[193] Koonz, *Mothers in the Fatherland,* p. 145.
[194] Frevert, *Women in German History,* p. 219; Koonz, *Mothers in the Fatherland,* p. 145.
[195] On women social workers in Nazi Germany, see Carola Sachße, *Industrial Housewives.* On women in the resistance, see Koonz, *Mothers in the Fatherland,* chap. 9; Gerda Szepansky, *Frauen leisten Widerstand;* and Dorothee von Meding, *Mit dem Mut des Herzens.*

ing 3.5 million members in 1941, organized support services in neighborhoods. On the whole, the Nazi strategy to win women over by addressing pragmatic concerns and involving them in hands-on projects paid off. It fostered a certain feeling of solidarity and unity across classes and generations of women, which in turn underscored the Nazi principle of "Volksgemeinschaft." It also disguised the fact that Nazi ideology created differences among women, differences that proved fatal to those the Nazis considered racially or politically undesirable. The vision of women's unity in the Third Reich was deceiving, but the majority of German women rarely protested against the new and deadly dividing lines.[196]

Alice Hamilton spoke sharply about policies aimed to ensure the "return of women to the home and to womanliness."[197] Hitler's intention to "elevate the mother as a citizen" fulfilled only superficially the goal of greater recognition of motherhood that maternalists on the left and right had advocated during previous decades. By subordinating maternalist policies to racist ideology, the Nazis perverted the life-affirming principles of earlier advocates for mothers' pensions and maternity leave.[198] Only Aryan mothers, healthy and politically loyal, who produced healthy Aryan offspring, could benefit from state programs like tax-free loans for newlyweds. Through nazified education, party youth organizations, and general terror, the state tried to ensure political loyalty. Women who would not or could not meet these standards were publicly humiliated, sterilized, tortured, sent to concentration camps, and murdered.

Although Alice Hamilton could not predict the extent of the genocide to come, she observed many of the public and personal consequences of the regime with chilling clarity during her visit to Germany, in letters home, and in a series of articles that the *Survey Graphic* published between September 1933 and January 1934.[199] Friends from her university days in Germany, as well as social justice feminists and members of the WILPF whom she and Addams had met almost twenty years before, were under

[196] Benz, *Frauen im Nationalsozialismus*, pp. 14–16.
[197] Alice Hamilton to Jane Addams, Berlin, April 22, 1933, reprinted here in the Epilogue.
[198] Whether Nazi family politics constituted a continuation or a break with earlier advocates of maternalist policies has been hotly debated. See Koonz, *Mothers in the Fatherland*, pp. 5, 14, and Gisela Bock, "Die Frauen und der Nationalsozialismus." On racist maternity policies, see also Gisela Bock, "Antinatalism, Maternity and Paternity in National Socialist Racism," in Gisela Bock and Pat Thane, eds., *Maternity and Gender Policies*, pp. 233–55. On social policy in Nazi Germany, see Michael Prinz, "'Sozialpolitik im Wandel der Staatspolitik'?—Das Dritte Reich und die Tradition bürgerlicher Sozialreform," in Rüdiger von Bruch, ed., *Weder Kommunismus noch Kapitalismus*, pp. 219–44.
[199] Alice Hamilton, "Below the Surface," *Survey Graphic*, September 1933, pp. 449–54; "Sound and Fury in Germany," ibid., November 1933, pp. 549–54; and "Woman's Place in Germany," ibid., January 1934, pp. 26–29, reprinted here in the Epilogue.

life-threatening siege, in prison, or exiled. Jews in Frankfurt and Hamburg were terrorized, fleeing the country, and committing suicide. Some acquaintances remained. "We have met very lovely women, all of whom you know, and I have never felt so full of admiration for my own sex," Hamilton wrote Addams. She reported that women's organizations had disbanded rather than "consent to turn Nazi," and none from "the old suffrage and reform groups" would be attending international meetings.[200] Nazi leaders would have preferred a takeover of the BDF to its dissolution, since that would have assured representation in the ICW, even if the regime generally denounced all forms of international cooperation.

Alice Hamilton's articles in the *Survey Graphic* offer a remarkably lucid analysis of the effects of Nazi rule on the three areas of German society that must have concerned her first and foremost: organized labor, the women's movement, and the Jewish community, to which many of her friends and acquaintances belonged. She returned home "a passionate democrat."[201] In Germany, radical feminists and pacifists who had been part of the transatlantic dialogue faced a choice of exile or arrest. Many of them managed to escape. Two decades of traveling within the international women's movement had made them feel more at ease in foreign cultures, and members of WILPF could rely on a network of women pacifists. Neither foreign governments nor international organizations could effectively stop the repression and annihilation of opponents of the Nazi regime, but the member organizations of WILPF resolved to register a formal protest with the foreign ministry in their country should German members be arrested. As a British WILPF member reported to Addams on an "emergency meeting" of the German WILPF in Cologne: "I am afraid that it is true that our members, in common with all other pacifists, will be in constant fear of arrest. The only hope I can see is that I do not think that people like Hitler and Göring pay much attention to women's activities, and they may escape that way."[202]

The most prominent German women pacifists could not entertain such hopes. Anita Augspurg and Lida Gustava Heymann received the news of the Nazis' seizure of power while vacationing at Madeleine Doty's house on the Spanish island of Mallorca. Outspoken radical feminists, pacifists, and supporters of the Bavarian republic after the revolution of 1918, they had long been on the Nazi hit list. They knew they were in acute danger, but continued their trip through the Mediterranean before deciding not to return to Germany. Their journal, *Die Frau im Staat* (Woman in the State),

---

[200] Alice Hamilton to Jane Addams, April 22, 1933 and July 1, 1933, reprinted here in the Epilogue.
[201] Hamilton, "Sound and Fury," p. 549.
[202] Edith Pye to Jane Addams, London, March 3, 1933, Jane Addams Papers, SCPC (and *JAP*, reel 24). The letter also mentions the WILPF resolution.

ceased publication immediately. Heymann and Augspurg stayed in permanent exile in Switzerland.[203]

Another German participant at the Women's Peace Congress at The Hague, Munich WILPF organizer Constanze Hallgarten, also fled initially to Switzerland, later emigrating to the United States via France, Spain, and Portugal. Helene Stöcker, who was in Czechoslovakia in January of 1933, likewise sensed immediate danger. She returned to Berlin to settle her affairs and emigrated to Switzerland within a few days. Stöcker arrived in the United States at the end of 1941 after a two-year odyssey through England, Sweden, the Soviet Union, and Japan.[204] Like many refugees from Germany, they expected a rapid collapse of the regime, staying in neighboring countries and continuing their flight as the Nazis extended their grip. By that time, entry into a truly safe haven like the United States had become all but impossible.[205]

Life in exile proved depressing and difficult. Women who had largely been self-sufficient now had to rely on financial help from friends, and their standard of living declined. The headquarters of WILPF in Geneva served as a meeting point for exiled German pacifists. In April of 1934, Emily Balch reported to Jane Addams that Heymann, Augspurg, Gertrud Baer, and the Berlin pastor Friedrich Siegmund-Schultze were well. Balch had also been visited by Alice Salomon, who was researching a book on the origins of schools of social work, with a grant from the Rockefeller Foundation.[206] Sometimes WILPF could even provide employment. When Gertrud Baer was exiled in 1933 because of her Jewish ancestry, WILPF headquarters immediately offered her asylum. From April to September 1933, she was paid $100 a month to prepare a WILPF congress. But even in the relative safety of Switzerland, Baer feared German spies.[207] Occasionally, American foundations or the newly founded Hospites, an organization of American social workers, offered grants to colleagues who had lost their jobs in Nazi Germany or who needed support in exile.[208]

The Nazi regime remained somewhat responsive to international pres-

[203]   See Karl Holl, "German Pacifist Women in Exile," and Heymann and Augspurg, *Erlebtes, Erschautes*.
[204]   Christl Wickert, *Helene Stöcker*.
[205]   For a broader overview of German-speaking women refugees in the United States, see Christine Backhaus-Lautenschläger, . . . *und standen ihre Frau*.
[206]   Emily Greene Balch to Jane Addams, Geneva, April 2, 1933, and April 24, 1934, Jane Addams Papers, SCPC (and *JAP*, reel 25).
[207]   Pye to Addams, March 3, 1933; and Balch to Addams, April 24, 1934.
[208]   The minutes of a Hospites board meeting from January 1934 list among the grant recipients Alice Salomon, her fellow social worker Ruth Weiland, Salomon's colleague Siddy Wronsky, Marie Lüders, sociologist Marie Baum, and social worker Frieda Wunderlich. See Elisabeth Clark to members of the Board of Hospites, New York, January 9, 1934, Jane Addams Memorial Collection, University of Illinois at Chicago Circle (and *JAP*, reel 26).

sure. Marie-Elisabeth Lüders, imprisoned for four months in 1937, was released after international protests.[209] Afterward, she lived under a publishing ban. It may have been the threat of international protests that saved Alice Salomon's life. As a Jew, Salomon felt the impact of the new powers instantly. Charlotte Dietrich, whom Salomon had chosen as her successor as the head of the Women's School for Social Work in 1925, immediately joined the Nazi Party in 1933. Salomon was prohibited from entering the school she had founded. She did succeed in dissolving the German Academy for Women's Social and Pedagogic Work and destroying its records before the stormtroopers could enter the building. Convinced that emigration only made sense for people under forty, Salomon decided to stay in Germany and use her international connections to assist younger men and women, Jews and Christians, who had decided to leave. She became a member of Martin Niemöller's Confessional Church (Bekennende Kirche).[210] But her old networks eroded quickly. "So many friends have left [since you were here]," she wrote Alice Hamilton in November 1934, "and others are planning to follow them and the air is getting rather thin which surrounds us."[211]

In May of 1937, the Gestapo made the choice for her. Citing her international travels as suspicious, they forced Salomon to emigrate or be sent to a concentration camp. Unlike many other refugees, she had enough time to settle her affairs and destroy incriminating papers before she departed for the United States. She arrived in New York later that summer.

Even for the woman once dubbed "the German Jane Addams," the country that had been hospitable to her before World War I and supported her in the early 1920s had changed. She was sixty-six, the Great Depression was in its seventh year, and New York was full of German refugees looking for jobs. It was difficult to find gainful employment. Many of her old friends were unavailable, and Salomon had to make new connections through *Survey* and various foundations. "If Jane Addams had been alive or if Lillian Wald was not so ill," Salomon wrote to Joanna Colcord of the Russell Sage Foundation, "everything would have been done for me without my saying a word or making a suggestion. But my generation is going and all the friends I have now know very little of my work."[212] For many years, Salomon tried unsuccessfully to market her memoirs. She died an American citizen in New York in 1948.

Thus ended a half century of eloquent dialogue between American and

209   Marie-Elisabeth Lüders, *Fürchte Dich nicht*, pp. 130–40.
210   Salomon, "Character is Destiny," pp. 293–302.
211   Alice Salomon to Alice Hamilton, Berlin, November 24, 1934, *JAP*, reel 26.
212   Alicia [*sic*] Salomon to Miss Colcord, New York, July 24, 1934, Survey Associates, box 162, file 1251, Social Welfare History Archives, University of Minnesota, Minneapolis. On Salomon's years in exile, see Joachim Wieler, *Er-innerung eines zerstörten Lebensabends*.

German social justice feminists. Between 1885 and 1933 their contact shaped approaches to social reform on both sides of the Atlantic. Reaching beyond their national boundaries, each group was enriched by its relationship with the other. Initially they drew on each other to enhance their standing within their own political cultures. Their differences prompted them to view each other as prototypes that illuminated the limitations of their native polities. Their similarities helped them learn from each other and apply what they learned to their own reform efforts. This combination of differences and similarities forged relationships that deepened over time, becoming both more professional and more personal. During World War I, cooperation between American and German women consolidated a new international effort to merge women's rights and human rights. After the war, their cooperation weathered the crises of famine and revolution in Germany and political reversals in the United States. Their dialogue ceased only with the Nazis' eradication of social justice feminism in Germany.

This dialogue was constructed by a generation of women reformers born in the 1860s and 1870s, who rose to national prominence in their respective political cultures around 1900, gained unprecedented power in the years before 1914, struggled to meet the challenges of new circumstances in the 1920s, and passed from the scene in the early 1930s. In the half century after 1930 new social, economic, and political forces hardened national boundaries. The international political culture that these women nurtured before 1914 had few heirs. Their organizations persisted after 1930—most notably WILPF—but on both sides of the Atlantic, women's political cultures tended to be absorbed within male-dominated groups that were themselves embedded within national political structures. Partly because they offer us an alternative to those structures, the women whose writings are included in this book illuminate possibilities for the future as well as their struggles in the past.

PART I

Promoting a Dialogue: American Women Forge Ties with German Activism, 1885–1908

"Family of Mrs. Motto making artificial flowers in a very dirty tenement, 302 Mott St., New York City," a photograph taken by Lewis Hine for the National Child Labor Committee, 1911. Courtesy of the Library of Congress.

1. Florence Kelley Tells American Suffragists to Attend to Working Women

In this 1885 letter to the editor of *New Era*,[1] Florence Kelley praises the example of the leading German-American socialist newspaper, the New York *Volkszeitung*, for consistently publicizing the concerns of working women and girls. Kelley tries to shame middle-class American suffragists into following the *Volkszeitung*'s example. By discussing examples of the working-class legislation that suffragists should be supporting, she offered political guidance that readers were not currently getting from the suffrage press. She argued that since the success of the suffrage movement depended on the support of working men, suffragists should cultivate the respect of working men by advocating "working-women's protective laws."

The *New Era* was a Chicago suffrage periodical launched by Elizabeth Boynton Harbart in January 1885. Invoking "the sacred rights of motherhood," Harbart demanded suffrage for women on the grounds that "the hand that rocks the cradle shall help to rule the world." Married to a reform-minded Chicago attorney, she had earlier edited the "Woman's Kingdom" in the Chicago *Inter-Ocean*, one of the most popular newspapers in the United States. Her *New Era* failed financially in less than two years, perhaps because it voiced such a multiplicity of concerns, ranging from temperance and popular amusements to the organizational structure of the suffrage movement, that it failed to establish a consistent readership.

Letters from the People
Heidelberg, Germany, March 1885

Dear Mrs. Harbert [*sic*]:

I have read with great interest the accounts of the Washington convention, and I have slowly arrived at a criticism which will seem too heterodox, but if you will think it over will find true, nevertheless.[2]

---

[1] Florence Kelley Wischnewetzky, "Letters from the People," *New Era* (Chicago), May 1885; emphasis in the original.

[2] The Seventeenth National Convention of the National Woman's Suffrage Association met in Washington, D.C., in January 1885. The convention devoted a considerable amount of discussion to resolutions condemning Christian and Jewish clergymen for their opposition to woman suffrage. The primary object of the NWSA was the passage by Congress of a constitu-

I do not think that our movement, in its present phase, represents the mass of American working women *in practical work*. That is, our organs and conventions discuss *higher* education and the laws affecting married women's property, and the need of property-holding women getting school suffrage, as work to be done hand in hand with agitation for the ballot; but I look in vain for their discussing laws for keeping little girls out of factories and in school; for their having hearings before the legislature in support of factory acts, or acts to secure the mill hand weekly payment of her wages, though the hearings in favor of the property acts aforesaid have been frequently and well reported.

When I want to learn anything about immediate practical work in the interests of working-women, I am obliged to lay aside my various organs of the movement with a sigh, and turn—it was a great surprise to me to make the discovery—to the organ of the working-men—the N.Y. *Volkszeitung*. For instance, this (March 7th) week's *Volkszeitung* brings me the following, which I might much better have expected to find in the *Woman's Journal*:[3]

A Bill Which Must Not Become Law

The bill introduced last week by State Senator Titus, by which imprisonment for debt is to be abolished, is one of the highest importance to all working-women and girls. In 1867 the legislature inacted a law intended to compel the payment of wages to women and girls, on penalty of imprisonment. In 1878 the amount of unpaid wages for which imprisonment could be imposed was fixed at $50, and in 1880 these provisions were changed by the adoption of the new civil code so that such imprisonment should not exceed fifteen days. The adoption of Senator Titus' Bill would remove all punishment from "sweaters" who do not pay their employees, and it is earnestly to be wished that the Assembly may reject it, for most of the employers who plunder women and girls avoid having property which can be seized, and if this penalty of imprisonment should be removed, their employees would be placed wholly at the mercy of conscienceless rascals. <u>It is the duty of the Working-men's Associations so to protest against this bill that the members of the Assembly may take good care not to vote for it</u>.[4]

The underscoring is my own. It strikes me as putting our workers and our organs in a very bad light, when the working-men are left to take care

---

tional amendment prohibiting the states from disfranchising United States citizens on account of sex.

[3] The *New Yorker Volkszeitung* (1878–1932), owned not by a party but by an independent board, was the most prestigious and influential German-American socialist newspaper. In 1900 it introduced a women's page. The *Woman's Journal*, founded in 1869, was the official publication of the American Woman Suffrage Association.

[4] The editors have not been able to learn anything further about Titus or his bill.

of such a measure as this without even a word of approval from us, much less such initiative work of our own in behalf of the bill as we are in duty—*and in policy*—bound to give it. For what can we expect but contempt from working-men, if while we take good care of laws for the benefit of property-holding women while working for the ballot, we leave the working-women's protective laws to the working-men to care for? And yet the working-men are the majority of voters, and every time we go to Congress or a legislature, we appeal to a body elected by working-men; and it is arrant nonsense to suppose that we can get on without the sympathy and support of that portion of them now organized and organizing, and therefore easily accessible to suffrage work, provided the movement commands their respect.

The foregoing extract is only one of a dozen in the course of a month. Factory hours restriction law in Michigan; the employment of primary school girls during school hours in Brooklyn factories, the bill (affecting chiefly women and girls) prohibiting the manufacture of cigars in tenement houses in New York City, the eight-hour laws for the states of New York, Vermont, Connecticut, and Maine, not a word of one of them in our organs, and all carefully and elaborately treated in the working-man's organs! It makes me thoroughly uncomfortable. It seems to show such a one-sided activity on our part, such a want of sympathy with the hard-struggling thousands whom we, of all people, ought to represent, and defend, and protect.

I am eager to see a copy of THE NEW ERA, and hope to find the new organ which represents the great west in advance of its elder sisters in this respect. It seems to me that they have not kept pace with the changed condition of the women of the country in this respect, and I do not hesitate to criticize them in this way, because I am criticizing them even more vigorously through their own columns as you doubtless see from your exchanges. Hoping that you will pardon the length of this letter, and with a very earnest wish to call the attention of our workers to the subject of it, I am,

With great respect very truly yours,
Florence Kelley Wischnewetzky

2. Kelley Urges American Suffragists to Adopt a Program

Established in Beatrice, Nebraska, in 1883, the *Woman's Tribune* covered the woman suffrage movement in Nebraska and reported events affecting

the movement nationally. Its editor, Clara B. Colby, was a leading speaker and organizer for woman suffrage in Nebraska.

In this first of two letters to the *Tribune* (written early in 1885, but not published until September),[5] Kelley calls upon readers to develop a "a set of principles clearly formulated," offering the example of the German Working Men's Party as her model. Even more important, she insists that the suffrage movement develop a program that moved beyond the perspective of middle-class women. She encourages the American suffrage movement to imitate the example of German socialists and address the class inequalities that afflict working women, thereby more effectively reducing the total sum of social inequality.

"Correspondence from Heidelberg"

Heidelberg, Germany

Dear Mrs. Colby:—I thank you very much for the specimen of the WOMAN'S TRIBUNE which came yesterday. I had not seen it before. I like the tone of the TRIBUNE immensely and wish it all success. I hope our best energies in the West may be led to concentrate upon it; It is so very necessary to have two or three organs clear in tone and *rich in substance.*

I have one subject heavily upon my mind. If I had been in America I should have brought all the vigor I possess to bear in bringing this subject before the convention. At present I am hammering upon it in the *Woman's Journal* and in my whole private correspondence. *We need a program.* Our platform of one plank [of] the ballot is not enough. The maxim *Equality before the Law* is not enough, though it is good as far as it goes.[6] (For instance, neither of them has any *immediate* bearing upon the question of equal pay for equal work.) We want a formulated program defining our general objects first and our immediate practical demands second: In my work for instance, I am constantly hampered for want of it. If, for instance, I want to criticize the actions of the German Working Men's Party here in Germany in any given case, I have their program at hand, a program adopted sixteen years ago, modified at succeeding annual conventions and freely ratified every year. Candidates are elected on pledges to support this program, organs are conducted in accordance with it, speeches of representatives in the superial parliament are criticized with it as a standard, and friends defend and enemies attack a set of principles clearly formulated and universally acknowledged as the principles of the party.

But when I want to defend our movement against some wild charge,

<hr>

[5] Florence Kelley Wischnewetzky, "Correspondence from Heidelberg," *The Woman's Tribune* (Beatrice, Nebr.), September 1885, 1; emphasis in the original.

[6] "Equality Before the Law" was the motto printed on the *Woman's Tribune* masthead.

when I want confidentiality to affirm what it is pledged to do, in general, and what it demands for today and tomorrow while working for the ballot, I have to hunt up some single resolution of some single convention, or some good word of a known leader, or the motto of some organ: and it is most unsatisfactory. I am in danger of quoting some momentary piece of political tactics for an eternal principle of the movement, and some transitory observation as a part of the creed.

At present in writing an elaborate criticism upon Mr. Lawrence Gronlund's chapter on Woman, in his "Cooperative Commonwealth," I feel this disadvantage sorely.[7] It is clear as daylight what he wants; but when he says what the Suffragists want (besides suffrage), he has me at an infinite disadvantage for he can assert what he pleases and I have no formulated declaration of general principles and special demands with which to confront him. I must bring up our whole array of reports of conventions, resolutions, arguments, petitions, etc., where half a dozen lines ratified by successive national conventions as the principles of the party would be worth the whole collection.

It is no slight task to prepare such a program. If every one concerned would begin to think about it now, and discuss it personally until the next Washington convention, I think it would still take three days of debate to make such a program as it would stand here, year after year, as this program of the German Workingmen's Party does.[8]

For we have the interests of more than half the nation to represent, and times have changed so infinitely that the old general demand for equality of the sexes is not comprehensive enough. At the close of the war [it] answered very well, but then the inequality of the sexes was the greatest that there was, even outweighing the inequality between the Blacks and the Whites, now that is all past. The inequality between the millionaire capitalist and his employee on the verge of pauperism, on the verge of starvation, is greater than the difference between the millionaire and his wife, and the employee and his wife though the employee may have a vote (which he must use as commanded) and the fashionable lady none. To make the employee's wife the equal and leave her there is cruel disregard of her human needs, and to make the millionaire's wife his equal is to add almost nothing to her present power. . . . The mere demand for equality of the sexes is

<hr>

[7]   Lawrence Gronlund, a Danish immigrant who had studied law in Germany, worked as an attorney in Chicago in the 1870s. His extremely popular 1884 book, *The Cooperative Commonwealth: An Exposition on Modern Socialism* (New York: Lovell, 1887), was the first full statement of modern socialism published in the United States. While it owed a strong debt to Marx, this and his later writings interpreted socialism in a religious light, viewing moral questions as more important than economic issues.

[8]   The National Association for Woman Suffrage held an annual convention in Washington, D.C.

good as far as it goes; but to make the working women the mere equal of the working man in these days of wages reductions, lockouts, short time, voting to order, and the rest of the workingman's hardships, is a task which will not arouse much enthusiasm among thinking people. Our demand must be more comprehensive. . . .

When I want to learn anything definite about the status of working women in America, I have to turn my back to our organs after searching them in vain; and I find full particulars in the "New York Volkszeitung," the organ of the German Workingmen and the "Sozialist" the central organ of the Socialistic Workingmen's Party . . . .[9] It seems as if we were indifferent to the interests of the majority of our fellow country-women and cared only for the minority when we fight married women's property acts through the legislatures and [leave] the factory acts that protect unmarried, non-property-holding workinggirls to the workingmen to take care of and not even discuss them, sometimes fail even to record their passage. In this respect we are far behind the English suffrage movement which, while concentrating attention upon that fraction of the ballot which it has the best chance of getting, i.e., for property holding women, never loses a chance of lending a hand to the working women, watches new laws, criticizes old ones, investigates the manner in which beneficial ones are embraced and has succeeded in suspending that most corrupt law which exists in some of our own states, licensing prostitution that is fostering vice chiefly at the cost of the women of the working class.[10]

I cannot judge from the convention number of the WOMAN'S TRIBUNE, whether it differs in this respect from our other organs and I am waiting with great interest for the next number. With great respect, very truly yours,

Florence Kelley Wischnewetzky

[The above was the first communication received from our German correspondent. Although it was laid aside to make room for other interesting

---

[9] For the *Volkszeitung*, see Part I, document 1, Florence Kelley Wischnewetsky, "Letters from the People," note 3. *Der Sozialist* was the national weekly paper of the Socialist Labor Party, headquartered in New York.
[10] In 1874 the National Society for Women's Suffrage, headquartered at Manchester, proposed a bill to Parliament that would have extended suffrage to widows and unmarried women, but explicitly excluded married women. In 1884 strategies supporting limited forms of woman suffrage were renewed during the debates attending the passage that year of expanded provisions for male suffrage. The formation in 1874 of the Women's Protective and Provident League (later called the Women's Trade Union League) drew the support of many politically active middle-class British women. The public regulation, and hence legal recognition, of prostitution through the Contagious Diseases Acts was repealed by Parliament in 1883, after a thirteen-year campaign by Josephine Butler and the Ladies National Association for the repeal of the Contagious Diseases Acts.

letters, yet it contains valuable suggestions and criticisms which make it timely for any issue.—EDITOR]

3. Kelley Describes the German Working-women's Movement to American Suffragists

In this second of her letters written to the *Woman's Tribune* (though the first to be published),[11] Florence Kelley tries to build a bridge between supporters of woman suffrage in Germany, who before 1900 were almost exclusively SPD activists, and middle-class advocates of woman suffrage in the United States.

Aiding that cross-Atlantic, cross-class bridge was the publication of August Bebel's recently translated *Women in the Past, Present and Future*, which Kelley recommends as a pathbreaking analysis of the rights of women. Bebel's emphatic support of women's civil rights, including suffrage, placed him in the vanguard of social democratic attitudes toward the "woman question" and at the same time rendered his views acceptable to middle-class American readers. While Bebel claimed a connection between socialism and women's emancipation, none actually emerged from his argument. That connection had only just been made in Engels's *Origin of the Family, Private Property and the State* (1884). Yet Bebel's prominence within the SPD, which rested partly on the vigor of his theoretical writings, partly on his effectiveness as the head of the SPD delegation within the Reichstag, merged theoretical acuity and civil activism in ways that made him especially appealing to Florence Kelley.

Class divisions within Germany and the public activism of women associated with the SPD informed Kelley's effort to connect American suffragists with German social democrats. She overlooked the fact that bourgeois women's groups were already pushing for greater educational and professional opportunities, if not for suffrage. Instead, she emphasized the backwardness of German middle-class women on the suffrage question. No middle-class suffrage league existed in Germany until 1902, and the League of German Women's Associations did not support woman suffrage until 1911. The General German Women's Association (Allgemeiner Deutscher Frauenverein, ADF, founded in 1865) chiefly promoted women's education and access to employment.

[11] Florence Kelly Wischnewetzky, "Movement Among German Working Women," *Woman's Tribune*, May 1885. *New Era* published another letter from Kelley in July 1885, which resembles the one published here.

Kelley clearly hoped for more from her middle-class American readers than she expected from the middle-class women's movement in Germany. She heaped scorn on the latter as a way to prod the former into new forms of cross-class activism.

"Movement Among German Working Women"

I see from their letter of greeting to the Washington convention published in the TRIBUNE of March that our fellow workers, Mrs. Foster and her daughters, share the prevailing belief that there is no woman suffrage movement in Germany, and that Madame Guillaume-Schack is about to make a new departure in trying to organize one in the next month.[12] The trouble is that outsiders, not Germans, do not look in the right place for the German movement and naturally do not find it, though it is neither young nor feeble, much less waiting to be born. We Americans naturally look to women of the comfortable, intelligent class to take the lead in such a movement all the world over, because they have done so in England and America, and finding that those German women who are comfortable are rarely intelligent, and that the few exceptions are well nigh in despair because their movement finds so little support among the women who ought to work for it, we naturally conclude that universal torpor reigns among German women.

The secret to this matter is that in Germany, the most intelligent women are with a few noble exceptions, the uncomfortable ones, *i.e.* the women who work for wages or try to bring up their children on the inhuman wages of their husbands. They are the working-women, and the wives of 750,000 voters who comprise the workingmen's party. Among these women there is no torpor prevailing. Those of them who are not clear themselves as to what ought to be done are eager in response to such noble exceptions among the more favored class as Madame Guillaume-Schack, Madame Hageman and the others who are now earnestly preaching woman's need of the ballot and of careful scrutiny and sharp criticism of legislation

[12]   Rachel Foster Avery (1858–1919), American suffragist. She came to the attention of the *Tribune* in 1882 when she directed the Nebraska campaign for a state suffrage amendment. In 1885, the year this article was published, she studied at the University of Zurich, where she met Florence Kelley. Two years later, she funded the publication of Kelley's translation of Friedrich Engels's *The Condition of the Working Class in England in 1844*. She served as secretary of the World's Congress of Representative Women at Chicago in 1893, the first secretary of the IWSA (1904–1909), and vice president of the NAWSA from 1907 to 1910.

Gertrud Guillaume-Schack (1845–1903), German feminist and socialist, promoted progressive sex reform, partially modeled on the work of Josephine Butler in England. In association with the SPD, she also founded the short-lived Verein zur Vertretung der Interessen der Arbeiterinnen (Association to Promote the Interests of Working Women) in 1885.

touching women.[13] These workingwomen are far better off than their working sisters in America in one single respect: they are represented in the Imperial Parliament by four and twenty workingmen voters, all pledged to a clearly formulated program, the first demand of which is universal suffrage.[14]

American women who read German can readily learn what the actual state of things is in Germany upon the woman question by reading a little book recently published by August Bebel, the leader in Parliament of these twenty-four representatives of woman suffrage.[15] The book is entitled "Die Frau in der Vergangenheit, Gegenwart und Zukunft" (Women in the Past, Present and Future), and may be had at trifling cost from Herman Nitzsche, 548 Ninth Avenue, New York City. This book has been translated into English by Dr. Adams-Walther, an English lady who graduated in medicine in one of the Swiss universities, married a German physician, is practicing medicine in Frankfurt, and is the leading spirit of all movements in that part of Germany for the improvement of the condition of women in general and of teachers and wage-earning women in particular. Dr. Adams-

---

[13] The socialist movement had not yet developed a settled position on the question of protective labor legislation for women, and would not do so until ten years later. Clara Zetkin (1857–1933), German teacher, revolutionary, journalist, pacifist, and feminist, head of the Women's Socialist International from 1907 to 1914, led the way in defining the need for special laws for women.

The editors have not been able to identify Madame Hageman.

[14] The Imperial Parliament or Reichstag was formed by Chancellor Otto von Bismarck in 1871 when the empire was established as a justification for Prussian rule over other German states. Very weak in relationship to other branches of government, including the monarchy and various government ministers, the Reichstag was designed by Bismarck to reduce and contain the influence of bourgeois liberals. By introducing universal manhood suffrage in Reichstag elections, Bismarck assumed that the liberals would be outnumbered on both their left and right, and that internal divisions would render the body ineffective. Kelley's estimate of the parliamentary power of the SPD was therefore somewhat exaggerated, implying as she did that the Reichstag was equivalent to the British Parliament or the U.S. House of Representatives. Nevertheless, since the SPD obtained a new level of power within the Reichstag in the elections of 1884, her glowing report has some validity.

The Social Democratic Party endorsed woman suffrage implicitly in 1875, when it called for universal, equal, direct suffrage for all citizens, but not until 1891 did the party explicitly begin to promote female suffrage.

[15] August Bebel (1840–1913) was a member of the Reichstag from 1871 to 1913, and joint chairman of the SPD from 1875 until his death. At the time of Kelley's letter, Bebel's command of the party was increasing, due to the German government's intensified campaign against the SPD. That campaign undercut centrists within the party, strengthened the party's left wing, and by enforcing prohibitions against party activity outside the Reichstag, highlighted Bebel's capable and energetic leadership within the Reichstag.

The first English language edition of Bebel's book had just been published as August Bebel, *Women in the Past, Present and Future,* translated by Dr. H. B. Adams Chapman Walther (New York: John Lovell, 1884). Since the original title of Bebel's book, *Die Frau und der Sozialismus* (1878), caused it to be banned, he had issued a new edition with a new title in 1883: *Die Frau in der Vergangenheit, Gegenwart und Zukunft.* Subsequent editions after 1890 resumed the title, *Women and Socialism,* which after 1910 was translated as *Women under Socialism.*

Walther's translation of August Bebel's book is now in press in London and will doubtless be reprinted in America in the course of the summer, meanwhile the German edition is to be had as before suggested, of Nitzsche in New York. This work has been published in three editions, bought chiefly by workingmen and their wives, widely discussed by their organs all through Germany and accepted as formulating the workingmens' standpoint upon the question. It had not appeared in its present form at the time of Mr. Theodore Stanton's "Woman Question in Europe" or Mr. Stanton, who in his own fine article so justly attributes to the workingmen the lion's share of the progress, little as it is, which the woman question has made in France, [and] would certainly not have let the most insufficient essays of Frauleins Hirsch and Marie Cahn [sic] stand as descriptive of the state of the present German woman question.[16]

How wide awake the German workingwomen are as to their own interests, may be judged by the following petition recently forwarded to the Imperial Parliament by three hundred and thirty workingwomen of Danzig. It is directed at the bill now before Parliament and supported by the Ultramontane Party for restricting the work of women and children equally.[17] The petition reads as follows:

> It is proposed to forbid the employment of women in factories on Sundays and holidays and to shut them out of certain employments wholly. It is even proposed to limit the employment of married women in cities to six hours, so placing them precisely on the level of children.
>
> In such an attempt there is something utterly insulting and humiliating for the German woman. How can such an attempt at "protecting" the German woman be justified?
>
> Have the workingwomen who, in the bitter struggle for existence, nobly toil to maintain themselves and their families deserved *such* "protection?"
>
> Have not the workingwomen proved themselves quite as conscientious and trustworthy as the male workers? Are not their services in many fields of labor fully equal to those of men?
>
> They place industrious, independent women side by side with children!
>
> We do not ignore that these bills are intended to defend the workingwoman against over-exhaustion and to make home life possible for them—but legal enactments have no power to accomplish this.
>
> Want forces the workingwoman into industrial activity. To limit her in her

---

[16]   Theodore Stanton, ed., *The Woman Question in Europe; A Series of Original Essays* (New York: Putnam's, 1884). See the Introduction, note 57.

[17]   The port city of Danzig was then part of Prussia. "Ultramontane" was a derogatory term for Catholic-dominated political parties, suggesting that their primary loyalty lay in Rome with the Pope.

work without granting her any compensation for her loss, is simply to make it harder for her to live honestly.

There is certainly much to be done in the way of protecting working-women. We would suggest the need of safeguards against accidents and preventable disease, the appointment of women overseers in factories, the arrangement of separate washing and dressing rooms and other measures equally practicable and beneficent.

But we hereby protest against the limitation of the work of women, and against the attempt to place selfsupporting working women at a disadvantage as compared with workingmen, and we petition the Parliament to defend us against the proposed "protection."

So much for the three hundred and thirty workingwomen petitioners of Danzig. Next as to their representatives in the Reichstag. Representative Grillenberger, speaking March 11th on the question and in the name of his twenty-three colleagues of the workingmens' party said:

Gentlemen, we are not of the opinion that the labor of women can be limited to the same extent as that of children, and the entire prohibition of the work of women is utterly foreign to our intention. On the contrary, we believe that in a wisely organized society the work of women could be most admirably utilized for a multitude of industries for which the male hand is not adapted. But as matters stand to-day, women are employed in a great number of works in which they do not belong, where masculine muscles alone are in place. When it goes so far that women are made to do the heaviest work in iron and steel works, the state of things is utterly ruinous to their health.

We demand that night work for women in factories be forbidden outright. We demand that in occupations especially injurious to the health and morals the employment of women be forbidden. But we can never consent that in employment where men and women work side by side, a shorter working time be enforced for women than for men as the Ultramontane Party's bill proposes. It is Utopian to demand such a provision from our present society, it cannot be enforced under our present method of production, because it would be equivalent to prohibition of women in factories. We hope much more in this direction from the enforcement of the normal working day for all workers.[18]

This is a clear and vigorous statement of the Workingmens' Party towards the working women whom it represents, and I think it justifies me in the assertion that in having these four and twenty representatives in the Imperial Parliament, the German workingwomen are far better off than

[18] Karl Grillenberger (1848–1897) was a locksmith and proofreader who became an SPD delegate to the Bavarian parliament and a member of the Reichstag.

their toiling sisters in America. In any case, the woman question and the movement of German women centre in the activity of the workingmen, the workingwomen and the Workingmens' Party, and she who watches the activity in this part of the German people soon grows reconciled to the torpor of the women of the comfortable class. It comes to seem less shameful for the German nation that its more prosperous daughters care nothing for a respectable education and they bow down in worship of the man who is chiefly responsible for the vile legislation that presses upon women to an extent undreamed of in America.[19] These comfortable laggards are, after all, a minority of the women of Germany; the kernel of the nation is its working class, and this kernel is developing in a way in which it behooves us to watch, study and learn from.

Florence Kelley Wischnewetzky

4. Kelley Explains Illinois Factory Laws to German Social Democrats

With this 1894 article Florence Kelley resumed her dialogue with German social democracy.[20] This time, from a position of substantial power in the United States, she tells readers about her work as the Chief Factory Inspector of Illinois. Offering glimpses of her day-to-day struggle to implement pathbreaking social legislation, she presumes that her audience is curious about how social justice was being advanced in what German readers might consider a province on the margins of civilization. Her tone is that of a social experimenter wondering which forces would prevail—those favoring her efforts or those opposing them.

Kelley had drafted the legislation that she now enforced, including the provision that created the Illinois factory inspectorate with its requirement that five of the twelve deputies be women. Although she does not try to explain why she and other women led the movement that established the Illinois Office of Factory Inspector, she does remark upon some peculiarities of the American setting that account for the intensity of her struggle as the enforcer of new social legislation. The lack of compulsory school attendance laws and the ethnic diversity of the working class highlight the weakness of organized labor and help explain what she was up against, as does

---

[19] Kelley was referring to Otto von Bismarck, Prussian prime minister. By "vile legislation" she meant the laws prohibiting women from taking part in political meetings.

[20] Florence Kelley, "Die Fabrikgesetzgebung in Illinois," *Sozialpolitisches Centralblatt,* July 30, 1894; translated by Corinna Hörst and the editors, emphasis in the original.

the power of the state supreme court to declare her legislation unconstitutional. These differences between Germany and the United States amplified her struggle and made immediate success unlikely. Indeed in 1895 the Illinois Supreme Court did declare the regulation of women's working hours to be unconstitutional. Nevertheless, Kelley remained optimistic. She shared her readers' social democratic belief in the capacity of state officials to channel social change in a positive direction, and describes here how she used her position to harass employers who exploited the labor of children, tenement sweatshop workers, or women wage-earners.

"The Factory Laws in Illinois"
by Chief Factory Inspector Florence Kelley in Chicago

Just last year, factory inspection was introduced to Illinois by means of the passage of a law notable for the drastic character of its few regulations.

This law creates the position of the Inspector, who is assigned an assistant and twelve deputies, five of whom have to be women. The inspectors are required to inspect all factories, industrial establishments, workshops, and even tenements in Illinois in which clothing is produced. They must also prosecute all violations of the law. Punishment is at the judges' discretion; however, it must amount to at least $3 plus court costs, and a single violation of the law will not exceed $100 plus court costs.

The provisions of the factory law mainly cover three topics: child labor, the conditions under which clothes may be finished, and the working hours of female workers.

Regarding child labor, the regulations of the Illinois factory law are basically as follows: No child under fourteen years old may be employed in any factory or industrial establishment. Children between fourteen and sixteen shall only be employed if they provide the employer with a certificate, confirmed by the father, mother, or guardian, that gives detailed information about their date and place of birth. The inspector is also responsible for asking for a medical certificate for children who are in poor health or physically underdeveloped. The office of the industrial establishment is required to maintain a complete list with the name, age, address, and beginning and ending dates of employment of every child, even if the child has only been employed there temporarily. At the request of an inspector, the age certificate, the health certificate, and the list with the names of all children not yet sixteen years old must be presented. Further, a similar list of names must be posted on the wall of every room where children under sixteen are employed.

As the turnover of children is almost continuous in all industrial establishments where children are employed, it is very difficult for employers to comply with this demand. A certain manufacturer of candy usually employed 190 little girls between nine and sixteen, without any control by the state. After the law was enacted, the manufacturer asked for an age certificate from every child who was working for him. In six weeks, he collected more than 700 certificates, although the number of children working in his factory never exceeded 190 during this time. The explanation for this phenomenon was that the work did not require any training or skills, could therefore be done by any child, and was correspondingly badly paid. As a result, the children were not tied down but came and went from day to day just as they pleased. With such constant changes in the workforce, it proved to be impossible to keep the lists in the office and on the walls up to date. The manufacturer was prosecuted because of these incomplete lists, and a $25 fine and $25 court costs were imposed on him. After that he decided no longer to employ children unless they had passed their sixteenth birthday. Nearly all employers who primarily employed children in their factories had similar experiences, for example manufacturers of paper boxes, cigars and tobacco, men's clothing, etc.

Therefore, within the first half year after the enactment of the law, a very significant decrease of child labor has been achieved in Illinois.

Child labor regulations are especially significant because of two facts characteristic of American conditions, namely the lack of compulsory school attendance and the ethnic diversity of the working class. Except for Massachusetts, Connecticut, and New Jersey, there is no compulsory school attendance worth mentioning. In Illinois, one finds children who have never been to school and who cannot distinguish the letters of the alphabet, although they were born in Chicago. . . .

It will therefore be very interesting to see whether school attendance rises during the next year because of the exclusion of children from factories or whether, because of the lack of enforced compulsory school attendance, boys not yet allowed to work in factories will become shoe cleaners, newspaper boys, peddlers, errand boys etc., and girls will enter domestic service, which factory girls not unreasonably detest.

The group of inspectors is representative of the population of Illinois. Three are American-born with American parents, five have Irish parents, and one has German parents, while one has immigrated from Ireland, one from Sweden, and one from Russia, the last a Jew. As a result, the Inspection Office has at its disposal four languages that are widely used among the working class in Illinois, namely English, German, and Swedish and the dialect of Russian Jews. Sometimes, it is regarded as a hindrance that no one among the inspectors speaks Bohemian, Polish, or Italian, although a large part of the working class is only accessible with the help of these languages. . . .

The judge's position regarding the protective regulations of the laws against child labor becomes clear in the fact that fines of $3 to $20, in addition to court costs, were imposed in seventy-six cases out of a total of eighty-two prosecutions instituted by the inspectors because of violations of the child labor law in the course of 120 days.

The law is narrowly limited in that it only applies to factories and workshops, not to commercial establishments and their workers. It also does not include any regulations about protective devices at machines, even when fourteen-year-old children are working at those machines, which happens very frequently and is very dangerous. . . . Manufacturers who give clothing to contractors to be finished are urged to keep an exact list with the names and addresses of those contractors (sweaters). These contractors have to keep similar lists if they pass out clothing to homeworkers. Copies of these lists have to be given to the health authorities. As the number of names that must be submitted amounts to 28,000–30,000 in Chicago alone, the supervision of homework is a sheer impossibility. Twelve inspectors already have to inspect around 66,000 factories and workshops in the state of Illinois.

Therefore, these paragraphs of the law would have been a complete pretense if far-reaching additional regulations had not existed saying that if inspectors find vermin or contagious diseases in a homeworker's place, all products intended for the market have to be destroyed immediately by the health authorities. This paragraph is pushed into the forefront as much as possible, and therefore homework is regulated somewhat, although insufficiently. As long as homework in the garment industry is not suppressed altogether, satisfactory supervision is impossible in that field. . . .

The third and by far most popular regulation of the Illinois law concerns the working hours of female workers and reads as follows: "No female person shall work longer than eight hours a day or forty-eight hours a week in any factory or workshop." The working day in Illinois was completely unlimited until this law. For example, one case known to me is a print shop where a number of young girls were working continually for twenty-four hours, from 7 o'clock in the morning until 7 o'clock the next morning, and then—without a break—until 4 o'clock the afternoon of the second day. A break was only introduced after one girl had fainted. In a second case, a girl known to me was working, also in a print shop, from 7 o'clock in the morning until 11:30 at night. One night when she was walking home, she was attacked and nearly killed. Such cases are not rare. In every branch of business it was once a rule that female workers did overtime during the high season—and every branch had its own high season. This did not involve a violation of any law. Nowadays, unlimited working hours still exist in most other states as they did in Illinois until a short while ago. Wherever the normal working day has been introduced, it applies only to women and young workers, and then it still allows ten hours of effective work every day.

The new Illinois law, introducing regular, fixed working hours without exception, caused a big sensation. The working class had eagerly supported the law and strongly and energetically insisted that it be implemented. Those manufacturers who most depended on female workers felt terribly injured, not only because they now had to let their workers work in shifts, which was more expensive, but also because their competitors in neighboring states did not have to comply with similar regulations.

This regulation has been heavily opposed, while other paragraphs of the new law came into force relatively peacefully. About one hundred of the richest manufacturers of this rich state have even gotten together to determine whether the law is constitutional. Already today measures are being taken, with the help of Habeas Corpus proceedings, to shorten the long way to the Supreme Court. They hope by the summer to dispose of the question, whether the working hours of female workers in the factories and workshops of Illinois can be legally fixed or not.

The *Manufacturers Association* does not simply disapprove of the law but ignores and violates it and openly defies the inspectors in every respect.[21] However, a number of manufacturers, among them some of the largest and most powerful in the state, were willing to comply wholly with the law, right from the beginning. So did the Western Electric Supply Works, which employed 300 women and girls among its 700 workers. In this establishment it has always been the custom to employ female workers for $13\frac{1}{2}$ hours effectively during the months of January and February. Some girls suffered greatly under such overexertion, but they could not refuse to stay at their workplace until 9:30 p.m., because it was made clear to them that they would lose their jobs if they did so. This year, however, the law was strictly complied with and the consequence was that in spite of the bad business of a bad year, thirty-five more new female workers were employed during the high season than in the previous good year. After seven months of experience, the corporation as well as the female workers were completely satisfied with the shortened work day. President Enos Barton recently explained to this author that if the new law is declared unconstitutional by the Supreme Court, Western Electric Works will adhere to the eight-hour day. Things are similar in many even larger establishments, especially where female workers have joined their male coworkers and formed effective organizations, stimulated remarkably by the current lawsuit determining the law's constitutionality.

[21]   The Illinois Manufacturers' Association was formed in 1893 for the explicit purpose of fighting Kelley's 1893 law. In 1895 IMA members helped found the National Association of Manufacturers.

5. Kelley Reports on Women Factory Inspectors to a German Audience

This brief history of women factory inspectors in the United States was the second of Kelley's many articles published in *Archiv für Soziale Gesetzgebung und Statistik.*[22] (Her first, printed two years earlier in 1895, reviewed factory laws in the United States generally.) "Women Factory Inspectors" analyzes the inclusion of women in the ranks of state officials capable of intervening in the relationship between capital and labor. Kelley writes from personal experience, not only as the industrializing world's preeminent woman factory inspector, but also as the person responsible in 1889 for getting the first women factory inspectors appointed in the United States.

The topic offered Kelley ample opportunities to examine the gendered structures of social change and to compare German and American political cultures through the lens of gender. She suggests that more women were appointed as factory inspectors in the United States than in Germany or England because women's voluntary organizations were better at mobilizing public opinion. Hull House was her prime example.

Yet she notes that the American political context also produced weaker state initiatives: no workers' insurance existed in the United States; civil service laws were weak; and factory inspectors lacked the authority that they enjoyed in Germany or England. Thus the greater number of women factory inspectors bore an inverse relationship to the power of the state itself. Insisting that gender is irrelevant to the woman factory inspector's performance, Kelley challenges the reigning view in both Germany and the United States that women inspectors should be hired on gender-specific grounds, either for their ability to examine women's worksites or to elicit information from women employees.

Kelley's article was written at the height of the appointment of women factory inspectors in the United States. After 1900 the number of women inspectors declined, partly because women's activism broadened to include a variety of other concerns about the industrial workplace, partly because the appointment of inspectors became increasingly subject to patronage politics.

---

[22]   Florence Kelley, "Die weibliche Fabrikinspektion in den Vereinigten Staaten," *Archiv für Soziale Gesetzgebung und Statistik* 2 (1897): 128–42; translated by Corinna Hörst and the editors.

Kelley thought that civil service reform would foster a more professional inspectorate, but expresses little confidence here that such reform will be enacted. Her optimism about the future of American political culture rested not on the German example of state officials, but on the strength of reform activism among middle-class women, which in the 1890s had created dramatic new opportunities for her and other American women social reformers.

"Women Factory Inspectors in the United States"
by Florence Kelley
Chief Inspector of Factories and Workshops for Illinois

The institution of factory inspection in the United States and Canada was created according to the English model. As in England, inspectors visit and supervise factories, mines, businesses, and many other places of employment. As in England, they are authorized to prosecute all employers who violate the laws pertaining to factories and workshops.

In America, there is no workers' insurance, and the worker and his family are inadequately protected from accidents for which employers are liable. Under these conditions, the role of factory inspection gains additional significance for the worker.

The American factory laws encompass many regulations for the protection of workers' life and health, specifically concerning hygiene in the food and clothing industries, as well as age limitations and compulsory school attendance for children who are employed. Some of the inspectors' duties are highly technical, while others are easy for any person of average intelligence to carry out.

Women have worked as factory inspectors in America for seven years. In the beginning there was only one, but since then the number of female factory inspectors has increased to twenty in the United States and three in Canada. Therefore, we can draw on some experience in considering the aptitude of the female sex for the profession of factory inspector.

In the United States and particularly in the [states of the] West, there is in general no insurmountable obstacle to women's employment in most professions, although people tend to demand especially convincing reasons for hiring a woman instead of a man. Where no legal civil service regulations exist, or where they do not guarantee women equal candidacy, there is a tendency to hire enfranchised men. But even in those places this is not a consistent rule. Thus in 1893, Governor Altgeld appointed a woman to the office of chief factory inspector of Illinois and another woman as her assistant, although the law prescribed the appointment of only five women as deputies and left it up to the governor to fill the posts of chief inspector and assistant with friends and political supporters.[23]

Those who advocate appointing women as factory inspectors support the general principle that all professions and occupations should be open to those who want to pursue them. They further emphasize that experience has shown that women are capable of filling the posts they aspire to and of carrying out the duties connected with those positions.

Nevertheless, the first appointment of a woman factory inspector was deliberately called an experiment and a completely new venture unparalleled in America or even in England, where the idea of factory inspections originated. Indeed, before 1889, women already held offices administering schools and charities. These, however, were only honorary positions without pay and without such demanding duties as those of factory inspectors, with their daily "hikes" from site to site. In the last seven years, a considerable number of women have been entrusted with the most varied positions in factory inspection. The matter has now lost its novelty and is seen as something entirely natural.

The movement for appointing women as factory inspectors began in the New York Working Women's Society, a small group of women from both the wealthy, influential class and the working class. This union circulated petitions and composed resolutions.[24] In 1889 and 1890, it was finally supported by other philanthropic groups and labor unions in bringing the proposal concerning the nomination of female factory inspectors to the legislature. The proposal to add women as officials to the Office of Factory Inspection was only made for humanitarian reasons; in no way was it a goal of the general workers' movement, although it found support among the unions.

From New York, the agitation spread to Pennsylvania and there it was promoted in the same manner. A women's union was formed on the model of the New York society. This new group also consisted of various wealthy and independent women, and a small number of very intelligent women dependent on wage work, primarily stenographers, typists, and reporters. Women factory workers did not belong to the group, although the others tried incessantly to persuade them to join. At that time, there were no women's unions in Philadelphia; however, there were a number of lively women's chapters of the Knights of Labor. Although Pennsylvania

[23] German-born John Peter Altgeld (1847–1902) was elected in 1892 by a reform coalition within the Democratic Party. His pardon of the anarchists accused of masterminding the 1886 Haymarket massacre guaranteed his defeat in 1896, and hence Kelley's failure to be reappointed.

[24] The goals of the New York Working Women's Society, as defined in their 1892 *Annual Report*, were "to found trade organizations in trades where they do not exist and to encourage and assist existing labor organizations to the end of increasing wages and shortening hours."

was already the second-largest industrial state in the union, it had no factory inspection, so agitation was not simply concerned with hiring women as inspectors, but rather introducing factory inspection itself. The movement received significant support from the unions and the workers' press.

In Illinois, the supporters of the movement were members of Hull House, an institution serving social purposes, consisting of educated men and women who lived in one of the poorest industrial areas of Chicago. They tried to share the privileges and benefits of civilization with their neighbors and give them more than the residents of these large industrial districts, populated with new immigrants, could as a rule obtain for themselves. For many months, systematic agitation was used to attack the sweating system. The result was that the Senate and the House of Representatives of the State of Illinois finally sent a commission to Chicago to investigate the conditions in questionable workshops. Members of Hull House, who were particularly familiar with the areas where workshop conditions were least healthy, served as guides for the commission's inquiry. The commission's findings resulted in extensive legal regulations, which not only limited the operation of sweatshops, but also established an Office of Factory Inspection to carry out the measures. Regulations were also established for hiring women as inspectors. These regulations are still in effect today. Here too, the movement was initiated by philanthropists and reform organizations. . . .

The first female factory inspector in America was appointed in December 1889 as secretary of the Pennsylvania Department of Factory Inspection. . . . In Illinois, Rhode Island, and Pennsylvania, the laws that introduced factory inspection also required that half of the officials had to be women. . . .

. . . [I]n seven years, seven states and provinces have appointed twenty-three women as factory inspectors. In none of these states or provinces were such appointments turned down by the legislatures, and the fact that one state legislature after another passed laws pertaining to the appointment of women as inspectors appears to prove that these appointments correspond to public opinion.

Here it should be emphasized that the appointment of women did not keep up with the growth of factory inspection during the period. The number of inspectors in New York went from eighteen in 1890 to thirty-four in 1897, while the number of women officials amounts to only seven. . . . Other states have only male factory inspectors. . . .

The reason that the appointment of women has not kept up with that of men is not because the appointed women are unsuitable. It must rather be sought in other causes, which put the entire issue of factory inspection in a bad light and which have slowed down its development in America. Namely, in the United States, with the exception of New York and Massachusetts, inspectors are not hired on the basis of their qualifications, but solely in consideration of how much their official occupation will further party goals. In this preposterous system women suffer the most. Were the appointments to occur on the basis of the candidates' qualifications, there would literally be a revolution in almost all inspection departments in America, and a large number of well-educated women and women of the working class would hold honorable positions. Unfortunately, however, the distribution of government posts is decided above all by considering enfranchised men, and women are usually only appointed when the law unconditionally demands it.

Concerning the aptitude of the female sex for the post of factory inspector, I must say that on the basis of my past experience, women possess the qualities necessary for this job just as much as men. Above all, good health and a clear mind are necessary; without them nothing can be achieved. Also, one needs to be of an appropriate age, not too young and not too old, the latter because of the daily stress of the profession. Further, the inspector should not be nearsighted, so that he can recognize children who may try to escape his notice in large factories, for example at the far end of a long hall. Sharp eyes are also of primary importance in fulfilling the duties of the position in other respects. Officials must also be able to move quickly in case they need to catch children who want to slip away. Morally, an inspector should be honest, to deter bribery, and loyal, to promote thorough and exact inspection. They must have the energy to enforce the law regardless of plausible excuses. Furthermore, a certain cunning is necessary in dealing with shady employers and parents, who want to get around the law and let their children work even though they are under the minimum legal age. Now, anyone can see that women have all these qualities as well as men. . . .

With the exceptions of New York and Massachusetts, no exams are required before securing these positions. . . . [but] there are already signs that things will get better in [New York] as a result of the statutory reorganization of civil service law. Thus recently, a woman passed the exam after she received a degree from Smith College, wrote a dissertation on factory inspection, traveled for several months through various states in order to gain practical knowledge for her future profession by direct observation, and was helped by the inspectors who accompanied her on her examination of factories.[25]

In stark contrast to such preparation, the first chief inspector for the state of New York, appointed in 1886, several years before the civil service

[25] The editors have been unable to identify this Smith graduate. A later example of such writing is Belva Herron, "Factory Inspection in the United States," *American Journal of Sociology*, 12, no. 4 (January 1907), 487–99.

law came into effect, was an active politician, so ignorant that he could not write a letter. Naturally, he was not able to gain any respect or authority. The actual director of the office was his assistant, an extremely capable man of high character, who after ten years of service was fired in 1896 for political reasons. Both men, the capable and the inept, were hired and fired solely on the basis of party considerations. In Pennsylvania, the chief inspector changes with each governor of the state, so that the present chief is already the third one since the establishment of the office in 1889. Such a process naturally subjects the Office of Factory Inspection to the same corruption that predominates in all branches of civil service under the spoils system. Inspectors are hired who can hardly prepare the required reports of their daily achievements. Positions are even filled with people who cannot function because of old age or sickness. This applies to both men and women. Thus sickly and uneducated women were appointed because they were friends of active politicians, or because their deceased husbands had served as brave soldiers in the war that ended thirty-two years ago.

Only a fundamental change in the system of appointment can enable us to judge properly the advantages and disadvantages of female inspectors. Up to now, agitation for appointing women was partly based on the absurd system of political interests. When, therefore, the New York Working Women's Society turned to the legislature for help in 1888 and 1889, their most impressive argument was the description of the incompetence of the male personnel in the Office of Factory Inspection. It was said that they were so dependent on politicians that it would be extremely useful to appoint a few women who were not engaged in politics and who, with the continual stimulus and moral support of the union, would dutifully and permanently carry out the factory laws. . . .

Women of the working class have proven to be the best and most active factory inspectors, particularly those nominated by the unions. First, they are used to hard work and they have a particular interest in protecting their fellow workers. Although generally uneducated and without technical training, these women are endowed with special advantages because they are eager and accustomed to continuous work. But the fact that they come from the unions confirms the employers' conviction that factory inspection is a measure that has been forced upon them by the workers in their interest, not the interest of the whole society. They do not see it as a measure that should simply prevent the exploitation of the working class and keep them from being destroyed totally, body and soul. . . .

. . . [I]n some states there is a division of labor, so that one group of inspectors concern themselves with only technical matters, while the other group deals with those affairs that do not require a technical background. Thus in Massachusetts, . . . [t]wo female inspectors are entrusted with carrying out regulations dealing with the age and school attendance of children who work, and the working hours and sanitary conditions for women and children. In general, they oversee all legal measures in all factories except those employing only men.

Other states, such as Illinois and Rhode Island, do not employ this division of labor, and the same duties are fulfilled by all officials, whether men or women. In Pennsylvania, some female inspectors perform all the inspection functions, while others check only regulations having to do with women and children. . . .

In the years 1888–90, when the question of hiring women as inspectors still stood unanswered on the agenda of public opinion, all sorts of views were expressed. Because of a lack of experience, these were necessarily based on probabilities. Thus opponents of this innovation argued that the health of prospective female inspectors would not be able to bear the stress of the daily burdens that the men continually suffer, and that women wearing long and bulky clothing would be endangered as they passed by machines. The women would be exposed to unbearable aggravation and would be unable to enforce recognition of and obedience to the law in the face of the resistance and ridicule they would experience in the factories and workshops. In addition, they were said to lack the necessary technical know-how.

The advocates of female inspectors, on the other hand, generally gave the following arguments: First, the appointment of female inspectors would increase the overall efficiency of factory inspection. Second, women would bring to light and eliminate grievances that up to that time remained undiscovered and had not been remedied because of a lack of female inspectors. Further, this profession would open for women a new and worthwhile career, and finally, in this way, people would acquire an interest in factory inspection who previously had hardly known of it or had not been concerned with this important institution. . . .

If one considers the movement for the appointment of women as factory inspectors as an effort to open up a new sphere of influence for women, one cannot characterize it as successful: appointing twenty-three female inspectors in seven years does not mean much. Nevertheless, one can assume that once women have been hired, and after more and more civil service exams offer women increased opportunity on the basis of their capabilities, the number of female inspectors will multiply much more quickly than in the last seven years. Up to now in most states the most ignorant politician has had a better chance [of being appointed to the position] than a well-prepared male or female candidate.

Concerning the alleged damage to the health of women inspectors in carrying out their professional duties, experience proves that they are indeed affected by having to climb up and down many steep staircases, day in and day out in all weather, by having to move between operating machines, and by the many temperature changes, as well as by the various levels of foul air present in many industrial settings. The often very cold and changeable winters in some of our industrial states have a further adverse effect. Both male and female factory inspectors have to protect themselves against such circumstances. The traditional long skirt is undeniably a hindrance when walking in rain or in slush. But skirts have already been shortened considerably by the introduction of the bicycle, thereby eliminating this artificial hindrance to female inspectors' productivity and easy mobility. It would be very desirable if all female inspectors would always wear the short, light, and comfortable dress of the bicyclist during work. Women inspectors who cannot part with corsets, high heels, and the many heavy petticoats and kid gloves of our grandmothers will not, of course, be able to keep up with the endurance and the accomplishments of their colleagues who wear the practical clothes of today's businesswomen.

In the work of inspection itself there is nothing detrimental to health. It will be easier for the average woman to go up and down stairs in factories without elevators, or to stand when observing children or machines, than it is for the washerwoman who has to bend over her tub all day, or the saleswoman who has to stand behind the counter. The female factory inspector is able to use different muscles in her work, and she has a great deal of elbow room. In addition, she always has the opportunity in every factory she visits to rest for a short time, because she must fill out the control lists. If a woman inspector dresses appropriately and otherwise pays proper attention, there is no hazard in her work. Female inspectors who were hired in 1889 and 1890 are still working in Pennsylvania and New York and their health has in no way been affected, thus decisively disproving the argument that women's health cannot withstand the demands of the profession.

It was once believed that female inspectors would be subjected to ugly insults while carrying out their duties. Yet experience has proven this fear, strongly and frequently emphasized in 1888–90, to be groundless. A female inspector entering a factory identifies herself to the factory owner with her badge, the official card, and the appointment form from the governor. This authorization ensures every person a cordial reception, including factory inspectors, both men and women. Besides, every case of hindering a civil servant from carrying out his or her duties is punished as a special violation of state laws. But if an employer really ventured to make the work of a female inspector impossible, would it not be especially desirable that the women and children in precisely this factory make their conditions known to the woman inspector?

One of the arguments most often expressed at the beginning of the movement was the widespread view that the grievances of women and girls in factories and businesses did not come to the notice of male inspectors because women, and especially girls, did not like to tell men about the impropriety and harassment they suffer. In the course of my four years as chief inspector for the third largest industrial state in the union, I have found that the distinction between male and female inspectors makes no difference with respect to workers' bringing complaints. Each year our department receives a large number of complaints in the mail. These complaints are handed to our officials who work in the area of the factory or workshop where the grievance is said to exist. If the official to whom the complaint is given to verify is clever and versatile enough, if he pays attention to the details of the work, he usually succeeds in getting to the root of the problem very soon. This is valid for male inspectors just as much as for females.

During the performance of his duties the inspector receives few or no complaints, and women and children avoid speaking with a female inspector just as much as with a male inspector. This is confirmed by the experience of female inspectors, not only of Illinois but of all states. Complaints about moral offenses of employers, supervisors, or other employees are directed neither to male nor to female inspectors. We are hired to inspect and to prosecute violations of the law; we are not a counseling but rather an executive authority. For that reason workers do not entrust us with their personal concerns, although they expect us to duly and effectively check the execution of decreed regulations of the factory laws and if necessary to enforce them.

The worker avoids speaking with an inspector in the factory because he knows that punishment goes with every violation of a factory law, and that he could be suspected of having acted contrary to the employer's interests if an employer or foreman is punished. Workers are less fearful of making written complaints to the Office of Factory Inspections. Almost half of these complaints are signed by the people making the complaint, with addresses; the rest remain unsigned or they carry fictitious names. The complaints are very often justified, although exaggerated in form. They do not, however, concern moral lapses, and they could be directed to women as well as men.

In ending this discussion we should point out one more element that furthered and will continue to further the development of the question of female factory inspectors. In the United States, continuous clear agitation for specific proposals usually paves the way for legislative innovations that improve working conditions. The more the people approve of these proposals, the more likely it is that the proposals will attract the legislators' attention. It is much easier to find approval by appealing to the sympathy of the masses for the welfare of helpless working women and children than to find it by suggesting absolutely necessary measures to protect the lives, bodies, and health of men, who are the fathers, husbands, and breadwinners of the same women and children. It is not easy to gain the sympathy of the whole population for these male workers, because it is assumed that they can protect themselves and that they can achieve what they need by virtue of their right to vote, without appealing to the support of public opinion. We encounter this phenomenon in the development of factory legislation in each of our industrial states.

We have seen how, in harmony with this perception, the question of appointing women as factory inspectors arouses the interest of philanthropic groups. The presence of only a few women in the factory inspection department not only kept this interest alive but also increased it considerably. In hundreds of women's clubs and scholarly institutions, an effort has been made in the last year to hold speeches and lectures on child labor, the sweatshop system, working hours for women and children, and other related topics, using reports of factory inspectors as sources. In a country where only the women (of the higher classes) have leisure time and increasingly take an active part in political life—even where they are not entitled to vote—their interest is of the greatest value. It is of even greater value the more it is based on growing understanding. It even seems to us that such interest, on the part of hundreds of intelligent women scattered across the industrial states, would be more lasting and effective in the development of factory legislation than the existence of twenty or a hundred women occupied directly with factory inspection. On the other hand, the existence of these working female inspectors is the best stimulus for the growth of those sympathies, and precisely this condition constitutes one of the most compelling reasons for the appointment of women as factory inspectors.

6. Kelley Analyzes American Sweatshops for a German Audience

Sweatshop labor offered good opportunities for international comparisons because it occurred in all industrializing nations, yet each dealt differently with the problem. Writing for a German audience about her American experience, Florence Kelley describes both those aspects of sweating in the United States that resembled the process elsewhere, and features that were peculiar to the United States.[26]

General to sweatshops everywhere were wages too low to sustain life,

---

[26] Florence Kelley, "Das Sweating-system in den Vereinigten Staaten," *Archiv für Soziale Gesetzgebung und Statistik* 12 (1898): 208–32; translated by Corinna Hörst and the editors.

which then were supplemented by public relief or charity, thereby unfairly subsidizing the employer. The spiraling decline of the garment industry under the effect of this unfair competition drove out the "better" garment employees, and remaining workers were unable to reverse the descent. In the United States, as elsewhere, the power of unregulated capital, the deskilling of labor, and the seasonal nature of the garment industry also contributed to the creation of sweatshops.

To describe the peculiarly American characteristics of sweatshop labor Kelley draws heavily on her experience as Chief Factory Inspector—a position German readers could be expected to respect. She writes authoritatively about massive immigration, weak laws, cumbersome legislative procedures, the lack of adequate statistics, a gigantic domestic market, and—what her readers might not have expected—middle-class women in the social settlement and consumer movements.

Kelley had recently agreed to head the newly formed National Consumers' League, and she was turning away from the state-centered activism that made her so visible to German social democrats. Her hopes for effective action against sweatshops now rested with middle-class consumers. Nothing typified better the difference between her own and German political culture. To readers accustomed to depictions of the power of the state, she patiently sketches the obstacles to state action and insistently portrays the efficacy of consumers' organizations.

After almost fifteen years of building her political agenda upon a German model, Florence Kelley was now pursuing another path—one that recognized the weakness of state solutions and the strength of civic action in her native land. In the years ahead her contact with German political culture would be primarily through women's organizations.

"The Sweating System in the United States"
Florence Kelley

"Sweating system," a phrase used so inconsistently that we need to define it for this essay, refers to the principal way labor is organized in the garment industry. First, fabric is cut in the workroom of the wholesale merchant. He passes it on to a contractor, in whose shop, located in or behind a tenement building, the goods are finished; then they are returned to the wholesale merchant. In some cases fabric may pass from the contractor's workshop to the home of a woman who sews buttonholes and does hand stitching. But this does not change the nature of the system. Its essence is not in the work of the buttonhole maker or the homeworker but in the unified operations of the wholesale merchants, who have large amounts of capital and who employ the contractors who oversee people in the tenements. . . .

The extent of the sweating system and of homework cannot be determined accurately. The United States Census has never dealt with this subject. The Bureau of Labor has never investigated the sweating system in its annual or special reports. . . . Factory inspectors' reports describe the sweatshops, but they do not give current and comprehensive statistics.

The situation is further complicated by the fact that different states have different legal definitions for these workshops. Until this year, for example, Pennsylvania inspectors were not permitted to oversee workshops employing fewer than five people except when there was a woman or a child among them. Many tailoring workshops have two, three, or four men, but no women or children. In previous years, these workers have therefore not been included in the official statistics for Pennsylvania. In Illinois, on the other hand, every room is called a workshop where a piece of clothing is made for sale rather than for the personal use of the owner and his family. But the small number of inspectors—twelve for 6,707 workshops and factories, employing 200,140 workers in all branches of the industry—makes it impossible to visit each house where a woman produces shirts, coats, undergarments, or hand-sewn clothes for the sweatshop operators. The total number of persons employed in these trades in Illinois can therefore only be estimated. . . .

The reports of the Bureaus of Labor of the different states contain much material that is not statistical but that forcefully describes the horribly uniform misery inherent in these trades. Among these sources are the reports of the Bureaus of Labor Statistics of Ohio (1895), Illinois (1892), New York (1884), and Missouri (1897). All of the reports of the New York factory inspectors from 1886 to 1897 discussed the sweatshops. The reports of the factory inspectors of Pennsylvania from 1893 to 1896 prepared the ground for the improved law, which was passed in the state in 1897. These reports seem to indicate clearly that the system is expanding everywhere it has appeared, and that the measures designed to regulate and control it have been inadequate. . . .

The relatively few ready-made clothes produced in Chicago before 1885 were the product of a few factories that primarily employed girls as machine workers. Most of these workers spoke English. Wages were high, even though the quality of the products was poor. Only recently have high-quality goods been produced as well. Beginners earned four dollars a week, the most efficient workers sixteen. Skilled girls averaged about ten dollars a week during high season. Few of the small number of factories which existed then were steam-powered, and it was an exception before 1885 to find machines operated by a foot pedal.

This situation changed when Russian Jews and Bohemians began to settle in the city. The latter group came in large numbers at about the same time as the Jewish immigration peaked. These newcomers did not know

"Making Party Favors in the Kitchen," an illustration from Albert Kohn, *Unsere Wohnungs-Enquête im Jahre 1911*, a tenement house survey published in Berlin in 1912.

anything about steam power and did not mind depleting their life's energy on a foot pedal. They had no fixed wages or working hours and no regulated work conditions. They preferred to work under foremen who knew their language, respected their religious holidays, observed the Sabbath, and labored along with them at the machines while directing the work of the shop. The workers avoided the factories, except for the person who customarily picked up the fabric at the factory and was responsible to the owner. The others provided their own machines and during the first month contributed to the rent of the small workshops if necessary. These workshops arose in the midst of the Jewish and Bohemian quarters. From these conditions emerged the comprehensive system of garment production known as the sweating system.

The "kitchen tailors" lost all but the very best custom work. The individual worker in his decent little shop could not compete with the workers of the sweatshop. They were able to keep the machines busy day and night during the high season because they divided the labor and worked in shifts. Women and children were employed to perform the simpler tasks of this inferior work.

The girls in the coat factories now had to compete with men who were content to earn the lowest wages and to work unlimited hours. The men brought the fabric home at night and the next morning delivered the finished clothes, which they had sewn during the night with the help of their wives and children and, if necessary, even some neighbors. Wages fell, working hours increased, and the need to organize became ever more urgent. But there was an irreconcilable quarrel between the girls and the men. The girls could not understand the men's language and despised their poverty and their half-civilized behavior. They mistrusted the men and hated them for having ruined their trade. It was never possible to unite these hostile elements. The better elements gave up the trade and found other work. Almost all factories closed down, the sweatshop replaced the factory, the higher and more progressive organization of labor had to yield to a cruder one. It was a step backward.

In the meantime, the garment industry in Chicago has expanded tremendously. Twenty-four enormous wholesale establishments as well as many other businesses supply not only Chicago and Illinois with ready-made clothes but also the entire Northwest and Southwest. It is no exaggeration to maintain that Chicago supplies eighteen of the forty-four states of the Union with clothes. Much capital is required to bring these finished goods to market, and the large size of the market area increases the costs even further. A peculiar example, which happened during the smallpox epidemic of 1894, will illustrate this point. In a tenement building in Chicago where some people had been infected with smallpox, I found a suit being worked on which had been commissioned by a clothing merchant in Helena, Montana, a flourishing city about 1200 miles northwest of Chicago. The clothing merchant had taken his customer's measurements, shown him samples of his products, and then phoned the order to the wholesale company in Chicago whose agent he was. The suit had been cut according to the measurements and would certainly have been delivered a week later to the unsuspecting customer in a distant city if an inspector who was looking for another tailor had not by accident entered that infected workshop. . . .

Several hundred sweatshop victims who produce coats and knee-pants are simultaneously wage laborers and regular recipients of relief. They work during the season and receive public and private assistance the rest of the time. When the relief worker refuses to grant assistance because a man capable of working belongs to the family, that man often leaves. Since his abandoned family cannot be left to starve and freeze during the cold American winter, they receive temporary public relief during December, January, and February. As soon as work starts again, the runaway husband and father returns to his family and resumes their support. Where and how he lived in the meantime remains his secret.

Workers like these cannot be expected to influence legislation in their own interest or to sway public opinion. The sweatshop victims have not succeeded in organizing themselves so that they can improve their condition through their own efforts. Differences in race, religion, language, sex, age, and past experience make organizing impossible. In Chicago, sweatshop workers include Irish, Germans, Swedes, Norwegians, Poles, Bohemians, Russian Jews, Italians, and Danes. There are men and women, boys and girls, with women and children in the majority. Catholics, Protestants, and Jews mistrust each other. This diverse population will not have a common language for many years to come, much less the common traditions, experiences, and customs they need in order to gain even the most modest victory in the economic struggle. . . .

By no means do I consider immigration to be the cause of the poverty and lack of organization that distinguish the garment industry in the entire civilized world. It provokes the interest of the government in Vienna, Paris, Berlin, and London as much as in Chicago. But I believe that the rapid development of the garment industry, followed by the miserable living conditions, squalor, and poverty of immigration, has agitated public opinion more deeply than in trades whose development proceeded along more typical lines. The indignation among the public, which considers such a debasement of economic activity as alien and which does not want it to take root in American soil, is not likely to die away until successful measures have been taken and implemented. This explains why several states have passed drastic laws in rapid succession, designed to cure the sweatshop evil. . . .

The continuous debates about the sweating system always overlook the fact that the stream of unskilled laborers pouring into the sweatshops can be stopped. It is entirely within the power of the American republic to educate all children in existing vocational and technical schools so that they do not grow up to become victims of their own ignorance and incompetence. . . .

The second method that has been suggested for abolishing the sweating system is the organization and information of consumers. This has been used consistently for years by the cigar workers' trade union by means of their label. No worker in any branch of industry who is respected in his trade union forgets to demand the blue union label when buying cigars. The retail price of cigars produced by trade union members is not any higher, because the retailers take advantage of the trade union's publicity. But even if the union label did raise the price a little, workers are too accustomed to it to give it up.

The cigar workers' efforts to educate consumers were successful only because the workers were intelligent, and because they had a strong organization with enough money to advertise the union label and to prosecute imitations and falsifications. Education of consumers by workers presupposes that the workers themselves are organized and educated. Since the sweatshop victims lack this kind of education almost completely, and since their weak trade unions fight each other continuously, there is not much hope that this method can be used in the near future.

More promising seems to be the strong movement among middle-class women who organize middle-class and working-class consumers. This movement was conceived by the Consumers' Leagues of New York, Philadelphia, Boston, and Chicago. These consist of women who reject homework and the sweating system but who cannot obtain guarantees from their merchants that the goods they purchase were not produced in sweatshops. Up to now their membership has not been large enough. Also, their publicity efforts have been too weak to force the retail merchant to demand from manufacturers the same guarantee that the conscientious mother buying clothes for her family demands from him.

The Consumers' League of New York has been in existence for almost eight years and has been concerned primarily with conditions in retail shops. Since the League was very successful in this arena, it changed its constitution and enlarged its field of operations in order to attack the sweating system through the retail merchant. In addition to committees of women volunteers who visit stores and who in the future will also inspect clothing factories, the League intends to employ its own inspector. The inspector and the volunteer committees must convince themselves that working conditions not only comply with the factory law, but also with the demands of the League, namely, that the goods are not produced in domestic workshops. If they are convinced and if the company gives a written guarantee that the goods were manufactured in the factory, the League recommends these goods and adopts the same means as the cigar workers union to ensure their sale. Such a guarantee is legally binding, and a company who gave it with deceitful intentions could be legally prosecuted because it sold goods under false pretenses. The Leagues of different cities have joined forces to achieve their goal. It is possible that this will result in a reform of the conditions of production of those goods bought by the more intelligent and conscientious part of the population. It remains to be seen whether the wives of workers will be attracted to this movement as well. An attempt in this direction was made when the wives of cigar workers and women from the neighborhoods of university and social settlements were pulled into the movement.

The following excerpt from the constitution of the Consumers' League of Chicago illustrates its new area of activity.

Article I. Goals:
1. To use the power of demand in order to regulate the supply.
2. To make the buyer responsible for the quality of goods, their conditions of production, and their method of distribution. Shoddy and poorly made goods, devoid of substance and taste, are produced because consumers demand and buy them. The sweating system continues because the goods produced by it find buyers and the children and women in the shops are not protected because the buyers do not care.
3. To inform consumers about the methods of production, about the origins of household goods such as wallpaper, boots, shoes, coats, hats, caps, rugs, glass, china, etc.
4. To identify the goods produced in sweatshops and to recommend goods produced under healthier working conditions.
5. To induce merchants to abandon the evils to which employees in their shops are often subject, by pointing out to consumers those stores which can be regarded as models in this respect.

While the agitation against the sweating system has for many years been carried out by the working class, this is the first attempt by middle-class consumers to protect themselves against the danger of infection, which is always and everywhere inherent to the system. It has been a great disadvantage for consumers that sweatshop victims were unable to make themselves understood. These workers who can neither read, write, nor speak English and who have no other common language were incapable of conveying the necessary information to this important part of the population.

Most American women, even the wives of better-off workers, are freed from the burdens of housework to a greater extent than elsewhere. Central heating systems, the pipes for hot and cold water in every modest household, the use of gas instead of petroleum lamps, of gas for stoves instead of coal or wood, the common use of various types of mass-produced food—these and a thousand other circumstances leave spare time to housewives whose husbands and sons work and are likely to have to work all their lives. A large part of that free time is wasted in aimless shopping and other self-centered amusements, but by no means all of it. In their clubs and in philanthropic and educational associations, these women develop activities useful for the common good, for which they did not have time in the past. These associations are responsible for the laws that commission women as factory or school inspectors. These laws have provided better care for helpless, sick, and criminal children, made school attendance compulsory, and enlarged the opportunities for instruction and for many other kinds of necessary public activities.

For several years, the club women have devoted their attention to those industries which women once carried on at home, but which then left the home, taken over by men seeking profit. They realize that most of the products of these industries are bought by women, and their social consciences awaken. They are concerned not only that the clothes they buy may have come in contact with infectious diseases during production, but also that the workers who produce them have to be supported by relief during part of the year, and during the rest of the year are subjected to inhuman labor. At first this awakening of social conscience was more or less sentimental. Women who bought garments produced in sweatshops also listened to lectures and sermons about poverty and misery in the garment trade, and about the means necessary to cure those conditions. But now they declare that the production of clothing, food, furniture, and books is a social function and that the buyer can demand a guarantee that the conditions under which they are produced shall not endanger the health of his family. This new women's movement, based on a higher sense of obligation and on distaste for the present method of garment production will, it is hoped, greatly facilitate the reorganization of the garment trade and the elimination of the sweating system.

The agitation against the sweating system and the education of consumers has been promoted most forcefully by the social settlements. More than forty of these exist in the United States at this time. These settlements are established by men and women who live voluntarily in the poorest sections of the cities in order to help their neighbors, the majority of whom are recent immigrants, to a larger share of the advantages of the city life. . . . It is impossible to live in an area where the sweating system exists and not feel the urge constantly to speak out about it. The agitation of the settlement members is particularly effective because their statements are based on personal observation and they have a reputation for avoiding imprudent remarks. They are therefore asked to serve as witnesses in all official inquiries about the system.[27]

The third path taken to abolish the sweating system has as its goal the organization of the workers in these trades. . . . All efforts designed to motivate sweatshop victims so that they can work, live, and fight, together with other workers outside their workshops and their neighborhoods, must be supported. . . . But such labor organizations do not offer a direct remedy against the sweating system. The victim's hope to become a contractor himself some day makes him ineffective in the fight against the system.

The fourth remedy is difficult to apply because the subject is still so new. Legislation dealt with the sweating system for the first time ten years ago. Illinois passed its law in 1893, Pennsylvania in 1895 with improvements in 1897, and Ohio in 1896. The laws of New York and Massachusetts, which have been improved several times, were first passed in 1888. . . .

The reason why this legislation appears inadequate can be stated briefly: it permits the continued existence of the sweating system and it alleviates only its worst abuses. The regulations are only partial and ineffective. . . .

American legislation is at best a most peculiar process, which passes through a number of different phases. First, there is agitation in the press and among the public (in this case by the trade unions, the women's associations, and the settlements). Petitions are sent to Congress and to the legislatures of individual states. The legislative bodies appoint investigative commissions and finally pass a law. The trade unions used to be content at this stage, since they assumed that the law would implement itself. But painful experience has shown that the implementing of a law that deals with economic loss is the most difficult part of the process. The appointment of officials to enforce the law meant only too often the virtual abolition of the law, since under the spoils system, these officials did not fulfill their obligations. But even when officials dutifully carry out the law, the people affected by it will violate it until an exemplary case has been tried, not only in the local courts but in front of the state or federal supreme courts as well. Such a process can take two to seven years. Because of the restrictions of state and federal constitutions, it is extremely difficult to pass a flawless law that is safe from being declared unconstitutional. Two important regulations designed to control sweating have been declared invalid for that reason: the New York law which prohibits the production of cigars in domestic workshops, and the Illinois law which prohibits the employment of a female worker for more than eight hours a day.

In spite of such difficulties, it is important to campaign for such legisla-

---

[27]   This link between the voluntarism of the social settlement movement and state legislative measures was one that Kelley later characterized as "investigate, educate, legislate, enforce." As she saw it, voluntarism had a place at all four of these stages.

tion in order to educate public opinion. Those who sponsor a law create more public interest than those who advocate a theory or a principle will ever be able to do in this pragmatic country. . . .

It is hardly necessary to speak here of attempts to use the sweating system as an argument for federal restrictions on immigration. Nobody seriously believes that in order to boost a few debased trades, it is necessary to close the ports of America to immigrants who escape from religious persecution or from the poverty of Sicily and Calabria.

7. Mary Church Terrell Speaks in Berlin

After graduating from Oberlin College in 1884, Mary Church Terrell traveled and studied in Germany in the late 1880s. There she appreciated the absence of the "color line" that had dominated her life in the United States. Her skin color was light, and Germans often thought she was Spanish. Conscious, however, that her education had prepared her for a life of usefulness, she returned to the United States determined "to promote the welfare of my race." When she went back to Berlin in 1904, she spoke as a leader of the African-American women's movement.

More than any other single individual, Terrell bridged the gap between the white and black women's club movements. As president of the National Association of Colored Women in the late 1890s, Terrell viewed the "race question" as more urgent than the "social question." Until World War I most blacks were excluded from industrial work, so protective labor legislation and other issues arising from the industrial workplace were less important to her than those related to lynching, disfranchisement, and discrimination. Nevertheless, Terrell's commitment to the "woman question" was integral to her concern about the progress of her race, and she was well known to American social justice feminists. With Jane Addams and Florence Kelley, she became a charter member of the National Association for the Advancement of Colored People in 1909. She picketed the White House with the National Woman's Party on behalf of suffrage during World War I, and in 1919 she returned to Europe for the Second Women's Peace Congress at Zurich.

At the 1904 Berlin congress, Terrell presented a revised version of her 1898 address to the National American Woman Suffrage Association, "The Progress of Colored Women." [28] She offered a moving portrayal of the

[28] Mary Church Terrell, "Die Fortschritte der Farbigen Frauen," in Marie Stritt, ed., *Der Internationale Frauen-Kongreß, Berlin 1904* (Berlin: C. Habel, 1905), pp. 567–73; translated by the editors. Some parts of the translation follow an address that Terrell delivered before the NAWSA in 1898. In the German original, Terrell uses the terms "schwarz" (black), "farbig"

achievements of black women against a background of racial violence and injustice. She raised concerns central to the black women's club movement: the intellectual and moral education of black children; race segregation in the nation's professions and trades; the sexual morality of black women; and the power of women's collective action to improve the lives of black people. Terrell demonstrated an astute understanding of the causes of low wages for black women when she pointed to the "overcrowded . . . avocations in which colored women may engage." Her criticism of American labor unions as "hostile against the colored" was well deserved.

Conscious of her nationality as well as her race, Terrell concluded with a generous expression of gratitude for the support and encouragement that black women had received from white women in the United States. Many, she said, had "penetrated deeply into the problems of the colored race." Herself a fine example of cross-race cooperation, Terrell hoped for as much from her listeners.

The Progress of Colored Women
Speaker: Mrs. Mary Church Terrell-Washington

In 1861 war had broken out between the Northern and the Southern States of North America. As is well known, the former were victorious. If that had not been the case, I would probably be living on a plantation in the Southern states of North America in the chains of slavery, enslaved in body and mind, instead of addressing you today as a free woman. I think my appearance before this illustrious gathering deserves attention for two reasons. First, I am the only woman at this congress representing a race that has only enjoyed the riches of freedom for less than forty years. Second, I am the only one whose parents were in fact slaves, and I have only Providence to thank that I escaped that fate. You look at me and think for yourself: a white crow indeed. But I am present in your midst tonight happy and in good cheer, again for two reasons: First, I am happy for the emancipation of my race, and then for the general elevation of my sex.

If fifty years ago somebody had had the courage to predict that a woman with African blood in her veins would travel from the United States to Berlin to address the International Women's Congress of 1904, that person would have been thoroughly laughed at or even declared ready for the madhouse. I am not exaggerating. In those days of oppression and despair, colored women were not only refused admittance to institutions of learning, but the laws of all states in which the colored element dominated, ex-

---

and "Farbige" (colored and the colored), "afrikanisch" (African), "Afro-Amerikaner" (Afro-American), and "afrikanisch-amerikanisch" (African-American). (In German, nouns are capitalized and adjectives are not.) In translating, we have followed her terminology.

cept for two, went so far as to make it a crime to teach them. Not only could they possess no property, but even their bodies were not their own. Nothing, in short, that could degrade or brutalize the womanhood of my race was lacking in this system from which colored women fifty years ago had little hope of escape. So gloomy were their prospects, so fatal the laws, so pernicious the customs, only fifty years ago. But from the day their fetters were broken and their minds released from the darkness of ignorance to which for almost three centuries they had been doomed, from the day they could stand erect in the dignity of womanhood, colored women have forged steadily ahead in the acquisition of knowledge and in the cultivation of those virtues which make for good. To use a thought of the illustrious Frederick Douglass, if judged from the depths from which they have come, colored women need not hang their heads in shame! For not only are colored women handicapped on account of their sex; in some parts of the United States they are baffled and mocked on account of their race. Desperately and continuously they are forced to fight that opposition, born of a cruel, unreasonable prejudice which neither their merit nor their necessity seems able to subdue.

The progress that colored women have made along these lines, in spite of the almost insurmountable obstacles in their path of life, is therefore a true miracle of our time. Intellectually and morally they are making rapid progress, and their prosperity is also increasing visibly. Colored girls have been graduated with honors from the most famous universities in the United States, from the best high schools and other institutions of higher learning, have even received graduate degrees and have thus forever settled the question of their capacity and worth. A few years ago a large number of young white men and women, among them a colored girl, competed for a scholarship, entitling the successful competitor to an entire course through the Chicago University. The result of the examination was that the prize was due to the colored girl and that she received the scholarship. Wherever colored girls study, their instructors bear testimony to their intelligence, diligence, and success. Among teachers for colored children, 80 percent are women.

Ever since the publication, in 1773, of a book entitled "Poems on Various Subjects, Religious and Moral," by Phyllis Wheatley, negro servant of a white man, Mr. John Wheatley of Boston, colored women have from time to time given abundant evidence of literary ability.[29] In sculpture we are represented by a woman upon whose chisel Italy has set her seal of ap-

[29] Phillis Wheatley (c.1753–1784), African-American poet. Taught to read as a child in Boston by the children of her master, she published her first poem in 1770. She and her poetry received much attention, and were frequently cited as proof that black people were educable.

proval; in painting by Bouguereau's pupil, whose work was exhibited in the last Paris Salon, and in music by young women holding diplomas from the first conservatories in the land.[30] Then there are several female lawyers as well as quite a number of women doctors and dentists whose practice is lucrative and large.

In business, colored women have had signal success. Several years ago, a colored woman owned the principal ice plant of Halifax, Nova Scotia, which recently sold for a high price. In Alabama there is a large milling and cotton business, belonging to and controlled entirely by a colored woman. Usually, however, colored women who want to engage in an occupation still face great obstacles. There are relatively few professions and trades open to them. So overcrowded are the avocations in which colored women may engage and so poor is the pay in consequence, that only the barest livelihood can be eked out. Chiefly, colored women work as teachers, attendants to children and the sick, seamstresses, laundresses, chambermaids, and cooks. It is difficult for them to achieve anything outside of these occupations. This is sometimes the result of their own negligence, but more often of bitter and cruel prejudice against their race. As long as the labor organizations of the United States are as hostile against the colored as they are now, it will be impossible for them to advance in the trades. Already those colored people who have enough intelligence and insight and are troubled by these hostile movements against them do everything possible to fight them. They hold a brief for the high value of labor at all times and encourage young people to devote themselves more emphatically to industry and to acquire dexterity and manual skills.

The fact that members of the African-American race were enslaved until fifty years ago has of course not always promoted the moral education of the colored woman. In the Southern states of North America, colored girls are lacking the natural protection of adults who usually guard youth and innocence. Public opinion and the law do not protect colored girls either. And still, statistics compiled by men not inclined to falsify in favor of my race show that immorality among colored women of the United States is not so great as among women in other countries who are in similar circumstances and are exposed to the same temptations.

They engage indefatigably in public works of all kinds that they may benefit and elevate their race. By banding themselves together in the interest of education and morality, by adopting the most practical and useful means to this end, colored women have in the last thirty years become a great power for the good. A number of kindergartens have been established and successfully maintained by different organizations, religious

---

[30] Adolphe William Bouguereau (1825–1905), a popular French painter of the neoclassical style.

and secular, and through the intermediary of the National Association of Colored Women, which at this time has about 10,000 members and of which I have the honor to be Honorary President.[31] Day nurseries for children of colored workers have been established; object lessons are given concerning household affairs; classes for English and German literature as well as for other branches of knowledge have been established; and homes and asylums for fallen women and seduced girls have been founded and all works of charity supported. In short, we did everything that was in our power.

In their earnest endeavor to work at their own elevation, colored women have often been supported and encouraged by their more fortunate sisters of the dominant white race. Many of them penetrated deeply into the problems of the colored race. They treat their sisters with darker skin fairly and kindly and bestow every possible assistance upon them. There are a great many women of the dominant race in the United States who are as close to the ideal of perfect womanhood as can be found anywhere in the civilized world. Without the sympathy and the energetic participation of those women the lot of colored women would be sad and hard. It is therefore my great pleasure to express to the white women of the United States, speaking publicly and in a foreign country, my thanks and the thanks of the 3 million black women for whom I speak here tonight. Surely, my white sisters could not send more able and noble representatives here than Susan B. Anthony, the true Abraham Lincoln of women's emancipation, and May Wright Sewall, Anna Howard Shaw, Hanna G. Solomon, Mary Wood Swift, and Ida Husted Harper, who are among us tonight.[32]

[31]   The National Association of Colored Women, an umbrella organization that brought together scores of organizations, was founded in 1896. It took as its motto "Lifting as We Climb." By 1914 the NACW claimed 50,000 members in twenty-eight state federations and over a thousand clubs. Through this and other organizations, black women participated in coalitions that advanced progressive reform.

[32]   Susan B. Anthony (1820–1906), American suffrage leader and cofounder of the NWSA (1869) and the ICW (1888).

May Eliza Wright Sewall (1844–1920), American educator, clubwoman, suffragist and pacifist. Sewall founded the Girls' Classical School in Indianapolis. She was president of the National Council of Women (1897–1899) and of the ICW (1899–1904).

Anna Howard Shaw (1847–1919), American minister, lecturer, and suffragist. She served as vice president of the NAWSA from 1892 to 1904 and as president from 1904 to 1915.

Hannah Greenbaum Solomon (1858–1942), American clubwoman and welfare worker, was the first president of the National Council of Jewish Women. Her work in the National Council of Women brought her to the 1904 congress of the ICW in Berlin.

Ida Husted Harper (1851–1931), American journalist and suffragist, biographer of Susan B. Anthony and collaborator on the *History of Women's Suffrage* (volumes 4–6). She attended the ICW congresses in London and Berlin.

Mary Wood Swift, a dear friend of Terrell's from her public school days in Oberlin, Ohio, accompanied Terrell to Berlin in 1904. Swift was the wife of the pastor of the Central Congregational Church in Fall River, Rhode Island.

If I have succeeded at interesting just a few women outside of North America in the fight that the colored woman is waging in the United States to free herself from the condition of degradation and ignorance that was forced upon her for more than three hundred years, then my mission here in Berlin will be happily fulfilled. In any case, I wanted to bring forward to this meeting the facts that bear witness to the progress of colored women. Thanks to the activities of our opponents, the vices and mistakes of the African-American race are better known abroad than their virtues, abilities, and good deeds. The evils committed by this race are being trumpeted in an exaggerated way from the North Pole to the Cape of Good Hope, while the good deeds are only carried gingerly on the wings of rumor. If I have succeeded at convincing you, ladies and gentlemen, that the colored man is not as black as he is usually painted, that he leads a constant and courageous battle to secure the highest goods of his life; if I could convince you, that we endeavor with all our hearts, souls, and minds, with supreme effort, to free ourselves from the yoke of oppression and condemnation to become truly free women and men—if I could convince you of that, then my trip of many hundred miles has not been in vain. In spite of unmerciful opposition and almost insurmountable obstacles, today's Afro-American shows an amount of progress in education, industriousness, and financial affluence that has never been achieved in such a short time and under such discouraging circumstances as long as the world has turned. And if you should ask me which special phase of the development of the Afro-American is most promising for surmounting the present difficulties, I would answer without hesitation that it is the work of regeneration and uplifting of the race undertaken by our colored women. No race can despair, whose women are as inspired by their sense of duty. They happily shoulder the responsibilities that only they can successfully take on.

8. Jane Addams Praises German Labor Legislation

On a lecture tour of the Northeast in 1908, Jane Addams echoed many of Florence Kelley's 1885 arguments about Germany. Many newspapers reported her speeches.[33] The *Boston Journal* declared on March 23, "Miss Jane Addams, Woman Suffragist Says Germany is Our Leader."

[33]   This is the version printed in the *Boston Globe*, March 23, 1908.

In her talks Addams first described the American need for legislation to protect women workers. Then she pointed to the German example of social and labor legislation that valued human life above wealth. Comparing Germany and the United States on education, industrial accidents, unemployment, health insurance, and old age pensions, she praised the German model, and used it to legitimate legislation for American working women.

Addams invoked the German example at a crucial moment for American social justice feminists. Her speaking tour occurred just weeks after the U.S. Supreme Court ruled favorably on the constitutionality of state laws limiting the work day for women to ten hours. In *Muller v. Oregon*, a landmark decision rendered on February 23, 1908, the court opened the way for the kind of legislation that Addams championed in her tour. Florence Kelley and the National Consumers' League had initiated that court decision. Although Kelley had left Hull House in 1899, she and Addams remained devoted friends, and Addams now assisted her by promoting the new labor legislation that the court had made possible.

Germany Far in the Lead

Has Better Labor Laws, Miss Addams Says

Early Realized Importance of Protecting Working Class

United States Behind in Factory Legislation

An audience composed largely of women crowded Faneuil hall yesterday afternoon and gave Miss Jane Addams of Hull House, Chicago, an unusually warm greeting. The meeting was held under the joint auspices of the Women's trade union league and the Boston equal suffrage association for good government.[34] Most of these present were clearly people who are interested in the practical methods of present-day philanthropy and students of social questions from the churches of Boston and vicinity and the organizations devoted to these questions.

Miss Addams' topic was "The Relation of Women to Industry and Social Legislation," and she treated the whole subject from a broad humanitarian standpoint.

---

[34] Founded in 1903 at a meeting of the American Federation of Labor in Boston, the Women's Trade Union League was a cross-class organization. It studied the plight of women in industry, lobbied for protective legislation, trained women as union organizers and leaders, and published *Life and Labor*. Upper- and middle-class members put up bail for arrested strikers and marched with them on picket lines. Mary Kenney O'Sullivan (1864–1943), one of the founders, began her career as a labor organizer in Chicago, where she became friendly with Jane Addams; she was living in Boston by the time Addams gave this speech there.

A resolution favoring a postal savings bank was voted by an unanimous standing vote.

The meeting was called to order by Miss Emily Balch, professor of economy [*sic*] at Wellesley college, who spoke briefly of the work which Miss Addams had done in Chicago through Hull house. She said that in days gone by, meetings in Faneuil hall had been devoted almost entirely to politics, but latterly it was being used more for the consideration of social questions, showing that these questions were the problems of the hour.

Factory Girls

Miss Addams was roundly applauded when she stepped forward. She is a fine type of the cultivated, broadminded, kindly and sympathetic American woman. She is of middle age and above the medium height. Her voice is neither resonant nor very powerful, but it is clear and distinct. Her style is simple and forcible and without oratorical frills.

She first pointed out a great change in the lives of working women which had been brought about by the changed industrial conditions which took from the home of the people those activities which were formerly among the household duties of women, such as spinning and weaving. These are all done in factories, and women are no longer able to control their labor at these industries as formerly. The man who owns the machinery and the factory now controls the labor, and, of course, it was natural that women should be trained to operate the machines, and so women have gone in great numbers into these factories. They are usually very young women— between the age of 16 to 21, and hundreds below the age of 15.

The fact of the factory woman's youthfulness, she said, complicates the situation, for it makes difficult that kind of voluntary organization that should be of benefit to them.

"Now," said Miss Addams, "what are we doing for the health and education of these young women? Women suffer more than men from many of the physical conditions imposed on them by this work. It is important that these young women should be so protected during their work and so educated that they may not be unfitted for subsequent domestic work.

"We are behind Germany in these things. The United States has less regulations, in certain sections, concerning the labor of women than either Russia or Italy. Our regulative legislation comes under two heads: First, regulations which shall preserve our standard of living; second, those regulations which tend to elevate the standard of living. It is about this standard of living which all the battles of labor are fought. The standard of living is the test of our civilization.

Industrial Accidents

"Something should first be done about industrial accidents. Some years ago when they investigated in Buffalo and other places the cause of poverty, it was found that most of it was traceable to either the death or disablement of the wage-earner. Germany considers this thing very carefully. The government realizes the importance of this matter—the importance of the health and strength of the working unit to the family and the community.

"In certain rubber industries the government has said that four hours shall constitute a day's work, because more than this is imperiling the health of the workers. Out in the Wyoming valley 1000 or more miners are killed and injured every year. This is a terrible waste of life. This subject is just beginning to be studied in this country."[35]

Miss Addams said the German government has also studied carefully the subject of employment, and if a large enterprise is to be started in a community, it is first ascertained what the benefit is going to be to that community. If it appears that the prospects are not clear and that it is liable to create a class of unemployed, the men at the head of the enterprise are told that it would be well not to start such an enterprise. The problem of government in Germany has come to be largely one of reasonable industrial legislation, and if human life is more important than wealth, it is the duty of all governments to work along these lines. You cannot separate the producers and consumers, as the producers are usually the best consumers.

Protects Unit of Labor

"The German law long ago," she said, "discovered that if their nation was to go forward the power would come from the humblest people, for it was found that in the peasant and the artisan classes were the great reserves of power. It was after the revolution of 1848 that the Germans began to realize this and they at once began that system of education by which a boy when he goes into a factory is not tied to a machine. The government sees to that. They also saw the importance of the play instinct in the boy. That, too, was a useful force to develop.

"The result," she continued, "has been that Germany, by protecting its units of labor, leads the world today—all traced to the German respect for life and human power. There the government has educated ability and then protected it. There the state guards its own while at work and sees

[35] Germany began to impose limits on the workday for adults in 1891, with legislation limiting women's work to eleven hours. The editors believe that Addams was mistaken about the four-hour day in the rubber industry.

that they are protected when sick and old age overtakes them—not thrown aside as in this country when either of these conditions arise."

The large bodies of immigrants to this country should be unified, she said, on the old simple, human basis, and government should afford the necessary protection. The immigrants are too simple to be affrighted by the factory situation. It seems natural to them to work. We should look more carefully to the protection of our most valuable asset—the human being that works, and especially the woman who works. Legislation must shape itself to these ends.

PART II

GERMAN REFORMERS CONSIDER THE AMERICAN EXAMPLE, 1891–1914

Portrait of Alice Salomon, taken for the 1904 ICW congress. She gave this copy to May Wright Sewall, inscribing on the back, "My fatherland is where I am useful." The photograph was taken at the renowned Hof-Atelier Elvira in Munich, a studio of women photographers that Anita Augspurg had helped to found in 1887. May Wright Sewall Collection, Library of Congress.

1. An Early Report on the New York Consumers' League

The New York Consumers' League was less than a year old when German readers learned about its unusual approach to social reform. In the United States, consumers' leagues became one of the chief lobbying agents for the passage of social and labor legislation, with sixty-four locals throughout the country by 1904.

Although the author of this unsigned article[1] was largely accurate, expectations arising from German political culture led her to make one revealing error: she characterized league members as coming from the "richest" New York women and insisted that "no workers' association started this movement, or even suggested or stimulated the creation of this league." In fact, although the city's "most influential" women did help create the league, the "richest" women—wives of robber barons, for example—did not. Moreover, working women were decisive in its founding. Presumably, the author emphasized the role of middle- and upper-class women in class-bridging coalitions—unusual in Germany at the time—to define a model that her German audience might imitate.

League members came chiefly from the upper-middle class—the old middle class that was in place before 1880, when massive immigration re-populated the working class and the reorganization of business management lifted most of the native-born working class into managerial status. The league's beginning can be traced to the Working Women's Society, which in 1888 organized a face-to-face meeting between working women and the middle-class consumers of their products. Society members appealed for middle-class support of their demands for better working conditions. Two years later the New York City Consumers' League was formed in response to a report written by Alice Woodbridge, a department store clerk, about her coworkers' need for improved working conditions.

The first European consumers' league was formed in Paris in 1902. Maud Nathan, president of the Consumers' League of New York City, proposed the creation of a German league in a speech to the 1904 Interna-

---

[1] R.S., "Vorgehen amerikanischer Frauen zur Lösung der sozialen Frage," *Volkswohl*, 1891, pp. 28–29; translated by Corinna Hörst and the editors.

tional Congress of Women in Berlin, and the Berlin Käuferbund was chartered in 1907. Some of the most prominent women social reformers provided leadership for the Berlin league. Indicating the German league's closer tie with state officials, Martha Bethmann Hollweg, the wife of the Prussian minister of the interior, served as its first president. By 1909 German consumer leagues claimed a membership of 423, located primarily in Protestant cities, augmented by eight affiliated organizations with 25,000 members.

The periodical *Volkswohl* (People's Weal) was edited by Viktor Böhmert and Wilhelm Bode for the Zentralverein für das Wohl der arbeitenden Klassen (Central Association for the Welfare of the Working Classes) from 1876 to 1915. Wilhelm Bode (1862–1922), teacher and editor, headed a temperance organization from 1892 to 1899. Viktor Böhmert (1829–1918), social politician and author on economic issues, edited the *Arbeiterfreund* (Worker's Friend, founded by W. A. Lette in 1847) between 1873 and 1914, and from 1875 to 1903 was Professor of Law and Political Science at Dresden Technical University. Among other reports on reform issues at home and abroad, *Volkswohl* featured short contributions on the public and private reform agenda in the United States during the Progressive Era. Authors were usually only identified by initials, and we have not been able to discover the identity of "R.S."

American Women Act to Solve the Social Question
by R. S.

New York, January, 1891

American women are working very hard through an organization of their own to contribute to a solution to the social question. A number of the richest and most influential women in New York, including German women, have just founded a "Consumers' League." The goals of this league are quite similar to those of a boycott, but it does not go so far as to violate the conspiracy law.[2] The members of the League have committed themselves to buy goods from what they call "fair houses." These shops and stores fulfill certain conditions concerning the treatment and wages of their employees, most of whom are women and children.

A fair house is a store in which equal pay is offered for equal work, regardless of sex; in which wages are paid weekly; in which "cash girls" (little girls who bring the customer's money to the cashier or take purchased goods to be wrapped and then return them to the customer) receive at

[2]   The "White List" of the New York City Consumers' League was designed precisely to avoid the legal problems associated with blacklists, which were outlawed in an attempt to prevent organized labor from blacklisting certain employers.

least $2 a week; in which the working day is from eight o'clock in the morning until six o'clock at night with a three-quarter hour lunch break; in which during the three summer months a half holiday is granted every week, usually Saturday afternoon; in which employees get at least one week of holiday without salary deduction during the summer; in which overtime is paid; in which workrooms are separated from lunchrooms and where the rooms meet sanitary regulations; in which, in accordance with the law, there are seats for saleswomen and they are allowed to use them; in which humane and proper treatment is the rule; in which loyal and continuous service is appreciated; in which no children under fourteen years of age are employed.[3]

The Consumers' League has a committee of five members who visit the department stores and shops of the city and then report on their compliance with the requirements of the League.[4] In accordance with the report, a list is published with the names of those stores the League considers worthy of patronizing. This is called the "White List," and the members of the League have committed themselves to favor the listed stores whenever possible. The White List is regularly revised, and every month it is published in one of the daily newspapers. The expenses of the League are supported through voluntary donations. No one is forced to contribute, and a new member need only sign her name and declare that she agrees with the purpose of the League.

The requirements mentioned above suggest that the goal of the League is a boycott. But since no one is intimidated or constrained from shopping at stores that do not comply with the League's conditions, a violation of the conspiracy law is hard to establish. The object is to bring as many customers as possible to the "fair houses," and as a consequence other shops are less profitable. Store owners cannot become members of the League.

It remains to be seen whether the League will be successful. Last summer, its founders started investigating conditions at the big stores. By the time the League was founded, they could already distribute a list of stores and shops located all over the city. No workers' association started this movement, or even suggested or stimulated the creation of this League. As stated above, the richest women of New York are among its members.

Four years ago, a similar movement was founded in Washington and was very successful. Housewives were asked to sign an agreement not to shop in

---

[3] This list of employment conditions was longer than that provided in most New York League literature, which tended to emphasize compliance with state laws, a ten-hour day, and no employment of children under fourteen. Although the league began by focusing on department store clerks, it quickly expanded its scope to include industrial work.

[4] Enforcement of the terms of the League's "White List" was the weakest link in the chain of its efforts. When the National League was founded in 1898, Florence Kelley was hired to head it partly on the basis of her enforcement skills.

stores that were open after six o'clock at night and that did not permit employees a weekly half holiday during the summer. This movement achieved so much public support that the large stores—which are the decisive factor—did not hesitate to cooperate for long. Small shops and stores later followed on their own.[5]

It is often said that rich people have no compassion for the workers. This is not true, especially not true of women.

2. Minna Cauer Describes the American Women's Movement

Minna Cauer wrote this article[6] the same year that she cofounded the Mädchen- und Frauengruppen für soziale Hilfsarbeit (Girls' and Women's Groups for Social Assistance Work). The text was published just before the Columbian Exposition as a brochure to inform German women about the women's movement in the United States. Cauer helped organize the German delegation to the World's Fair but did not travel to Chicago herself. In fact, she never visited the United States; overseas travel was more common for the generation of middle-class woman activists who followed her.

Minna Cauer did eventually meet American women. She was the chief organizer of the International Congress for Women's Work and Endeavors, held in Berlin in 1896 and attended by a number of American women, among them the lawyer and peace advocate Belva Lockwood. Later, Cauer attended sessions of the 1904 quinquennial meeting of the International Council of Women in Berlin, along with such prominent members of the American women's movement as Susan B. Anthony, May Wright Sewall, Anna Shaw, Mary Church Terrell, the journalist Ida Husted Harper, Bryn Mawr president M. Carey Thomas, and Maud Nathan of the New York Consumers' League. Although Cauer was quite critical of this congress and thought that the delegates were more concerned with their elegant appearance than with the topics under discussion, she reported on the gathering in her periodical *Die Frauenbewegung* (The Woman's Movement).

[5] This is the only reference the editors have ever seen to a Consumers' League in Washington, D.C., in the 1880s. NCL records first mention a Washington chapter in 1912.

Economies of scale enabled large stores to comply with Consumers' League requirements more easily than could smaller retailers or producers. In this way the League's goals were compatible with the growth of larger producers and retailers.

[6] Minna Cauer, "Die Frauen in den Vereinigten Staaten von Amerika," pamphlet, Berlin, 1893; translated by Corinna Hörst and the editors.

130

GERMAN REFORMERS CONSIDER THE AMERICAN EXAMPLE

While Minna Cauer's essay is filled with errors and cannot be taken as an accurate account of the American women's movement in the nineteenth century, the basic contours of its argument hold. Moreover, the essay shows us how one relatively well informed reformer viewed the women's-rights tradition of her American counterparts. Cauer's chief points—that the American women's movement was rooted in the "country itself," and that it sought to improve the "general welfare" of American society—were designed to win German approval for the "Americanism" of strong women. Yet these points also had a great deal of historical validity, and they help us understand a subtle aspect of the appeal of American social women reformers to their German peers: they demonstrated that nation-building was women's work.

Cauer's factual errors reflect her generation's reliance on secondhand information about American women. Nevertheless, she consistently returned to her main theme, women's contribution to the unity and the welfare of a nation, an opportunity that—in her eyes—German women had missed during and after the unification wars twenty-five years earlier.

Women in the United States of America
by Minna Cauer

The following study was written because of the great interest that the successes of the American women's movement have provoked in Germany. Our country is only slowly comprehending the great, important, so-called woman question. "The Americanism," which is what this element of the social question is called, causes much suspicion. People fear, with justification, that the American situation will influence the development of this vital matter in our country.

The following pages intend to prove two things. First, that the nature of the American women's movement is rooted in that country itself; and second, that from the beginning, women in the United States identified with their country and never lost sight of how they could contribute to its general welfare.

The importance of the last point will be stressed in the following pages.

With all the emphasis on an independent and distinctive development in Germany, there are three elements of the American women's movement which can guide us: freedom in the education of the female sex, the assumption of social duties by women, and a better legal position. The goal is the same everywhere: the development of women to be worthy, useful, and important to the whole society. Different times call for different women. A telegram on May 16th reported from Chicago that the International Women's Congress, which was supposed to coincide with the World's Fair, opened May 15th, in Columbus Hall. It was said that five thousand women participated. The coming months will bring many different reports about this wonder of our century. For the first time, women will act independently and purposefully. In the development of the burning women's question, much, if not everything, depends upon the seriousness, calm, and grace with which women plead for their own cause.

The works of women from all countries are exhibited there, and there are women representatives of all nations. Women should remember what the context of the following study is: women's close identification with the history of their fatherland and a holy duty to participate in solving questions to the benefit of mankind.

Minna Cauer
Berlin, May 1893

During the last decades, it has become customary in Germany to speak about America as an "Eldorado" when referring to the women's movement and the woman question. Friends and enemies love to point to the country across the ocean as proof of their love or hatred. The more resistance the [members of the] first group find in their own country, the more they make the mistake of seeing the perfection and realization of their wishes and desires in their enthusiasm about America. The second group imagines the scenes of horror that would result, within the framework of old and established ways, as soon as the weaker sex got a more liberal education and greater independence. As usual, an accurate picture is in the middle. The high expectations of both male and female advocates of women's emancipation in the United States have not been achieved, nor are American women nightmares. Most of the time, people speak without personal observation or experience, and easily neglect a calm discussion of America and its peculiar development. They particularly forget that from the beginning, the American woman interacted constantly with her country.

Women have always had a peculiar, privileged position in America. The reason for this lies in the development of the country and in the fact that even today, women are in the minority. The nature of the American women's movement and its successes are due to the fact that from the beginning, since the separation from England, the American woman has always felt like an integral part of her country and acted accordingly. Eduard Lasker remarked in [his] article "Talent and Education" that the German woman leads a comfortable life because she does not feel in any way that she has a mission to do something for the general welfare of the people.[7]

---

[7] Eduard Lasker (1829–1884), politician and founder of the National Liberal Party. A member of the Prussian parliament (1862–1879) and the Reichstag (1867–1884), Lasker was critical of many of Bismarck's policies, particularly the anti-socialist laws.

Cooperation and participation in the welfare of the whole, compassion and happiness, and feelings of responsibility make the American women's movement appear so important. This is also the secret of their success.

The woman question is the same across the ocean as here. Its development depends on the circumstances of the country and on unpredictable, coincidental conditions. It cannot be solved by emphasizing just one aspect because it is at the same time an economic, a commercial, an educational, and a family question. Its development demands first of all the destruction of current barriers to the education of girls. The artificial restriction of their abilities as well as the artificial education of their inabilities has to be stopped. Not only in America, but everywhere, the present time calls for genuine, true, and noble women. A nation rises and falls according to the position of its women. The ideal "woman of the future" is the woman who also operates outside of the family, who invests time and power in acquiring skills to work for the common welfare. The women in the new world have understood this task from the beginning. . . .

During the first activities of the colonies against the mother country, energetic and politically active women appeared who stood in close contact with Samuel and John Adams, Jefferson, Washington, and Dickinson.[8] Those names alone guarantee that this connection concerned important issues. With good reason, American women of today in their struggles for more political rights and more general rights point to their foremothers from whom they learned to be brave. . . .

Convinced about the importance of education, these women wrote to the men in Congress: "If you complain about the education of sons, what should we say in regard to our daughters? Every day demonstrates to us the horrible lack of a good education. If you want great statesmen, diligent philosophers and heroes for our country, you should above all raise learned women."[9] . . .

Germany's women continued to dream at the feet of Goethe and Schiller. . . .

The first question that occupied women's minds, after the foundation of the new nation and the healing of the war wounds, was education. Mrs.

[8] John Dickinson, the least known of Cauer's list of patriots, was the author of *Letters from an American Farmer in Pennsylvania* (1768), which mobilized opinion against the Townshend Duties. He was also the chief author of the Articles of Confederation in 1776, and later a Federalist supporter of the Constitution.

[9] The quotation comes from Abigail Adams's personal correspondence rather than an official petition. This quotation paraphrases sentiments associated with "Republican Motherhood," or the belief that a republic needed to create democratic sources of leadership and responsible citizenship, and that mothers could play a patriotic role by encouraging such leadership and citizenship. Abigail Adams (1744–1818) was the wife of John Adams, second president of the United States.

Emma Willard did outstanding work from 1819 on.[10] . . . Back then, women were working in all fields: we find the first doctors, authors, and speakers. They tried to exert influence on the prison system and on guardianships for the poor, and they took stands in the press on all questions of public life. Those things did not come easily for these women and even in the United States, they had to gain ground step by step. Of course, these advocates felt stable ground under their feet. Time and again, they pointed out: "Our fathers fought for human rights, our rights are part of them. As mothers of sons and daughters, we should not only think about the former, because neglecting the education of our daughters and disrespect for their position would lead to the decline of family life." . . .

Summing up the first period of the American women's movement, it can be said that the warm and noble participation of the female sex during the war of independence and in the development of the country gained women a privileged position in the United States. Noble men of the nation are convinced that the state can only become vigorous and powerful if women stand on the same level as men, and that in a free country even women should be granted liberties in regard to their education. All this provides a broader basis for the American women's movement from the start, one that does not exist in Germany. Closely linked are questions about education, the legal position of women, and their free participation in the cultural life of the nation. Thus in that first period lie all the roots of the present time in which the woman in the United States has gained complete freedom regarding her choice of occupation. . . .

The women's movement experienced a radical boost when the slavery question was pushed to the forefront. . . . Men and women joined the Anti-Slavery Association and women especially appeared in the forefront. They were inspired by two fighters from the South, the sisters Sarah and Angelina Grimké, daughters of a rich planter from South Carolina, who set a noble example and freed their slaves.[11] The sisters hurried North to tell, eloquently, about the horrible situation in the South. Angelina wrote to [William Lloyd] Garrison, encouraging and concurring, and thanked him

[10]   Emma Willard (1787–1870), author of the widely read *Plan for Improving Female Education* (1819), unsuccessfully attempted to raise funds for a female academy from the state of New York. Willard then (1819) established her school in Troy, New York, in response to the decision of the city government to raise $4000 by taxation for a female academy. By 1831 when Elizabeth Cady Stanton attended it, her school was large and successful, with one hundred boarding students and more than two hundred day students. Governor Clinton went to the New York legislature, not the U.S. Congress, on Willard's behalf.

[11]   Sarah Grimké (1792–1873) and Angelina Grimké (1805–1879) are well characterized by Cauer as being central to the antislavery movement. During their public speaking tour of New England in 1837 they were criticized by local ministers for addressing "promiscuous assemblies"—consisting of both men and women. The Grimkés' spirited defense of their right and the right of all women to speak out on moral issues launched the women's rights movement.

GERMAN REFORMERS CONSIDER THE AMERICAN EXAMPLE

for his appearance in Boston, where he energetically defended his view-point in front of a furious mob. The highest moral courage, the strongest belief and will power was necessary to fight this strenuous and difficult bat-tle. Only as the slaveholders started to put prices on the heads of signifi-cant abolitionists, only as they dared to demand special laws for the press, did the Northern states revolt and give the opponents of slavery a foothold.

One has to bear in mind two points in the development of the slavery question—its amalgamation with the woman question, which caused a con-flict among abolitionists, and the opinion of the clergy in the two matters. The slavery question suffered because of the link to the woman question, since the question about the equality of men and women caused a debate about general social conditions that led far away from the original, limited goals. The most active abolitionists did not want to hear anything about the equality of women, especially the clergy. The women, on the other hand, who stood up for the good cause with word and deed, and who had fought and suffered like the men, could not and did not want to do without their rights any longer because they had assumed the same social duties as men. Especially because of speeches about freedom and oppression, about equality and inequality, which were given daily in many different cities, women came to realize how trivial and nonexistent their own rights were. The clergy . . . did not want to hear anything about the equality of women. The words of the apostle Paul, "Let your women keep silence in the churches," became their motto. . . .

In the general congress about the slavery question that took place in London in 1840, the antagonism erupted dramatically.[12] The Union sent, among their delegates, eight women, most of whom belonged to the strict sect of the Quakers. The English people were dumbfounded about women participating at the congress. But they calmed down when they actually saw the modest women. Nevertheless, the participation of women at a congress of men could not happen in the old Europe. The European men did not win great laurels in the debates about whether they should allow or deny the participation of women during the sessions. The men from the other side of the ocean fought against such narrowmindedness, which only al-lowed women to listen to the meetings from behind a curtain and a railing. The debates about this issue had a dramatic effect. The majority, among them most of the clergymen and even the American ones, voted against the admission of women. . . .

On the evening of this memorable day, two representatives of the female

[12]   Cauer is referring to the World Anti-Slavery Convention, called by the British Foreign and Anti-Slavery Society in London in 1840, which invited "friends of the slave of every nation and clime." The controversy over the seating of accredited female delegates from the Massachu-setts Anti-Slavery Society and the Boston and Philadelphia Female Societies demonstrated the recent split in the American abolitionist movement.

sex walked for hours up and down the foggy streets of London in deep rage. One was Lucretia Mott, a delegate, the other one was Mrs. Stanton, who had listened to the negotiations during her honeymoon.[13] On the pavement of "Old England" they decided to establish a league for women's rights. What the women of the New World had experienced at the hands of the men of the Old World and parts of the clergy gave rise to a different kind of women's movement: the right to vote was now put on the agenda.

Eight years after the congress and the two women's conversation, the "Women's Rights Convention" was founded. The declaration of human rights [*sic*], which represented the cornerstone for the liberation of the colonies from England, was used as the foundation for this convention as well.[14] That declaration of the women presents their case so convincingly that one can understand how amazed the world was. But there is such bitter and hard criticism in the allegations against the state, the law, and society that their declaration would have been suppressed in some countries of the Old World. In this declaration, equal rights in education, a choice of occupation, and the right to vote were demanded for women. . . . Free development in all directions but also the fulfillment of all duties by the female citizen of a republic: these are the ideals of the American women's movement.

If we look at several of the women's colleges in the United States, we cannot remain without a smattering of envy because they are so well provided for. . . . Wellesley College is especially well off in this respect. It was

[13]   Lucretia Coffin Mott (1793–1880), American abolitionist and woman's rights pioneer. A Quaker minister, she was one of the organizers of the 1837 Anti-Slavery Convention of American Women. In 1848, she and Elizabeth Cady Stanton called the women's rights convention in Seneca Falls, New York.

Elizabeth Cady Stanton (1815–1902), leader of the American woman suffrage movement from its inception in 1848. With Susan B. Anthony she founded the NWSA in 1869; they worked closely together promoting woman suffrage throughout their lives. In 1876 she disrupted the Philadelphia Centennial Exposition to present the Woman's Declaration of Rights. Two years later she persuaded a U.S. senator from California to introduce to the U.S. Congress a federal woman suffrage amendment, which was reintroduced in every succeeding Congress until it was finally adopted in 1920.

[14]   "A convention to discuss the social, civil, and religious rights of women" was announced in the local newspaper, Stanton later wrote. Drawing on their experience of anti-slavery gatherings, Mott, Stanton, and others drew up a "Declaration of Sentiments and Resolutions," taking the Declaration of Independence as a model. The resolutions did indeed discuss "social, civil and religious rights." Stanton suggested including the demand for women's suffrage in the list of resolutions, but Mott considered it too daring. Only through the intervention of black abolitionist leader Frederick Douglass was it presented to the floor, and it was the only resolution not passed unanimously. None of the women present felt she could serve as a chairperson, so Lucretia Mott's husband James filled the post. At the conclusion of the meeting, sixty-eight women and thirty-two men (a third of those present in the Wesleyan chapel) signed their names to the Declaration of Principles. The convention in Seneca Falls is generally considered the birth of the organized woman suffrage movement in the United States.

founded in 1875 by Mr. Durand and his wife, who after the loss of her only child, spent their entire fortune during their lifetimes to establish a model college. It features the so-called cottage system. Spread out on the large property around a castle-like main building are several little houses in which the girls live, supervised by teachers. The institute is managed by a female president; there are around seventy teachers and around six hundred students. Professors from nearby Boston or Harvard Universities give weekly supplemental lectures in the various disciplines. The whole institute demonstrates such an immersion in the female soul, such fine judgment of the female nature and her needs, that the college can truly be regarded as a model institute . . . .

Nevertheless, this does not mean that North America gave its daughters such liberties happily and voluntarily. On the contrary, American women had to fight their way, step by step. Yet since the principle "free women citizens in a free state" must be valid in the republican system of the Union, more and more people are convinced that the most capable and the most significant people, no matter whether man or woman, should have their day.

It has become customary in Germany to dismiss the actions of free, independent women with the word "Americanism." Anxious people warned German maidens of their strong-willed, self confident sisters in the New World. As with all new ideas and the attempts to realize them, extravagant action easily takes center stage. The German woman should realize that a feeling of close unity with the fatherland has to be her first duty. Then she might not pass such harsh judgment if brave women stand up for more freedom in female education. . . .

With this firm belief, American women have been at work for the last twenty years in a movement unique until now, which boasts the largest association in world history. This movement is linked to the family question; it concerns the vice of alcoholism, which, in the nerve-stimulating climate on the other side of the ocean, is an even bigger destroyer of families than here. The action of the women in this area is called the women's crusade against alcoholism. It started in 1873, when fifty ladies established an organization after listening to a stirring lecture by a Dr. Lews [*sic*] from Boston.[15] . . .

In less than twenty years, the society founded at that time has 200,000 members. There are only women, and along with honorary members and children's groups, they constitute an association with over half a million members. The organization is exemplary. The headquarters is in Evanston,

[15] Dio Lewis (1823–1886), a popular speaker on questions related to women's health, sparked the founding of the WCTU.

near Chicago, and the president is Miss Frances Willard.[16] The huge organization is administered from this suburb of Chicago, from a small, friendly house in Evanston. Its members travel throughout the world to work, according to the spirit of the society. All official employees are centered in Evanston; it is a magnificent bustle of treasurers, telegraph operators, stenographers, typewriters, and so on. All official employees are paid. The organization is a joint stock company with a capital of 150,000 pounds sterling, it owns a house, and the women manage the capital. The organization is called "The Woman-Christians-Temperance-Union" [English in the original] and even though the name sounds religious, the society is independent of any ecclesiastical influence. The whole organization was thought of by women, started by women, and is being managed by women. . . . The principal work was first only directed toward alcoholism and therefore toward the enactment of a law to prohibit the serving of all drinks which lead to alcoholism. Soon it was realized that laws alone did not achieve much, . . . The organization expanded to the point where over forty departments have been established. It has become more and more involved in all cultural tasks. To mention only a few, there is, for example, a department that deals with the education of black people, and another one that examines the influx of immigrants. The organization directs its attention especially toward German immigrants as they open beer and liquor establishments, as their first step in the New World. The department of Sunday schools is in the hands of the organization, which gives them a very powerful position. The department for literature produces hygienic, statistical, and educational material. The prison system is being tackled, along with public morality, the poorhouses, and the management of orphanages. . . .

Nothing remains distant or foreign to the women. Here one can see a picture of how, in a future state, female nature will express itself for the public welfare. . . .

This women's crusade is welcomed by many in the Union because it supports the public welfare. The "American Woman Suffrage Association" [English in the original],[17] however, is in general less popular. The dislike

16 Cauer's emphasis on the Woman's Christian Temperance Union was appropriate, since under the leadership of Frances Willard (1839–1898) between 1879 and 1898, the WCTU politicized more women's lives than any other organization in the nineteenth century. Its policy of "Do Everything" carried members beyond temperance to address a wide range of other issues, such as prison reform and child labor.

17 The American Woman Suffrage Association, formed in Boston in 1869, the same year that Stanton and Anthony launched the NWSA in New York, differed in the degree to which they gave woman suffrage priority above all other reforms. The AWSA endorsed the Fifteenth Amendment to the Constitution, which provided for black male suffrage, and generally took a more moderate approach. The NWSA did not endorse the Fifteenth Amendment because it introduced the word "male" into the U.S. Constitution for the first time.

GERMAN REFORMERS CONSIDER THE AMERICAN EXAMPLE

is not so much against the women's goal—to gain the female vote—but against the first supporters of this idea, who took such harsh and bitter actions that they harmed their cause.[18] In 1871, at a meeting in Washington, a milder tone was set, which still continues, and this leads to the hope that this demand of the women in the Union will slowly gain more life and meaning. The story of this question is told and discussed in detail in a work by Lady Stanton, Susanne Anthony [sic], and Mathilde Joslin Gage [sic].[19] The book not only proves the intellectual strength of the three American women, but also gives an insight into the political and judicial system of North America.[20] To go into that aspect of the women's movement in more detail would require an extra booklet. . . .

The women's movement in the United States is often seen as an example and model for the women's movement in other countries. In one big and important point, it can definitely be an example: the fulfillment and assumption of obligations for the public welfare by the female citizens. Even the most ardent opponents of the woman question cannot hold anything against that. But women's goals and actions in a particular cause have to be adapted to the characteristics of the nation and of the women in that nation. Morality, good habits, and a struggle for the ideal will gain the upper hand where there are noble and decisive women full of character.

Since this report was finished, the women have moved into their own palace at the World's Fair.[21]

For the first time, a woman's architectural designs were used . . . .[22]

The costs of the project are supposed to be 480,000 marks. Women have helped indefatigably and with full devotion. Some assisted with large financial support, others helped with their skills. The interior decorations, the

[18]   Cauer mistakenly suggests that the American Woman Suffrage Association was the more radical, when contemporaries considered it the less radical of the two suffrage groups.
[19]   For Susan B. Anthony, see Part I, document 7, Mary Church Terrell, "The Progress of Colored Women," note 32. Mathilda Joslyn Gage (1826–1898) became president of the NWSA in 1875. Stanton, Anthony, and Gage coauthored the 1876 "Declaration of Rights" for women; all three women coauthored the first three volumes of the monumental *History of Woman Suffrage* (1881–86).
[20]   *A History of Women Suffrage* concentrates on the history of the NWSA and not its competitor, the American Woman Suffrage Association. The two merged in 1890 to form the National American Woman Suffrage Association.
[21]   At the 1893 Columbian Exposition in Chicago, women for the first time organized a separate exhibition about their cultural achievements, in a specially designed Woman's Building. See the following document, "A German Report on the International Women's Congress at the Columbian Exposition."
[22]   In 1891, Sophie Hayden (1868–1953), the first woman to graduate from the architecture program at MIT, won the Board of Lady Managers' competition for the Woman's Building; it remained the major work of her career.

woodwork, the paneling, the wall painting, and the metalwork were done by women, supported in their project by the government. The women of North America look with pride at their achievement. They have experienced that work, striving, and unity have their noble reward.

German women can also participate happily in this success. Many of their works have been sent there.

German women have not a single hall of fame in their fatherland; they are not permitted to participate in the important higher education; the government does not make it easy for them to follow the way to their ideals and goals. Only the consciousness of giving something noble and encouraging to their own sex, and therefore also to their fatherland, supports the women, steels their courage and inspires their endurance. Across the ocean, women have also struggled, fought and suffered.

Large cultural tasks cannot be resolved easily.

3. Käthe Schirmacher Reports on the International Women's Congress at the Columbian Exposition

The vitality of women's organizations at the Columbian Exposition of 1893 reflected their growing importance in American society. Some contemporaries called it a "woman's fair." The meetings of the World's Congress of Representative Women attracted about 150,000 participants from thirty-one countries. In eight consecutive meetings, the delegates debated women's contributions to literature, art, and science, as well as educational and household issues, women in industry, women and charity, moral questions and social reform, religion and politics. Some 330 women presented papers. The German delegates argued mainly for women's access to higher education and the professions, the main demands of the German bourgeois women's movement at the time. In contrast, they might have listened to Jane Addams's talk on organization among working women, or heard Florence Kelley—recently appointed chief factory inspector for Illinois, and listed on the program as "expert, U.S. Department of Labor"—speak on trade unions.

This report by one of the German delegates conveys her amazement at the "bold new world" of American women's political activism.[23] Käthe

[23] Käthe Schirmacher, "Der internationale Frauenkongress in Chicago," *Nationalzeitung*, June 25, 1893; translated by Corinna Hörst and the editors.

Schirmacher was as much captivated by the "exciting and fruitful" socializing at the Palmer House Hotel as by the internationalism generated at the
sessions of the congress. At the same time, her account reflects on the
starkly different perceptions society held of these women in Germany and
the United States.

In Chicago, many European women, especially German women, experienced for the first time large-scale public sympathy for women's political
activism. European women made their American counterparts aware of the
international scope of their movement, while "the Americans represented
for the Europeans the guarantee that their most audacious dreams and
hopes would come true." Schirmacher introduced some of the most
prominent leaders of the American women's movement to her readers, emphasizing that professional and politically active women were only "unusual" by German criteria, but were increasingly accepted by American
society. Here Susan B. Anthony is not considered an "unfulfilled spinster"
but rather a "heroine." Schirmacher's description of women lawyers, doctors, and preachers as "serious and polite," a "multicolored picture of self-
confident womanhood," counteracted the firmly entrenched German
image of the "emancipated woman" as a bad imitation of the male.

Käthe Schirmacher came to Chicago by invitation of the Columbia
Damen Club, a German-American women's club, which had originally
planned to invite Helene Lange. At the congress, she presented a lecture—in English—entitled "The Marriage Prospects of the Modern
Woman," in which she explained how such prospects in Germany had
been diminished by demographic and economic factors, and by women's
growing desire to gain economic independence and be treated as intellectual equals. Herself a member of the progressive wing of the bourgeois
women's movement at that time, Schirmacher considered American
women more radical in all matters of moral, social, and political reform
than their German counterparts.

The following report was printed in the *Nationalzeitung*, a liberal Berlin
daily, about four weeks after the Women's Congress closed. In later, more
detailed accounts and lectures, published in a collection of essays (*Soziales
Leben*, Paris 1897), Schirmacher was critical of the exhibition in the
Women's Building, judging large parts of it amateurish.

Käthe Schirmacher
The International Women's Congress in Chicago

In the week from May 15 to May 23, Chicago was the head and the heart of
the women's world, site of a gathering, a fusion of related elements, an organization of power, which had never been seen before. Female leaders

and female demands, also unknown until now, emerged forcefully. The European delegates who up until now had only expected the fulfillment of their ideals with the coming of the millennium, have observed this bold new world with incredulous European eyes.

The meetings of the International Congress took place in the Art Palace, located near Lake Michigan.[24] At the time of the congress, many doors had not been hung, many walls were without decoration, there was still rubble in front, the asphalt of the driveway had just been laid, and the garden was still empty and barren. Other rooms in this half-finished building, however, were complete and decorated with wonderful art—pictures, statues, and antique busts that stood out oddly against the modern surroundings. Both main meeting rooms, Columbus Hall and Washington Hall, were decked with flags of all nations. The star-spangled banner, the black-white-red flag, the Union Jack, the licking dragon of Japan, and others covered the wooden walls.[25] Both halls, each with enough room for about three thousand people, were filled to the last seat in the morning and the evening, as were all the other rooms in which smaller meetings were held. On one day there were at least twenty-three sessions, but neither the speakers nor the audience grew tired.

This was due to the atmosphere that pervaded the women's congress. It can be described with the word "goodwill," a goodwill of the individual, the masses, and the press. Curiosity, however, was also part of it, especially on the evening when the American women—the favorites of the American audience—appeared as speakers. But in the long run curiosity was not the main motif, because the speakers from the floor were also welcomed with great interest and listened to with great attention that evening. The majority of the audience came to this meeting, as to other meetings, because of their interest in the subject and in the leading figures whose life and activities they had been following for years.

In the clever and energetic Mrs. Sewall, the American audience saw a woman who through her energy and vivacity, through her far-reaching sympathies and connections, had a leading role in organizing the congress.[26] She was welcomed with applause whenever she appeared. The audience listened to her and let her scold and criticize them, responding to whatever Mrs. Sewall's clever and quick wit inspired her to do at that mo-

[24]   The Chicago Art Institute was incorporated in 1879 as the Chicago Academy of Fine Arts. Since 1893 it has occupied the Renaissance building on Lake Michigan, erected in Grant Park in connection with the World's Columbian Exposition. The meetings of the World's Congress of Representative Women were held here.
[25]   The "black-white-red flag" is a reference to the flag of Imperial Germany from 1871 to 1918.
[26]   On May Wright Sewall, see Part I, document 7, Mary Church Terrell, "The Progress of Colored Women," note 32.

GERMAN REFORMERS CONSIDER THE AMERICAN EXAMPLE

ment. Eventually they were completely obedient to the gavel in her hand, the American equivalent of the president's bell. The audience not only submitted to her resolute hand but also willingly followed the quiet influence of Mrs. Rachel Foster Avery, a paragon of femininity.[27] Although a mother, she had been serving the congress constantly over the last year as its secretary.

The audience acted most enthusiastic when Susan B. Anthony appeared.[28] Forty years ago, together with her friend Elizabeth Cady Stanton, she was the first woman to think about the emancipation of women.[29] She was the pioneer for the political right to vote, for women's higher education, and for female clothing reform. Today, she is the most popular woman in America. Seventy-two years old, in German terms she is an old lady, an old spinster who missed her calling. In American terms she is a heroine who, despite scorn and derision, insisted upon her case and now is beginning to reap what she has sown. She is a gaunt person, with white hair, the keen eyes of a falcon, and a wonderful mouth. She has the look of those who have walked lonely paths. Although she wears an expression of determination, a good-natured smile plays about her lips, as if she is used to people's foolishness and can no longer get angry about it.

It is impossible to mention the names of all the leading American women who participated in the general and the sectional conferences or to describe all these interesting characters in detail. Still, I want to mention those who are unusual by German criteria. Think what you will. The fact is that these women exist in America, that they are organized, and that they appeared forcefully at the congress.

A woman preacher would be unusual at a German, and even at a European, meeting. "Reverend" Annie Shaw is unmarried and has chosen theology as her profession.[30] In the presence of eighteen other women preachers of various denominations, Annie Shaw gave the Whitsunday sermon on the morning of May 21. She is an ordained Methodist minister, while her colleague who read the liturgy was from a nondenominational parish. The service had every shade of religious belief and nonbelief. Annie Shaw, in her simple black gown, told the audience what we are accustomed to hearing from wise, omniscient men, what we consider the heritage of Lessing, Schiller, and Goethe, but what has not yet gained entry

[27] For Rachel Foster Avery, see Part I, document 3, Florence Kelly Wischnewetzky, "Movement Among German Working Women," note 12.
[28] For Susan B. Anthony, see Part I, document 7, Mary Church Terrell, "The Progress of Colored Women," note 32.
[29] For Elizabeth Cady Stanton, see Part II, document 2, Cauer, "Women in the United States," note 13.
[30] For Anna Howard Shaw, see Part I, document 7, Mary Church Terrell, "The Progress of Colored Women," note 32.

into our modern churches: We believe in one God and love unites us all. This female Methodist let everyone understand the "one God" in her own way. Besides, Annie Shaw was a favorite of the congress audience for her warm personality. She knew her audience and can be cheerful as well as serious. With her rhetorical skill and her willingness to help out whenever there was a need to fill in unforeseen pauses, she soon won everyone's heart.

Rhetorical skills were also displayed by Mrs. Ellen Foster, a cheerful and impressive personality.[31] She is a lawyer, her husband's partner, and she had already used her substantial influence in the legislative process. Although her home was once set on fire in retaliation, she has not lost her sense of humor and continues her work, confident and calm, as lawyer, consultant, and even as friend of the legislature.

To influence legislatures, to have direct representation for their interests and ideas—that is what American women ask for today in the name of justice. They have societies for female suffrage, and they have formed the temperance association, which has the same goals as the ones on the Continent except that the American association consists exclusively of women. They founded this society to improve morality, declaring themselves openly against today's double standard for men and women. None of those present in Chicago will forget seeing these noble women on stage. They spoke seriously and politely about something that is emerging only slowly with much conflict and anger in Europe, about conflicts and indignities as yet understood by few: that nothing can be done to women without harming the rest of the world; that ruling the world without women means running a machine on half power; and that what people call the "sphere" of the women has barely been a small hemisphere.

Everyone who has thought about the question of morality knows that this can only be tackled seriously where woman are doctors. That is so in the United States, and the list of famous women at this congress would be incomplete without the name of Dr. Stevenson, who was trained under the direction of Professor Huxley.[32] Today she is a women's doctor in Chicago, and even during the congress she kept working in her practice. That is why this stately figure, this smart attractive face was not seen as often as we wished. But she was always with us in spirit.

[31] [Judith] Ellen Horton Foster (1840–1910), American temperance leader, lawyer, and Republican organizer. She was a delegate to the founding convention of the Women's Christian Temperance Union in 1874, and in 1888 organized the Woman's National Republican Association.

[32] Sarah Ann Hackett Stevenson (1841–1909), American physician. She was the first woman member of the American Medical Association (1876) and the Illinois State Board of Health (1893). She studied for a year in London with Thomas Huxley (1825–1895), a well-known British biologist and advocate of Darwinism.

Around this core of American women, there were the foreign delegates. Canada was best represented with about fifteen delegates, Germany with six, France with two, England with five, Denmark and Sweden each with two. The Swedish government had insisted, with the explicit permission of the king, on sending Countess Thorberg-Rappe as the official delegate to the women's congress. Finland had sent two young youthful representatives, Mrs. Nordquist and Miss Toppelius. Greece had sent the amiable Mrs. Parren, an intimate friend of the crown princess. Italy and Bohemia each sent one representative; the latter, Mrs. Humbal-Zeman, distinguished herself with her excellent command of the English language. The Russian delegate could not come and the Spanish representative was still at sea. But Brazil and Syria were represented. India's delegate only appeared on paper because Pundita Ramabai, the leader of India's women, thought it would be better to stay at her position in India.[33]

It is difficult to describe the warm welcome the delegates experienced in Chicago. During the meeting, they were guests of the National Council, an association of American women made up of representatives from fourteen large national women's organizations.[34] Their chief task is to tend to all things of interest to women, to create a unified organization and mutual acceptance. The Palmer House Hotel became the headquarters of the delegates; and the cheerful activities, the babel of languages, the socializing, were exciting and fruitful. But this sympathy reached beyond the circle of the National Council and the walls of the Palmer House. No matter how well or how poorly the delegates spoke, no matter whether they spoke English or their mother languages, the congress audience was always delighted to receive them, another sign of friendly relations among people of different nationalities. They listened carefully to the reports about foreign countries. Everyone saw internationalism growing steadily, like a chain of hands coming together for the work in common. For the Americans, the Europeans symbolized the global aspect of the women's movement; the Americans represented for the Europeans the guarantee that their most audacious dreams and hopes would come true.

These days of momentum and excitement have surely made some European delegates, now tamed by their own experiences and disappointments, ask themselves: Is this just a dream? Is there such public sympathy? Is it possible that vanity and individual temperament can diminish completely and everyone accept each other? For clarification, they might have turned to one of these women, who seemed extremely quiet and sedate, and asked:

[33] The editors have not found biographical information about Countess Thorberg-Rappe, Mrs. Nordquist, Miss Toppelius, Mrs. Parren, Mrs. Humbal-Zeman, or Pundita Ramabai.
[34] The National Council of Women of the United States was founded in March 1888. It attempted to unite women's organizations of all types, ranging from literary clubs and temperance unions to suffrage associations and labor organizations, a goal only partially realized.

Are these facts? Is there genuine work behind these words? Are people only carried away by talk? The most wonderful moment of the congress might have been the answer: "No one is exaggerating. The women who work for the movement are working with their full souls, mostly unselfishly. They know that they do not only work for themselves but also for the future. Of course, even we have to deal with jealousy and rudeness, it even happens to us that the jangling bells drown out the finer instruments. But the public has started to choose the best ones, and our women are usually kind and without envy."

If you add Mrs. Potter Palmer's words—"Women should learn not independence but responsibility"—to the axiom of the congress—"You cannot rule the world nor complete it without us"—and if you reckon in the final thought of the meeting that every country should establish a council of all women's associations and then unite all these councils into an international organization, then you have a picture of the International Women's Congress in Chicago.[35]

Surely, no one can give written proof of all that happened there. How could you describe all those beautiful women, imposing in their rich, colorful dresses, with their wise faces, their freed and graceful movements? There were so many distinctive personalities here, but none of the type that the "emancipated women" have been accused of having created, with imitation male features. It is also hard to give an adequate impression of American eloquence. The new woman is very genuine, without any artificial touch. On stage, the woman speaker is a complete, outspoken individual who does not hold back her ideas and risqué remarks, who says what needs to be said at the moment. That is why the American audiences are so intimate with their favorites. No one minds if a woman tells her life story in front of a large audience. It gives the speech and the meeting some color and originality.

Originality and sincerity was also evident in the kind of hospitality the delegates experienced. It was not rare that a woman from Chicago, who had listened to one of the speakers and who liked the speech, would go up to her on the street and ask the speaker to spend an evening with her family.

Among the most colorful aspects of the congress were the receptions and social events. Various Chicago women's clubs, the ladies of the National Council, and the head of the congress, Mrs. Potter Palmer, had invited the congress participants to these gatherings. Every one of these

[35] Bertha Honoré Palmer (1849–1918), Chicago society leader. As chairman of the Board of Lady Managers of the World's Columbian Exposition, she personally secured many of the international exhibits in the Woman's Building by approaching governments and royalty. After the Fair, Palmer served as vice president of the Chicago Civic Federation.

functions was a multicolored picture of self-confident womanhood. Every way of thinking, every nationality, every kind of individual was present there. There were also all kinds of dresses, from the most expensive to the most simple. The reception at Mrs. Potter Palmer's house was especially successful. Every room in the house is a jewel, and the house itself was the jewel box, with its brown square stone blocks and sparkling windows looking out on Lake Michigan. A garden, clad in the delicate green of the late American spring, separated the house from the street, muffling the noises of Chicago. But all the unfinished properties around here never let one forget that the house is on American soil, in the New World that has united all the elements of the Old World. It is an immense melting-pot of contrasts, the crucible of the future. It is a land of which is said in one of the country's national anthems: "to worship the world others have died, to free the world is the goal of our life."[36]

4. *Die Frau* Reviews Elizabeth Cady Stanton's *Eighty Years and More*

The following review of Elizabeth Cady Stanton's autobiography[37] appeared in *Die Frau*, the most widely read publication of the bourgeois German women's movement and, according to its subtitle, "a monthly magazine for all aspects of women's lives in our time." The author, Helene Lange, edited the magazine from 1893 to 1916, when she was joined by her lifelong friend Gertrud Bäumer, who in turn became sole editor from Lange's death in 1929 until *Die Frau* ceased publication in 1944.

Especially during the years before World War I and again in the second half of the 1920s, *Die Frau* reported widely on women's education in the United States, on the American women's movement, and on the lives of prominent American women such as Frances Willard, Susan B. Anthony, Harriet Beecher Stowe, Helen Keller, and Jane Addams. Writings by American feminists like Charlotte Perkins Gilman, Jane Addams, and Margaret Sanger were translated into German after the turn of the century, but there was no German edition of Elizabeth Cady Stanton's memoirs. This ex-

[36]   The original reads "Die Welt zu heiligen, sind andere gestorben, die Welt befrei'n sei unseres Lebens Ziel!" This is probably a free translation of "Land where our fathers died / Land of the Pilgrim's pride / From every mountainside / Let freedom ring."

[37]   Helene Lange, "Eine amerikanische Führerin der Frauenbewegung," *Die Frau* 6 (1898/99): 224–29; translated by Corinna Hörst and the editors. The editors have restored the original English in quotations from Stanton, despite the changes in meaning that Lange introduced into the German version of the article.

plains why Lange does not present her readers with a mere review of the book, but comments extensively on Stanton's life. Like Minna Cauer in the preceding selection, Lange sees in the work of the American women's movement and the life of one of its preeminent leaders an inspiring example for the women in her own country.

An American Leader of the Women's Movement
Helene Lange

A recently published book by Elizabeth Cady Stanton, *Eighty Years and More*, offers compelling evidence for the minor verity that a human being, too, is a native product, a child of maternal soil. No where else but in the United States of North America could this book have been written, this life been lived.

Mrs. Cady Stanton is one of the few survivors of a great epoch, who experienced the development of the women's movement nearly parallel to that of the antislavery movement. A few years ago, her eightieth birthday (Elizabeth Cady Stanton was born November 12, 1815) was celebrated like that of a queen. She sums up her life in this book. And the final judgment of the reader is: this life was worth living.

From childhood on, she was concerned with the "women's movement." The little girl soon realized that something was not right. Like Charlotte von Kalb, whose grandmother, disappointed at not having had a grandson, said, "You should not be here," Elizabeth Cady had a father, an excellent lawyer in the state of New York, with the same attitude.[38] Comforting his eleven-year-old daughter after the death of his only son, he said, "I wish you were a boy." But how different was the effect on the sensitive German aristocratic woman who complained with emotion, "As a child I have cried enough to last me a lifetime" and on the energetic American, who pragmatically sat down and thought about the solution to the problem of "boyhood." She decided to come close to being a boy by studying Greek and learning how to ride. She translated this approach into action, only to hear, after her first success in Greek studies, the same fatherly sigh: "Ah, you should have been a boy."

In her father's office, where the little girl came and went unnoticed, she listened to the complaints of hundreds of women who, as victims of harsh marriage laws, asked the lawyer in vain for help. The young law interns enjoyed teasing her. One day when she was wearing nice coral jewelry, she

---

[38] Charlotte von Kalb (1761–1843), German writer, close acquaintance of Friedrich von Schiller (1759–1805) and Jean Paul (1763–1825), and inspiration for many women figures of the German classics. In her memoirs, von Kalb recalled the disappointment of her parents, who would have preferred a son.

had to listen to one of them say, "If in due time you should be my wife, those ornaments would be mine; I could take them and lock them up, and you could never wear them except with my permission. I could even exchange them for a box of cigars, and you could watch them evaporate in smoke."[39] That is how the main thread of her life was chosen. From her childish decision to cut all the harsh laws against women out of her father's books, her determination rose slowly but steadily, to help women to fight for their rights.

A happy childhood, spent enjoying the New World's characteristic free contact between the sexes, the delightful natural life that is totally strange to us Europeans, eventually yielded to serious duties. At twenty-five, Elizabeth Cady married one of the most eloquent and earnest leaders of the antislavery movement: Henry B. Stanton.[40] At her firm request, the word "obey" was left out of the wedding ceremony, since she was not willing to obey someone with whom she entered a relationship on equal ground. The marriage has in every respect been happy. Seven children have been raised and they have taken up respectable positions in the world, although—or perhaps because—their mother understood the need to combine, with a big heart, more than just house and family.

Even the honeymoon trip was characteristic. The destination was London, where, in 1840, the great antislavery congress was taking place.[41] Some of the most famous American female leaders had come over. Admission was denied to them because of their sex; they were compelled to listen in silence to the "platitudes of the men about 'woman's sphere.' " Stanton and the great William Lloyd Garrison spoke up for the rights of the women, but in vain, so that only silent protest remained for them.[42] "After

[39] Under New York law as under English common law, everything a woman owned became her husband's property upon their marriage. A woman could not hold, buy, or sell property, sue or be sued, enter into contracts, or keep her own wages. Various forms of married women's property laws were passed in all states between 1839 and 1895. The first, passed in Mississippi, served primarily the interests of fathers who wanted to protect their estates from improvident sons-in-law. In states where the women's rights movement was more prominent, more comprehensive laws were passed, most notably in New York, where the lobbying of Susan B. Anthony and Elizabeth Cady Stanton helped to secure the Married Woman's Property Acts of 1848 and 1860. These gave wives in that state the right to own, buy, and sell property; to sign contracts; to sue and be sued; to keep their own wages; and to be joint guardians of their children. By the mid-1870s, married women's property laws had been passed in most northern states, and by the turn of the century in most southern ones.
[40] Henry Brewster Stanton (1805–1887), American lawyer and abolitionist, was active in the American Anti-Slavery Society. Following the World Anti-Slavery Convention, he lectured on anti-slavery topics in Great Britain. He was a New York State senator from 1849 to 1853 as a member of the Free Soil Party; later, he helped to organize the New York Republican Party. After the Civil War, he worked as a journalist for the New York *Tribune* and the New York *Sun*.
[41] For the World Anti-Slavery Convention, see Part II, document 2, Cauer, "Women in the United States," note 12.
[42] William Lloyd Garrison (1805–1879). Prominent reformer and abolitionist.

battling so many long years," said Garrison, "for the liberties of African slaves, I can take no part in a convention that strikes down the most sacred rights of all women." That is how he shared the coerced silence with the women, after he had traveled three thousand English miles to speak about the subject that was most important to him. The women have never forgotten that. Then and there the seeds were planted for the American women's movement.

For some time the young wife [Elizabeth Cady Stanton] was wholly occupied with motherhood. With characteristic thoroughness, she observed babies and discovered that human mistreatment was even here, too, the source of most illnesses and misery. She allowed her baby freedom of development, regarded thought and reflection as better than "maternal instincts," and did not hesitate to propagate with her usual liveliness these ideas, which seemed extremely heretical to her nurse.

Fate brought her from Boston and Chelsea to Seneca Falls, New York, where she lived for sixteen years. Here she began her public career. At a meeting with Lucretia Mott, she strongly expressed the "general dissatisfaction" she felt about the "woman's portion as wife, mother, housekeeper, physician, and spiritual guide."[43] The call to the first "woman's rights convention" (July 14, 1848) was issued at this meeting. This date is for the women's movement what July 4 is for the republic. The convention took place at a Methodist church. "The house was crowded at every session, the speaking good, and a religious earnestness dignified all the proceedings."[44]

The women were not spared the ordeal that is inseparable from those first serious steps. The press raised an outcry: "It seemed as if every man who could hold a pen wrote a sermon about the woman's sphere." Nevertheless, the ice was broken. The antislavery press remained faithful; one convention followed another; men like Garrison, Phillips, and Emerson participated. And one of these meetings caught the attention of Mrs. John Stuart Mill, who wrote that article, "The Enfranchisement of Women," in the *Westminster Review* (October 1852), one of the starting points of the English women's movement.[45] The fact of this article, incidentally, exposed the superficiality of Laura Marholm, who wanted to ascribe the origin of the women's movement to two men, Mill and Bebel.[46]

[43] For Lucretia Mott, see Part II, document 2, Cauer, "Women in the United States," note 13.
[44] For the Seneca Falls convention, see Part II, document 2, Cauer, "Women in the United States," notes 13 and 14.
[45] Harriet Taylor (1807–1858), British feminist, wife and collaborator of philosopher and economist John Stuart Mill (1806–1873).
[46] Laura Marholm was a pseudonym for Laura Mohr Hansson (1854–1905), a German writer. Born in Latvia, where she started as a journalist, she moved to Germany after her marriage to writer Ola Hansson, living first near Berlin and later in Bavaria. A member of the literary circle Schwarzes Ferkel (Black Piglet), Marholm wrote dramas, essays, and short stories.

Shortly thereafter, a friend entered Elizabeth Stanton's life, with whom she worked for half a century, the two complementing each other wonderfully: Susan B. Anthony.[47] She was a deeply religious person, without any dogmatic beliefs. For her, "work is worship. . . . In ancient Greece she would have been a Stoic; in the era of the Reformation, a Calvinist; in King Charles's time, a Puritan; but in this nineteenth century, by the very laws of her being, she is a Reformer."

She was a Quaker who fought both inner and outer conflicts to gain her freedom. As a teacher she knew how to get respect even from the loudest boys. One day, she entered a class that was feared even by the male teachers because of a fifteen-year-old barbarian, who tried at once to play a trick on her. The gentle Quaker woman calmly gave the boy a strong beating. That was an early demonstration of what characterized her later public career: she knew what to do in every situation.

Instead of the alphabet books and textbooks, larger issues were slowly emerging: the temperance question, the antislavery movement, and the suffrage issue were taking hold of her. She joined Mrs. Stanton. And fifty years later, that woman wrote:

So entirely one are we that in all our associations, ever side by side on the same platform, not one feeling of envy or jealousy has ever shadowed our lives. We have indulged freely in criticism of each other when alone, and hotly contended whenever we have differed, but in our friendship of years there has never been the break of one hour. To the world we always seem to agree and uniformly reflect each other. Like husband and wife, each has the feeling that we must have no differences in public.

Long trips broadened Susan's horizons. She was even in Berlin during the 1880s.[48] As a guest in the house of the U.S. minister to Berlin, Mr. Sargent, she sent her mail to the post office in the official envelopes of the suf-

---

Among her works are *Das Buch der Frauen* (1894, translated as *Modern Women*, 1896), *Frau Lilly als Jungfrau, Gattin und Mutter* (1896, translated as *Frau Lilly as Maiden, Wife and Mother*, 1896), *Wir Frauen und unsere Dichter* (1895, translated as *We Women and Our Authors*, 1899), and *Die Frauen in der sozialen Bewegung* (1900, Women in Social Movements). Her writings were also translated into Norwegian and Russian. The focus of Marholm's writings is the "woman question" of her day. Social, cultural, and economic themes do not figure prominently in her analysis. Contemporary feminists criticized her substantially, especially the two volumes of *Zur Psychologie der Frau* (1897, translated as *Studies in the Psychology of Women,* 1899) in which traditional views of the "feminine nature" prevailed.

For August Bebel, see Part I, document 3, Florence Kelley Wischnewetsky, "Movement among German Working Women," note 15.

[47] For Susan B. Anthony, see Part I, document 7, Mary Church Terrell, "The Progress of Colored Women," note 32.

[48] Susan B. Anthony toured Europe for several months in 1883. Beginning in March, she traveled through Italy and Switzerland, then went to Germany, where she visited Munich, Nuremberg, Cologne, and Heidelberg. During the first week in May, she was a guest of the Sargents (see note 49) in Berlin. She then went on to Paris, England, Ireland, and Scotland.

frage movement, which bore the inscription: "No just government can be formed without the consent of the governed."[49] An official of the post office returned a whole pile of these letters, saying, "Such statements cannot be sent by mail." After that, she was not unhappy to return to her home country and to her friend.

And now they set to work, basically disseminating their ideas. From New York to San Francisco they gave speeches, in large cities and small towns, in churches, schools, barns, on a wagon in the open field, on Mississippi riverboats. One day, Miss Anthony was even invited to talk at a mental asylum— a valuable opportunity, said one of her followers, to talk to her equals, "for is not the right of suffrage denied to 'idiots, criminals, lunatics, and women'?"

This work was intensified when the Lyceum Bureau was established in Boston, New York, and Chicago.[50] The Bureau engages an assortment of speakers to bring education and reform ideas to the most distant places of this large republic. Mrs. Stanton also enrolled and from 1869 on, for twelve years, eight months of the year, she went on long, difficult pilgrimages from Maine to Texas, preaching tirelessly about the economic, judicial, and political liberation of women. A European speaker who steps out of her comfortable coupe, to be welcomed by friendly hosts and led to a lavishly decorated hall, can scarcely imagine these kinds of trips. Overworked mothers brought along their babies, who sometimes accompanied the speaker with crying. Roofs leaked water onto the speaker's platform. Sometimes she had to drive for hours through the snow, and she even at times got stuck in it. These were experiences Mrs. Stanton talked about with humor. On a trip through Canada she even got to know what it was like to sleep in a bed where a family of mice had established themselves, which had been given to her by the farmers without any "ceremonious changing of bed linen."

[49]   Aaron Augustus Sargent (1827–1887). Influential member of the Republican Party; U.S. minister to Germany in 1882. His wife was a treasurer of the NWSA in the 1870s.
    The NWSA was founded in May 1869 by Susan B. Anthony, Elizabeth Cady Stanton, and others, after the convention of the Equal Rights Association in New York City split over whether the demand for women's suffrage should be put aside until African-Americans had received the right to vote. Although Anthony and Stanton temporarily aligned themselves with southern Democrats, the NWSA set a precedent for women organizing independently of male-dominated politics. After the election of 1872, the differences between the two factions began to fade, but they did not merge into the National American Woman's Suffrage Association until 1890. The official mottoes on the NWSA stationery were "No just government can be formed without the consent of the governed" and "Taxation without representation is tyranny."
[50]   The Lyceum was a system of adult education stressing lectures, debates, and reading. It also promoted the establishment of libraries and museums and the improvement of district schools. Founded in 1826 and flourishing particularly before the Civil War, the lyceum system was a forerunner of the Chautauqua movement, university extension programs, and commercial lecture bureaus.

GERMAN REFORMERS CONSIDER THE AMERICAN EXAMPLE

These Lyceum trips were undertaken with special eagerness in 1876. The women decided to declare July 4, the hundredth anniversary of the republic, as "Women's Day."[51] A "Woman's Declaration of Rights" was prepared, but when they asked for an opportunity to read the declaration in public at the centennial celebration, it was denied. But on the morning of July 4, after the last words of a solemn reading of the Declaration of Independence of 1776 had faded away, one could see a few women, with Miss Anthony as leader, walking with calm determination through the rows of civic officials and foreign guests, who politely gave way. The women handed the chairman their declaration and he accepted it from the women in the confusion of the moment. In this way it became part of the historical record.

The details of the subsequent work in the service of the women's movement do not matter. Everything came from the same spirit of calm determination that knew how to operate without any "scenes," without any insincere pathos or putting on airs. One day, as cool as you please, Mrs. Stanton went into a polling station, and one of the distinguished citizens of the city announced her, saying, "Mrs. Stanton is here, gentlemen, for the purpose of voting. As she is a taxpayer, of sound mind, and of legal age, I see no reason why she should not exercise this right of citizenship." Reading Mrs. Stanton's short description of the ensuing confusion, one is reminded a little bit of the scene in the city hall of Heilbronn, which Goethe described with such high spirits.[52] Mrs. Stanton read out her rights to two civil servants and they pulled their hats over their faces "whether from shame or ignorance, I do not know." The third civil servant took the ballot box and put his hand over the opening. Mrs. Stanton calmly put the ballot in his hand, giving him the responsibility for curtailing her civil rights, and then left. An extensive *History of Women's Suffrage,* which Mrs. Stanton wrote together with Miss Anthony, contains a large amount of valuable material

[51] The NWSA had hoped to use the huge centennial exhibition in Philadelphia during the summer of 1876 to bring women from all over the country together and draw attention to the inequities they still suffered. The Centennial Commission denied the requests of the NWSA to present a Declaration of Rights for Women similar to that of the Seneca Falls Convention at the Fourth of July celebration held in Independence Hall. The NWSA requested a large number of tickets but received only five, which did give Susan B. Anthony and four others the opportunity to walk up to the podium at the moment the audience rose to greet the guest of honor, the emperor of Brazil. The startled chairman, president pro tempore of the U.S. Senate Thomas Ferry (1826–1896), grasped the parchment Anthony handed to him. On their way back, the women scattered handbills with the text of the Declaration, seized a bandstand opposite Independence Hall to read the Declaration before a large crowd, and managed to distribute more copies before adjourning to a church for a five-hour meeting. The AWSA did not associate itself with the Declaration, much less with its presentation, but got a little wall space in the exhibition to present some printed matter.

[52] Lange is here referring to a scene in Johann Wolfgang von Goethe's drama *Götz von Berlichingen.* The protagonist, the knight Götz, has been accused of disloyalty to the Emperor and has to defend himself before a council in the city hall of Heilbronn.

GERMAN REFORMERS CONSIDER THE AMERICAN EXAMPLE

about the first stages of the movement that has led to the total acceptance of women's political equality in four states.[53]

The most prominent element of Mrs. Stanton's character as a leader was her complete lack of preconceived ideas. This was only possible to such a degree in a country like America, in such a young union of state systems, where fundamental laws are created and changed every day, so that they hardly reach the stage where age is equated with divinity. It was precisely this absence of preconception that she applied to the analysis of the sexes and their duties. She simply would not understand why man has an advantage over woman, why he can decide about everything on the earth that pertains to both of them. Sometimes she used a harsh word, but usually she saw the present condition with humor, as only temporary. She tried to contribute as much as possible to changing that condition with speeches, activities, and the distribution of leaflets. Here she chose her audience very carefully: "I never offer a leaflet to a man with a small head, high heels on his boots, and his chin high in the air because I know that he, according to the nature of the earth, envies a superior woman. I do not offer a woman a leaflet who has the 'prunes and prisms expression'[54] because I know she will say 'I have all the rights I need.' " And with reference to the word "obey" in the wedding ceremony, she still holds the conviction that she had back then. She simply sees it as a violation of "the thirteenth amendment of the federal Constitution which says that neither slavery nor compulsory servitude should exist in the United States of America."

The same absence of preconception has led to a strange work which would have been a double impossibility in the old Europe: *The Woman's Bible*. It was based on the wish to take away the ground from those people who abuse the authority of the Bible for their hostile attitudes against women and progress. For this purpose, all the text parts of the Bible that refer to the role of women underwent criticism. It was a strange and absolutely unscholarly criticism, however. The text was not actually criticized; the content alone was subjected to unfavorable commentary from a modern standpoint. From a scholarly standpoint, it is an impossible book, sys-

[53] *The History of Women's Suffrage* was published in six volumes. The first two, edited by Elizabeth Cady Stanton, Susan B. Anthony, and Mathilda Joslyn Gage, were published in Rochester, New York, in 1881; the third volume was published there in 1886. Volume 4, edited by Anthony and journalist Ida Husted Harper, was published in Rochester in 1902. Volumes 5 and 6 were edited by Harper and published in New York in 1922. Although up to 1890 this work is primarily a collection of sources about the NWSA rather than about the entire women's suffrage movement and all volumes suffer from serious pro-NWSA bias, there is no better single record of events and legal gains for the cause of women's suffrage in the United States.

[54] Nineteenth-century women who wished to have small mouths and be judged as feminine repeated the words "plums, potatoes, prunes, prisms" to achieve the desired effect of pursing the lips.

GERMAN REFORMERS CONSIDER THE AMERICAN EXAMPLE

tematically though a very interesting one, since it shows that women have begun to have their own opinions about spiritual and practical problems and have started to voice them, though still with undeniable naïveté. When deep knowledge and a secure legal and civil position will have assured the evolution of woman's skills, the way she looks at such problems will not lead to such curious and strange things as *The Woman's Bible,* but to meaningful support of the cultural work of humankind. So those who come after us will be happier than we are, but sometimes one wants to join the deep sigh of this brave, earnest leader of our movement: "It is nice to know that our descendants will enjoy life one day, but when one craves a free breath, such reflection is not satisfying." Perhaps the old woman who looks as if she has another decade or more to live, will be allowed, in our fast moving time, to have more than a view from Nebo into the holy land.[55]

5. A German Sociologist Describes American Women Factory Inspectors

In 1906, after completing her dissertation "The Verein für Sozialpolitik and the Effects of Its Work on Labor Legislation," reformer Else Conrad visited the United States. Her reports to readers of *Die Frau* examined professional employment for women, including occupations of interest to women social reformers. They illuminated features of the American economy and polity that opened opportunities for women reformers, but—as in this article on factory inspectors[56]—emphasized American backwardness in the area of state regulation. In other parts of the series, Conrad reported on welfare secretaries, nurses, federal and postal employees, librarians, and sales and office clerks.

Conrad's report on factory inspectors strongly reflected Florence Kelley's views. Kelley probably also supplied many of the sources cited in Conrad's footnotes. Here in only slightly altered form we see many of the same points that Kelley had made in her *Archiv* articles ten years earlier: governmental regulations were weak, capital strong, and the wage-earning population consisted almost entirely of immigrants. The work of factory inspectors was therefore more urgently needed in the United States than in Germany, where they fit into a larger pattern of regulation. Possibly as a

---

55   Mount Nebo, the summit from which Moses viewed the Promised Land (Deuteronomy 34:1).
56   Else Conrad, "Frauenberufe in Amerika," *Die Frau* 15 (1907/08): 557–63; translated by Sally Robertson. Italics indicate emphasis in the original.

consequence, American women factory inspectors were treated more equally with men than was the case in Germany.

Women's Occupations in America
by Dr. Else Conrad

VI. The Factory Inspector

With the exception of Russia, America is the most primitive of all civilized countries with respect to the status of protective legislation. Of the fifty-two states and territories of the North American union, eight still have absolutely no restriction on child labor, and thirty-two have no ban on night-time labor.[57] Among the states which have passed child labor laws, seven provide for no kind of factory inspection, so that a violation of the law would be penalized only in response to a specific complaint from interested parties.

There are various reasons for America's backwardness in this area.

Primarily, it is consistent with the uniquely American spirit to allow the greatest possible freedom to rule everywhere, leaving everyone to his own devices and avoiding government intervention into economic life wherever possible. The Manchester doctrine of "laissez faire laissez passer" has not yet been completely overcome there. This effort to restrict government intervention as much as possible finds a certain amount of justification in the fact that there is no trust in government organs over there. The lamentable corruption, the great dishonesty, which rules in all areas of political life, generally keeps the best elements out of government—particularly state government—positions, which is why an increase in government influence and government bureaucrats naturally meets with resistance.

In addition, the phenomenally rapid industrial development of the United States gave all competent people the opportunity to work their way up, and it is therefore viewed as the personal fault of individuals if they remain on the lowest level and thus subject to the exploitation of employers. In fact, there are very few "true Americans" among the simple factory workers.

Furthermore, the rich industrial magnates, without an equally powerful class of landed gentry to counter them as in England, have such a powerful voice in the legislative process that they have probably been able to keep protective legislation in check while protecting their products with high duties.

[57] *Child Labor Legislation Handbook*, 1906, pp. 8ff., edited by the National Consumer League, New York City. [This footnote is in the original.]

Doubtless the most serious reason, however, is that industrial legislation is not a federal matter, but a state matter, and that therefore the only result of one state's conscientious action is that the industry affected by the restricting legislation moves across state boundaries or loses in a competitive battle with industry in other states which do not have such restrictions. . . .

Only twenty-seven states[58] place any restrictions whatever on women's work. Of those, fourteen limit the work day for women and juveniles (usually those younger than eighteen) to ten hours, and a few others limit the work week to sixty hours, with Saturday afternoons free. Thirty-one require the provision of seating opportunities for women in all factories and stores in which women are employed. Of course, there are also many laws dealing with separate dressing rooms for the two sexes and protective regulations regarding machinery. Above all, it should be mentioned that a number of states have established by law a normal working day at least for state and municipal offices. An Act of Congress establishes the eight-hour work day for all federal offices.[59] Only Utah and Wyoming limit working hours for men.

Even if we recognize these last-mentioned favorable laws with no reservations, American protective legislation must still be described as extremely in need of reform, in view of the fact that the overall level of restriction on woman and child labor is still minimal. This is beginning to be recognized, even over there. This is particularly true since Florence Kelley, a former Chicago factory inspector, whom I had the opportunity to get to know personally in a lengthy discussion, has been working for some years with all the energy at her disposal to win her nation over to the idea of a Federal child labor law. She is working with the Child Labor Committee, which has established a footing in fourteen states and gathers its supporters from church communities, women's clubs, and employees' and employers' organizations . . . .[60]

Now we come to our actual topic, the female factory inspectorate, which we felt had to be preceded by this short overview of worker protection legislation in America. For purposes of comparison with the German situation, it must be noted that the division of labor between the different American administrative departments is significantly different from ours. Some tasks which fall to factory inspectors here are assumed by the health

[58]   Labor Bulletin of the Commonwealth of Massachusetts,–190. [This footnote is in the original.]
[59]   Belva M. Herron. Factory Inspection in the United States. *American Journal of Sociology*. January 1907, Vol. XII, No. 4. The University of Chicago Press. [This footnote is in the original.]
[60]   In 1883, Congress standardized the work day for all federal agencies at forty-two hours a week. Offices opened at nine a.m. and closed at four p.m., six days a week, with a half hour for lunch. In 1892 Congress enacted a eight-hour law for all "laborers, workmen and mechanics" employed by the U.S. government, which provided better enforcement than a similar law passed in 1868.

department there, and others which are the responsibility of the police in Germany are carried out by factory inspectors in America.

There are female factory inspectors in only seven states, and there only in the last eighteen years at the longest. New York, the most populous state and a very industrialized one, was the first to appoint such an official in 1890. Massachusetts and Wisconsin followed suit the following year, Rhode Island in 1894, and so on. In those seven states, the law expressly prescribes the appointment of at least one female inspector, and the New York law adds that the number must not exceed ten.

I obtained the following information from a survey of all factory inspection operations employing female staff.[61] The state of New York currently employs eight women along with twenty-eight men, who must inspect all kinds of factories, as well as homework establishments. This completely equal use of the two sexes does not occur for reasons of principle, but for reasons of practicality, because the number of male inspectors is too small to meet all the needs. The entire territory is divided mechanically into districts, with one male or female inspector at the head of each district. Thus male and female salaries are also equal. When I asked whether the women were successful in these positions, I was told that there was a decided need to attract women to work as inspectors, but that they were not suitable for all kinds of work and that, therefore, the way they were used in New York was not the proper way. Men are preferable as heads of an entire district, I was told. . . .

Unfortunately, as with most American government positions, politics all too often plays a role in factory inspection, so that it is not uncommon for a poorly suited person to be entrusted with the tasks of factory inspection simply because some family member has risen to a position of prominence in the political party in question. This was even admitted by many at the last congress of factory inspectors. For example, a young former cigar worker declared there quite openly that he had only obtained his position as a factory inspector because he had worked so energetically as district chair for the election of the current governor. A woman adorned with jewels who was the next to step to the podium also confessed that she had secured her position merely by being the sister-in-law of the former governor—It also happens occasionally that an especially competent and experienced factory inspector must step aside to make way for a political minion.

[61]   The National Child Labor Committee (NCLC) was founded in 1904 by Florence Kelley and other reformers. Modeled on the New York Child Labor Committee, established the year before, the NCLC successfully campaigned for child labor legislation in many states, and for the federal child labor laws passed in 1916 and 1918, which were later nullified by the Supreme Court. By 1914, the Committee had almost nine thousand members and had succeeded in passing a fourteen-year age limit in thirty-five states.

GERMAN REFORMERS CONSIDER THE AMERICAN EXAMPLE

For these reasons, the assessment of women's success as factory inspectors is too disparate in the different states to be able to obtain a clear picture from the American experience of the significance and suitability of women as factory inspectors.

It is not uncommon for the female inspectors to be accused of being too ladylike, and of not dressing in accordance with their tasks. Some accuse them of having taken the job only for the money, but considering it below their dignity to actually do the work. And it is said that they let themselves be led through the factories, thus seeing what the company wants them to see. Above all, they are accused of knowing nothing about machinery. These accusations are undoubtedly justified in many cases, but they should be directed primarily at those who select such unsuitable persons for the jobs. Such deficiencies obviously have nothing to do with the suitability of women in general for the job. This can be seen in all cases where political considerations are eliminated from the appointment process. In those cases, it is openly acknowledged that the female factory inspectors do a competent and unique job and that they are undoubtedly necessary.

Let us add here the judgment of an American industrialist regarding female factory inspectors: "The best and most thorough inspection of my factory was done by a woman. The women work at this job with more dedication and stronger personal interest than the men; they put their whole being into it."

6. Alice Salomon on American
Settlement Work

After the 1909 ICW congress in Toronto, Alice Salomon traveled to the United States for the first time. Reports on the English and American settlement movements had inspired much of her work, and she was eager to visit as many settlements and other social reform institutions as she could during her short stay. Salomon would remain encouraged by the reform efforts of American women for the rest of her life. In 1909, she reported on their activities to her German audience[62] and began a relationship with Jane Addams that ended only with Addams's death in 1935.

"Soziale Arbeit in America" was published as a brochure as well as in *Leben und Wirken* (Life and Work), the monthly journal of the Baltic women's movement. The journal advocated higher education and the right

[62] Alice Salomon, "Soziale Arbeit in Amerika," *Leben und Wirken* 4 (1909/10); translated by Corinna Hörst and the editors.

to work for middle-class women as well as the protection of working women, and it discussed questions of childrearing, psychology, literature, and art. The editor-in-chief, Else Schütz, published the journal in Riga, Latvia. Among the contributing editors were Salomon, Anna Pappritz (who led the fight against state-sanctioned prostitution), and Käthe Schirmacher.

Here as in numerous other publications, Salomon emphasized the fact that women's reform activities were by far more accepted in America than in her home country. Salomon was particularly impressed that American women had achieved the goal of the German women's movement, namely, to "completely assume 'cultural' tasks." American women, therefore, had more opportunities to exercise civic duties. By labeling social service as patriotic, Salomon echoed one of the main arguments of her own movement. She also pointed to the settlements' contributions to American democracy: they educated immigrants "to be capable of self-administration, conscious of their civil duties, and aware of the use of democratic rights."

For Salomon, the settlement movement epitomized American social work because its Americanization work was central to the building of the American nation. Coming from a relatively homogenous society, it was hard for her to envision an ethnically diverse nation whose "cultural standard . . . is constantly threatened by the masses of immigrants."

Salomon's description of the American striving for social justice contrasted with the prevailing German stereotype of the "land of dollars." She was quite aware that rapid industrialization had resulted in unregulated and dangerous workplaces, problems that the German state had tried to address since the 1880s. On the other hand, the immense material wealth of American society had produced generous support for women's social reform projects, whereas women's reform work in Germany was characterized by "depressing money worries" and "petty and meticulous economizing."

In 1909 and in future visits, Salomon saw the larger American financial endowments and the greater involvement of women as the main differences between American and German social reform work. She tried to convey to her readers the professionalism, "the devotion and social consciousness" of American women activists, which she wished to pass on to the students of her Women's School for Social Work.

Social Work in America
by Dr. phil. Alice Salomon

Probably nowhere but in the large cities of the United States could we find the expression of two opposite ideals so close together. There, alongside the pursuit of dollars, the accumulation of wealth, and senseless luxury

GERMAN REFORMERS CONSIDER THE AMERICAN EXAMPLE

amounting almost to wastefulness, civic spirit celebrates its highest triumph, and devoted brotherly love and cooperation are developing. Possibly those who can satisfy every wish, who can have everything that can be bought with money, realize the uselessness and emptiness of a life directed only toward exterior, materialistic luxury and restless employment. Possibly business sense as an end in itself, extreme luxury, and hedonism collapse because they have reached their limits. The command of all the money in the world, if it becomes a habit, does not bring happiness, or even satisfaction.

But here, in contrast to the effects of materialism, new and higher ideals, purer, life-affirming joys, are coming into being. Alongside the dollar kings of Wall Street and the unsympathetic female hothouse plants who are always thinking up new opportunities to spend the money their husbands earn, we meet men and women who have turned away from employment for materialistic success and chosen to focus on the welfare of society and the nation. They devote themselves selflessly to pedagogical, philanthropic, and social duties to serve their fatherland as true citizens.

The leaders of this movement have been able to create so much sympathy for social ideals that they have even proposed new and higher goals for business. They oppose the pathological excesses that mark the development of capitalism and the culture of materialism. They oppose it with a higher stage of development, with new blossoms of an intellectual-moral culture, with self-conscious citizenship and willingness to sacrifice. . . .

It is characteristic of social endeavors in the United States that they do not start so much with the needs of the individual—the needy one—but with the society, the nation. Social workers do more teaching and educating in the higher sense of cultural work, rather than charity work. There are no model institutions to fight against infant mortality as in France, no sanitariums for people with lung diseases as in Germany, no extraordinary orphanages and houses of refuge as in England. The settlements for immigrants in the crowded immigrant quarters are the most peculiar and remarkable sign of the American sense of citizenship—the sign of American social work. They are peculiar and remarkable for more than one reason. First, because of their goals, as centers for immigrants of various nationalities, centers for their education and their sociability, centers that try to turn Galicians and Italians, Jews and Irish, Bohemians and Greeks, into Americans. They try to prevent these immigrants from the lower races, with their low standards of living, from persistently driving a wedge into the American population, as an alien element, threatening the vitality and advancement of the nation with low living standards, cheap labor and wage cutting, bad health, untidiness, and the danger of epidemics, alcoholism, and vice. The community cannot bear these alien elements. Therefore the strangers must be assimilated and brought up to the level of American workers.

It is not so much individual destitution, which is probably less severe among immigrants here than in their native countries, as these social considerations that generate settlement work and determine its direction and goal. Because of the community, the individuals are dealt with, taught the language and the laws of the country, and protected from the exploitation that awaits immigrants in numerous forms. . . . Without knowledge of the customs of the country or the ability to speak the language, a sad fate often awaits the immigrant if there are no friends to protect him and enable him to get to know and use the nation's laws and institutions.

This is one side of settlement work that is different from the social needs and endeavors of most European countries. In Germany, we usually deal only with natives of our own country. We can assume a minimum of knowledge and skills as common property, because of compulsory school attendance and the military. We know that the political parties try to expand their scope of attention beyond the sphere of work and daily life. Our whole welfare system supports the relief of material distress; it attends to the needs of the individual, although social aspects are becoming more and more significant. In America, however, the cultural standard of the whole nation is constantly threatened by the masses of immigrants—around half a million every year, most of whom stay in the cities of the east—if they are not successfully freed from their language barriers and their material, intellectual, and moral isolation.[63]

The settlements are peculiar and remarkable, not only in their goals, but also in their means and methods. Their work is not done as in Germany by large charity organizations of men and women who only spend a fraction of their time doing social work, alongside their occupational and domestic duties and their various other interests. Settlement work—which demands undivided attention from the individual—is done by many people as a life's work and a full-time occupation, often unpaid. Not only single men and women but also couples sacrifice their own homes, even renounce a private, independent sphere and live in a modest room in the social settlement house, in the middle of a crowded immigrant quarter. At Hull House in Chicago, the most important settlement in the United States and the brilliant creation of Jane Addams, there are about fifty inhabitants. According to a cooperative plan, they share the costs of the common household, take their meals at a common table, and spend their free time together in the common living rooms. Some raise the means for their support out of their own pockets, so they can dedicate themselves to settlement work

[63]   In the year of Salomon's visit to the United States, 750,000 immigrants entered the country. In several years during the period 1905–1914, the number was over a million.

GERMAN REFORMERS CONSIDER THE AMERICAN EXAMPLE

completely. Others support themselves with the income of an occupation that allows them to work for the settlement only in the late afternoon and evening.

The communal living of these social workers does not resemble a cloistered life far from the world and its restless bustle, or a quiet island. They live in the midst of crowds of people struggling for survival, where they can get to know their joys and sorrows, their temptations and passions, their strength and helpfulness.

The original idea of the settlement founders is expressed here. Canon Barnett, the director of Toynbee Hall, once said: "In order to love, we have to know the ones we are supposed to love."[64] Only someone who lives with and among the people can recognize and assess their needs and initiate reforms that are not based on unrealistic theories, but are adjusted to the real needs. Indeed, the leading settlement workers—Jane Addams in Chicago, Lillian Wald and Mrs. Simkhowitsch [sic] in New York—can be found in all public offices and administrative bodies; they are in demand as respected members of all government commissions that promote social reforms.[65]

Although these settlement workers, who primarily look for practical results and do not seek any kind of recognition, sometimes do not even publish reports about their work, they are generally perceived as experts on all social problems.

It is typical of the American situation that sex does not matter in this kind of work. Women often hold leadership positions in mixed settlements. It is seen as a natural division of labor that the men do the financial and technical tasks while the women completely assume the intellectual, in a higher sense, the "cultural" tasks. And the effectiveness of the settlements is seen as the highest cultural work. Hull House, the most remarkable settlement, is typical of the social work done in American cities. There, the methods applied are the same as in New York, and the reforms which have been realized reach far beyond the borders of the city.

In an immigrant quarter of Chicago, which is increasingly populated by

---

[64] Samuel Barnett (1844–1913), Anglican priest and social reformer, founded the first settlement, Toynbee Hall, in London's impoverished East End in 1884. It served as a model for settlements in the United States and worldwide. His wife, Henrietta Octavia Rowland (1851–1936), was also a reform activist and remained one of the leaders of the international settlement movement after his death.

[65] Lillian Wald (1867–1940), American public health nurse, settlement founder, and social reformer. In 1895, Wald established New York's Henry Street settlement. A close friend of Jane Addams and Florence Kelley, Wald often hosted guests of the ICW or the WILPF at her settlement. She was a cofounder of the National Child Labor Committee and of the American Union Against Militarism, which later developed into the American Civil Liberties Union.

Mary Simkovitch (1867–1951), American settlement worker and social reformer. The founder of New York's Greenwich House (1902), she became president of the National Federation of Settlements in 1917.

Jews and Italians now that the Irish have left, this splendid institution that developed gradually from modest beginnings is supposed to "provide a center for a higher civic and social life; to institute and maintain educational and philanthropic enterprises, and to investigate and improve the conditions in the industrial districts of Chicago."[66]

At home before I left, my friends and colleagues who know American conditions well told me that Hull House is the greatest attraction of Chicago. In Chicago itself, the words were confirmed: "Nowhere else in the world can you find such great ideas, such an intellectual center, in such a modest milieu and plain surroundings." It is wonderful what social concern has created here with relatively simple means.

The courses of the clubs and the social events of Hull House are visited weekly by nine thousand people, a crowd equivalent to the number of students at the University of Berlin. Yet all of these visitors are entertained and taught by unpaid volunteer workers, and not in large auditoriums where hundreds of people listen to some scientific or political lecture (whether with interest or passivity), but in small groups, in clubs where every limb must work as in a vital organism, to use and develop its power in the service of the whole.

The clubs constitute the main work of the settlements. There are clubs for men, for women, for children, and for families, and they meet once a week or more in the rooms of the settlement. At first they meet under the direction of a social worker, but as soon as possible, the members of the club take over its administrative tasks and explore possibilities for education and entertainment. . . .

These clubs correspond more or less to the efforts that have been started by various groups in Germany.[67] They have similar aims to our kindergartens, vocational training courses, athletic clubs, college extension classes, homes for working women, Young Men's Christian Associations and young women's societies, labor union halls, and schools for home economics. But the neighborhood is the central link in the settlement. The settlement creates and combines all the efforts for a quarter of the city. As some immigrant groups are deeply rooted in the neighborhood, a child can gradually move from the kindergarten and the children's clubs into institutions for adults. The center in which the child seeks education, entertainment, and social life will be maintained throughout his life. Social relationships are created here, not only between the leaders of the clubs and the members, but also among the members, who all belong to the

[66]   Salomon is here quoting from the Hull House charter.
[67]   Salomon is referring here in part to her own work, the Mädchen- und Frauengruppen für soziale Hilfsarbeit in Berlin.

164

working class. People form friendships here which last all their lives. Here, the natural desire for diversion, joy, entertainment, and pleasure is channeled in healthy directions. What this means for the youth can only be understood by those who know the fate of young lads and girls who do not speak the language of the country and who go to bars and dance halls after a hard day's work. What, in fact, can be considered an innocent pleasure— a good meal, a dance—can become a disaster here where temptation awaits foreign, helpless, and inexperienced creatures.

The settlement houses—above all Hull House—put a special emphasis on maintaining a social life and satisfying the need for entertainment through dances and theatrical plays. There are regular dance classes at Hull House because the social workers increasingly see dancing as recuperation and fun for young people who have to do mechanical, monotonous factory work, always straining the same few groups of muscles. In these dance classes, which usually bring together two hundred people, decent middle-class manners and rules are maintained and enforced. These well-organized festivities are not only very good substitutes for public dance halls; they are really an outlet for the high spirits of the youth, which have to be suppressed during the long working day. . . .

The theater is employed as a means for education and discipline. The theater club had the courage to perform dramas by Ibsen, Italians and Greeks performed classical plays in their mother tongues, and the children's and youth theater clubs provided an excellent opportunity to influence language and manners, during the rehearsals.

Finally, a special characteristic of settlement work is that all these social and pedagogical efforts—influenced by the democratic constitution of the country—consciously work toward educating the people to become useful citizens and to be capable of self-administration, conscious of their civil duties, and aware of the use of democratic rights. This happens, according to the practical sense of Americans, not through theories, lectures, or political discussions, but through teaching little children in the clubs to participate in the administrative tasks of their organizations. . . .

All the education, teaching, and social life that the settlement provides the people of the neighborhood serve only one purpose: to win useful citizens for the community.

The creation of a number of charities, and the stimulation of social reforms that only indirectly serve charitable purposes, is only possible because the settlement workers know the needs and troubles of the working people. They establish baths and homes for single, young male and female workers, as well as day nurseries and kindergartens. In Hull House an experiment has recently been started to revive the traditions of craft and folk art that the immigrants remember from their home countries, and to establish a little store where their products are sold.[68] A small museum shows the primitive working methods and the various materials still being used in the textile industries of some Southern European countries and still practiced by the old immigrants. The museum is supposed to create among young factory workers an interest in the development of their industries and their technical equipment, and to put in historical perspective the daily mechanical work process and the creation and development of the products, of which they themselves see only parts.

Most settlement houses are also centers for summer recreation programs. Again, it is characteristic of the American situation, as an immigrant country with a mostly young and healthy population, that establishments for working-class vacations are more important than sanitoriums and summer camps for weak children. Cures seem to be less important than prevention. The great intensity of work within fewer working hours and the hot summer climate make a rest seem desirable even for the healthy worker. This rich country provides money for such purposes more readily than our country, which is only slowly beginning to show some sympathy.

In examining the settlement, one thing should not be neglected. All cultural efforts are generously aided by the people who have benefited from nature's incredible wealth, still hidden in woods and mines. These people not only feed and dress hungry children and support the material needs of the poor, they give of their wealth to satisfy the hungry spirit, and they are not afraid that education and knowledge will make people demanding and dissatisfied. They give money to build settlements, to create a center for social life—a people's home or a club—and they donate with a broad mind and full trust to the social work leaders who have proven themselves capable of carrying out their plans. The social work of the settlement does not have to deal with the depressing money worries that often paralyze us, nor with the petty and meticulous economizing which we German women have to do in our clubs and associations and which takes away much of our power and energy. This rich endowment makes it possible for the settlements to become centers for everyone who is interested in social work or seeks advice, information, and ideas. Doctors, politicians, lawyers, and philanthropists meet here during dinner as guests of the settlement house workers. They want to receive or give, learn or support. Conferences and conventions are held here with people who in some way want to improve the lot of the working people and to enhance the common welfare. Hull

---

[68] The Hull House Labor Museum was established in the tradition of Ruskin's Arts and Crafts Movement, to preserve the traditional skills that immigrants brought from their home countries, both through lectures and practical demonstrations. Addams was especially concerned that the children of immigrants not lose respect for their parents' skills, even if they were of little monetary value in the New World.

GERMAN REFORMERS CONSIDER THE AMERICAN EXAMPLE

House has hosted union meetings and peace conferences as well as conventions of suffrage societies, consumer leagues, and the league for juvenile courts.

The leaders of the settlements have made themselves agents for all the demands that can lead to social reforms. They have helped to create juvenile courts and public playgrounds, they have established libraries and art exhibitions, they have fought for protective legislation and Sunday closing of stores, and they have helped found the School for Social Science and Social Work.[69]

The value and meaning of the settlements for the whole of public life lies in the knowledge of the practical conditions and requirements of the neighborhood that the settlement workers inhabit. A person who has lived and worked in such a house, according to one of the leading women in New York, can never call people "cases" or see them as statistics, but must remember that they are all human beings with the same inclination to do good or bad as oneself. The settlement has failed its mission if it does not plant these beliefs into the consciousness of everyone who works there. Further, it has to communicate that everything the people ask for is included in one demand: "Equal chances in competition, equal opportunities for everyone."

Although we German women have different tasks in social work and use different forms and methods, we can and must learn one thing from the settlement workers: their devotion and their social consciousness, which puts the goal of wanting to help before one's self, and which does not look for wealth and glory, but follows the meaningful words inscribed on the wall of the Hull House auditorium:

> Act well your part—
> There all the honor lies! [English in the original]

---

[69]   The Chicago School of Civics and Philanthropy was a private training school for social workers, established in 1903 by settlement founder Graham Taylor (1851–1938). Salomon was undoubtedly comparing it with her own school, founded only a year before her trip to the United States.

7. A German Translation of *Twenty Years at Hull House*

After the turn of the century, some of the writings of American social justice feminists were translated into German. As a result, German women reformers no longer had to rely on secondhand accounts like Helene Lange's review of Elizabeth Cady Stanton's autobiography or on the rare original that made it to Germany. In addition, visitors from the United States and returning immigrants supplied oral and published accounts of the work of American social reformers. Sometimes Americans sent materials on request, as Jane Addams did to Alice Salomon, Anna Lindemann, and Sister Maria (see documents in Parts II and IV).

The following letters to Jane Addams and the forewords to the German edition of her *Twenty Years at Hull House* point to the importance her book had for German women social reformers. Alice Salomon's letter[70] was part of her sporadic correspondence with Addams after 1909. In the first part of Addams's autobiography, which Salomon reviewed in *Die Frau*, she found many similarities to her own life, most notably their enforced idleness after the end of formal schooling—"the unnatural lives of wealthy girls"—and the efforts of socialist party politicians to win them over. Their admiration led Salomon and a group of Berlin social reformers to secure the German translation rights for *Twenty Years at Hull House*. Else Münsterberg was eager to translate Addams's book. Even without a German version, Salomon would have assigned the book to her students at the Women's School for Social Work, since she expected them to read English.

When Addams's autobiography first appeared in 1910, at least two translators approached her and her publisher, Macmillan, for the German rights, suggesting that a German market existed for the writings of America's leading social reformer. One of them, Friedrich Siegmund-Schultze, had himself founded a settlement in Berlin in 1911; the other, Else Münsterberg, was a member of Salomon's "Mädchen- und Frauengruppen" and the daughter of prominent Berlin alderman and social reformer Emil Münsterberg. It is not clear why Addams decided to grant the permission to Münsterberg. Perhaps she embraced the idea of a translation by a young

---

[70] Alice Salomon to Jane Addams, Berlin December 11, 1911, Jane Addams Papers, SCPC, series 1 (and *JAP*, reel 6).

woman who had lived at the Greenwich House settlement in New York and was thus familiar with the American context, or perhaps Münsterberg simply asked first. Undoubtedly, she had the strong support of Alice Salomon, who knew Addams personally.

Else Münsterberg's letter to Jane Addams[71] stresses the importance of making Addams's writings accessible to a wider German audience. In 1913, the German translation of *Twenty Years at Hull House* was published by Beck in Munich, rather than by the Berlin publisher that Münsterberg alludes to in her letter. Münsterberg's foreword to Addams's autobiography is part of the following selection. The book found a substantial and generally enthusiastic audience. Many reviews stressed Addams's compassionate work in the slums of Chicago and praised her as a model for women around the world.

In her preface to *Zwanzig Jahre sozialer Frauenarbeit in Chicago*,[72] Alice Salomon introduces Jane Addams as an "outstanding social politician in the United States," a position no German woman was even close to at the time. She identified with Addams's motives for her work, particularly with her concept of social work as a calling rather than a profession, a concept they both defended as the field professionalized.

Alice Salomon to Jane Addams

11. Dec. 1911

Dear Miss Addams:

I suppose you will not remember my name and that we met some years ago when the International Council of Women held their meeting at Toronto and when we all came to Chicago. And I will not take much of your time, but I feel bound to express how deeply your book "Twenty Years in Hull House" has moved me and how very very grateful I am to you for it. It is a book of power—and it truly gives strength to know how you have fought with all the inner as much as with the outward difficulties, which all of us who try to help and to better the social conditions have to meet.

I really came across the book by mere chance—and it is a shame that

---

[71] Else Münsterberg to Jane Addams, Berlin, September 28, 1912, Jane Addams Papers, SCPC (and *JAP*, reel 7); translated by Sally Robertson. There is a notation on the manuscript: "?? submitted to Macmillan Oct. 26. Permission granted by McM. Oct. 29."

[72] Alice Salomon's and Else Münsterberg's forewords to *Zwanzig Jahre sozialer Frauenarbeit in Chicago* were translated by Corinna Hörst and the editors. Italics indicate emphasis in the original.

1911 letter from Alice Salomon to Jane Addams. Swarthmore College Peace Collection.

people hear nothing about American books in Germany. Miss Münster-berg, whose father was a very close friend of mine, talked to me about the usefulness of a translation—and in order to adorse [endorse] her I sent for it—and literally spoken I have lived under its impression since long weeks [*sic*]. I have written something about it for our magazine "Die Frau" and I shall send a copy to you as soon as it is out and I hope and trust that you will feel that you are well understood at this side of the Atlantic as well as

GERMAN REFORMERS CONSIDER THE AMERICAN EXAMPLE

on the other.[73] It was all like a dream to me to read of your life and work. It is all so different from what we have to do here—and yet (I have worked since 14 years in Berlin along very similarly [sic] lines) I feel, that the real conflicts and difficulties are just the same. "The subjective needs" of settlements or of social work as we do it almost express the same thoughts which have been the "Leitmotiv" of my life since I was first awakened to see the way out of the unnatural lives of the wealthy girls—and all the different attempts of the Socialists and "single-tax people" and others brought back all the days of my youth, when "Bebel" and "Damaschke" and all these people thought it worth while to try and convert me to their creeds.[74] And much more than that: all the same thoughts and troubles about the way of really helping our poorer brothers, the constant difficulty, how to arrange our own life according to our belief in social justice. But after all this the difference between your strength of mind and soul—and my poor small attempts. The difference between what you have done for your country and my small influences.

But I know I must not keep you any longer. I only wish to let you know how wonderfully your book will help us in Germany. I think of reading it together and discussing some of the problems next winter with the advanced pupils of my school for Social Service. I know it will help many of them in their struggles and doubts.

I hope Hull House will have a peaceful Xmas—not one with a coal-makers strike as we are going to have, it seems. And I do wish with all my heart your work will be successful during the coming year.

Will you kindly remember me to all Hull House residents who know me: Miss Lathrop, Miss Abbott, the Borosinis, etc.[75]

Yours very truly
Alice Salomon

[73] Salomon's article appeared as "Das Lebensbild einer Bürgerin," *Die Frau* 19 (1911/12): 200–229 and 290–99.

[74] For Bebel, see Part I, document 3, Florence Kelley Wischnewetsky, "Movement among German Working Women," note 15.

Adolf Damaschke (1865–1935), German politician and economist, had fought for property tax reform since the turn of the century and later influenced the sections on property rights in the Weimar constitution.

[75] Julia Clifford Lathrop (1858–1932), American social worker, reformer, and first head of the Federal Children's Bureau (1912–1921).

Edith Abbott (1876–1957), American social reformer and social work educator; Grace Abbott (1878–1939), American social reformer, head of the Children's Bureau from 1921 to 1934. Both sisters were living at Hull House when Salomon visited there. It is unclear which of them Salomon means.

The Borosinis were probably the family of the Austrian Victor Borosini (no dates available), a Hull House resident before 1914.

Else Münsterberg to Jane Addams

Berlin, W. 10 Dörnbergstr. 7
September 28, 1912

My very dear Miss Addams,

A year ago, when you gave me your permission through Miss Smith to translate your book "Twenty Years" [English in the original], I set myself the goal of expressing my gratitude by finishing the translation. It is now finished, but I cannot send it to you yet, because I have not been able to find a publisher for it. Now it finally seems that I will succeed in reaching an agreement with a Berlin publisher. I have another request of you: to authorize the printing of the German version of the book without illustrations, with only your picture, namely the picture which I am enclosing with this letter, which Dr. Alice Salomon gave me, and which she clipped out of "Life and Labor" [English in the original].[76] May I request that you send me the original photograph from which this picture was made? For I fear that this picture belonging to Dr. Alice Salomon would not reproduce well. The publisher insists on omitting the other illustrations because they would increase the price of the book to such an extent that it would hinder its sale in Germany.

The winter program of the Women's School for Social Work in Berlin, directed by Dr. Alice Salomon, has just appeared. It includes a course called "Problems in Social Work: with reference to Jane Addams' book 'Twenty Years at Hull House [English in the original].' " In this way, the things that captured the interest and enthusiasm of those of us who know the book will now be made accessible to wider circles. May it bear fruit!

I cannot close without thanking you once again for granting me permission to work on your book. From the beginning to the end, I have not ceased to be grateful for that.

With warm regards, I am sincerely yours,
Else Münsterberg

Twenty Years of Women's Social Work in Chicago

Preface

In England, certain kinds of books are called "books of power" [English in the original]. They are the books that bring everything strong and great to life in the reader. They are the books that empower him to new thoughts and action. Jane Addams's book, made available to a wide German audi-

---

[76] *Life and Labor* was the periodical of the Chicago Women's Trade Union League.

ence by this translation, is such a "book of power" [English in the original]. It is the book of an important person, who has recognized goals beyond herself as the duty and essence of her life, who holds the thought of social service high and sacred like a confession of faith.

It will win new supporters for this creed. It will strengthen the convictions of socially inclined people, and it will lead them back to the right path in hours of doubts and turmoil.

The book is a *human* book in the best and deepest sense of the word. It is the autobiography of a woman who is revered in her home town of Chicago and is called its "first and foremost citizen," a woman who is considered an outstanding social politician in the United States of America. Her opinion is heard by the highest administrative bodies in her country, but what she says also holds true for the masses of the American people. The book is an autobiography that tells about the influences of her youth, her activities, and her work during the best years of her life, between thirty and fifty, told by herself. She looks back from the peak of a rich human life, to render an account for herself and others. It has been a human life rich with inner, not outer sensations, rich and delectable in the biblical sense, meaning troubles and hard work. But troubles and hard work were not the result of an outer necessity or an early developed determination and conviction, but the fruit of an inner struggle about the great questions of life and the course of humanity.

First there was this fight and struggle with her own soul, a restless youth which did not alternate high spirits and great social efforts with a life of self-improvement and a cultivated idleness, but combined them, like the youth of many human beings. Then the moment of awakening, when, forever inextinguishable, her task in life appeared before her eyes with a power that forced her into action. And finally the twenty years of social work with ever new problems, doubts, battles, and victories. All this is so true to life, so human and plain that it strikes a chord in every human being.

Because of this the book deserves the attention of the German audience. Because of this, its contents appeal to the educated of all countries.

Those who have participated in any form of social or social-political effort in Germany during the past twenty years, those who have followed the various attempts at solving the social problems of the developing industrial state, will read Jane Addams's account *objectively* and with great interest. It was due to her personality and activity that—under similar conditions— charity and social policies were created on untouched terrain in a rapidly developing industrial city that did not have any traditions of social assistance. The same necessities that drive us in Germany have led her from charity into social politics; from the desire to be a culture bearer for the poor classes to the task of first satisfying their primitive needs; from work-

173

ing according to her own methods and goals to accepting and appreciating other directions in charity work; from discussions with religious and political circles that tried to win her over, to her own firm worldview. The book will enrich our lives because it touches on all the experiences that we have had to undergo in our own social work and on those issues where we are still trying to find our way. Some readers will find a piece of their own experiences or an account that will make them understand their own development so much better. Nevertheless, our own shortcomings and weaknesses become clear when we measure ourselves against the personality of Jane Addams!

But the power that the book *radiates* lies precisely in the fact that it goes beyond a strictly businesslike account of the social problems and successes of her work. It shows us what a strong and pure person can create and that even strong and efficient people go through doubts and disappointments. The power that makes the book *vivid* lies in the fact that it teaches us that great things can be achieved in the social field. Yet they can *only* be achieved, if one contributes not only time, money, heart, and intellect—but completely gives his own self, *his entire personality*.

The leitmotiv that is interwoven with the book is written above the text in invisible characters—"Only those who lose themselves can find themselves."

Jane Addams's book is religious and secular at the same time. *Religious and secular* in the sense that all religion, all piety, for her means only that one has to prove himself in the world, that the lives of the faithful must rise to meet religious conscience, that faith needs to be converted into action, that one's beliefs and one's life must be unified.

The book is an awakening! May its words ring in many hearts!

Summer 1913
Alice Salomon

Preface

The original title of the book before you is "Twenty Years at Hull House." In the United States the institution of Hull House does not require further explanation. We avoided the name in the title of the German edition and substituted the activity that has its center at Hull House. "Twenty Years of Women's Social Work in Chicago!" Jane Addams herself says that it might be a little early to look back after only twenty years. "One's fiftieth year is indeed an impressive milestone at which one may well pause to take an accounting. . . . I have found it difficult to make a faithful account of the years since the autumn of 1889 when, without any preconceived social theories or economic views, I came to live in an industrial district in Chicago." Why was the book written in spite of the difficulties of judging objectively the people and conditions that one is close to? "Because settlements have multiplied so easily in the United States I hoped that a simple statement of an earlier effort, including the stress and storm, might be of value in their interpretation and possibly clear them of a certain charge of superficiality. The unworthy motive was a desire to start a 'backfire,' as it were, to extinguish two biographies of myself . . . that made life in a settlement all too smooth and charming."

With Jane Addams's permission I have reproduced her book in an abridged version; however, I only left out those passages that bear little interest to the German reader.

Jane Addams has dedicated the book to the memory of her father. I translated it in memory of mine.

Summer 1913
Else Münsterberg

8. A German Activist Responds
to *Twenty Years*

Else Münsterberg's translation of *Twenty Years at Hull House* had a considerable audience in Germany, especially but not exclusively in social reform circles, as the following selection[77] and the letters by Sister Maria in Part IV show. Anna Lindemann's enthusiastic response is an example of how the dialogue between German and American women reached into the everyday lives of leaders in the German suffrage movement.

Anna Lindemann's connections to Chicago social reformers were manifold. Mary McDowell (1854–1936), head resident of the University Settlement, visited her during a trip to Germany in 1911, and was impressed by Lindemann's work for the national and international suffrage movements as well as by her English skills. Jane Addams and Lindemann met at the 1913 congress of the International Woman Suffrage Association in Budapest. After her return to Chicago, Addams provided Lindemann with several of her books, as she continued to do when friends and colleagues abroad asked for them. But Lindemann was disappointed in her hope of meeting Addams again at the 1915 congress of the IWSA in Berlin, since the German committee (under Marie Stritt) withdrew its invitation after war broke out in August 1914.

---

[77] Anna Lindemann to Jane Addams, April 24, 1914, Jane Addams Papers, SCPC, series 1 (and *JAP*, reel 7). Italics indicate emphasis in the original.

Frontispiece and title page of German edition of *Twenty Years at Hull House*. This copy was originally part of the collection at Friedrich Siegmund-Schultze's settlement in Berlin.

GERMAN REFORMERS CONSIDER THE AMERICAN EXAMPLE

Zwanzig Jahre sozialer Frauenarbeit in Chicago

Von

Jane Addams

Berechtigte Übersetzung von Else Münsterberg

Nebst dem Bildnis der Verfasserin und
einem Geleitwort von Alice Salomon

C. H. Beck'sche Verlagsbuchhandlung Oskar Beck
München 1913

Anna Lindemann to Jane Addams

Stuttgart-Degerloch
April 24th, 1914

My Dear Miss Addams,

Among my faults there is one that almost looks like a virtue. But it is a very vicious little devil in its true nature. I always want to do things well—and the amount of procrastination that leads to can hardly be conceived! When I got the books you sent me last summer, I wanted to read at least one of them before I wrote and I started at once. But then one evil befell me after the other—my lady-help fell ill and I had to nurse her, the housemaid was called home, and at the same time the garden was full of fruit to be preserved, my chief yearly work had to be done for the municipal yearbook which comes out in the autumn, *and* elections went on for our large sick-fund, for which women have votes and eligibility.[78] I do not remember a more horrid summer and autumn in all my life. In the end I broke down in health and the doctor sent me away the day before Christmas. I was so dead tired that I had *no* feeling but pure relief at the thought that somebody else must do all my work for the Christmas festivities! I was away two months, and then at last I found time and strength to read "20 Years [at] Hull House." I cannot tell you how much I enjoyed it. The subject matter of the book is most intensely interesting. It is interesting where your experience is the same as we have in the old world, and even more interesting where you are dealing with the problems special to your own country and own city. But far above all this I enjoyed meeting you yourself in your book! You have enlarged the word "American" for me. I know it is only my mistake and the slightness of my experience, but I did not know before there would be in America people of your type. Everybody I think must love both you and your father in the early parts of the book; and during all the varied experience of the later times I still see the same little girl, wondering, observing; it has been a great delight to me to see how you have taken each new experience, gone through it to the very end, made the mistakes enthusiastic and believing minds must make, and come out of it—having gained for yourself and your work what there was to be gained and leaving behind with some gentle irony at your own former self all that had proved illusory. I just marvel at the way you have kept free from any reactionary spirit! It seems to me that there is in you something of what we consider the very best in our German character—the nature of the true student,

[78]   After the introduction of mandatory health insurance for some occupational groups in 1884, sick funds were administered locally or in the different branches of industry. The exact date when women received active and passive voting rights for the sick funds has not been established, but the funds constituted an important exception to the general disfranchisement of women in Germany.

who devoutly and reverently seeks truth and never himself—I have left my copy for a time in England, to be read and enjoyed by some of the nicest women in the world, the "Sisters of the People" in Katherine House, Fitzroy Square.[79] It makes me quite glad to think how many thoughts will be going your way from that little corner, a home of very pure devotion to mankind. Since then, I have heard many people speak with admiration of your book and your work, I have read a number of reviews of the German edition. But I just want to tell you: they all *admire* you and think your work wonderful. But I feel glad and happy that I have met you and have now come to know you much better still by your own book (even its literary shortcomings have made me understand your nature still better!), and if I am to tell you the outcome of it all, it is that I have not troubled to stop at admiration, I have gone straight on to loving you, dear Miss Addams!

I hope you are well and living and working to the joy of all around you (we all are around you, you know!), and the better for your journey to Europe last year! Shall we see you at the Berlin Congress in 1915?

Mit herzlichen Grüßen
Ihre[80]
Anna Lindemann

---

[79] Katherine House was a women's settlement in London. Although the English settlement movement was a predecessor and in many respects a model for the American movement, women were not as central to the English movement.

[80] Translation: "With warm regards, yours."

PART III

THE DIALOGUE CHANGES

DURING WORLD WAR I

The American delegation to the 1915 congress at The Hague. Jane Addams is second from left in the first row; Alice Hamilton is second from left standing in second row; Emily Balch is on the far left in the third row; Madeline Doty is sixth from the right in the last row (wearing beret); Mary Chamberlain is fourth from right in last row. Swarthmore College Peace Collection.

1. A Sympathetic Journalist Describes German Women's War Efforts

The following article,[1] published in a California suffrage periodical in November 1914, showed how war changed the terms of the dialogue: women's social welfare work could be put to belligerent as well as peaceful purposes. Mabel Harding, a former correspondent for a British newspaper who probably lived in Berlin, praised the war-oriented welfare work of German women, including Alice Salomon.[2] Her article was consistent with the policy of the German government of encouraging foreign correspondents to make the German case in neutral countries, especially the United States. The goal of preserving American neutrality was important to German policymakers, who hoped to keep the vast material and human resources of the United States out of the war as long as possible. Given the sizable German-American population and the respect for German culture in the United States, this goal seemed plausible. It was complicated, however, by reports of Belgian civilians suffering under German occupying troops.

As part of this battle over American public opinion, American correspondents based in Brussels or Berlin were invited to follow the German army. Harding pursued a different path and sought to engage the sympathies of American middle-class women by describing the social welfare work of German women. In this way her article illuminated the centrality of women's welfare work within the construction of the modern state both in Germany and the United States.

Established in San Francisco in February 1912, shortly after the enactment of woman suffrage in California, *The Woman Citizen* was designed to help women "use the newly acquired ballot intelligently and effectively for the furtherance of their individual and collective interests." Like other suffrage periodicals, *The Woman Citizen* declared itself "absolutely independent of any and all political organizations and associations." Consistent with that nonpartisan stance, and with the deep investment of women's public culture in peace organizations, *The Woman Citizen* in 1914 and 1915

[1] Mabel Harding, "German Women and the War," *The Woman Citizen*, November 1914.
[2] London *Standard*, a daily newspaper founded in 1873.

printed several articles critical of the European war. In the same issue in which Harding's article appeared, another declared: "Civilization here as well as there will be injured and delayed." Thus the appearance of Harding's article, which uncritically praised women's social welfare work within the German war effort, was all the more surprising. Frequent articles about women in foreign lands help account for its publication, as might the large German-American community in California. Merchants with German names advertised regularly in *The Woman Citizen* and might have encouraged the publication of an article praising the German home front.

German Women and the War
by Mabel Harding
Formerly Correspondent of [the] "London Standard"

The German Red Cross sent out its first call for women volunteers in August, and the response was a striking tribute to the organization and patriotic enthusiasm of German women.[3] In Berlin alone over 40,000 women responded in a few days; such was the extraordinary promptness of their response that it almost seemed that practical womankind dropped everything to fill in their country's emergency while time was precious. Women clerks left their offices, school girls cut short their courses at the gymnasium, cooks and servants left good positions, and even char women in the government buildings left their pails on the stairs the morning the call was sent out, wiped their hands on their coarse aprons and offered their services at the hundreds of little offices under the sign of the Black Eagle.[4] What of it if everyone couldn't nurse? They had it all worked out in their minds. Nursing entailed a lot of cleaning, sick men wanted the right kind of meals, and men in a hundred difficulties wanted a woman's hand. Within three days the examining doctors had drafted into active service 3,000 of the most desirable volunteers, while the rest were dovetailed into innumerable services, under not only the Red Cross or as nurses, but a score or more of other volunteer societies which rapidly organized to meet the changing emergencies of the times.

The Women's Red Cross organization throughout Germany has worked out as admirably as it did in Berlin. It is a complete and efficient micro-

[3]   The International Red Cross was founded in 1859 by the Swiss Henri Dunant to help victims of war. In 1866, German organizations with origins in the early-nineteenth-century Napoleonic Wars formed the "Patriotic Women's Associations of the Red Cross" ("Vaterländische Frauenvereine vom Roten Kreuz"). At its second conference in Berlin three years later, the association committed itself to assistance in peacetime and consequently became one of Germany's major charity organizations. During World War I, roughly 118,000 women and 133,000 men worked for the German Red Cross.
[4]   The heraldic animal of the Hohenzollern.

cosm of the Germany army. Divided by the Kingdoms and Duchies into eight separate organizations it is now controlled by a large central committee with headquarters at Berlin, which is composed in turn of representatives not only of the various Red Cross organizations, but of many kindred affiliated bodies. This centralization enables it today to set its machinery in motion all over the country, and in an incredibly short space of time, to mobilize, besides the volunteers, a fully qualified army nursing service that has been trained under military inspection. These branch organizations, however, control their own funds and activities, and also the activities of their affiliated societies. It is through these affiliated societies that the German Red Cross is perhaps the most varied and comprehensive of any country in the world. Besides the supervision of its large and splendidly equipped hospitals, its training schools, clinics, dispensaries and ambulance stations, it controls much baby welfare and care community work, home nursing, visiting and relief work. Just like the Red Cross organization itself every affiliated body has to conform with the standards of the military regulations in the matter of nursing. Consequently, the volunteer worker who undertakes the duties of home nursing, welfare work or visiting, is as much at the top-notch of true German efficiency as her paid professional sister of the actual army service or on the great hospital staffs. . . .

But it is not only in active service in immediate connection with the fighting that German women are showing their powers of effective organization. Again, with the knowledge that the centralization of tangent forces means an efficient system of relief, they have welded their great unions and suffrage societies into a Women's National Service League.[5] Here, working together in admirably organized co-operation, we find the suffrage unions, the National Council of Women, the Union of Women Workers, and the Social Service organizations.[6] To them has been handed over the great work of caring for the wives and families of the soldiers at the front. Their representatives confer with the official relief bureaus and city councils. The employment bureaus are under their control, and feasible schemes

[5] During the first week of the war, the BDF, religious and social democratic women's organizations as well as the Patriotic Women's Association of the Red Cross (Vaterländische Frauenvereine), created the Women's National Service League (Nationaler Frauendienst) to coordinate the voluntary social work of women from all classes. The organization worked closely with local bureaucracies and private charities, but also organized talks and published pamphlets on women's part in the German war effort. The founding of the Nationaler Frauendienst was proof that the "domestic truce" all parties in the Reichstag had agreed upon was not confined to male politics.
[6] By "National Council of Women," Harding probably means the "League of German Women's Associations" (Bund Deutscher Frauenvereine). By "Union of Women Workers," she probably means the social democratic women's organizations. Like the majority of the SPD, social democratic women pledged to keep a "domestic truce" ("Burgfrieden") after the war broke out and, at least on the local level, joined bourgeois and church women's organizations in the war effort.

for the prevention of unemployment among the women workers of the country and soldiers' families are being put through under their active management. Now is their greatest opportunity in a generation to show the value of women's organization and their comprehension of their country's needs. They have stepped into the breach caused by the withdrawal of the masculine population, and are giving the lie as never before to Bismarck's never-forgotten platitude: "War is none of women's business."[7] To the Kaiser, also, they are proving that Kirche, Küche, and Kinder do not entirely fill the horizon of German women, and that it is a very fortunate thing for him today, at any rate, that they have not taken his sage advice and kept only to these essentially feminine occupations.[8]

Without the women's co-operation in many other ways Germany would be having a very bad time indeed. It is their philosophical adaptation of the present crisis alone that has enabled the domestic and retail trade of the country to carry on its increasingly desperate struggle for existence, while in the harvesting emergencies of the past two months they have unquestionably saved millions of marks to Germany's fast depleting larder. Whole fields of corn all over the country have been bound and stacked by women workers, aided by the younger children, and the earth prepared for autumn crops of root vegetables.[9] No special appeal had been sent broadcast throughout the country for them to undertake this work; they just knew it had to be done—and so it was done.

Meanwhile, the National Council of Women, working in co-operation with the National Service League, is endeavoring to solve the women's unemployment problem. Large workrooms have been opened where the destitute are employed in making clothing for the fighters. Women who have children to care for or who are unable to go out are humanely supplied with work at home and paid the regular rate for home work. In a good number of instances these "amateur" home workers are absolutely incompetent to turn out satisfactory work and naturally find it hard to compete with the regular workers. Shirts which no man could get into without help, socks without heels, are the output of some of these amateurs. Therefore, another class of voluntary helpers has been formed to go round and show the incompetents how to knit and sew. Now, by an Imperial order, clothing must be cut according to army regulations, and garments not conforming to these are rigorously excluded from the commissariat wagons.

Another responsibility which the Women's National Service League has taken upon itself is the regulation of the price of food. Like the Housewives' League of America, its members are keeping a tight lookout on the

[7]   Otto von Bismarck (1815–1898), prime minister of Prussia, founder and first chancellor of the German empire (1873–1890).
[8]   The kaiser was William II (1859–1941), German emperor and king of Prussia (1888–1918). "Kirche, Küche, Kinder" means "church, kitchen, children."
[9]   By "corn," Harding means wheat.

THE DIALOGUE CHANGES DURING WORLD WAR I

market prices, visiting the shops and ascertaining the purchase prices of food, and are advising the city councils on matters of dietary [sic].[10] Professional household economists are visiting women in their homes in order to show them how to make nourishing dishes from cheap materials, classes are being held at which the value of foodstuffs are demonstrated, while excellent lessons on stretching the penny to its utmost value are enabling mothers with the thinnest of purses to just make both ends meet. . . .

The Kaiserin, who with her daughter and daughter-in-laws, is perhaps the busiest woman in Germany at the present time, goes the round of hospitals nearly every day, meets the incoming trains with the wounded soldiers, God-speeds the outgoing men.[11] She also consults with the women's committees on plans for the prevention of unemployment and the care of the children and wives of the combatants. The Kaiserin's visits have brought her many revelations. While unofficially visiting at one of the large free meal depots one day she noticed a very old woman waiting in the crowd for her meal ticket. She went up to her and asked her how many sons she had in battle. "Nine," came the answer. "Ah," said the Kaiserin, "you have given more than I have, for I have but seven," and she kissed the old woman's cheeks and went away. . . .

And it is not only the poor who are being catered for. In the Kurfürstenstrasse, Berlin's Fifth Avenue, a band of society women have opened a suite of beautifully arranged rooms for the benefit of free-lance journalists, actresses, writers, stenographers and secretaries, who, owing to the war are having just as hard a time as the families of the combatants to make both ends meet. Every day from twelve till two these women entertain numbers of these hard-pressed better-class workers as their guests to a substantial luncheon. This kind of help is typical of the innate good sense of the German women who know where to differentiate between charity and tactful assistance. The collection of walking-sticks is another war duty which has been taken up by women of leisure. Districts are canvassed on the house to house basis for any sticks not actually in use. They are then collected and conveyed to the hospitals for the benefit of the wounded soldiers. Thousands have already been dispatched, but the trainloads of wounded men crowding into the capital and other large cities render the collection a daily task.

In every occupation, in every walk of life, the women of the Fatherland

[10]   The Housewives' League was founded in 1911 by Mrs. Julian Heath, at one time the chair of the Jacob Riis Settlement House and of the New York City Federation of Women's Clubs' home economics department. The purpose of the League was to enforce sanitary laws and other retail regulations by making housewives into inspectors.

[11]   The kaiserin was Auguste-Viktoria (1858–1921), wife of William II. During the war, Auguste-Viktoria more than ever served as a model for German women and was especially praised for her hands-on approach. Her tireless work undoubtedly encouraged upper-class women to engage in the war effort.

are doing their level best to help the men folk in the great crisis through which they are passing. Not only are these German women thinking and helping in the present, they are looking forward with increasing attentiveness to the future. They are asking themselves what it will mean to them when thousands and thousands of the flower of German manhood are rendered crippled and helpless, while many thousands more will never return to their country to take up their responsibilities and duties. To the women of Germany the rebuilding of the country will be dedicated in one of the crucial periods of her history. Today, Germany possesses nearly 10,000,000 women bread winners, tomorrow she will possess many more. The terrible depletion among the men must necessarily open to women in the future unprecedented and unsuspected opportunities in the new Germany. Their responsibility as heads of families will be increased, too. And most of all, it will be seen whether the Government will recognize the services rendered by women in the time of war by granting them some of the privileges and rights they have so long unsuccessfully demanded—or just done without. Already in Germany is growing the feeling among progressive women that after the war is over the great awakening that all women will have received will be the commencement of a new era for German womanhood. A new world of civic duties will devolve upon them. The suffragists already herald the new opportunity. That is why they have just opened this month in Berlin a school for women under the directorship of Dr. Alice Salomon, of the National Council of Women. Here the citizen duties of women together with the work they can perform on public care committees and councils are being most ably expounded, and lastly, under the tuition of Dr. Gertrud Bäumer, one of the most prominent and progressive of German suffragists, the possibilities that women will have to face after the war are being canvassed with great frankness and the assurance of power already theirs.

War is a terrible medium to bring about women's participation in the affairs of their country, but in Olive Schreiner's fine phrase from "Women and Labor," "On that day, when woman takes her place beside the man in the governance and arrangement of external affairs of her race will also be that day heralded the death of war as a means of arranging human differences." [12] If this be true, then let every woman bend this crisis to the good that clearly begins to appear, even from the appalling horror of this time of fratricidal murder. The spiritual bond which unites the progressive women of all nations should be strengthened by the universal suffering

[12] Olive Schreiner (1855–1920), British (South African) writer, feminist, pacifist, and social reformer. Schreiner was a delegate of the aborted mission of British women to the Peace Congress at the Hague in 1915. *Women and Labour* (1911) was her most influential political treatise.

THE DIALOGUE CHANGES DURING WORLD WAR I

which the war entails, and enable them to gird on their armor and wage war against WAR.

★   ★   ★

Patience, have faith and thy prayers shall be answered.—Longfellow

2. German Radical Women
Organize for Peace

Lida Gustava Heymann and Anita Augspurg were for many years the leading figures of the radical wing of the bourgeois German women's movement. Advocating higher education, protection for working women, and woman suffrage, raising their voices against the sexual double standard, they turned to international peace work in 1914. This account of their wartime activities was written after their exile from Germany in 1933, when the Nazis came to power, and they, as supporters of the Weimar government and as pacifists, were vulnerable to imprisonment. In Switzerland at the time, they decided to stay and never returned to Germany. In the following years, they jointly drafted their memoir, first published in 1977.[13] Without access to any personal papers or to their archives, which were destroyed by the National Socialists, Augspurg and Heymann had to rely on their recollections. Although the memoir is written from the perspective of their later life, it offers a compelling account of their experiences during World War I, including the organization of peace conferences by German social justice feminists and by socialist women. No American women attended the socialist conference, but their presence was well-noted at the conference that Heymann and Augspurg attended.

Women's Work for International Reconciliation and Job Creation
Lida Gustava Heymann and Anita Augspurg

Throughout the war years, we always placed international reconciliation in the foreground of the absolutely necessary social work. Everyone who came into contact with us was influenced in this sense. The boundless mis-

---

[13] From Lida Gustava Heymann and Anita Augspurg, *Erlebtes, Erschautes. Deutsche Frauen kämpfen für Freiheit, Recht und Frieden* (What we lived through, what we saw. German women fight for freedom, women's rights and peace), ed. Margit Twellmann (Frankfurt: Helmer Verlag, 1992), pp. 137–50. Translated by Tammy Huck. Italics indicate emphasis in the original. Reprinted courtesy of Ulrike Helmer Verlag. The memoir was first published in 1977.

ery of the countless, completely destitute German refugees who had been driven out of foreign lands, as well as that of the female intellectual and manual laborers in Germany, had forced us to assist in the social arena. But many of us soon became aware that through our welfare services and creating work for women, we were more or less indirectly prolonging the war. Those of us who recognized this soon turned to exclusively political activity, which we had promoted, despite all peril, since the beginning of the war, as much as is possible during wartime. Any public statement against the war was impossible. All of the German women's organizations, including the social democratic ones, had fallen prey to the national war frenzy; they devoted themselves completely to the war effort. They could not be counted on for political action. General meetings could be held only in some local groups of the German Union for Woman Suffrage in order to thoroughly discuss political and pacifist themes. At such meetings, all the events of the war were discussed and strongly criticized in the spirit of international solidarity. Through resolutions and petitions[14] to the Reichstag, we raised sharp protests against the German invasion of Belgium and against all the rapes and barbarities by civil and military authorities during the four-year war, insofar as they came to our attention, as well as against the annexation desires which soon emerged. Heated discussions occurred at these meetings, which took place in Hamburg, Bremen, Breslau, Frankfurt, Munich, Stuttgart, and several smaller towns, for some of our members as well had gradually fallen prey to the general war psychosis so that numerous resignations followed. Spies sneaked into the meetings, which were soon prohibited by the government. After that, we met in our homes, but even there the spies knew how to find the way and inform on us. From year to year, from month to month, greater difficulties arose.

Despite it all, we remained in constant contact not only with the women of the neutral but also of the warring countries. In October 1914, a letter was directed to the women of all countries, which expressed the solidarity of German women with those of other countries and which made it clear that men alone governed the fates of peoples and ruled over war and peace, and that the women of all nations, ever since matriarchy was displaced by patriarchy, had to bear the same fate of suffering. It closed with the words, "We want to extend our hands to each other beyond the World War, greet each other with mourning, bowed heads, more united than ever in the knowledge that only when women are freed and help rule their states will the world remain spared the recurrence of a similarly horrible experience."

Communications intended for the public were exchanged with women

[14] The exact text of all the protests and petitions can be found in "Women's International Reconciliation Work During the World War," available from I. Fr. Fr. Fr. Geneva, Rive 3, case postale 174. [This footnote is in the original.]

of the warring countries at Christmas, Easter, and on any occasion when opportunities arose during the war years. To publish such letters involved difficulties. Only too often, the military authorities prohibited printing, and so they had to be distributed by illegal means.

Pre-Conference and Preparation Work for an International Women's Congress for Ending the World War

The written communication with Aletta Jakobs [*sic*] continued, but for our ever-growing unrest, everything proceeded far too slowly.[15] Every day, countless people were killed, tortured, in trenches and military hospitals, and for what? The hope that the war, as was predicted in Germany at the beginning, would be over by Christmas 1914 and the "victorious German troops" would be home again, had long since vanished. Finally, on February 12 and 13, 1915, women met in Amsterdam for a preliminary discussion to convene a women's congress *against the war*. It had turned out that not one of the international women's organizations was still aware of what it owed to its international spirit. They all failed as a group, only individual women did not; a new women's Internationale arose from them: women's solidarity had thus proven itself, despite everything! . . .

[A] pre-conference drafted a provisional program for the International Women's Congress, which was to be held from April 28 to May 1, 1915, at The Hague. The congress's goal was threefold: to represent a women's protest against the war and its human butchery; to proclaim the demand of equal political rights for women; and to try to bring about the end of the war. Two principles were established and thereafter strictly adhered to: discussions about relative national responsibility for the present war and the manner in which it was being conducted were not allowed, nor were resolutions calling for a regulation, that is, humanization of the conduct of the war. The conference instructed the Dutch women to issue invitations to women of all countries.

Almost everywhere, publicity had to be arranged with the greatest caution. We had scarcely ten weeks for the preparatory work; at a time when the mail functioned poorly, letters were often checked or disappeared, and the military issued new traffic and other regulations daily, the work was made very difficult.

[15]   Aletta Jacobs (1854–1929), Dutch physician and suffragist. The first woman doctor in the Netherlands, Jacobs fought against bad working and housing conditions, advocated birth control and family planning, and was involved in the campaign for woman suffrage beginning in the 1890s. She was central in organizing the Women's Peace Congress at The Hague, and afterward ran the office of the International Women's Committee for a Permanent Peace in Amsterdam. In August and September of 1915 she traveled to the United States; in 1919 she accompanied Jane Addams to Germany.

The few days in Amsterdam had newly revived our courage to face life and our capacity for work. . . .

Twenty-eight German women came to the congress at The Hague in April; a much larger number would have participated if lack of pecuniary means had not hindered them on the one hand, and, on the other, the military authorities in different towns had not denied passports at the last moment, as for example to Frida Perlen in Stuttgart, with the explanation "that your visit to The Hague must be prohibited, because the assumption is justified that German interests will be endangered by your participation." [16]

The German women were in a difficult position with the mood that prevailed against Germany in Holland because of the German conduct of the war, that is, only in public, not with their international colleagues, who agreed with them that soldiers are as alike as peas in pods and that a nation's women cannot be held responsible for military atrocities. The conduct of the German women during the congress again stirred sympathetic feelings among the Dutch for the German people. In any case, as we later learned, the German envoys reported to their government that the German women attending the congress had made a good impression for Germany. Besides, the presence of twenty-eight women proved that there were real pacifists among the women in Germany who were ready to stand up for their convictions, even at a time in which they were viewed as traitors by their own people for this reason.

Twelve countries—Belgium, Canada, Denmark, Germany, Great Britain, Holland, Italy, Norway, Austria, Sweden, Hungary, and the United States of America—were represented at the congress by fifteen hundred delegates. . . .

Jane Addams had declared herself willing to preside at the congress. She made the voyage to Europe with forty American women on the *Noordam* and was supposed to arrive in Holland four days before the congress began.[17] The *Noordam* was stopped in Dover, and it appeared that Jane Addams and the American delegates would be detained. Nevertheless, they arrived shortly before the opening date.

The International Women's Congress at The Hague in 1915

Only those who took part in the preliminary work and the congress itself can imagine the difficulties, the spiteful opposition, the intensely burning chauvinism, that had to be overcome everywhere; only they can appreciate what it meant that a congress of this size was successfully convened during the war, a congress for ending the World War and against all wars.

[16]   See also Part III, document 3.
[17]   The American delegation was made up in all of forty-seven women.

THE DIALOGUE CHANGES DURING WORLD WAR I

Many international and national organizations that had refused to seize the initiative now sent delegates or declarations of support, including, among others, the International Congress of Socialist Women, which had met from March 26 to 28 in Bern. Greetings arrived from Selma Lagerlöf, Ellen Key, Olive Schreiner, Rosa Mayreder, Charlotte Despard, Emily Hobhouse, and others.[18] Greetings came from Italy from 20,000 women, from Sweden from 24,151, from Norway from 24,000. A greeting with 3,000 signatures came from the small Dutch town of Zaandam and so on and so on, proof that women had only needed a stimulus in order to rely on their own senses and rebel against the insanity called "war."

The congress proceeded in the greatest harmony; no discord disturbed it. In vain, the press waited, with close attention, for "the bombs to finally burst." It seemed unthinkable to men that, during wartime, women from warring countries could peacefully discuss with each other ending the war and a better future. Each day, they buried their hope anew, the sensation they ardently hoped for failed to appear; the women present felt it natural to work together in good fellowship with women of warring countries toward the same goal.

The resolutions were the final result of long negotiations and of many suggestions on which individuals, national committees of many countries and the international committee appointed in Amsterdam had worked for months. . . .

How much disaster, brutality, destruction of cultural treasures, and brutalization of humanity would the world have been spared if women's advice had been followed in 1915. . . .

Work in Germany for The Hague Resolutions, Measures by the Authorities

When the first German edition of the Hague resolutions, printed in Holland, was out of print, we wanted to have a second one printed in Munich. The Bavarian Ministry of War prohibited the printing on the basis of the

[18] Selma Lagerlöf (1858–1940), Swedish novelist, was awarded the Nobel Prize for Literature in 1909.

Ellen Key (1849–1926), Swedish teacher, essayist, pacifist, and reformer, was convinced that maternal compassion would bring about peace and stayed on the sidelines of the women's peace movement during and after World War I.

For Olive Schreiner, see Part III, document 1, Mabel Harding, "German Women and the War," note 12.

Rosa Mayreder (1858–1938), Austrian writer, painter, feminist, pacifist, and social reformer, cofounded the General Austrian Women's Association in 1893 and was president of the Austrian branch of WILPF after 1919.

Emily Hobhouse (1860–1926), English reformer and social worker, was active in relief work in central Europe during and after World War I.

The editors have been unable to identify Charlotte Despard.

laws of the state of war, as well as every kind of duplication and circulation, as well as public discussion of these resolutions, for the duration of the state of war in Bavaria. Violations would be punished with imprisonment of up to a year. All efforts to lift the ban were futile.

Now, Bavaria was not Germany; we tried to have the printing done in Hamburg. The same ban was in effect there; we turned to Frankfurt am Main. It almost seemed as though we would succeed there, but in the end there were insurmountable difficulties. After much back and forth, we managed to print them in Stuttgart and from there the distribution in the German empire was carried out. Members of the Reichstag and Landtag were sent copies and Bavaria as well was thoroughly covered, because, according to the ban's wording, technically nothing stood in the way. But in October 1915, the acting general command in Württemberg also prohibited any further distribution of the Hague resolutions as well as all printed or otherwise duplicated communications and promotional literature of the National Committee of Women for a Permanent Peace.

Reactions of Radical Socialist Women and Other Women

The German Social Democratic Party had completely failed at the beginning of the war. World fellowship was forgotten, chauvinistic patriotism fervently erupted. As a whole, the Social Democrats in the Reichstag had approved war loans as in other parliaments. For the first time, on September 10, 1914, Karl Liebknecht, Franz Mehring, Rosa Luxemburg, and Clara Zetkin protested against such actions.[19] The German radical socialist women not only took up the fight against the imperialistic war, but also against the patriotism of the party's executive board, of the Reichstag faction, and of the immense majority of the party press. The government summoned up all the resources of power afforded by the state of siege against these Socialist women. With only a short break, Rosa Luxemburg sat in prison until the outbreak of the revolution. Lore Agnes was sent to prison.[20] In 1915, Clara Zetkin was in custody for months; when she became very ill, she was released on bail. These women had not just the government against them, but were fought against and spied on by their own comrades, be-

[19] Rosa Luxemburg (1870–1919), Polish-born German revolutionary and agitator, advocated a humanitarian theory of Marxism. After her release from prison during the German revolution of 1918, Luxemburg and Karl Liebknecht (1871–1919) demanded political power for Workers' and Soldiers' Soviets. They were both assassinated by reactionary troops on January 15, 1919.

Franz Mehring (1846–1919), radical journalist, was the historian of the Social Democratic Party and biographer of Karl Marx.

For Clara Zetkin, see Part I, document 3, Florence Kelley Wischnewetsky, "Movement among German Working Women," note 13.

[20] Lore Agnes (1876–1953), German socialist Reichstag deputy from 1919 to 1933.

cause they remained loyal to the principle of international solidarity and turned against the war of conquest of capitalistic imperialism. Clara Zetkin was removed as editor of *Gleichheit*, which she had directed for twenty-seven years. Frida Wolff, party secretary in Breslau, and Luise Zietz, Hamburg, member of the party executive board, were both relieved of their duties.[21] Clara Zetkin explained: "The fact that the politics of war have led to a split in social democracy is largely the work of leading women, a very large number of the female party members went along with the opposition, among them those recognized as the best agitators and organizers."

As the secretary of the International Office of Socialist Women, Clara Zetkin sought and found solidarity with international socialist women; they managed to convene an International Socialist Women's Conference in Bern from March 26 to 28, 1915. Delegates from Russia, Poland, Holland, Germany, England, Italy, France, and Switzerland were present. The negotiations clearly revealed two trends: the revolutionary, which hoped to bring about the end of the war more quickly through a revolutionary fight or civil war; and the pacifist, which wanted to save the Internationale from collapse. . . .

A majority of the German representatives belonged to the Karl Liebknecht-Rosa Luxemburg group. This group was already beginning to separate from the chauvinists and to fight against their government. Rosa Luxemburg was already in prison; such were events in her own land. On the international scene, however, they believed they had to display maximum complacence—because they were the delegation of the country that at that moment was victorious on all fronts. If the conference, which had been prepared with so much difficulty, had failed, they would have been held responsible for it. The chauvinists of all countries, first and foremost Germany's social patriots, would have found great pleasure in this failure. And for this reason Clara Zetkin made concessions to the pacifists, which meant weakening the revolutionary content of the resolutions. . . .

In a manifesto, the conference asked the socialist women of all countries to take up the fight against massive killing and for the social revolution. Approximately one million copies of this manifesto were illegally distributed in Germany alone. The Socialist Women's Conference in Bern undoubtedly paved the way for later socialist conferences in Zimmerwald and Kiental, and it is indisputable that it was once again the women, first and foremost, who successfully made socialist men aware of the duty of international solidarity.[22]

Besides the women who worked on the Committee of Women for a Per-

---

[21] *Gleichheit* ("Equality"): the journal of the Social Democratic women's movement.

Luise Zeitz (1865–1922), German socialist and, together with Zetkin, the main organizer of the SPD women's movement.

[22] From September 5 to 8, 1915, a few dozen European socialists opposed to the war met in Zimmerwald, Switzerland. They ultimately rejected Lenin's resolution to turn World War I

manent Peace and the socialist women, there were also a number of German women who, during the World War, tried to maintain international relations and to fight against war and for pacifist efforts, such as Lili Jannasch and Elisabeth Rotten, among others.[23] They too were exposed to continual persecution. Lili Jannasch sat in preventive detention for months under hardly pleasant conditions.

3. A Mainstream German Woman Activist
Opposes Pacifism

The German delegates to the Hague congress represented a radical minority within the bourgeois German women's movement. The mainstream adopted a decidedly different stance, as seen in the following article from *Die Frauenfrage* (The Woman Question), the official publication of the League of German Women's Associations (Bund Deutscher Frauenvereine, BDF).[24] When the Women's Peace Congress was convened, the League's member associations voted unanimously that participation was "incompatible with the patriotic sentiments and national duties of the German women's movement." In the weeks before the congress, they declared any "propaganda for the congress" as a "breach of the solidarity of the German women's movement." After the congress, the League's president Gertrud Bäumer had to defend this internal resolution and the decision to deny a "responsible position" to any woman who attended the congress publicly.

Dismissing pacifists and radical suffragists from the German women's movement, the BDF saw itself as the only legitimate representation of German women. They considered the meeting at The Hague a conference of private persons, without a mandate from German women and even without a true understanding of the meaning of the war. Bäumer labeled the goals and proceedings of the congress "superfluous, untimely, impossible, and tactless." She rejected the concept of arbitration, which constituted the heart of the resolutions at The Hague, although she tried not to denounce

---

into a European civil war. At a second conference in nearby Kienthal from April 24 to 30, 1916, the workers of all countries were called upon to resist the war.

[23] Lilli Jannasch (b. 1872, d. after 1937), German writer and pacifist, one of the most perceptive critics of German militarism.

[24] Gertrud Bäumer, "Der Bund deutscher Frauenvereine und der Haager Frauenkongreß," *Die Frauenfrage* 17 (1915/16): 82–85; translated by Sally Robertson. Italics indicate emphasis in the original.

the delegates to The Hague altogether as "betrayers of the fatherland." Nevertheless, the work of the BDF throughout the war was fully dedicated to supporting the war effort.

Although the war made Bäumer and her fellow leaders in the BDF uncompromising patriots, she remained optimistic that ties to foreign women's movements could be "reattached," since women in the warring countries were now united by the "deeper, more fateful fellowship" of mothers who had to deal with the "contradiction between motherhood and heroism." Caught in a narrow nationalist paradigm, she could not envision an alternative route to a transnational dialogue.

The League of German Women's Associations and the Women's Congress at The Hague by Gertrud Bäumer

To date, we have intentionally avoided any public discussion of the Women's Congress at The Hague and have publicized only as much regarding the position of the League of German Women's Associations with respect to that event as was indispensable for providing complete clarity on this point. We did not even do that until the German propaganda committee itself turned to broad sectors of the public with letters [to newspapers] that led to the misconception that the organized German women's movement had something to do with the event.[25]

The members of the League are familiar with the League's declarations, the first of which followed the newspaper notices disseminated by the German propaganda committee in the winter, and the second of which was sent out immediately before the congress. The first was passed by the smaller League executive committee, while the president was instructed to write the second by a unanimous vote of the overall board of directors in its meeting of April 16. At this meeting, the board also had to decide to what extent they considered the question of delegations to the congress to be a statement of solidarity within the German women's movement. As a result of this discussion the following resolution was adopted unanimously by the members of the board, that is, by the representatives of fifty-six associations.

The League of German Women's Associations has refused to participate in the International Women's Congress at The Hague. It declares propaganda for the congress or participation in the congress to be incompatible with the patriotic sentiments and national duties of the German women's movement.

[25] "German propaganda committee": Bäumer means the women pacifists like Heymann and Augspurg who encouraged German women to attend the Congress.

Based on the unanimity demonstrated in the associations of the organized women's movement regarding rejection of the congress, the League must regard any propaganda for the congress by German women to be a violation of the solidarity of the German women's movement. The League declares any such propaganda, as well as attendance at the congress, to be incompatible with any kind of responsible position and work within the League of German Women's Associations.

This declaration was sent to our associations with the comment that it was not meant for the public, but as information for the associations about how the board viewed the obligation of a statement of solidarity on this matter. Many on the board expressed the desire to be allowed to use this declaration to clarify our position to the public as well. These wishes were denied with the reasoning that the purpose of the declaration was not to publicly stigmatize those who attended the congress but to communicate to our associations that the League considered a uniform position on this issue to be their duty.

It turned out, however, that, in our concern about keeping the truce, we overestimated the loyalty of the friends of the congress. Through a breach of confidence, the occurrence of which in our ranks we are ashamed to acknowledge, our declaration was provided to a few newspapers of radical orientation, which published it along with their commentary. Even then we refrained from further public discussion of the matter. It now seems, however, that the response to the consideration which we showed toward a vanishing minority of German women was that misconceptions are being spread regarding the position of the League which we would not be able to correct were we to continue our discretion. And it could be that, under certain circumstances, these distortions might reach persons at home and abroad whose opinion is more important to us than attacks by people who two years ago celebrated the female civil war of the suffragettes and now protest against the male war as a bloody insanity.

Therefore, in order to avert the danger of people going fishing all over the place in the dark, we once again declare the following.

The statement of the League that participation in the congress at The Hague is incompatible "with the patriotic sentiments and national duties of the German women's movement" is a reflection of the views of all of the associations of the League. We were able in our resolution itself to refer to the unanimity that moves the German women's movement in this regard. It was also confirmed afterward by the fact that the League did not receive a counterdeclaration against our resolution from a *single* association board. We received a total of six declarations against the League's position from individuals. The board of the German Federation for Woman Suffrage also sent us a declaration addressed to them by two suffrage societies. Finally,

198

the Women's League of the German Peace Society, which is unaffiliated with our League, sent us an announcement "on behalf of those of their members who are also League members," but, without having asked these members, as they themselves informed us.

Thus we can certify that there has never been a question on which the League of German Women's Associations was so absolutely of a single mind as on the decision that participation in this congress is "incompatible with the patriotic sentiments and national duties of the German women's movement." . . .

I find in the journal *Neues Frauenleben,* which is published in Vienna as the official organ of the General Austrian Women's Society, in a report on the congress at The Hague, an article by Leopoldine Kulka which states that the "German leaders of the League view women's fight for peace as a betrayal of the fatherland and its men." [26] This oversimplification of our position seems to me to be representative of the interpretation under which our decision is circulating.

Therefore, let me express it here with absolute clarity: the German women do not view women's fight for peace as a betrayal of the fatherland. Rather, they found the form imposed on the fight for peace by the organizers of the congress at The Hague to be incompatible with their patriotic sentiments. . . .

The Hague congress intended to unite four goals. It intended, in the words of Rosa Mayreder, to affirm "the international solidarity of women, which is one of the ideals underlying the women's movement" in its independence from the events of the World War.[27] It intended to support peace in principle as well as a regulating of international relations which would completely eliminate war in the future. Thirdly, it intended to contribute toward a shortening of *this* war. And it intended, last but not least, to promote women's suffrage. In our opinion, the first was superfluous, the second was untimely, the third was impossible, the fourth was tactless, and the combination of the four intentions in one event was full of the deepest contradictions.

On the first point, as the president of the League of German Women's Associations, I am anxious to emphasize that it is our conviction that the deep internal relationships created between the women's movements in the various countries by virtue of their shared history, though they will

---

[26] Leopoldine Kulka (1872–1920), Austrian author and feminist. In her twenties, Kulka joined the General Austrian Women's Association, the radical wing of the bourgeois women's movement; she published its periodicals *Dokumente der Frauen* (Women's Documents) from 1899 to 1902 and *Neues Frauenleben* (Women's New Life) from 1902 to 1919. She became vice president of the Association in 1911 and founded its "peace section" in 1917.

[27] For Rosa Mayreder, see Part III, document 2, Heymann and Augspurg, "Women's Work," note 18.

probably be interrupted by the war, will not be shaken. . . . And we German women are not at all denying this fellowship. When the war broke out, Mrs. Creighton, president of the English League, said in a circular to the presidents of the national member organizations of the International Council of Women that, throughout this time, we should attempt to bear in memory how we came to know each other as colleagues during the International Congress in Rome, and we agreed from the bottom of our hearts with the sentiments and the will expressed in this request.[28] Likewise, we are deeply grateful for what the members of the English Women's League are doing for German civilian prisoners and their families—just as we are doing as much as we can here to aid the families of the English civilian prisoners. The Women's League of Canada, on their own initiative, inquired as to the exact situation of the German and Austrian prisoners in Canada and sent us the report. The National Council of Women of the United States sent us a sum of money to support our war services. All of this is evidence that despite everything which necessarily separates us today, there remains an unshakable fellowship of women around the world . . .

Even far beyond the bounds of the women's movement, can we ever forget the fellowship of mothers trembling for heroically sacrificed life on both sides of the battle fronts? Must not a new, even deeper, more fateful fellowship between the mothers of different nations be created from the heart-wrenching experience of the tragic contradiction between motherhood and heroism, for which thousands upon thousands of women around the world must now seek a solution? We are certain that we will feel that fellowship once we are allowed to reattach the strings which are now torn.

But would not this very experience, this very tear-burdened fellowship, be made intolerably alien and shallow were the women to come together today and forge resolutions arising from women's sentiments, while the men face each other in the performance of their most sacred duties? The "solidarity of women's perceptions" touches me much more deeply in the declaration with which the Frenchwomen explained their rejection of the Hague congress, which was not read because of the attacks on Germany, than in the colorless conference style of these international protestations.[29] I *understand* the passion with which the Frenchwomen think of their home and their men. I *understand* that this passion (of love, not of hate!) is larger, closer, more sacred to them than "ideals of humanity," and I empathize with them when they are unable and unwilling today to sepa-

[28]   The sixth quinquennial congress of the ICW convened in Rome during the summer of 1914.
[29]   On the French declaration, see Part III, document 4, Chamberlain, "The Women at the Hague."

rate their living maternal instinct, which is tied to child and home and native soil, from their theoretical motherhood. For that is the deepest core of our resistance to this international congress: we cannot make ourselves "international" today! We—particularly we women!—cannot set aside from 9 to 1 and from 4 to 8 the deepest, strongest, most intense experiences that burn within us and, as theoretical ghosts of our true selves, ascend into an international fourth dimension. It is of course impossible to reach agreement with anyone who cannot empathize with this, anyone who therefore did not perceive the congress as a most deeply inappropriate expression, as an internally impossible profanation of the great shock experienced by women of all affected nations in the internal conflict with their ideals. The German women, however, with few exceptions, were unanimous in their perception that participation in the congress was "incompatible with their patriotic sentiments." . . .

There is no German woman who does not long for peace from the bottom of her heart, not just for her own sake, but for that of the world, life, and culture, so that we can all begin to rebuild what has been destroyed. But for every German woman, peace is a German question to the same degree that, for all other nations involved, it is a matter of their own existence. . . .

[T]he whole congress was based on the conflict between the male and female perspective. Still, we find the emphasis on this dichotomy of intellectual worlds to be deeply injurious at this moment when we feel more strongly than ever the common precious asset of "fatherland," to which the German war poet added, "motherland, childland," at a time when we understand more clearly than ever what it means to us as women to be "citizens," and when men and women must rely on one another more than ever. We certainly do not want, in the words of Rosa Mayreder, to "sell our birthright for a mess of pottage." But there are truly enough forms in which women today can practically espouse a belief in life, love, and reconciliation.

For all of these reasons, the League of German Women's Associations refused to attend the congress. (It was truly not out of the concern attributed to us as an "ameliorating circumstance" in the most grotesque of the protests of which we learned: "We, who advocate for a permanent peace, can very well understand that the League cannot immediately support all of the advances of the women's movement, for many professional organizations belong to the League who are dependent on the disciplinary power of the male state or must fear their male masters"!) Thus it was not out of "fear of the male master" and not out of opportunism of any kind, but precisely out of the feeling of responsibility for our own movement that the League took a position against the congress. . . .

There were twenty-eight German women at The Hague, none of whom holds a seat on the board of the League or any of its member associations. This means *that the German women's movement was not represented at The Hague.* And if the plan to hold a women's congress at the same time and place as the peace talks is carried out, and the German action committee elects the twenty German delegates to that congress in accordance with the Hague resolutions, then the participation in this future congress will not be an activity of the German women's movement but a private activity of twenty German women.

4. An American Report on the Hague Congress

Combining social justice values with social science methods, *Survey* was the leading social reform periodical in the United States between 1902 and its demise in 1952. During most of that time it was edited by Paul and Arthur Kellogg, midwesterners who transformed the magazine from its stodgy predecessor, *Charities,* the official publication of the Charity Organization Society edited by Edward Devine. Florence Kelley, Jane Addams, and other leading reformers served as coeditors of or wrote regular columns in *Survey,* and reformers often met to discuss strategy at *Survey's* offices in the Charities Building in New York City. There they would have met Mary Chamberlain.

Chamberlain, a staff writer for *Survey,* volunteered to cover the extraordinary international meetings of women activists at the Hague in 1915 and in Zurich in 1919. A delegate to both congresses, she wrote vibrant, sympathetic accounts that evoked the drama of each gathering.[30] Although trying to maintain her objective stance as a journalist, Chamberlain disclosed her feelings of "tenderness and sympathy" for the many of the participants. Her deft sketches of their personalities warmed her account, as did her willingness to personalize her own impressions. She described each national delegation, their travail in traveling to the congress, and how they approached the major issues. She captured the political identity of the delegates and the political tenor of their debates. With insight and humor, she humanized the ponderous issues raised at the congress—the "pro-Ger-

[30] Mary Chamberlain, "The Women at The Hague," *Survey,* June 5, 1915, pp. 218–22, 236. Italics indicate emphasis in the original.

man" problem, the question of territorial conquest, disarmament, and the quest for permanent peace.

The Women at The Hague
by Mary Chamberlain
of the staff of *Survey*

The four of us sat over coffee in the café of the Hotel Central in The Hague.

Soldiers in peaked caps, loitering with their sweethearts, passed the window; bicyclists zigzagged dangerously through the crowd; and once in a while, the last bit of Dutch picturesqueness—the wooden shoes, flaring white head-dress and gold hair-pins of a peasant woman, kept us aware that this black-coated orthodox stream of passersby was not the ebb and flow of Broadway. Inside the vermillion trimmings and gold braid of smart uniforms gave color to the stodgy gathering of Dutch folk, and a jolly American ragtime, though bereft of the American café dance-floor, lightened the heavy menu of fish and meats and compotes.

The International Congress of Women was over. The four of us were journalists—tired with taking notes, seeking interviews, hurrying to meetings, straining our ears to foreign languages. We were in danger of losing sight of the spirit of the congress in our zeal to "get a story" from some delegate, in our efforts to straighten out names and numbers and speeches. Now for the first time we were trying to touch this spirit and to clear our vision by an exchange of impressions.

"It was bourgeois," said the Socialist, "a gathering of sentimentalists. The real people who want the war stopped are the working people and they would have nothing to do with this congress. To me it seemed barren and cold. Why, I've heard a little East Side striker rouse a meeting to a pitch of enthusiasm that was never touched by those club women and suffrage leaders."

"Self-control, you mean, not lack of feeling," objected the short-story writer. "I felt a great swell of emotion under the reserve of those women from warring nations. Constraint was necessary or it would have burst on the meeting like a shower of shrapnel."

"And as for the delegates from neutral countries," added the newspaper woman, "I'm sure the minds of many of those women were poisoned for the first time with the fear of war. For the first time I believe that hundreds of Dutch women in the audience realized that war would mean the flowers of Holland soaked with the blood of the recruits drilling there in front of the Dierentium where the congress met."

From the press-table of the congress back to America, to England, to

Germany, to Scandinavia, I knew criticisms had gone as diverse as these. With them had gone others less honest, less intelligent, more partisan. The newspapers of the countries from which the delegates came denounced the congress as "pro-German," as traitorous, as hysterical, as base and silly. Some people claimed an influence for the congress far wider that it can attain for years, others decried it as futile.

Bewildered by this wrangle and confusion, I left my friends in the café and went to Jane Addams to ask her opinion of the congress. For three days, Miss Addams had, as president, steered the business of the congress through a sea of resolutions, amendments, and suggestions given her in French, German, English and Dutch. She was thoroughly acquainted with the hitches and obstacles that clog every international conference and had been most closely in touch with the members of the congress.

"The great achievement of this congress," said Miss Addams thoughtfully, "is to my mind the getting together of these women from all parts of Europe, when their men-folks are shooting each other from opposite trenches. When in every warring country there is such a wonderful awakening of national consciousness flowing from heart to heart, it is a supreme effort of heroism to rise to the feeling of internationalism, without losing patriotism."

With a rush of tenderness and sympathy I remembered some of the women who sat beside Miss Addams on the platform at the congress—frail little Miss Courtney and Chrystal Macmillan, British to the fiber yet offering a hearty second to many resolutions proposed by German delegates; Lida Gustava Heymann, whose honest straightforward ways made one smile at the insinuation of a congress packed with German spies; valiant Eugenie Hamer who pushed through from Belgium with five companions; warm-hearted Rosika Schwimmer from Hungary; and Frau Leopoldine Kulka of Austria, with her quiet blue eyes and patient face.[31]

---

[31]   Kathleen Courtney (1878–1974), British suffragist and peace activist. She attended the women's congresses at the Hague and Zurich and was a cofounder of the WILPF as well as president of its British section for ten years.

Chrystal Macmillan (1882–1937), British feminist and attorney. She served as a secretary of the International Women Suffrage Alliance from 1913 to 1920, was one of the initiators and secretary of the Women's Peace Congress at The Hague, and was a delegate of the Women's Congress to the Paris Peace Conference in 1919.

Eugenie Hamer (dates unavailable), Belgian pacifist. She was vice president of the Belgian Women's Alliance for Peace Through Education.

Rosika Schwimmer (1877–1948), Hungarian feminist and pacifist, founder of the Hungarian Feminist Association and editor of A Nö (Woman) from 1907 to 1928. During World War I, Schwimmer's campaigns for peace and neutrality led to the founding of the Women's Peace Party and to the Women's Peace Congress at The Hague. She also initiated private missions, including Henry Ford's controversial Peace Ship. Schwimmer was ambassador to Switzerland during the short-lived Hungarian democracy in 1918–1919. She escaped to Vienna in 1920 and emigrated to the United States in 1921, in the midst of the Red Scare. American citizenship was denied to her, and she remained stateless. She dedicated the last years of her life to a campaign for world government.

THE DIALOGUE CHANGES DURING WORLD WAR I

Nearly everyone of those women who sat there side by side so dignified and courteous, had brothers, husbands or friends facing each other in maddened fury or even now mown down by each other's bullets. It was a great test of courage for these women to risk the bitterness of their families, the ridicule of their friends and the censure of their governments to come to this international woman's congress. In the midst of the war tumult which is making all Europe shake, it meant a far sweep of imagination to realize that the feelings of mothers, sisters and wives are the same in all countries and it took the finest generosity for these women to associate themselves in a discussion of means to restore international good will.

The congress that bore this fruit was planned with doubt and misgivings. When the International Alliance for Women Suffrage held its last congress at Budapest in June, 1913, it was decided to hold the next convention at Berlin in June, 1915. Meanwhile the war broke out, kindling its hatred between nations and burning away all thought of an international suffrage gathering. However, a few broadminded women still held fast to their ideals in the midst of these rough realities. Among them, the Dutch National Committee for International Interests, a sub-division of the Alliance for Women Suffrage, ventured to lift up its voice. It proposed that the congress which it was impossible to hold at Berlin should be convoked instead in the Netherlands.[32]

The twenty-six separate countries affiliated with the international alliance were approached, but the answers received, were on the whole discouraging. The idea itself met with general favor but it was considered advisable to refrain from holding official assemblies. Therefore, the only chance of success lay in consulting the prominent women of the different countries, both belligerent and neutral.

This consultation took place with the result that a meeting was held on February 12–13 in Amsterdam, attended by a number of British, German, Dutch, and Belgian women. Here the plans for the International Congress of Women were laid, the preliminary program was drawn, invitations were sent out, committees appointed and the emphasis of the congress turned from political equality to peace.

The next difficulty in the path of the congress confronted, not the central committee at The Hague but those who desired to take part in the conference. It was one thing for these women to accept the invitation to the congress; it was another for them to reach Holland.

Of 180 British women accepting the invitation to the congress, two only arrived—Kathleen Courtney and Chrystal Macmillan, English suffragists

---

For Leopoldine Kulka, see Part III, document 3, Gertrud Bäumer, "The League of Women's Associations," note 26.

[32] Alliance for Women Suffrage: Chamberlain means the International Woman Suffrage Alliance.

and members of the International Committee on Resolutions, who reached The Hague a week before the congress opened. The other 178 were first pared down to 24 by the secretary for Foreign Affairs, who advised the home office to limit the issuance of passports. Reginald McKenna, British secretary of state for Home Affairs, has explained this action by stating that his colleague in the Department for Foreign Affairs believed that so large a number of English women in a city near the scene of war and infested with the enemy's spies would constitute a danger for the country.[33] Therefore 24 delegates were sorted out, representing the most important organizations and seeming most prudent in giving out information. In doing this Mr. McKenna was careful to make it understood that these delegates had received no official character.

The reason for the non-appearance of these twenty-four picked delegates is not quite so clear and must be explained as the "fortunes of war." When a member of parliament who objected to the participation of English women in the congress, asked Mr. McKenna if any of the twenty-four had actually reached The Hague, the secretary replied: "No, indeed. You know that all communication between England and Holland was interrupted after the delegates received their passports."

But while these twenty-four women were waiting at Folkstone for any sort of boat to convey them to Holland, Miss Courtney and Miss Macmillan were making up in quality of membership what England lacked in quantity. It was the hard work and perseverance of these two women that made one almost forget the small proportion of delegates from this allied nation in the membership of the congress. One Canadian delegate, Laura Hughes of Toronto, crossed the Atlantic to represent the colonies.[34]

The action of the British government in suspending traffic between England and Holland was also responsible for nearly cutting off the American contingent from the congress. For four days the steamship *Noordam*, loaded with ammunition for the Dutch government in the hold, and with forty-two peace delegates to the Dutch capital in the first cabin, lay at anchor off Diel.[35] The delegates sent telegrams to the American ambassador at London and the American consul at Dover; they held meetings to devise ways and means to investigate the halt; finally they settled down to face the fact that they were as nothing compared to the transference of troops to France or the movements of the British fleet. Then just as mysteriously as

[33]   Reginald McKenna (1863–1943), British statesman. As First Lord of the Admiralty, McKenna initiated a massive battleship construction program that was fiercely opposed by Winston Churchill and David Lloyd George, who wanted to spend more money on social reform. McKenna prevailed, and his program gave Great Britain a considerable advantage at the beginning of World War I. He served as Chancellor of the Exchequer during the early period of the war but resigned when Lloyd George became prime minister in December of 1916.
[34]   The editors have been unable to identify Laura Hughes.
[35]   Chamberlain probably means the seaport of Deal, about ten miles north of Dover.

THE DIALOGUE CHANGES DURING WORLD WAR I

she had been delayed, the *Noordam* was ordered to proceed, and we reached Rotterdam without meeting mines or further mishaps, the very day the congress opened.

Much has been said by the press and critics of the congress of the "Germanizing" of this peace meeting. The thirty German delegates and the fifteen Austrians and Hungarians present have been called the "Kaiser's cat's-paws," German spies and many other names. It has been suggested that the German and Austro-Hungarian governments were only too glad to be represented at a peace meeting; it has even been hinted that the expenses of the congress were met by German government funds. Strangely enough, the newspapers of a large country from which a large number of delegates were excluded by government orders,—Great Britain,—were loudest in proclaiming that the congress was steamrollered by the Germans!

As a matter of fact, the way of the German, Austrian and Hungarian delegates was not altogether paved with ease and cordiality. Although they finally received their passports without trouble, they were at first suspected by their governments and at all times they have been the butt of ridicule and calumny of the press and the general public. The union of German women, for example, has almost unanimously denounced the participation of German women in the congress.[36]

All the delegates openly declared that they did not represent the sentiment of the majority of women in their fatherlands, but only small, radical groups. Among them are women whose names are well known to the International Suffrage Alliance and in social work. Anita Augspurg and Lida G. Heymann of Munich are founders of the suffrage movement in Germany; Helena [*sic*] Stöcker and Fräulein Rotten of Berlin are, respectively, president for the League for the Protection of Mothers, and an officer of the League for the Care of Prisoners; Rosika Schwimmer of Hungary, represented the Association of Agricultural Woman Laborers, a suffrage organization of peasant women; Vilma G. Glücklich and Paula Pogány are the president and secretary of the Hungarian Feminist Alliance; Anna Zipernowsky is a member of the Hungarian Peace Association; Leopoldine Kulka and Olga Misar came as delegates of the Austrian Women's Union (suffrage); Bertha Frölich, as a delegate of the Society of Temperance women; and Darynska Golinska came from Austrian Poland with a memorial from the suffering Polish women demanding the rebuilding of an independent Poland as an "indispensable reservation" in a lasting peace.[37]

---

[36] By "union of German women" Chamberlain means the League of German Women's Associations.
[37] See Biographical Notes.

For Rosika Schwimmer, see note 31 of this section.

Vilma Glücklich (1872–1927), Hungarian suffragist and pacifist, cofounder and director of the Hungarian Feminist Association. Glücklich helped to organize the 1913 congress of the IWSA in Budapest and led the large Hungarian delegation to The Hague. Glücklich also

Likewise, Rosa Genoni of Milan, lecturer, writer and the sole delegate from Italy, did not claim to represent the widespread feeling of her country-women.[38] "The other women in Italy," said Madame Genoni, "were frightened to cross Germany into Holland, for they fear in Italy that war may break out any minute. Alas! in Italy they do not think only of peace. Everybody desires it perhaps, but first of all they think of national interest. Even the peace associations in Italy are drawn into the mesh of war."

From the Scandinavian countries came large delegations to the congress, representing in most instances the committees formed in these northern nations for the international congress. Among them stood out such names as Anna Lindhagen of Sweden, inspector of children's institutions and one of the seven women members of the town council of Stockholm; and Thora Daugaard of Denmark, representing 15,000 suffragists.[39]

No Russian or French woman attended the congress. Whereas the European press overlooked much that was of real and lasting importance in the congress, few papers failed to publish in full the manifesto of the Conseil National des Femmes Françaises and L'Union pour le Suffrage des Femmes, organizations representing more than 150,000 French women.[40]

---

attended the congress in Zurich and her Association became the Hungarian branch of the WILPF. From 1922 to 1925 she served as the organization's secretary in Geneva.

Anna Zipernowsky (died 1923), Hungarian pacifist. She cofounded the Hungarian Peace Society in 1895, founded the peace section of the Hungarian Women's Association, and was a member of the council of the International Peace Bureau.

For Leopoldine Kulka, see Part III, document 3, Bäumer, "The League of Women's Associations," note 26.

The editors have been unable to find biographical information on Paula Pogány, Olga Misar, Bertha Frölich, and Darynska Golinska.

Golinska's memorial: During the period between 1771 and 1792, the Polish state was dissolved, and its parts were apportioned to Russia, Austria, and Prussia. In the end, the Russian Revolution and the defeat of the Axis powers in World War I made a new Polish nation state possible.

[38] Rosa Genoni (dates unavailable), Italian fashion designer, teacher, and suffragist. After the Hague congress she was selected as a delegate to tour government capitals with Jane Addams, but had to return to Italy when her country entered the war. She obtained a passport to attend the 1919 congress in Zurich by persuading Italian officials that she would be studying women's fashions. Her 1906 book, *Per una moda italiana,* lent credibility to her claim. In 1919, she joined Addams, Gabrielle Duchène, and Chrystal Macmillan in carrying the resolutions of the Zurich congress to the Paris peace delegates.

[39] Anna Lindhagen (1870–1941), Swedish social worker, writer, and suffragist. A prominent campaigner for women's suffrage, she edited the women's journal of the Swedish Social Democratic Party and was elected to the Stockholm city council in 1911. Lindhagen was a delegate at the Hague congress in 1915 and helped organize the Swedish branch of the WILPF. She was prominent in the Swedish "Save the Children" campaign in war-ravaged Europe and in refugee work.

The editors have been unable to find biographical information on Thora Daugaard.

[40] Conseil National des Femmes Françaises (National Council of French Women), founded in 1901 as the coordinating body for all women's and children's organizations. L'Union pour le Suffrage des Femmes (Union for Women's Suffrage, UFSF) was founded in 1908, when suf-

The Manifesto is addressed "to the women of neutral and allied countries." It is a touching document courteously declining for French women a share in the congress and proudly declaring that "in order that future generations may reap the fruit of this magnificent display of self-sacrifice and death, French women will bear the conflict as long as it will be necessary. At this time united with those who battle and die, they do not know how to talk of peace."

The manifesto further proposes that French women can talk of peace only when justice has been triumphantly vindicated by the heroic defenders of the French nation.

In spite of this manifesto many letters were received from individual French women telling their desire to reach the congress and of the impossibility of traveling so far. Among them was a telegram of sympathy from Jules [*sic*] Siegfried, president of the Conseil National des Femmes Françaises, and a letter signed by Mme. Duchène, chairman of the Section du Travail du Conseil National and by some fifteen working women, which offered to "the women of other nations good wishes and assurance that we are ready to work with them more ardently than ever to prepare the 'peace of tomorrow.' "[41]

Russian women sent a letter expressing much the same sentiment as did the French manifesto, but the very feeling which kept these French and Russian women from the congress drove five valiant little Belgian women across the border into Holland from devastated Belgium. Eugenie Hamer and Mlle. Sarton, vice-president and treasurer of L'Alliance Belge des Femmes pour le Paix par l'Education, decided that no peace congress attended by German and Austrian delegates should pass resolutions without a hearing before Belgian women.[42] They determined not to vote but to

---

fragists discussed the continued absence of France from the IWSA. It united mainstream suffragists.

[41] Julie Paux Siegfried (1848–1922), French suffragist. She married a wealthy cotton merchant and future deputy of the French parliament, Jules Siegfried, with whom she constructed a life-long partnership in promoting liberal social reform. In 1901, she was cofounder of the Conseil National des Femmes Françaises and served as its president from 1912 to 1922. At her death she presided over seven different charitable organizations.

Gabrielle Laforcade Duchène (1878–1954), French journalist, pacifist, and political activist, involved in issues of child welfare, sweatshop regulation, and worker protection. She attended the Women's Peace Congress at The Hague and later worked to establish a French section of what was to become WILPF. Duchène did not receive a passport to attend the Zurich congress in 1919, but was one of the delegates who carried the recommendations of WILPF to the Versailles Peace Conference.

[42] The editors have been unable to obtain biographical information about Mlle. Sarton, treasurer of L'Alliance Belge des Femmes pour le Paix par l'Education (Alliance of Belgian Women for Peace Through Education). Founded in 1906 in Antwerp, the Alliance recruited a thousand members from Belgium before 1914, bringing together both liberals and Catholics. Several branches were created in various Belgian towns.

protest any measure, such as the calling of an armistice, which they deemed unjust to their country.

With three companions they obtained permission from the German authorities to go. They went by automobile to Esschen, where they were searched to the skin; thence they walked for two hours to Rosendahl across the Dutch border, and from there they traveled to The Hague by train.[43] Then when Mlle. Hamer finally reached the congress, it was Dr. Augspurg of Munich who welcomed them to a seat on the platform.

So, over seas and mountains, pushing aside dangers and obstacles, more than three hundred women "got together" with the Dutch delegates and visitors who crowded the meetings night after night. However any might criticize the proceedings of the congress, none could fail to admire the magnificent spirit of these women who dared clasp hands with women from an enemy country. Even if this international congress wields little influence, it was, as Miss Addams said, a lasting achievement in thus uniting from every corner of Europe different sympathies and beliefs in one great yearning for peace.

But as I talked with Miss Addams, another thought came into my mind. Was it not, I asked her, a higher test of courage than "getting together" when the trenches were bleeding with wounded comrades, to "stick together" until out of their common suffering these women evolved a charter of common aspiration? Someone in the café had spoken of a mutual distrust that seemed to constrain the delegates. Now, talking with Miss Addams, I realized how this mistrust had gradually melted. Like my socialist friend, I missed the flare of passion which kindles a meeting held to score a specific wrong; I revolted sometimes at dodging realities and floating in a cloud of theories; I, too, missed the vigorous robust solidarity of a congress bound together by the sense of the interdependence of labor. But more and more, I was feeling that strong, sober solidarity based on universal mourning.

"Everybody talks about victory," said Rosika Schwimmer in one of her stirring speeches, "but we women know that every victory means the death of thousands of sons of other mothers."

It was grief and sympathy that welded us together.

At the first session of the congress, without a dissenting voice, a motion was carried making the basis of membership in the congress the acceptance of two resolutions—that women shall be granted equal political rights as men and that future international disputes shall be subject to conciliation and arbitration.

---

[43] Esschen: Essen, town in the Belgian province of Antwerp, at the border to the Netherlands.

Rosendahl: a town in the south of Holland, about twenty miles north of Essen.

THE DIALOGUE CHANGES DURING WORLD WAR I

With the meeting-ground of the congress thus defined, the way was left open for debate and discussion on any other resolution to be considered. But so great was the unity of feeling that day after day of conferences slid by with no or little friction. Indeed, the monotony of accord caused us at the press-table to snatch and over emphasize the faintest spark of sensationalism—the harangue, for instance, of the militant suffragette who vowed that for every woman in England wishing to attend the peace congress 1,000 wished to fight; or the excitement of a Belgian lady who thought that the phrase "backward nations" referred to Belgium.

Many resolutions were passed unanimously such as those protesting women's sufferings in war, demanding democratic control of foreign policy, urging that the education of children be directed toward peace and that women be represented in the conference of powers after the war. Even the radical resolutions introduced by the American contingent went through without protest. Among these were resolutions calling for open seas and free trade routes, for the acceptance of the principle that investments in a foreign country be made at the risk of the investor, for mediation without armistice and for the establishment of a permanent international conference which shall deal with practical proposals for future international co-operation and shall appoint a permanent council of conciliation for the settlement of differences arising from social and economic causes.

From the German delegates came a resolution of even greater import which repudiates the right of conquest. This resolution affirms that there shall be no transference of territory without the consent of the residents and urges that autonomy and a democratic parliament shall not be refused to any people.

When the resolution came up for vote advocating universal disarmament and urging all countries to take over the manufacture of arms and munitions of war and to control international traffic in the same, a stir was created by a delegate from the United States who moved an amendment that "traffic in arms from neutral countries be prohibited." Miss Addams ruled the amendment out of order as bearing on present conditions, but added that she herself as an American citizen favored it.

Aside from the delay and slight confusion caused by tedious translation, there was but one hitch in the proceedings of the congress. It came after Madame Schwimmer's appeal for women to "call a thunderous halt *tomorrow* that shall overthrow the thunder of the trenches." By a rising vote the congress had voted to accept without debate this resolution urging the governments of the world to put an end to bloodshed and to begin peace negotiations. Then Mlle. Hamer, burning with the spirit of the French manifesto, pleaded for a peace based on justice "which would return to Belgium her liberty, independence, richness and prosperity." Unanimously the congress voted to insert in this most important of resolutions:

"The congress demands that the peace which follows shall be permanent and therefore based on principles of justice."

Thus "arbitration" bridged the one division of feeling in the congress which threatened a serious split.

What will come of it all?

That is what the world of practical people, who demand immediate results, is asking.

When I questioned my Socialist friend, she scoffed a little bitterly, "A lot of talk that will blow away with the delegates." But the newspaper woman reflected that it would leave its stamp on the woman movement in every country, and the magazine writer declared that its end was already attained in dispelling the idea of implacable hatred between women of warring countries.

The one immediate step of the congress was to delegate envoys, women from both neutral and belligerent nations, to carry the message expressed in the congress resolutions to combatants and non-combatant countries. Already Jane Addams, Aletta H. Jacobs, chairman of the executive committee of the congress, and Rosa Genoni of Italy, have been received by the court of Holland, have presented the resolutions to the prime minister of England and have come back to the continent in a tour which includes the capitals of Germany, Belgium, France and Austria[44] They will later be joined by Kathleen Courtney of England and Anita Augspurg of Germany, and will visit the neutral countries of Switzerland, Spain and United States. The entrance of Italy into the war will prevent these delegates visiting Rome as planned.

Meanwhile another group has been appointed to go to Denmark, Sweden, Norway and Russia.

To students of diplomacy and to the "practical" people of the world the expeditions will seem, like the congress itself, the action of visionaries. They will laugh at a "parcel of women" bearing resolutions to prime ministers who are vexed with the burdens of war. They will sneer at its futility and assail its temerity. But to others, and especially to us who attended the congress, the mission of these women will mean that the spirit of the congress will not be girded by the canals of Holland but will reach across trenches smoking with war.

[44] For Aletta Jacobs, see Part III, document 2, Heymann and Augspurg, "Women's Work," note 15.

THE DIALOGUE CHANGES DURING WORLD WAR I

5. Resolutions Adopted
at the Hague Congress

The women at the Hague Congress declared their special interest in opposing the war and linked the success of peace efforts to their enfranchisement. In the following resolutions, the congress endorsed measures for international cooperation, including an international court and a Society of Nations, general disarmament, national self-determination, and democratic control of foreign policy. The resolutions were printed in English, French, and German and distributed to European heads of state. Members of the U.S. Congress were also sent copies, since the success of the plan largely depended on persuading President Wilson to initiate and lead mediation as head of the neutral nations. Addams and other delegates of the congress met with him throughout the summer but found that he had started to shift toward preparedness and in any case preferred to act alone, even if he was sympathetic to the proposals of the Women's Peace Congress. *Survey* printed the resolutions of the Women's Congress; they were also part of a volume in which Jane Addams, Emily Greene Balch, and Alice Hamilton reported on the war in Europe and the Women's Peace Congress.[45] In Germany, hundreds of copies of the resolutions were mailed to politicians, civic organizations and private citizens.

**Resolutions adopted by
The International Congress of Women
The Hague, Holland
April 28 29 30, 1915**

I. WOMEN AND WAR

1. PROTEST

We women in international congress assembled, protest against the madness and the horror of war, involving as it does a reckless sacrifice of human life and the destruction of so much that humanity has laboured through centuries to build up.

---

[45] Jane Addams, Emily Green Balch, and Alice Hamilton, eds., *Women at the Hague. The International Congress of Women and Its Results* (New York: Macmillan, 1915), pp. 150 ff. Also in *Survey,* June 15, 1915, p. 218.

2. WOMEN'S SUFFERINGS IN WAR

This International Congress of Women opposes the assumption that women can be protected under the conditions of modern warfare. It protests vehemently against the odious wrongs of which women are the victims in time of war, and especially against the horrible violation of women which attends all war.

II. TOWARDS PEACE

3. THE PEACE SETTLEMENT

This International Congress of Women of different nations, classes, creeds and parties is united in expressing sympathy with the suffering of all, whatever their nationality, who are fighting for their country or laboring under the burden of war.

Since the mass of the people in each of the countries now at war believe themselves to be fighting, not as aggressors but in self-defense and for their national existence, there can be no irreconcilable differences between them, and their common ideals afford a basis upon which a magnanimous and honourable peace might be established. The congress therefore urges the governments of the world to put an end to this bloodshed, and begin peace negotiations. It demands that the peace which follows shall be permanent and based on principles of justice, including those laid down in the resolutions[46] adopted by this congress, namely:

That no territory should be transferred without the consent of the men and women in it, and that the right of conquest shall not be recognized.

That autonomy and a democratic parliament should not be refused to any people.

That the governments of all nations should come to an agreement to refer future international disputes to arbitration or conciliation and to bring social, moral and economic pressure to bear upon any country which resorts to arms.

That foreign politics should be subject to democratic control.

That women should be granted equal political rights with men.

4. CONTINUOUS MEDIATION

This International Congress of Women resolves to ask the neutral countries to take immediate steps to create a conference of neutral nations which shall without delay offer continuous mediation. The conference shall invite suggestions for settlements from each of the belligerent nations and in any case shall submit to them simultaneously reasonable proposals as a basis of peace.

---

[46]   Note. The resolutions in full are Nos. 5, 6, 7, 8, 9. [This footnote is in the original.]

III. PRINCIPLES OF A PERMANENT PEACE

5. RESPECT FOR NATIONALITY

This International Congress of Women, recognizing the right of the people to self-government, affirms that there should be no transference of territory without the consent of the men and women residing therein, and urges that autonomy and a democratic parliament should not be refused to any people.[47]

6. ARBITRATION AND CONCILIATION

This International Congress of Women, believing that war is the negation of progress and civilization, urges the governments of all nations to come to an agreement to refer future international disputes to arbitration and conciliation.

7. INTERNATIONAL PRESSURE

This International Congress of Women urges the governments of all nations to come to an agreement to unite in bringing social, moral and economic pressure to bear upon any country, which resorts to arms instead of referring its case to arbitration or conciliation.

8. DEMOCRATIC CONTROL OF FOREIGN POLICY

Since war is commonly brought about not by the mass of the people, who do not desire it, but by groups representing particular interests, this International Congress of Women urges that foreign politics shall be subject to democratic control; and declares that it can only recognize as democratic a system which includes the equal representation of men and women.

9. THE ENFRANCHISEMENT OF WOMEN

Since the combined influence of the women of all countries is one of the strongest forces for the prevention of war, and since women can only have full responsibility and effective influence when they have equal political rights with men, this International Congress of Women demands their political enfranchisement.

IV. INTERNATIONAL CO-OPERATION

10. THIRD HAGUE CONFERENCE

This International Conference urges that a third Hague Conference be convened immediately after the war.

11. INTERNATIONAL ORGANIZATION

This International Congress of Women urges that the organization of the Society of Nations should be further developed on the basis of a constructive peace, and that it should include:

    a. As a development of the Hague Court of Arbitration, a permanent in-

---

[47] Note. The congress declared by vote that it interpreted no transference of territory without the consent of the men and women in it to imply that the right of conquest was not to be recognized. [This footnote is in the original.]

ternational Court of Justice to settle questions or differences of a justifiable character such as arise on the interpretation of treaty rights or of the law of nations.

b. As a development of the constructive work of the Hague Conference, a permanent International Conference holding regular meetings in which women should take part, to deal not with the rules of warfare but with practical proposals for further international co-operation among the states.

This conference should be so constituted that it could formulate and enforce those principles of justice, equity and good will in accordance with which the struggles of subject communities could be more fully recognized and the interests and rights not only of the great powers and small nations but also those of weaker countries and primitive peoples gradually adjusted under an enlightened international public opinion.

This International Conference shall appoint:

A permanent Council of Conciliation and Investigation for the settlement of international differences arising from economic competition, expanding commerce, increasing population and changes in social and political standards.

12. GENERAL

The International Congress of Women, advocating universal disarmament and realizing that it can only be secured by international agreement, urges, as a step to this end, that all countries should, by such an international agreement, take over the manufacture of arms and munitions of war and should control all international traffic in the same. It sees in the private profits accruing from the great armament factories a powerful hindrance to the abolition of war.

13. COMMERCE AND INVESTMENTS

a. The International Congress of Women urges that in all countries there shall be liberty of commerce, that the seas shall be free and the trade routes open on equal terms to the shipping of all nations.

b. Inasmuch as the investment by capitalists of one country in the resources of another and the claims arising therefrom are a fertile source of international complications, this International Congress of Women urges the widest possible acceptance of the principle that such investments shall be made at the risk of the investor, without claim to the official protection of his government.

14. NATIONAL FOREIGN POLICY

a. This International Congress of Women demands that all secret treaties shall be void and that for the ratification of future treaties, the participation of at least the legislature of every government shall be necessary.

b. This International Congress of Women recommends that National Commissions be created and international Conferences convened for the scientific study and elaborations of the principles and conditions of permanent peace, which might contribute to the development of an International Federalism.

These commissions and conferences should be recognized by the governments and should include women in their deliberations.

15. WOMEN IN NATIONAL AND INTERNATIONAL POLITICS
This International Congress of Women declares it to be essential, both nationally and internationally, to put into practice the principle that women should share all civil and political rights and responsibilities on the same terms as men.

V. THE EDUCATION OF CHILDREN
16. This International Congress of Women urges the necessity of so directing the education of children that their thoughts and desires may be directed towards the ideal of constructive peace.

VI. WOMEN AND THE PEACE SETTLEMENT
17. This International Congress of Women urges that in the interests of lasting peace and civilization the conference which shall frame the peace settlement after the war should pass a resolution affirming the need in all countries of extending the parliamentary franchise to women.
18. This International Congress of Women urges that representatives of the people should take part in the conference that shall frame the peace settlement after the war, and claims that amongst them women should be included.

VII. ACTION TO BE TAKEN
19. WOMEN'S VOICE IN THE PEACE SETTLEMENT
This International Congress of Women resolves that an international meeting of women shall be held in the same place at the same time as the Conference of the Powers which shall frame the terms of the peace settlement after the war for the purpose of presenting practical proposals to that conference.

20. ENVOYS TO THE GOVERNMENTS
In order to urge the governments of the world to put an end to this bloodshed and to establish a just and lasting peace, this International Congress of Women delegates envoys to carry the message expressed in the congress resolutions to the rulers of the belligerent nations of Europe and to the President of the United States.

These envoys shall be women of belligerent nations appointed by the International Committee of this congress. They shall report the result of their missions to the International Women's Committee for Constructive Peace as a basis for further action.

6. Alice Hamilton and Jane Addams
Tour Europe at War

As Jane Addams's companion on her trip to the Women's Congress at The Hague, Alice Hamilton's outlook on the venture was much less enthusiastic than that of Mary Chamberlain. When Addams was chosen by the congress to present its resolutions to the governments of the warring countries, Hamilton accompanied her, but did not consider herself part of the delegation. As shown in the following report,[48] which appeared in *The Survey* as well as in their memoir, *Women at The Hague*, she was initially more interested in the medical aspects of the war than in the women's pacifist endeavors. Hamilton had her doubts about the congress and considered the resolution to send delegates to the warring and neutral countries singularly foolish, but she changed her mind after the delegation was received courteously by political leaders in Berlin, Vienna, and Budapest.

In addition to presenting the resolutions to state leaders, the women had informal meetings with journalists, pacifists, and anyone interested in the Women's Peace Congress. The delegation left Amsterdam on May 19, 1915. In Berlin, war met them "on all sides." Addams and Hamilton were on the one hand impressed by the efficiency that kept the war machine running and especially by the contributions of women to it, and on the other hand horrified by the thought of the casualties of this efficiency. They had to face accusations about the sale of American munitions as well as the rejoicing about the sinking of the *Lusitania* less than two weeks before their visit.

The trip gave the two women an opportunity to renew old acquaintances and establish new contacts in Germany. Alice Salomon welcomed them at her Women's School for Social Work, and Friedrich Siegmund-Schultze's East Side settlement sponsored a lecture by Addams about the work of Hull House. Marie Stritt, the internationally minded former president of the League of German Women's Associations and in 1915 president of the conservative German Federation for Woman Suffrage, met the delegation at the Dresden train station on their way to Vienna. The League itself, having denounced the congress altogether, viewed Addams's mission much more critically. When Helene Lange and Gertrud Bäumer invited her to speak at the Lyceum Club, they made it very clear that she could not talk

---

[48]   Alice Hamilton, "At the War Capitals," *Survey*, August 7, 1915, pp. 417–22.

about the congress at the Hague but only about her settlement work before the war.

They encountered many surprises. Former pacifists had turned into ardent supporters of the war, while on the other hand, members of the bourgeois women's movement were "much more moderate than we had been led to expect." In Vienna, an audience of women pacifists was "small and rather timid," but courageous enough to ask for a report. For Jane Addams and Alice Hamilton, the women's peace mission opened a window onto the warring societies. They found that "there is in the countries actually at war no such universal desire to fight on to the bitter end as we suppose over here."

At the War Capitals
by Alice Hamilton, M.D.

THE SURVEY has asked me to write the narrative of Miss Addams' journey to present the resolutions of what is now usually called the Woman's Peace Congress at The Hague to the governments of the warring and some of the neutral countries. The delegation consisted of only Miss Addams and Dr. Aletta Jacobs of Amsterdam; but Dr. Jacobs took with her a friend Frau Wollften Palthe of The Hague, and Miss Addams took me.[49] We two were not official members of the delegation and usually took no part in the formal interviews with ministers of foreign affairs or chancellors; so that my account of our wanderings must be confined to the unofficial parts, to the people we met informally and the impressions we gained as we passed through the countries, and stopped in the capitals and the life there.

There were absolutely no hardships encountered anywhere, not even real discomforts. Inconveniences there were in the shape of tiresome waiting in consular offices for passports,—a formality which had to be repeated in between each two countries; but aside from that, travel was easy and comfortable. The first government visited by the delegation was the Dutch, since the congress was held at The Hague, and after that came Great Britain where the delegation saw Mr. Asquith and Sir Edward Grey.[50] I did

[49]   For Aletta Jacobs, see Part III, document 2, Heymann and Augspurg, "Women's Work," note 15.
    Frederika Palthe [Frederika Wilhelmina (Mien) van Wulfften Palthe-Broese van Groenen] (1875–1960), Dutch women's activist and member of the IWSA. Palthe was a good friend of Aletta Jacobs, who spent the last years of her life in Palthe's home.
[50]   Herbert Henry Asquith (1852–1928), British statesman, member of the Liberal Party, and British prime minister from 1908 to 1916. Asquith supported Irish home rule and advanced some social reform legislation before World War I. Although Asquith felt that women should not participate in politics, he supported their enfranchisement in Britain because of their role on the war and favorable public sentiment.

not accompany Miss Addams to London, for just then I had an unexpected opportunity to go into Belgium and chose that instead, so that her experiences there I did not share in and cannot describe. The beginning of our joint pilgrimage was on May 19 when with the two Dutch women we left Amsterdam for the day's journey to Berlin.

Germany looked far more natural than we had been led to expect; indeed, the only unusual feature to my eyes was the absence of young and middle-aged men in the fields where the work was being carried on almost entirely by women, children and old men.

We reached Berlin at night and the next morning as we drank our coffee, Dr. Sudekum's card was brought up.[51] Readers of THE SURVEY will probably remember him as a prominent Socialist, a member of the Reichstag and an authority on city planning, who visited this country some two years ago and spoke in some of our large cities. We went down to meet him, but seeing no one in the room except a few officers, thought there was some mistake; when, to our surprise, a tall, blond soldier came up and saluted and we recognized that this was actually Dr. Sudekum. We had never supposed that he would actually be in the army though we knew that he was one of the military Socialists—indeed, one of those selected by the Kaiser to go on a mission to Italy and try to persuade the Italian Socialists that Italy should remain loyal to the Triple Alliance.[52]

We talked together and he told us of Italy's probable entrance into the war, insisting that it would be a matter of no military importance, but an act of unforgivable treachery. He had been up all the night before at the foreign office and his eyes had that dull hunted look that goes with sleeplessness and intense emotion. He was the first one to attack us on the subject of America's sale of munitions of war to the allies, an attack to which we became wearily accustomed before we left Germany and Austria. Dr. Sudekum was just back from nine days at the front and claimed that every

---

Edward Grey (1862–1933), British statesman who served as Foreign Minister from 1905 to 1916. His comment on the outbreak of World War I—"The lamps are going out all over Europe"—became proverbial. Grey was responsible for the secret treaty by which Italy joined the Allies and solicited U.S. support for Britain in World War I. Like Asquith, he supported Irish home rule and resigned when Asquith retired. In 1919 he was sent on a special mission to secure the United States's entry into the League of Nations.

[51] Dr. Albert Südekum, German politician (1871–1943) of the Social Democratic Party, was a member of the Reichstag from May 1900 to November 1918. He visited the United States at least once, and his contacts to Addams date back to this trip in 1910. Südekum served as the Prussian minister of finance from November 1918 to March of 1920.

[52] Südekum traveled to Stockholm and Rome in September of 1914 to explain the German social democrats' policy of support for the war efforts to Swedish and Italian socialists. In 1882, Italy had formed the Triple Alliance with Austria-Hungary and Germany. At the same time, a secret treaty allied it with France in 1902. Italy declared war on Austria-Hungary on May 23, 1915, days before the visit of Addams and Hamilton, and on Germany on August 28 of the same year.

THE DIALOGUE CHANGES DURING WORLD WAR I

shell which had fallen in that part of the line while he was there was an American shell. Nevertheless, he was most friendly and readily promised to do what he could to secure an interview for the delegation with Count von Jagow of the Foreign Office.[53]

After he left, I went out on a few errands and got my first impression of Berlin. The city, of course, was in perfect order, yet the war met me on all sides. The walls were placarded and the windows full of appeals for money for all sorts of objects; for blinded soldiers, for the relief of the widows of the heroes of a certain battleship, for a woman's fund to be made up of pennies and presented to the Kaiser, and much the most terrible of all— long lists of the latest casualties. But there were no wounded soldiers to be seen and no evidence of poverty and suffering, the relief work is apparently well done. Later on, when we were taken around by Dr. Alice Salomon, we saw how work has been provided for those who need it, for the women especially.[54] I had a curious sensation on that expedition of having seen and heard it all before: and then I remembered that just a little while ago in Brussels I had seen gentle Belgian ladies organizing work for the Belgian poor in exactly the same way the gentle German ladies were doing it for the German poor. And in Paris, and in London, it was the same.

We had been told before we went to Germany that the people were absolutely united in a determination to fight until Germany was victorious, that there were not a dozen men the length and breadth of the land who were even thinking, much less talking, of peace.

Of course, such unanimity is inconceivable in a nation of sixty-five million thinking people, and it was easy enough for us to convince ourselves that it did not exist. From the first we met men and women who were pacifists. The one who stands out most prominently in my mind, is the clergyman Sigmundt-Schultze, who is fortunately too lame to serve in the army. He has gathered around him a group of people, free from bitterness, and from ultra-patriotism, fair-minded, and deeply sorrowful over the war. Many of them belong also to a group that calls itself *Das Bund Neues Vaterland,* which stands for very much the same things as the Union of Democratic Control in England—that is, for a peace without injustice or humiliating terms to any people, no matter who is victor.[55]

[53]   Gottlieb von Jagow (1863–1935). Von Jagow was the secretary in Germany's Foreign Ministry from 1913 to November 1916. He supported the ambitious war aims of the nationalists and militarists.
[54]   Unemployment rose at the beginning of the war and for many working-class families the pay of a soldier did not amount to their prewar wages. Therefore, public and private welfare organizations organized work projects for women.
[55]   The Bund Neues Vaterland (New Fatherland League) was formed in Berlin in 1914 when the Deutsche Friedensgesellschaft (German Peace Society) failed to protest decisively against the war. It united conservatives, liberals, and socialists, opposed the annexation policy, and put forth a vision of a peaceful and democratic united Europe. From 1915 on, the organiza-

Of course, we also met people who held the point of view which we in America have been led to think universal in Germany. The Lusitania was still in everyone's mind and the first note from America had just been received.[56] I talked to many people who accepted the sinking of the vessel without questioning. She was carrying ammunition; she was armed; the passengers had been warned, and had no more reason to complain than if they had entered a city that was being besieged. These people were absolutely sure that Germany was fighting in self-defense only, and their respect for the military was so great that they looked upon the acts of the Belgian *franc-tireurs* as horrible crimes.[57]

Toward the invasion of Belgium most of them had held the belief that it had been a military necessity, but that there must be no permanent occupation. No one believed in the tales of atrocities. "If you knew our good German soldiers, you'd see how impossible all that is."

As for our selling munitions of war to the allies, the resentment it arouses is almost incredible. Many of them seem to suppose that all the ammunition used by the allies comes from America. The American wife of a German nobleman told Miss Addams that a widowed friend had come to see her, with a bit of shell some soldier had sent her from the front, saying that it was the shell that had killed her husband. And the woman had shown her the ghastly thing and said: "Look at it and tell me if it is an American shell."[58]

We stood up stoutly for our country, arguing that it was Germany that

---

tion experienced considerable pressure from the German government. The harassment did not stop when some leading members assumed official posts after the revolution of 1918. Renamed in 1922 the Deutsche Liga für Menschenrechte (German League for Human Rights), it strove for reconciliation with France and Poland, often on a personal basis, staged yearly antiwar marches, and lobbied for Germany's entry into the League of Nations. It was disbanded by the Nazis, but a few members founded new branches in exile.

The Union of Democratic Control was founded in England in August of 1914. A small organization with a prominent membership from Oxford, Cambridge, and Parliament, it blamed not only Germany but the British Foreign Office for the outbreak of the war. In November 1914 it had already drawn up terms for a negotiated settlement.

[56] When a German U-boat sank the British liner *Lusitania* on May 7, 1915, 128 Americans drowned along with over a thousand other passengers. The sinking exposed deep divisions in U.S. public opinion about whether to support military preparedness or neutrality. Many Germans felt that the torpedoing was justified, and it later turned out that the ship had indeed carried munitions destined for England, and that the German embassy had cautioned Americans in a small newspaper announcement against travel on British or French vessels.

[57] Free shooters: Belgian partisans during the German occupation in World War I.

[58] Possibly Neena Hamilton Pringsheim (dates not available), who hosted the group in Berlin and later appealed to Addams to help her in relief work for British and Russian soldiers interned in Germany. Neena Hamilton was an American lecturer and writer on art who received a doctorate from the University of Heidelberg in 1901; she had also studied in Berlin, Halle, Munich, and Paris. She married Hans Pringsheim in Germany and eventually moved to Berlin.

THE DIALOGUE CHANGES DURING WORLD WAR I

had prevented both Hague congresses from pronouncing against this very practice, that Germany had herself taken every opportunity to sell munitions to warring countries, that for us to change international law and custom in the middle of the present war in favor of Germany and to the detriment of the allies would be an unneutral act, but it was mostly useless.[59] I think we convinced, perhaps, two or three men. Most of them did not even listen to our explanations.

There was no difficulty in securing an interview for Miss Addams and Dr. Jacobs with Count von Jagow and although Dr. Bethmann-Hollweg did not consent to see the delegation, he granted Miss Addams an interview.[60] I waited for her in a spacious room in the chancery on the Wilhelm Strasse, looking out on a great shady garden right in the heart of Berlin. From there we went to pay some calls on men who we thought might throw some light on the question of the possibility of neutral nations acting as negotiators between the warring countries. It was very easy to secure the introductions we wanted, partly through Sigmundt-Schultze and partly through some friendly American newspaper men.[61]

We called first on Prof. Hans Delbrueck who lives next door to Harnack, his brother-in-law.[62] Miss Addams was greatly tempted to call on the latter,

[59] The two peace congresses at The Hague in 1899 and 1907 passed vague resolutions on disarmament and the use of certain types of weapons, and established an international court of arbitration. Few of the participating nations were genuinely committed to lasting peace efforts. The German delegation was especially reluctant to yield any rights of national sovereignty for the cause of peace.

[60] Theobald von Bethmann-Hollweg (1856–1921) was appointed German chancellor in 1909. His ambiguous and hesitant action during the war and his failure to assert the primacy of the civilian government over the military forced him to resign in July of 1917.

[61] Among those who apparently secured Addams the interview with Bethmann-Hollweg were Friedrich Siegmund-Schultze, Alice Salomon, and the American journalist Louis Lochner. Lochner (1887–1975) was a pacifist who had from the beginning of the war tried to win Wilson to the idea of continuous mediation. He was in Berlin during Addams's visit in May 1915 and was part of the Ford Peace Ship mission later that year. His leadership in the peace movement ended after World War I, when he became a foreign correspondent in Germany. He worked in the Berlin bureau of the Associated Press from 1924 to 1941, winning a Pulitzer Prize in 1939.

[62] Hans Delbrück (1848–1929), German military historian. Delbrück served in the Prussian Landtag (state parliament) from 1882 to 1885 and in the Reichstag (national parliament) from 1884 to 1890. He edited the influential Preussische Jahrbücher (Prussian annals) from 1883 to 1919. In 1896 he was appointed professor of history at Berlin University, a position he held until 1919. During World War I, Delbrück opposed the ambitious military leaders and pleaded for moderate war aims, peace negotiations, and the introduction of a democratic constitutional monarchy. He avidly opposed the Vaterlandspartei, a nationalist and militaristic party. After the war, he severely criticized the German military, but also opposed the idea that Germany alone was responsible for the war.

Adolf von Harnack (1851–1930), Protestant theologian and brother-in-law of Delbrück, father of women's rights activist Agnes von Zahn-Harnack and Elisabet von Harnack (see Part IV). Harnack taught at the universities of Leipzig, Marburg, and Berlin (between 1888 and 1921), where Alice Salomon took his classes. Harnack's teachings, especially the book Hamil-

THE DIALOGUE CHANGES DURING WORLD WAR I

for she has always had a great admiration for his book, *Das Wesen des Christenthums*. But Sigmundt-Schultze who was with us advised her not to, saying that she would only be disappointed, he had gone in heart and soul for the war.

The interview with Delbrueck was not enlightening. He did not seem to me wise or just, and his idea of the sort of intervention which would be of value in this crisis was so utterly un-American that we thought it hardly worth listening to. Briefly, he advised that President Wilson should use threats to the two chief belligerents and thus bring them to terms. "Let him," he said, "tell England that he will place an embargo on munitions of war, unless she will accept reasonable terms for ending the war, and let him tell Germany that this embargo will be lifted unless Germany does the same."

Miss Addams told him that such a move would be impossible, even if it were of any value; that for the president to use threats would be to lose his moral force, and that he would not have the country behind him. But Delbrueck waved aside as absurd both these objections. "Moral influence is nothing," he said, "what is needed is armed mediation. Your president has the right under your constitution to do this, he need not consult the country."

He went on to say much that he had already said in his article in the *Atlantic,* that Germany desires no new territory in Europe, but what she requires is colonies, and that he would be in favor of her evacuating Belgium on condition of her being given concessions in the Belgian Congo.[63] He was one of the Germans who could see no argument in defense of our sale of munitions and who considered the sinking of the Lusitania absolutely justified.

I found Maximilian Harden much more interesting.[64] He is a little man with a big head, almost all of it forehead and hair, his eyes tired and burnt out and his general aspect full of weary depression. People had warned us against him, calling him a fire-eater, one of the men who had done most to encourage the war. To us he seemed quite the contrary; he seemed to re-

---

ton mentions, were controversial within the conservative Protestant establishment. Initially deeply shocked by the war, von Harnack focused on his studies, but ultimately turned against the politics of the Vaterlandspartei. Although devoted to the emperor, he later supported the Weimar Republic.

[63]   Hans Delbrück, "Germany's Answer," *Atlantic Monthly*, February 1915, pp. 233–42.

[64]   Maximilian Harden (1861–1927), German writer and editor. Although he supported an imperialist foreign policy, Harden pleaded for reconciliation with France before 1914 and for domestic reform measures in Germany. Harden's enthusiasm for the war waned quickly, he was arrested, and his weekly, *Die Zukunft* (*The Future*), was censored. Harden supported a negotiated peace and realized early that Germany was drifting toward complete defeat. After World War I he continued his fight against militarism and nationalism despite an assassination attempt in 1922.

THE DIALOGUE CHANGES DURING WORLD WAR I

gard it as a terrible tragedy. He was very fair to our country, saying that Germany had no right to criticize our sale of ammunition to the allies. He said he had always told the Germans that since they had a great advantage in their enormous factories at Essen, England naturally must strive to offset it by an equal advantage, and this she had in her navy which enabled her to buy the supplies she could not manufacture.[65] He said it was poor sportsmanship for Germany to protest. As for help from the neutral nations in this crisis, he seemed to think it the only hope, and yet not an immediate hope.

Miss Addams was entertained by the large women's organization, the Lyceum Club, which has a beautiful building of its own.[66] We dined there with some of the leaders and afterwards there was a reception and Miss Addams spoke, but they did not wish her to speak of the peace congress or of her mission. As everywhere, excepting in Hungary, the women's suffrage organizations and the International Council of Women had pronounced against the meeting at The Hague and made it difficult for their members to attend. Nevertheless, when we talked to these women individually we found them much more moderate than we had been led to expect. Indeed, as I look back on our German visit, I can remember two persons who spoke to us with the sort of bitterness that I have heard from German-Americans over here, even though the war is so very close to them. I suspect that that is the real reason: that the tragedy is too great for rancor and uncharitableness. One women said to me, when I quoted something from this side of the water, "I am far past all that now. At first I was bitter, but that is gone now. I have almost forgotten it."

One must always remember that the Germans read nothing and hear nothing from the outside. I talked with an old friend, the wife of a professor under whom I worked years ago when I was studying bacteriology in Germany.[67] She and her husband are people with cosmopolitan connections, they read three languages besides their own, and have always been as far removed as possible from narrow provincialism, but since last July they have known nothing except what their government has decided that they shall know. I did not argue with my friend, but, of course, we talked much together and after she had been with us for three days she told me that she had never known before that there were people in England who did not

---

[65]   Essen and the Ruhr valley were at that time the center of German heavy industry.

[66]   Lyceum Club: a Berlin women's club formed to provide higher education for women when secondary schools and universities were still closed to them. Addams and Terrell attended the lectures of the club during their trips to Germany.

[67]   Hamilton is referring to Ludwig Edinger (1855–1918) and his wife Anna (1863–?), a social welfare leader and feminist who as a member of the German branch of WILPF attended the Vienna congress of 1921. Hamilton knew both from her studies in Germany (see the Epilogue).

wish to crush Germany, who wished for a just settlement, and even some who were opposed to the war.

Then she said, "I want you to believe this. We Germans think that the fatherland was attacked without provocation, that our war is one of self-defense only. That is what we have been told. I begin to think it may not be true, but you must believe that we were sincere in our conviction."

In Berlin we had bread cards and we ate war bread. At each meal the waiter asked for our cards and snipped off one of the three coupons, then he brought us one and a half *Brodchen*, quite enough for breakfast and more than enough for the other meals.[68] It was good bread something like a cross between rye bread and white bread. They told us that this excessive economy was not necessary, for as a matter of fact, Germany gets all the wheat she needs across the Russian border by bribing officials, but that the German government wished to train the people in habits of saving. It has certainly been successful. I could not imagine being wasteful of bread in Berlin. . . .

[Hamilton here provides descriptions of further travels in Austria, Hungary, Switzerland, Italy, France, Belgium, and England.]

It is hard to sum up general impressions from this journey, there are so many of them. One, however, I should like to speak of, for it is born in so strongly now that I am at home again. That is, that there is in the countries actually at war no such universal desire to fight on to the bitter end as we suppose over here. We judge largely by the newspapers which come to us from that side and which are, of course, strictly censored.

I find that people here are often indignant, if not actually resentful, at the mere suggestion that negotiations be substituted for force at the earliest possible moment. They seem to be so much impressed with the things that can be gained by war before war can be allowed to stop, but I believe that they do not realize what war has already cost the countries engaged in it and what more it will cost if it is to continue. The men at the head of affairs over there are not blind and they do realize it, and so do many thinking people in every country, and so would Americans if they could see for themselves and were not obliged to form their judgment simply on what the warring governments allow the newspapers to say. Those nations are committing race suicide and impoverishing their children and grandchildren, and they know it; yet they seem to be unable to find any way to end it. Surely it ought to be our part to keep our heads clear to see things as they are; and instead of hounding on the fighters to seek for some rational way out of it all.

[68] Brötchen: roll.

THE DIALOGUE CHANGES DURING WORLD WAR I

7. German Women Appeal to Jane Addams and Edith Wilson

After the armistice was declared on November 11, 1918, Germany faced starvation and revolution. The following day, representatives of the mainstream German women's movement, Gertrud Bäumer and Alice Salomon, appealed for aid in a telegram to Edith Wilson, the wife of Woodrow Wilson. German women pacifists, stressing that they were now "free voters of a free republic," sent a telegram to Jane Addams. The messages were intercepted by the State Department and released to the press by the War Department on November 14. Addams learned about them from newspapers. Only very liberal publications like *Survey* expressed sympathy for the defeated enemy. Many others, like the *Buffalo Enquirer*, ran hostile headlines: "Huns Use Women to Try to Evade Terms of the Armistice" (November 15, 1918). Reprinted here are the messages as they were reported in the *Chicago Tribune* on November 15, 1918.

While Edith Wilson never acknowledged the telegrams, Addams willingly identified their authors in later newspaper interviews. She praised Anita Augspurg as a "brilliant and earnest woman" and as a participant of the Women's Peace Congress at The Hague, and she clarified Bäumer's and Salomon's positions in the German women's movement. Addams's cautious remarks resulted in a number of hate letters. After consultation with the Women's Peace Party, Addams had planned a cautious, noncommittal response—"Peace Greetings. Understand Food Will Be Supplied"—but the Trading With the Enemy Act prohibited any private communication with Germany.

In the months following the message from the German women, Addams joined in the work of the American Friends Service Committee and eventually became central in the English and American postwar efforts to "Save the Babies."

Appeal of Berlin Women to President's Wife and Jane Addams for Aid

General Women Suffer Most

"Free Voters of Free Republic"

WASHINGTON, Nov. 14—The War Department tonight made public wireless messages from German women appealing to Mrs. Woodrow Wilson and Miss Jane Addams to save the women and children of Germany from starving.

The messages were picked up from the German wireless station at Nauen. Berlin, Nov. 12, 1918.

The message to Mrs. Wilson follows:

"To Mrs. Woodrow Wilson, White House, Washington, D.C.

"Madame: According to the terms of the armistice Germany has to surrender a very large part of the rolling stock of her railways. At the same time she has to feed the troops of her former enemies in the occupied provinces of Germany.

"The German women and children have been starving for years. They will die from hunger by millions if the terms of the armistice are not changed.

"We need the rolling stock of the railways to bring food from the farms to the cities. It will be impossible to feed the soldiers of the occupying armies if we cannot get large amounts of food from overseas.

"The women and children all the world over have been the innocent sufferers of this terrible war, but nowhere more than in Germany.

"Let it be through you, madame, to implore our sisters in the United States of America who are mothers like ourselves to ask their government and the allied governments to change the terms of the armistice so that the long suffering of women and children of Germany may not end in unspeakable disaster.

"For the National Council of Women of Germany.

"Gertrude Baeumer,

"Alice Salomon."

The message to Miss Addams follows:

"Poz, Nov. 13, 1918.

"To Jane Addams, Hull House, Chicago.

"German women, foreseeing entire famishment and mutiny for their country, urge their American sisters to intercede for relief of truce conditions regarding terms of demobilization, blockade, wagons, locomotives. We are all free voters of a free republic now, greeting you heartily.

"Anita Augsburg [*sic*]"

———

Miss Jane Addams had not received a message of appeal from the women of Germany late last night. She said she had no intimation regarding the identity of Anita Augsburg [*sic*].[69]

[69] It is unclear why the *Tribune* reporter could not obtain this information from Addams. In an interview with the Chicago *Examiner* the next day, Addams identified all three German women—Anita Augspurg as a pacifist, Alice Salomon as a social reformer, and Gertrude Bäumer as editor of the leading publication of the German women's movement.

THE DIALOGUE CHANGES DURING WORLD WAR I

8. An American Report
on the Zurich Congress

An event held parallel to the official proceedings at Versailles where the terms of the peace treaty were being negotiated by representatives of the victorious forces, the International Congress of Women for Permanent Peace met in Zurich in mid-May 1919. It attracted delegates from seventeen countries, both neutral and belligerent. Mary Chamberlain, still working for *Survey*, was a member of the American delegation to Zurich, as she had been in 1915 to The Hague. Again her report captured the spirit of the congress as it evolved during the five-day meeting.

Chamberlain's article[70] explored many features of the unfolding drama at Zurich—the statements exchanged by German and French women; the effects of revolutions in Russia and Germany; the refusal of the group to endorse revolution despite the predominance of left-wing political views; and, above all, protest against the British blockade of Germany. She described the different geopolitical perceptions of the blockade, which in some delegates' countries was hardly noticed but in others threatened a entire generation of children with starvation. Helene Stöcker estimated that 50 percent of the babies born in Berlin in 1918–19 had died. Children in Austria were suffering the most.

Along with the blockade, the vengeful peace terms cast a shadow over the congress. But delegates still hoped to create a greater awareness of international issues and to forge solidarity among peace-oriented women on both sides of the Atlantic.

The Women at Zurich
by Mary Chamberlain
of *The Survey* Staff

In the hall of the Glöckenhaus (Christian Association) of Zurich, two hundred women met together in the second International Congress of Women for Permanent Peace, on May 15–25.[71] They were from seventeen different countries; six more were thus represented than at the Hague in 1915 (see

[70]   Mary Chamberlain, "The Women at Zurich," *Survey*, June 14, 1919, pp. 426–28. Italics indicate emphasis in the original.
[71]   The proceedings of the Congress include the lists of the delegates. They can be located in *JAP*, reel 17.

Survey for June 5, 1915). Three women there had started in March from Australia, on being sent by the Union of Shorthand Writers and Typists at Melbourne. Four came from Holland, led by Doctor Aletta Jacobs, suffragist and internationalist, whose life labor was rewarded at the conference by the news that the Dutch parliament had passed the universal suffrage bill.[72] Six women from Norway, four from Denmark and eleven from Sweden had journeyed eight days through Germany—at ordinary times a three day's trip—carrying their own food and waiting sometimes all night long for trains that departed on helter-skelter schedules. Twenty-seven delegates, social democrats, independent socialists and one communist bore testimony of social and economic conditions from almost every large city of Germany.[73] Two delegates came from Soviet Hungary, four from Socialist Austria.[74] Twenty-six English women, including Mrs. Despard, veteran suffragist and daughter of General French; Mrs. Philip Snowden, Mrs. Pethick Lawrence, and Dr. Ethel Williams, who holds the diploma of public health from Cambridge University, brought to the conference such energy and ability that it seemed as though the meeting would not be swamped, as had been feared before calling the convention in Switzerland, by a superiority of Germans but by a superiority of British "generalship."[75]

---

[72] Holland was represented by Aletta Jacobs (see Part III, document 2, Heymann and Augspurg, "Women's Work," note 15), Cornelia Ramondt-Hirschmann, and Frederika Palthe.

Ramondt-Hirschmann [no dates available] was a pacifist who was involved in organizing the 1915 Women's Peace Congress at The Hague. From 1919 to 1937, she was a board member of WILPF and president of its Dutch branch.

For Frederika Palthe, see Part III, doucment 6, Alice Hamilton, "At the War Capitals," note 49.

[73] Germany was represented by twenty-five delegates, among them Anita Augspurg; Lida Gustava Heymann; Gertrud Baer; Auguste Kirchhoff; Frida Perlen; Constanze Hallgarten (1881–1969), a German pacifist who had attended the Hague congress and later headed the Munich branch of WILPF; and Margarethe Selenka (1860–1923), German journalist and pacifist, founder of the Committee for Rallies for the Peace Conference in 1898–99 and organizer of a women's peace demonstration, the first international organized political activity of women.

[74] Among the Austrian delegates was Leopoldine Kulka (see Part III, section 3, Bäumer, "The League of Women's Associations," note 2).

[75] Great Britain was represented by twenty-five delegates, including Kathleen Courtney (see Part III, document 4, Chamberlain, "The Women at The Hague," note 31); Chrystal Macmillan (see Part III, document 4, Chamberlain, "The Women at the Hague," note 31); Emmeline Pethick-Lawrence (1867–1954), British suffragist and social reformer, one of the three British women who attended the Women's Peace Congress at the Hague in 1915; Ethel Snowden (dates unavailable), British socialist and suffragist, who wrote about her experience at Zurich in *A Political Pilgrim in Europe* (1921); and Catherine Marshall (1880–1961), suffragist and pacifist who helped organize the Hague congress but did not attend and who held various offices at WILPF in Geneva in the 1920s.

The editors have found no biographical information about Dr. Ethel Williams or about Mrs. Despard, presumably Charlotte Despard, mentioned by Heymann and Augspurg (in Part III, document 2, Heymann and Augspurg, "Women's Work").

THE DIALOGUE CHANGES DURING WORLD WAR I

The Zurich Congress in session (1919). Archives, University of Colorado at Boulder Libraries (WILPF Archive).

Three delegates arrived from "the Irish Republic" and insisted (peacefully!) on their tables bearing a separate sign from the tables assigned to "Great Britain." A single delegate from Rumania represented the Balkan states; one from the Argentina [*sic*] sufficed inadequately for the vast tracts of South America, and Madame Rosa Genoni was the only Italian to secure a passport from the Italian government.[76] Though an internationalist by avocation, Madame Genoni is a designer of costumes by vocation and fully persuaded her government to let her attend the conference to study the fashions of "tout le monde!" The Belgian delegates who went to The Hague were said to have been threatened with expatriation if they appeared at Zurich, so that although Mlle. La Fontaine was a listener in the audience, no Belgian name appeared on the list of delegates.[77] Missing, too, were women from Russia and from countries in the Far East.

Almost at the end of the conference, three French delegates reached

[76] For Rosa Genoni, see Part III, document 4, Chamberlain, "Women at The Hague," note 38.
[77] Since peace was advanced by Germans and their sympathizers during the occupation of Belgium by Germany in 1914–18, after 1919 many continued to suspect peace advocates of being unpatriotic and pro-German.

Zurich, one from war-torn Nancy.[78] All members of the French branch of the Women's Committee for Permanent Peace, they had secured passports on various pretexts, but Madame Duchesne [*sic*] and the group of French working-women were held up relentlessly by the French government.[79] They contributed to the conference, however, by sending a carefully thought-out labor program and a beautiful message of greeting to their German "friends." Likewise, our delegation of twenty-six Americans, headed by Jane Addams, president of the conference, lost its labor spokesman, Rose Schneiderman, President of the Woman's Trade Union League of New York.[80] Miss Schneiderman, though in Europe, could not secure the necessary French visé to enter Switzerland.[81]

The congress of women at Zurich was not a revolutionary body. With the delegates paying their own expenses and summoned on another basis than that of purely labor or politics, it was bound to be a gathering of suffragists, teachers, social workers, wives. To untouched America it may seem wildly dangerous and radical, but in Europe, prepared and adjusting itself to social changes, it was no doubt considered very harmless.

To be sure there was a vigorous "left wing." But the temper of the meeting was tested when this factor introduced a resolution recognizing "the fundamentally just demand underlying most revolutionary movements," declaring sympathy with "the purpose of the workers who are rising up everywhere to make an end to exploitation," counseling against violence on either side in revolution and "*urging the possessing classes voluntarily to give up their special privileges and consent to the reorganization of industry on a democratic basis so that a new order may be inaugurated without bloodshed.*" In high tension the conference accepted the resolution in part—as far as the italics. There it balked at the attempt to split the united purpose of women, rich and poor, by propaganda for one economic class against another.

Léonie La Fontaine (1859–1949), Belgian pacifist and president (1913–19) of the Belgian National Women's Council.

[78]   The three French delegates were Andrée Jouve, a suffragist; Jeanne Mélin, who later attended the WILPF congress in Vienna; and Mlle. Reverchon. The editors have found no biographical information about these women.

[79]   For Gabrielle Duchène, see Part III, document 4, Chamberlain, "The Women at The Hague," note 41.

[80]   Rose Schneiderman (1882–1972), American labor organizer and social reformer. Schneiderman was president of the national WTUL from 1926 until it disbanded in 1950.

[81]   The United States was represented by twenty-six delegates, among them Jane Addams; Emily Greene Balch; Mary Chamberlain; Madeleine Doty; Alice Hamilton; Florence Kelley; Mary Church Terrell; Lillian D. Wald (see Part II, document 6, Alice Salomon, "Social Work in America," note 65); Alice Thatcher Post (dates unavailable), managing editor of *The Public*, a New York journal of finance, commerce, and political science who served as vice president of the American Proportional Representation League and vice president of the Anti-Imperialist League; and Jeanette Rankin (1880–1973), the first woman elected to the U.S. House of Representatives, from Montana, who voted against U.S. entry into World War I.

THE DIALOGUE CHANGES DURING WORLD WAR I

Nor did this international gathering pretend to represent the attitude of women in general. The women at the conference were the outsiders, the visionaries you might call them, who had clung to their ideals throughout the war. Several of the Germans had been imprisoned for opposing the war, many had been persecuted, practically all, from all countries, had been discredited for their principles.

When Fraulein Hymann [*sic*] of Munich dramatically clasped the hand of Madame Nénin [*sic*] from Nancy, none presumed to say France and Germany were united.[82] Instead, Fraulein Hymann herself begged the conference "to recall those women who do not think and feel with us, whose hearts are still filled with hate."

"We do not condemn them," she said; "we try to understand them. I am thinking first of all of the women of Belgium, France and Serbia who for years had no fatherland and whose fatherlands were occupied by foreign troops. Let us keep clearly and steadily before our eyes how infinitely more these women have suffered than those whose lands have not been invaded. Above all, I want to cry out to the French and Belgian women. We German women who think differently from you, who represent the point of view of the Internationale, who stretch out our hands to you and implore you to forget the crimes that German men and soldiers have committed in your country—remember that there are still women in Germany who love you, who have suffered with you through all these years in which war was passing over the earth."

This congress at Zurich was held, then, because, though separate in politics, religion, class, a handful of women in every country stayed steadfast to one great principle—opposition to war. At the Hague in 1915, when sons and husbands faced each other in enemy trenches, this opposition was voiced in the emotional (some have said sentimental) appeal to stop the spilling of blood. At Zurich, this opposition centered on the slower violence of starvation.

Here in this American land of plenty, the blockade fades into some invisible line beyond which, I realize vaguely, is intolerable suffering.[83] But in England, the blockade is a near thing over which English women are peering and beginning to ask if the warfare of the Allies is to be that same warfare against women and children waged by Germany. In Scandinavia and Switzerland the blockade is a hard reality, responsible in large part for the rationed bread, milk, and fat. In Germany the blockade is the heavy, high wall imprisoning a people—not in starvation but in under-nourishment which offers no resistance to old age, babyhood, disease or moral tempta-

---

[82] "Madame Nénin": Jeanne Mélin.
[83] The blockade of German ports was kept up after the armistice to compel German acceptance of the peace treaty, and was not lifted until July 1919.

tion. In Austria, in areas of the Balkans and further East the blockade means starvation and death itself.

Statistics are not compiled in a country swept completely with the turmoil of war. But from such figures as were obtainable, Dr. Stoecker, head of the Mütterschaft movement in Berlin, estimated that 50 percent of the babies born in 1918–19 had died.[84] Those who survived are fed upon meal mixed with water and, if fortunate, a little milk. Frau Lehmann of Göttingen had found that in her town 15,000 of the children in the anemic classes at school had developed tuberculosis and that among all the population the tuberculosis death-rate had increased by leaps and bounds.[85] Most pitiful of all, she said, was the influenza epidemic last year which swept away the young people of 15–20 whose resistance had been weakened by lack of food. Hardened to the loss of men at the front, to the loss of babies and old people, they could not bear this loss of the flower of the population on whom the future of the new Fatherland depends. The food ration received by the Göttingen townspeople consisted of 150 grs. of meat (1/2 bones) a day, a tiny piece of bread daily and one teaspoonful of butter to last a week for all purposes.

From Vienna Frau Kulke brought figures showing that the average weight of children of six years is 4 kilo (10 pounds) less than it should be and told how many children of 5, 6, and 7 are too weak to walk.[86] Among 15-year-old children the tuberculosis death-rate is 160 percent—where 6 died before the war 26 are dying now. As for babies, they cannot stand any slight infant malady—the death-rate is so terrific that funerals are held no longer, but parents wrap the little bodies in newspapers and take them on the trains at night to the cemeteries for burial. While before the war 900,000 quarts of milk were delivered in Vienna daily, now only 40,000 are available so that mothers are urged to nurse children up to 2 years although it is estimated that 80 percent of nursing mothers lost an average of 25 kilos (about 60 pounds) each in weight. Austria, according to Frau Kulke, is in a worse plight than India had been during any famine.

A few of the delegates to the conference were thinner than they were four years ago at The Hague. Several had red and pimpled faces, the result of rough sand-soap and ill-digested substitute food. But no one was starved, and some were as fat as the proverbial German Frau. More noticeable than the physical change was the mental change. Fraulein Hymann, indefatigable translator at the Hague, was now worn out by the middle of the day.

[84] Chamberlain means the League for the Protection of Motherhood and Sexual Reform (Bund für Mutterschutz und Sexualreform, BfMS).
[85] Henny Lehmann (dates unavailable), German writer and local political activist, especially active in child welfare causes.
[86] For Leopoldine Kulka, see Part III, document 3, Bäumer, "The League of Women's Associations," note 26.

Frau Hallgarten was the life of the picnic that we had on the mountain-side one afternoon.[87] She told merrily of her young son's excitement at finding two pieces of bread by his plate a few days before; she made light of her privations and said laughingly, "It is you who are starved with your ban on German music, not we." But later, as we bumped down the mountain road in the bus, little Frau Hallgarten shrank into the corner, the tears streaming down her fatigued face.

Thus nearly all the delegates from the Central Powers showed the strain of under feeding. On the one hand they were nervous and excitable, on the other dull and slow to keep abreast of events. Instead of leading the discussion as they did at The Hague, Miss Addams had to delay proceedings while some point was patiently translated over and over for the German-speaking delegates.

Moreover, many of us at the conference who had seen the refugees from France and Belgium driven from their wrecked homes felt that the German delegation should have condemned their country in no uncertain terms for this misery it had caused. Although they condemned war in general, and although Fraulein Hymann almost at the close of the conference, in the speech quoted above, shouldered in part the blame, we felt that the resolution offered by English and American delegates against the blockade should have been matched by one from the German side expressing their desire to repair the damage done to France and Belgium. I do not think this attitude was conscious. Rather it was because with senses dulled by their own present suffering they could not visualize the enormity of the suffering of others.

In spite of this German unresponsiveness, the conference did not lessen its protests against the blockade. Unanimously it passed a resolution urging "the governments of all powers assembled at the Peace Conference to develop the inter-allied organization for purposes of peace" and to take immediate action, first, to lift the blockade, second to organize all the resources of the world for the relief of the peoples from famine and pestilence, third to prohibit the transportation of luxuries until necessities are provided. This resolution, signed by Miss Addams, was sent to Versailles and brought back the answer of President Wilson, which has been reported incorrectly by the newspapers as an answer to a resolution on the peace treaty.[88] "Your message," replied the President, "appeals both to my head and to my heart, and I hope most surely that means may be found,

[87]   Constanze Hallgarten (1881–1969), German pacifist. She attended the Hague congress and headed the Munich branch of WILPF from 1919 to 1933. She also belonged to the German Peace Society and the German Union for the League of Nations. In 1933, she escaped from the Nazis to Switzerland and later moved to the United States.
[88]   Woodrow Wilson to Jane Addams, [Washington, D.C.], June 16, 1919, Woodrow Wilson Papers, Library of Congress.

though the present outlook is exceedingly uncompromising because of unfortunate practical difficulties."

Because the blockade rather than the peace terms threw the blacker shadow at the conference, I feel, unanimous verdict of the German delegates to the contrary, that hunger must dictate the signing of the treaty. On the other hand, the Germans seemed too stunned to grasp the severity of the terms. Most touching was the appeal of every delegate with whom I talked—"President Wilson will still help us, don't you think so?" They said that as liberals they were ground between two millstones by the treaty. On the one hand, the militarists are sneering, "We always told you what would happen when you got the peace you begged for;" on the other hand the Bolsheviks are saying, "The workers alone can be trusted; join us in the revolution."

Aside from the partition of Prussia, the economic clauses of the treaty—the loss of mines, the uncertain indemnity, the commercial discouragement—fell most heavily. Especially German women at the conference made a point of the five million "surplus" women at home. Drawn into industry, they would be compensated in some measure for the loss of marriage, they thought; with industry paralyzed as they predicted with the treaty in force, these women would prove a great moral responsibility.

Not a German delegate, however, spoke of the treaty in the same breath as the blockade with bitterness or indignation—only with a sort of hopelessness. "We cannot sign," they said, "and what will it matter—we cannot suffer more than now." It was the Allied delegates present who formed the second resolution sent to Versailles: "By guaranteeing the fruits of secret treaties to the conquerors, the terms of peace tacitly sanction secret diplomacy. They deny the principle of self-determination, recognize the right of victors to the spoils of war, and create all over Europe discords and animosities which can lead only to future wars. . . . With a deep sense of responsibility, this congress strongly urges the Allied governments to accept such amendments of the terms as may be proposed to bring the peace into harmony with those principles just enumerated by President Wilson upon the faithful carrying out of which the honor of the Allied peoples depends."

Like the resolution on the blockade, this second resolution was passed without a dissenting voice. But in the resolution of the League of Nations which followed, again the "left wing" of the conference pressed forward to condemn in toto "any order attempting to reestablish the principle of force" and to substitute clauses urging the "transformation of the capitalist system . . . so that mutual help may replace combat." And again the conservatives showed their majority. As it passed, the resolution endorsed the *principle* of the league of nations included in the treaty and protested against the exclusion of any self-governing state from the league, against

THE DIALOGUE CHANGES DURING WORLD WAR I

Anita Augspurg (left) and Lida Gustava Heymann (right) on the street in Zurich (1919). Between them is Mme Despard, whom they mentioned in their memoir of the Hague congress. Swarthmore College Peace Collection.

"one-sided" disarmament, against unequal trading opportunities, against any discrimination of women as league officers.

So there were scores of resolutions slowly discussed, translated, passed or rejected by the women who packed the Glöckenhaus hall: a resolution that changed the name of the body from the Woman's Committee on Permanent Peace, to the Women's League for Peace and Freedom; resolutions on education, on freedom of press and speech, on self-determination for small nationalities, on labor and feminist programs to be worked out by the permanent bureau which the conference voted to establish at Geneva.[89]

But what is the goal of a sheaf of resolutions, what is the use of a handful

[89] Soon thereafter, the name was changed to the Women's International League for Peace and Freedom.

of women flinging a few of their idealistic notions at the powerful and practical conference at Versailles?

First of all, I believe every such "getting together," however small and useless, helps to create the international mind and to throw back into each country some little reflection of another point of view. But that is just a theory. It helps, to quote Miss Addams, in "forming a similar opinion in all countries." But to reply more practically, I will repeat an incident that Miss Addams also brought out:

After the first congress met at The Hague, delegations of women went from country to country, presenting to statesmen, among them President Wilson, the resolutions passed at that conference. Nearly eight months later, when Miss Addams went to the White House for an interview on an entirely different subject, the President drew from his pocket a crumpled sheet of paper. "You see," he smiled, "I have been studying your resolutions hard." Not long after, President Wilson's Fourteen Points stirred the world—points in some ways so identical with the resolutions in his pocket that the latter must have played their modern part in shaping that powerful appeal. How can we say then that this second conference may not sometime help to turn these ideals into realities?

Sidebars: Message of the French Women to the German Signed by Twenty-five French Women

Today for the first time our hands which have sought each other in the night can be joined. We are a single humanity, we women. Our work, our joys, our children, are the same. French and Germans! The soldiers which have been killed between us are for both of us alike victims. It is our brothers and our sisters who have suffered. We do not want vengeance. We hate all war. We push from us both the pride of victory and the rancor of defeat. United by the same faith, by the same sense of service, we agree to consecrate ourselves to the fight against war and to the struggle for everlasting peace.

All women against all wars!

Come, to work. Publicly, in the face of those who have vowed eternal hate, let us unite, let us love each other.

Reply of the German Women to the French

We German women have heard the greetings of our French sisters with the deepest joy, and we respond to them from the depths of our souls. We, too, protest against the perpetuation of a hate which was always foreign to women's hearts. Our French sisters! It is with joy that we grasp your extended hand. We will stand and march together, in common effort for the good of mankind. On the ruins of a material world, founded by force and violence, on misunderstanding and hate, we women will, through death and sorrow, clear the road to the new humanity. As mothers of the coming generations, we, women of all nations, want love and understanding and peace. Despite the dark and gloom of the present we stumble, comforted, toward the sunshine of the future.

9. Florence Kelley Describes
the Zurich Congress

Florence Kelley had previously declared that her work on labor issues with the National Consumers' League prevented her from joining any other reform effort, including the peace movement. As a member of the War Labor Relations Board, Kelley held a position of considerable national power in enforcing labor standards. But when her pacifist views became known publicly, she was removed from the board. By 1919 she had nothing to lose in associating with the peace movement; and attracted by the chance to return to the scene of her student days at Zurich, she accompanied Jane Addams and the American delegation to the International Congress of Women in mid-May 1919. The experience changed her. Henceforth she counted herself as a member of the peace movement.

On her return voyage Kelley wrote candidly to Mary Rozet Smith about the congress,[90] describing the "weak sisters" among the American delegates as well as the "noble" Germans. Kelley knew that Mary Smith would be eager to hear about how her life partner, Jane Addams, had fared in presiding over the congress. She also knew Smith would forgive her for criticizing the woman they both loved. Laced into the breezy familiarity of her account was a somber recognition of the tragedy of recent events in Germany.

[90] Florence Kelley to Mary Rozet Smith, May 22, 1919, on board the S.S. *Rotterdam* (en route from Plymouth, England, to the United States), Jane Addams Papers, SCPC (and *JAP*, reel 12). The letter is annotated "Received by Jane Addams."

Florence Kelley to Mary Rozet Smith

Steamer Rotterdam, May 22nd 1919

Dear Mary,

I left Zurich last Thursday for Bern, Lausanne, Paris, Southhampton, Plymouth, and this ship. As you doubtless know, my going was an act of faith, not of conviction. When anyone asked why I was going, I said "To black J.A.'s boots and lug her suitcases." Of course, I was quite useless.

But next time I would go on my knees. It was *unbelievably wonderful.* There were twenty-five English women sitting with the Germans in front, and the Irish at one side, all alike engrossed in the common effort to do two things. First the English were obsessed with the passionate, overwhelming impulse to lift the blockade, modify the peace, and end the famine; second they wished greater power for women in the League of Nations, and many modifications in the provisions.

There were fourteen nations represented by 126 delegates when I left, and no one of the nature of Rosika or of Frau Selenka among the number.[91] I think we had more than our share of weak sisters with Mrs. Post, Mrs. Mead, Katherine Fuller (!), Marion Cothren, Mrs. Ford and Miss Barrett.[92] But then we were twenty-five all told, and no one was actively queer or obstructive.

The English leaders amazed everybody by emphasizing at every opportunity, that they were all Socialists. This included Mrs. Pethick Lawrence, Crystal Macmillan, Mrs. Snowden (of course), and all the lesser lights.[93] Hitherto, I have found it hard to *like* Englishwomen, but this time I found myself their humble admirer.

---

[91]   For Rosika Schwimmer, see Part III, document 4, Chamberlain, "Women at The Hague," note 31. For Margarethe Selenka, see Part III, document 8, Chamberlain, "Women at Zurich," note 73.

[92]   For Alice Thatcher Post, see Part III, document 8, Chamberlain, "Women at Zurich," note 81. Catherine Eastman Fuller worked as an editor in New York City. Marion B. Cothren, a New York City lawyer and publicist for woman suffrage, was the author of "ABC of Voting" and a member of the New York City Unemployment Commission. No further biographical information is available on these women.

Lucie Ames Mead (1856–1936) advocated world government as early as 1899. She was president of the Massachusetts Woman Suffrage Association between 1903 and 1906. Among her books are *Patriotism and the New Internationalism* (1906), *Swords and Ploughshares* (1912), and *Law or War* (1928).

Clara Ford, not an official delegate, was married to Henry Ford. Earlier in 1915 she had paid for 12,000 telegrams from Woman's Peace Party members to Woodrow Wilson demanding that he call a conference of neutrals.

Kate Waller Barrett (1857–1925), American social reformer and pacifist, was president of the National Council of Women between 1911 and 1916. Barrett attended meetings of the ICW in London (1899), Toronto (1909), and Rome (1914). In 1919 she attended the Zurich peace congress.

[93]   For Pethick-Lawrence and Snowden, see Part III, document 8, Chamberlain, "Women at

In Paris we saw much of Mme. Duchesne [*sic*] who hoped against hope for a passport until Wednesday, May 13th, when she finally wired that there was no hope.[94]

The solitary Italian, Rosa Genone [*sic*], arrived on Tuesday, May 15th, and Mrs. Swannick [*sic*] that evening.[95]

The French women who took part, and the one Belgian, Mlle. La Fontaine, were already in Switzerland, and needed no passports.[96]

Never have I seen so generous a spirit in any group of human beings. Even Dr. Jacobs was amicable from the word "go!"[97]

Needless to say, J.A. presided to the satisfaction of everyone (but me! I thought she wasted one afternoon). I heard people saying in the English delegation "What an excellent chairman, so fair, and not a moment wasted." In the Austrian delegation a woman was saying "she is so willing to yield and say that she is wrong. "I'm sorry I made that blunder"—I shall always hear her saying that, *and* she makes so few blunders."

No one who was not there can ever conceive what it meant to the German and Austrian women. Poor things! Starved in body and soul. I cannot think of them without tears. So noble and eager. The Bavarians feel that their great days have come and gone like a brief dream. Frau Baur [*sic*] a beautiful, loveable young woman was assistant Secretary of State and Frls. Augsburg [*sic*] and Heymann were members of the Bavarian Diet with seven other women, under Eisner.[98] But after he was assassinated by Count Arco Valley, and much violence and bloodshed followed, the[y] resigned in protest.[99]

Today for the first time in its history, Bavaria's army, railways and post office are controlled from Berlin. But women still have votes and our friends are convinced that Democracy has come to stay, whatever vicissitudes may arise.

Zurich," note 75. For Macmillan, see Part III, document 4, Chamberlain, "Women at The Hague," note 31.

[94] For Gabrielle Laforcade Duchène, see Part III, document 4, Chamberlain, "Women at The Hague," note 41.

[95] For Rosa Genoni, see Part III, document 4, Chamberlain, "Women at the Hague," note 38.

Helena Swanwick (1864–1939), British suffragist who chaired the British committee that helped plan the Hague congress. At the Zurich congress she was elected one of two vice presidents of the Women's International League for Peace and Freedom.

[96] Léonie La Fontaine (1859–1949), Belgian pacifist and president (1913–1919) of the Belgian National Women's Council.

[97] For Aletta Jacobs, see Part III, document 2, Heymann and Augspurg, "Women's Work," note 15.

[98] "Frau Baur": Kelley means Gertrud Baer.

[99] Kurt Eisner (1867–1919) was a leader of the Independent Socialist Party, formed by opponents to the war when the SPD voted for war credits. Eisner briefly headed the Bavarian government during a short-lived revolution in 1919. His political leadership was characterized by a faith in workers' councils and decentralized control from below. He was assassinated by Count Anton Arco-Valley, whose political loyalties were feudal and clerical.

There was great difference of opinion among the members about the draft of the League of Nations. When I left, a Committee was at work on a report to go to Paris, and the whole Congress on a long series of resolutions to go back to the national branches for study and for action in their own countries.

The public meetings were in the Aula of the University of Zurich where I was a student five and thirty years ago. The audiences were tremendous, many men being present and sympathetic in an extraordinary degree.

J.A. was at her very best. She loved the whole undertaking, tho I think the wide spread horror of the League of Nations, and especially of the Peace Terms among the members was a surprise and a disappointment.

The day before I left, May 13th, word came that she is to go into Germany. So she will not sail on the Noordam on May 23rd.

With dear love, Yours always.
Florence Kelley

PART IV

THE LIMITATIONS OF NATIONHOOD

IN THE 1920S

A. Americans Respond to Germany's Need

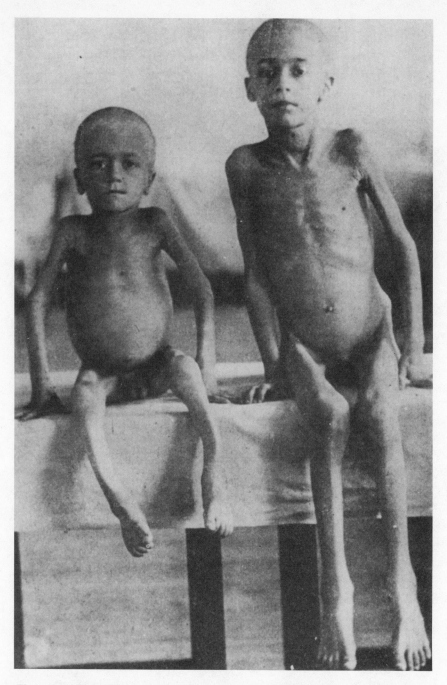

Therese and Aloisia Handl, starving children in Vienna, an illustration from *Survey*, July 15, 1919, p. 528. According to the caption, "The Next Generation in Vienna," this photograph represents "the average condition of children in Vienna" and was "brought home from the International Congress of Women for Permanent Peace, at Zurich, by Mrs. Florence Kelley." Social Welfare History Archives, University of Minnesota.

1. Addams and Hamilton
Tour a Ravaged Germany

After the women's congress at Zurich, Jane Addams and Alice Hamilton went to Germany, along with Carolena Wood and Aletta Jacobs, as part of a Quaker mission to distribute $30,000 worth of food and to investigate the effects of the famine. Since Herbert Hoover, then head of the American Relief Association in Europe, insisted that they wait until Germany had ratified the Treaty of Versailles, they had to spend two months in Paris, arriving finally in Germany on July 7 with the first civilian passports issued to Americans.

The differences between this and Addams's and Hamilton's previous trips to Germany could not have been more striking. Conditions in Germany were shaped by a war that had been fought and lost in the name of nationalism, and the two American reformers could not help but be touched by the consequences, especially the starvation of women, children, and the elderly. In this article,[1] they tried to reach beyond nationalism. Their observations also reflected Hamilton's medical training. They were shocked by the high incidence of famine-related diseases and the death rate among the elderly. More than once, Hamilton noted that the war had cost Germany its leadership in public health measures.

After their return to the United States, Addams and Hamilton published their report in *Survey*. They hoped that a sympathetic account would alter American public opinion on the defeated enemy; the relief campaign for German women and children had not been very successful. Their article was one of several on the postwar famine. Paul Kellogg, the editor of *Survey*, asked Addams for a second, even more sympathetic account that would clearly denounce the Allied blockade, but because she was already receiving a great deal of hate mail she declined his request.

This text also served as a basis for talks Addams gave to German-American audiences throughout the Midwest to support the Quaker mission in Germany. On visits to central Europe in 1920 and 1921, Addams witnessed

---

[1] Alice Hamilton and Jane Addams, "After the Lean Years. Impressions of Food Conditions in Germany After the War Was Signed," *Survey*, September 6, 1919, pp. 793–97. Italics indicate emphasis in the original.

the success of the Quaker programs. By the summer of 1920, the Quakers in cooperation with German welfare agencies were operating 3,400 soup kitchens, handing out more than 600,000 meals daily to children and teenagers. As the letters in this section show, many Germans saw the "Quaker feedings" (*Quäkerspeisungen*) as proof of the politics of international reconciliation, as well as of America's willingness to support the new republic.

After the Lean Years
Impressions of Food Conditions in Germany
When Peace Was Signed
by Alice Hamilton and Jane Addams

While we were in Zurich attending the International Congress of Women for Permanent Peace an invitation came to us to go into Germany with some members of the English and the American Society of Friends to discover how great was the need for food for the German children after the long years of hunger and to make arrangements for the distribution of such food and clothing as the Quakers had been able to collect. It may not be generally known that this society has been throughout the war laboring in the work of relief and reconstruction in France, Belgium, Russia, and Poland, is now planning to extend its work to Germany and Austria, and has in fact been sending supplies into both countries for several months. Dr. Hilda Clark and several other English Friends were planning their second journey into Austria but there were many delays before we were allowed to start into Germany.[2] As we were waiting in London for the peace treaty to be signed we saw something of the campaign which the English people were carrying on for feeding the rest of the enemy countries with the rest of Central Europe. There was the Fight the Famine Fund of which Lord Parmoor is president, the Feed the Children Fund, of which Mrs. Charles Roden Buxton is the leading spirit, the agitation led by the Women's International League, and many others, conducted with a freedom of speech in the Trafalgar square and Albert Hall meetings which was astounding to American ears.[3]

The four English members of the Friends' Committee who traveled

[2] Hilda Clark (1881–1955), British Quaker, relief worker and pacifist. Clark cofounded the Friends War Victims Relief in 1914. In 1919, she organized an elaborate scheme to feed two million starving inhabitants of Vienna.

[3] Charles Alfred Cripps, Lord Parmoor, brother-in-law of Kathleen Courtney (see Part III, document 4, Chamberlain, "Women at The Hague," note 31).

The editors were unable to find biographical information about Mrs. Charles Roden Buxton.

through the occupied region and entered Germany via Cologne, reached Berlin July 6; the three American members, Carolena Wood and ourselves, traveled from The Hague, crossing the border on the first civilian passports issued there after the war was technically over, and arrived in Berlin July 7.[4] We were equipped with letters from Mr. Hoover to his various representatives in German cities.[5] Dr. Aletta Jacobs, a Dutch physician who had been asked as a neutral to make observations on health conditions in Germany, was the fourth member of our party.[6] Dr. Elizabeth Rotten of Berlin, who has been acting as the representative in Germany of the work of the English Friends and is also head of the Educational Committee of the German Association for the Promotion of the League of Nations, was naturally our guide and adviser.

We saw, of course, all classes of the population but from the very first we made a special effort to see as many children as possible, so that we might know the effect of long-continued underfeeding as registered in their growing bodies. In each city, therefore, sometimes under the guidance of the workers or patrons of private charities, sometimes under city physicians and other municipal officials, and sometimes with well-known professors and child specialists, we visited the creches, the child welfare clinics, the playgrounds and outdoor sanitaria, the homes for convalescent children, the hospitals, orphanages, and always several public kitchens and the homes of workers.

Our impressions crowded each other so fast that they merged into one, an impression of mass hunger as we had never imagined it, hunger of millions continued month after month for three years or more; combatted desperately by the doctors, the experimental chemists, the government authorities, the social workers, even more desperately perhaps by the mothers who were urged on by the primitive passion to save their children from starvation; but combatted largely in vain because the necessary weapons

[4]   Carolena Wood (1871–1936). Born in Mount Kisco, New York, to a Quaker family, Wood studied at Union Theological Seminary. In 1915 she sailed with Addams and attended the Conference of Women for Permanent Peace in Zurich. There she interviewed German delegates about the effect of the blockade on children. She was a founding member of the American Friends Service Committee, created to allow conscientious objectors to do relief work in France in 1917. Eventually the AFSC raised three million dollars for relief in Europe. After traveling to Germany with Addams and Hamilton in 1919, Wood went on to bring Quaker-funded relief food to Poland and Silesia. In the late 1920s she joined peace missions that traveled to Central America and China.

[5]   Herbert Hoover (1874–1964), thirty-first president of the United States. Born to a Quaker family, Hoover became head of the Commission for Relief in Belgium in World War I. After working as United States food administrator—recruiting, among others, Jane Addams for lectures—Hoover administered American relief and rehabilitation work in Europe after the armistice.

[6]   For Aletta Jacobs, see Part III, document 2, Heymann and Augspurg, "Women's Work," note 15.

were not there. No specialist can fight tuberculosis with war flour and dried greens, nor can he keep alive a delicate old man on boiled turnips.

As nearly as we could learn up to the middle of 1916 the effects of the blockade were not severely felt, though people who worked among the poor knew that even then mothers of families were losing weight to an alarming degree and that the death-rate among the aged was increasing. Gradually, however, the important articles of diet—meat, milk, animal fats, then vegetable fats, eggs, wheat flour, began to grow scarcer, and the various substitute foods were of low caloric value, so that as the year went on the diet grew very poor. In 1917 it reached the low point of one-third or less than one-third of the standard adopted by all civilized countries as the minimum for a working adult. Then in 1917 the potato crop failed and the terrible "turnip months" came, remembered with horror in every city, but most of all in Saxony where for weeks at a time there was literally nothing in the market but white turnips, the coarse kind known as "Swedes."[7] Many people have acquired a permanent dyspepsia from the experience and for the old this diet was fatal. In Chemnitz the death-rate of those over 60 was only 166 in 10,000 inhabitants in 1914, but in 1917 it reached 430.[8] The village schoolmaster in Bärenstein, a little village in the Erzgebirge, told us that during those months in the morning session there would always be nine or ten children who would have to leave the room, vomit their breakfasts and stagger back to put their heads down on their desks and cry, too sick and miserable to sit up, much less learn their lessons.[9] We were constantly told that the amount of school work required of the children has had to be lessened in order to meet their lowered vitality and that, owing to their absolute inability to do the work, many children of the poor in Germany have practically lost four years of school life out of their possible eight. The numbers of school children was greatly reduced by actual illness. In Halle, we were told by one of the school doctors that the school population had fallen off by one-half since the war began.[10]

That these physical privations should have an influence on juvenile crime is only to be expected. Ruth van der Leyden and other probation officers of the juvenile court in Berlin told us much of the increased criminality among the former pupils of the higher grade school.[11] Those growing boys and girls who, owing to the shortage of labor during the long course of the war, undertook hard factory work, were simply unable to get enough to eat from the rationed supplies. From this root cause spread many thefts of food, falsification of bread cards, house-breaking into bak-

[7] Saxony is a heavily industrialized state in southeastern Germany.
[8] Chemnitz is one of the principal towns in Saxony.
[9] Erzgebirge: the Ore Mountains, in the South of Saxony, bordering on Czechoslovakia.
[10] Halle is an industrial town in central Germany.
[11] The editors have found no further biographical information on Ruth van der Leyden.

eries and mills, stealing potatoes and turnips in the fields, taking part in the fraudulent handling of food in the hope that some would be given to them, and so on. In addition to hunger, many of these children, unable to bear any longer the anxiety of their mothers, stole food to take home, reckless of the consequences to themselves. Of course they often stole money from their parents, sold the clothing of their brothers and sisters or such household articles as they could pilfer. . . .

We were constantly reminded that the paucity of food does not only affect the poorer people: indeed many working people with relatives in the country from whom they could obtain food fared much better than professional people and others who had no such connections. Often when asked a direct question, the professors in the clinics revealed the difficulty they had in providing for their own families. One of them, who kindly invited us to his house, showed us two blooming children of seven and eight, but the little war baby of two years had stopped growing when she was weaned, and developed rickets. With the utmost care she has been cured to the point of being able to walk, but she is tiny, white and thin, a great contrast to the other children. Another professor, who was taking us through a children's ward, admitted reluctantly that his daily food consists of a breakfast of black war coffee with bread and marmalade, no midday meal, and for supper soup and bread. He came back from the front to find that his wife had made a poor recovery from a serious operation and his two children were very much reduced, all for lack of proper food. He sent them to a seaside place on the Baltic, but there proved to be so little food there that he is obliged to save all he can to send food from Berlin.

Sometimes the tales of food shortage were touching. The editor of a large city newspaper told us he had been able the night before to take home a bottle of milk and that his little girl, who met him at the door, had shouted joyously to her mother that peace had come. We asked if she had found the milk as delicious as she thought and he said: "Oh, she could only feast her eyes on it. That milk was for the little sick one, there was not enough for two." Again we were told by a mother that her little daughter had asked her if it was true that there were countries in the world where there was no war and people could eat all they wanted. Perhaps it was these women who suffered most, these intelligent mothers who knew perfectly well how important proper feeding was and yet were unable to obtain the barest necessities for their children. One of them said to us that it was hardest at night after the children were in bed and one heard them crying and whimpering from hunger until they fell asleep and even after. She added, "I do not see how the women endured it who were obliged to sleep in the same room with their children and who could offer them no diversions in the evenings."

Many people kept conscientiously to the rationed food, though always at

AMERICANS RESPOND TO GERMANY'S NEED

a risk to their health. We met one young girl of wealthy family who is reduced to such a pale ghost of her former self that her parents are greatly disturbed. She has a large Bible class of working girls and, as they are unable to buy extra food, she has refused to eat anything but the prescribed ration. Others found it simply impossible to keep this up. Obviously, a woman who anxiously wonders whether the obligation to obey the law is as binding as her primitive obligation to preserve the health of her children, has taken the first step toward the illegal purchase of food. One woman who succumbed described her struggles: "My husband knew that I bought smuggled food for the children but he would never touch it himself. He died after a rather slight operation and I torment myself thinking that perhaps it was because he had no resistance left." [12] Another said: "My old father would not let me give him smuggled food till he had lost more than forty pounds in weight and my friends were reproaching me with neglecting him. Then he yielded and he always referred to it as 'the time my conscience died!' "

There were many wealthy people who were able throughout the period of the whole war to secure an abundance of food for their families, but even if all the food in the country could have been secured by the government and fairly distributed, the lack of fats and albumens would still have been disastrously great.

There is a general impression in America that this suffering from lack of food is now a matter of the past, but in point of fact the armistice was followed by the cessation of sea-fishing through the complete blockade of the North Sea, the demobilization threw back on the cities thousands of soldiers whom they were unprepared to feed, the surrender of rolling stock demoralized transportation still further, and the armies of occupation took possession of regions which had formerly supplied several large cities.[13] Thus Frankfurt am Main has lost its source of agricultural and dairy supplies to the French army.

Perhaps the best way to show the present state of things will be to describe some of the meals we saw in public and private institutions. We were in the kitchen of the great university hospital of Berlin, the Charité, at noon and saw the meal for 2,200 people. Since the revolution the hospital has had to adopt the *Einheitsessen,* that is, to give exactly the same food to everyone, from scrubwoman to head professor. We saw a tray of meat, about two and a half feet wide by 18 inches long, filled with chunks of lean beef, very stringy and full of bones, which had already been boiled for

[12] This may be a reference to Anna Edinger, for whose husband Ludwig Hamilton had done some research. He died in 1918. See Part III, document 6, Alice Hamilton, "At the War Capitals," note 67.

[13] On the blockade, see Hamilton, "At the War Capitals."

soup. This was for the 2,200 people. Of course they do not get it every day. The weekly allowance is 250 grammes (8 ounces) but after the bone has been removed it is not more than 150, which would make the daily allowance just the legal weight of a letter.

The allowance of bread is 335 grammes daily (11 ounces) but many of the sick cannot eat it, for it is made of meal ground very fine so as to retain all but 5 percent of the bran, which makes it irritating to a delicate stomach. Then they mix with the meal mixed dried greens and this makes the bread damp and liable to mould or sour in a few days. Yet if they cannot eat this there is no substitute. The allowance of white bread, made with the excessively dear American flour, is only one loaf a week for ten patients. Seafish stopped at the time of the armistice, rice, dried beans and peas are only beginning to come in, so the reliance has to be chiefly on green vegetables, of which the hospital is using ten times as much as before the war.

We saw the tuberculosis patients in the great wards for children—where before the war physicians from all over the world came to study the methods of treatment—fed with a soup of meal with dried greens and a little vegetable margarine.

"Something to Hope For"

In a *crèche* in Frankfurt they were giving emaciated and rachitic children a dinner of meal soup made with a pound of margarine to 100 children and in the afternoon a meal consisting of a mug of German tea, made from dried leaves of strawberry and other plants, without milk and with only three-quarters of a pound of sugar to forty quarts of tea. In Leipzig, we visited a *Landkolonie,* a large playground in which 625 children from six to twelve years of age spend the day and are given a midday dinner.[14] It consists of one pint of thin meal soup, to which had been added a little dried vegetable. Out of 190 children who were seated at one time in the dining room all except one were thin and anemic. The director made several announcements to the children—a hike for the following day, which he carefully explained was not compulsory, the time when the prize would be awarded for the best garden, and so on. All of these were received with a curious sort of apathy by the listless children, but when he said he hoped they would have milk in their soup tomorrow or the next day, the announcement was greeted by a shrill and spontaneous cheer. He turned to us with tears in his eyes. "I do not know where the milk is to come from," he said, "but one must give them something to hope for."

The meals for the grown people we saw in the many food kitchens, some

[14] Leipzig: one of the principal towns in Saxony.

maintained by the city, some by private charity. In Leipzig one could get for forty pfennigs two boiled dumplings of war meal with some dried pears which had been stewed with sugar.[15] It was probably a little over one-third of what a German would ordinarily eat at noon. The same was true of the meal served in Chemnitz, a soup of meal made with sauerkraut and potatoes and a little vegetable margarine. Both were more appetizing than the meals we saw served in Berlin, but scantier. However, in Berlin the price was a mark and a quarter or a half for meal soup, a dish of part dried and part fresh greens and potatoes, and sometimes a dessert of damp, grayish cake, which was so sticky and elastic one could draw it out like rubber, or aniline red jelly out of a still stronger and more unappetizing consistency, both, of course, sweetened with saccharine.

Food Rationing

It is needless to say that the lack of milk, butter, eggs, meat and fats is the serious side of the food shortage. Berlin's milk supply has fallen to a little over one-seventh of the normal, that of Chemnitz to less than one-eighth, of Frankfurt to less than one-twelfth. It is very strictly rationed to nursing mothers, children between one and four years and some of the sick. Children up to four get a pint a day, sometimes those up to six may get half a pint. Open tuberculosis calls for one pint a day, closed tuberculosis for none. Acute nephritis entitles the patient to half a pint, but not chronic nephritis, and if there is hemorrhage a case of ulcer of the stomach may receive a pint a day. This is only, of course, when the supply is sufficient.

The crops of this year are already supplying Germans with fresh vegetables; the potato crop, so important for the poorer people especially, promises to be fairly good, and the bread will be much better in quality and cheaper when the rye crop is harvested. But it is impossible to restore a starved population to a normal condition on fresh vegetables and cereals. It is absolutely necessary to have fats and albuminous foods. Germany has no animal fats because of the loss of cattle and the lack of rich fodder for the cattle which still remain. She has always imported this fodder in the form of oil cake and palm kernels. Germany has no source of vegetable oils, no nuts, no cottonseed. Therefore, she must, if her people are to be saved from the effects of malnutrition, buy in foreign countries the oils, fat meats and milk which she cannot herself produce. There is also need of sugar this year, since much of the sugar-beet land was sown to cereals. The important bacon, salt pork, suet, lard, butter, condensed milk, chocolate

---

[15] Pfennig, a German currency unit. There are 100 pfennigs to the mark.

and cocoa will necessarily be very expensive and beyond the reach of the poor and even the moderately well-to-do class.

The effects of underfeeding are registered chiefly in the increased tuberculosis rate at all ages, and in the increased death-rate among the old as is shown in Germany's statistics. During the third quarter of 1917, the deaths from tuberculosis had increased by 91 percent in women, only 40 percent in men. That same year the Prussian Home Office estimated the excess deaths among the old, those over 60 years, at 127,000, and among children under five at 50,000.[16]

Kayserling, one of Germany's foremost tuberculosis specialists, told us that the fight of almost forty years against tuberculosis was lost.[17] The Germans date their anti-tuberculosis campaign from about 1882 when Koch discovered the bacillus.[18] Since then their rate had fallen from over 30 per 10,000 of the population to less than 14. In the first half of 1918 it was already over 30 and is still rising and will continue to rise for some years. Nor does the death rate tell all the story. In Berlin the infection rate among babies—shown by the von Pirquet test—has increased threefold, the rate of tuberculous sickness among little children, fivefold. These children will not all die.[19] Many will live on to puberty and then fall prey to the disease, or if they are able to resist that period of strain, they will succumb during the twenties, under the strain of childbearing or heavy work. For the whole period of this generation, tuberculosis will claim a greatly increased number of victims and how far the health of the children of these war children will be affected, nobody can say.

Not only is the number of the tuberculous increased but the form of the disease is changed and German hospitals are now filled with varieties of the disease which used to be regarded as medical curiosities. We saw most pitiful cases among the children, multiple bone tuberculosis with fistulas, multiple joint tuberculosis, the slow boring ulcers of the face called lupus, great masses of tuberculosis glands such as we never saw in America, and that great rarity in civilized countries, caseating pulmonary tuberculosis in little children. Kayserling had said that the hunger blockade had shown that tuberculosis is a disease to be combated chiefly by nutrition, not by the prevention of infection, and that by long starvation it is possible to break

---

[16] By "Home Office," the authors probably mean the Prussian ministry of the interior.

[17] The authors probably mean the German physician Johann Carl Kaiserling (1869–?).

[18] Robert Koch (1843–1910), German physician and founder of medical bacteriology. Koch discovered the cause of tuberculosis while working as a member of the Imperial Health office in 1882. In 1885 he was appointed director of the Berlin Hygienic Institute and professor at Berlin University. He studied the origins of a number of diseases, including cholera, the plague, typhoid, and various tropical diseases and received the Nobel Prize for medicine in 1905. He visited the United States in 1908.

[19] Named after the Austrian Clemens von Pirquet (1874–1929), the Pirquet test is a skin test for the tuberculosis bacillus.

down racial immunity, if indeed there be such a thing. The forms of tuberculosis now common in Germany were formerly seen almost entirely among primitive peoples and it was supposed that the acquired resistance of civilized races made such things impossible, but that is now an exploded belief.

There is no space to do more than mention some of the other results of the long underfeeding of women, children, and old people. "Galloping consumption," fatal in four to sixteen weeks, used to be very rare; now it is the rule in young adults who develop tuberculosis after a decided loss of weight. Gastro-intestinal diseases of all kinds have, of course, greatly increased, especially ulceration. Rickets among children is enormously prevalent, scurvy less so, and the war oedema—which seems to be caused by an exclusively carbohydrate diet—has been brought under control and is hardly to be found except in isolated spots. The blockade of soap and soap fats has brought about not only an increase of skin diseases especially among babies, puerperal fever among women in childbed, from the lack of clean linen and the difficulty of securing personal cleanliness for the woman and the midwife. A further and more serious effect has been the gradual accumulation of household filth, which is shown by the fact that there are now in Berlin about 100,000 lice-infested houses and the municipality can see no way to get them cleaned unless they can provide cheap and abundant soap for the people. As typhus has smouldered in Berlin for months there is a very bad outlook for the city when once the cold autumn weather lights it up again in these vermin-filled houses.

In common gratitude we feel we must not close without referring to the fine spirit of courtesy with which the Germans received us. Doctors, nurses, men, and women who are working against tuberculosis, to keep babies alive, to keep children healthy, to prevent youthful crime and foster education, these people are way past the point of bitterness. What they are facing is the shipwreck of a nation and they realize that if help does not come quickly and abundantly this generation in Germany is largely doomed to early death or a handicapped life. For what Germany needs is more food for her children than normal children need, and more public care for her sick than she had before the war, more research, more experts. What she faces is a dearth of food and a crippling of all her institutions of relief and of learning.

The first cod liver oil, so terribly needed, reached Berlin this last May, a gift of the English Friends. The American Friends allowed our little group, Carolena Wood—herself a Friend—and ourselves to arrange for the purchase of $30,000 worth of condensed and dried milk, which seemed to us the most urgent need after we very reluctantly gave up cod liver oil. We left behind us a committee with headquarters in Berlin, consisting of Dr. Artur Levy, of the associated charities of Berlin, Dr. Elizabeth Rotten, who has been in cooperation with the English Friends throughout the war, Dr. Alice Salomon, the head of the school of philanthropy, Dr. Sigmund Schultze [sic], head of the city Jugendfürsorge Amt, and other experts in relief work, to take charge of the distribution of this food and if possible later consignments.[20] In Frankfurt the committee is represented by the head of the associated charities, in Leipzig by the head of the child welfare agencies, in Halle by the well-known Swiss scientist, Professor Abderhalden, in Breslau by the *Oberburgermeister,* and so on.[21] We had repeated interviews with all these people and are convinced that the supplies that are sent in will be distributed with the utmost efficiency by men and women conversant with the situation and experienced in modern methods of relief. All the money contributed will be sent to the Committee of American Friends in Philadelphia and will be expended in this country for food and medical supplies, both of these to be purchased and shipped most advantageously through the cooperation of Mr. Hoover.

2. A German Nun Writes to Jane Addams

The following two letters were written to Jane Addams by a German nun from the Rhineland.[22] They reflect both Addams's popularity in Germany and the belief of many Germans that Americans would help the defeated Germany, particularly by working for a revision of the Treaty of Versailles. Owing in part to Alice Salomon's writings about American women's activism and to Else Münsterberg's translation of *Twenty Years at Hull House,* Jane Addams was one of the best-known American reformers in Germany. Her visits in 1915 and 1919 reinforced that image.

Following the war, Addams received a number of letters with a similar content to these, often from total strangers. Sister Maria's request for American money was not unusual during the time of hyperinflation, when the ten dollars that Addams sent could go very far. In fact, Alice Salomon

[20]   Artur Levy (1862–1922), German welfare politician and president of the Center for Private Welfare (Zentrale für private Fürsorge).
   The Jugendfürsorgeamt was the municipal youth welfare work administration.
[21]   Emil Abderhalden (1877–1950), Swiss physician who taught in Berlin and Halle. During World War I, Abderhalden organized transports of wounded soldiers. After the war, he initiated several social reform projects, among them infant homes and care for the elderly. Breslau is a town in the industrial region of Silesia, in Southeastern Germany. "Oberbürgermeister" means "mayor."
[22]   Sister Maria to Jane Addams, Marienburg Convent in Vallendar near Coblenz am Rhein, April 5, 1920, Jane Addams Papers, SCPC (and *JAP,* reel 12); Sister Maria to Jane Addams, Marienburg Convent in Vallendar near Coblenz am Rhein, July 2, 1920, Jane Addams Papers, SCPC (and *JAP,* reel 13).

suggested in a letter to Addams that a hundred dollars would enable her to keep her school open for a year. It is, however, remarkable that Addams sent money to Sister Maria without getting more detailed information about the project, since her plea was only one among many. The fact that Sister Maria seemed very knowledgeable about Addams's writings undoubtedly helped to establish a relationship with her.

Like the letters of Alice Salomon and Anna Lindemann in Part II, Sister Maria's letter reflects the ability of educated German women to conduct the dialogue in English. To her, Addams's work represented universal sympathy and the fulfillment of people's needs across boundaries. Her writings had even replaced religious texts at Sister Maria's school for domestic science and social work. Sister Maria's letter is typical of the reverence Addams experienced outside her own country after World War I, at a time when her power in the United States had diminished. The German nun sees Addams as a powerful representative of her nation and of American traits. She conveys her hopes for reconstruction of the German nation-state with American help and the utilization of those traits of the American national character that she applauds in her letter. Her perspective on the German state of affairs was probably very different from the one presented to Addams on her trips when she chiefly talked to social work professionals and state officials.

Schwester Maria to Jane Addams

[note on original: "Answered + book + $10 sent."]

Marienburg Convent 5/IV.20.
in Vallendar near Coblenz am Rhein.

Dear Madam,
It is with a heart full of gratitude that I address a few lines to you knowing that the great work of charity in order to help our little starving children has been created by you. There was a Catholic magazine of our country telling our people how much we owe to you. I then only heard that you have been in Germany last year—I know you by your books and I do not wonder that you took the trouble of coming over to see by your own eyes how matters stand. You certainly passed Coblenz and I am so sorry that I did not know—I would have found my way to you to thank you for all the good you do for humanity by your books and deeds.[23]

It is so great a mission and just the mission of a generous woman—to

[23]   Coblenz is a town on the Rhine, close to Sister Maria's convent. Sister Maria is referring to the trip that Addams, Alice Hamilton, and Carolena Wood took in 1919 as part of the Quaker effort to supply food to Germany.

THE LIMITATIONS OF NATIONHOOD

spread pacifistic ideas. I read your book "Newer Ideals of Peace" and I wonder and admire how in 1907 you anticipated what has happened since that time. I read "The Spirit of Youth and the City Streets" telling me again with how much love for the poor and for the endangered youth your heart is filled. We appreciate especially your autobiographic "20 Years of Social Work" but I never could have it in English.[24] *Your* books I must read in the original and I dare ask you the great kindness to send it to me. We have a school for domestic and social science for educated girls—just a finishing school before they enter the world. Many of them take up a social job— there is so much to do everywhere and there is to built up family life [*sic*].

We must form their hearts and minds for sympathetic feelings and your broad love and your practical views are so precious as a model. I think God must love you very much, Dear Miss Adams [*sic*] for all the good you do for humanity. You teach practical love of God and that is what I want to have our girls realize and imitate.

There is a second request I dare address to you, because I have so much confidence in your kindness. Besides our school we have many poor orphan children needing food and clothing. Your supplies are supposed to be given to city-children and indeed they need them—We live in a little town and never have any support though we tried to ask for it.[25] So I determined to address to you in a personal way—as you are like a good friend to me by your books. May we hope that you can send us some money and supplies for our very much indebted big orphan house? Isn't it asking too much? I know you will do it whenever it is possible. So, Dear Miss Adams, let me thank you for so many good aspirations and inspirations your books have given to me. I am a Sister of Charity and therefore every idea of yours finds a quick response with me. *You* also know the *good* sides of our unfortunate and dishonored Germany and it is so comforting to think that you are just and true in your opinion of our country.

Your army of occupation knows our institution very well. There have been the staffs of 4 regiments alternating billeted in our house. We have been treated with all respect and kindness—and in order to enlarge my views I asked them many things about your country. There are *national virtues* and *principles* which you teach your children very early and that is the blessing of your nation. This is true culture I think. We have arrived to a state of terrible excesses in our own country. There is no religion anywhere and by consequences no moral. It is just dreadful how they lack the feeling of responsibility and of personal human dignity. I think there will be no change until there will be a *reform* of our schools teaching our children more human dignity and solitary responsibility, and teaching them to

[24] For the German translation of Addams's autobiography, see Part II, document 7.
[25] By "your supplies," Sister Maria probably means the foodstuffs distributed by the Quakers.

love and serve God. Your books will help to come to this end, teaching human sympathy. God bless you my Dear Miss Adams and He may give you many years to continue your great work for humanity.

Yours respectfully
Sister Maria

Marienburg July 2nd 20
in Vallendar on Rhine
near Coblenz Rhineland

Dear Miss Addams.

It was such an unexpected and charming surprise to find your kind letter and gift on my desk when I came back from Berlin where I had been send for some social studies. Let me thank you from all my heart also from Mother Superior's name. I knew you had so many people in all Europe and in your own country to assist that I scarcely dared hope that you would ever be able to listen to my personal request. Certainly I never expected a letter from your own hand and I cannot tell you how much it is enjoyed. Every morning at 7 o'clock *eighty-five* girls of the age of 17-18-19 years—a few are even 20—are listening to what you tell them about social work in Hull-house—your book is our breakfast-reading—We use to commence our day with some *religious* reading at breakfast—but it seems to me that your book leads towards the same goal, being a most powerful instruction about the "greatest thing in the world": fraternal charity. We read it in German, but our girls enjoy to take the original you sent us, to compare and to see the pictures. And we talk of the different subjects of social works with so much more interest, because your book shows the original state of need from which people has [*sic*] been released. There is so much profoundness of sympathy you teach the world and I think there is another ideal of peace—more effective than the league of nations that might be our salvation.

It seems to me that our ruined country, demoralized, degenerated in all its classes, more than ever needs good and virtuous and proud women of their own, to rise again. In our school,—a finishing school for domestic science and social work, we try to form caracters [*sic*] as our country needs them. It is a work which is supported by every woman of our time, able to influence our young girls by her personality. And therefore your book, Dear Miss Addams, will help us to form these young souls who look at you with admiration and veneration.

We had many American soldiers in our convent last year and they made us understand that America is not willing to "extinguish" our nation. I hope our government and people will turn towards the new world, which in the U.S. certainly represents a power destined to lead humanity for the time to come. May America U.S. [*sic*] understand her great mission in this sense.

THE LIMITATIONS OF NATIONHOOD

The refusal of ratification of peace treaty has caused many troubles, but I think your nation is right to do so.[26] There is too much growing and increasing of every power of human spirit in your country as to have it controlled by old Europe anxious not to loose [sic] his predominance in the world. And here we experience every day that U.S. without peace with Germany is more peaceful than the Entente nations which signed the peace-treaty.

Spa makes us expect a hard time to come.[27] There is only one comfort: the thought that God leads everything in the world for the best of humanity and that every nation has its mission in the divine world plan. We are not to perish yet—perhaps God has another mission for us in store—certainly all humiliations can be turned into a new spiritual worth, don't you think so, dear Miss Addams. I suffer so much from all the hatred in the world and therefore your broad love for everyone expressed is my comfort. That is what makes me write in such an inofficial way. I read a good deal of your books, as the American library at Coblence is kind enough to let me borrow them. All the aspirations you have, find a very eager response in my mind I believe. The other day—just the day of the conference at Spa—We heard the IXth symphony of Beethoven at Coblence so appropriate for the time,—and ending with the enthusiastic choir of Schiller: "Seid umschlungen Millionen—Einen Kuß der ganzen Welt—Alle Menschen werden Brüder—Über'm Sternenzelt muß ein lieber Vater wohnen."[28]—"We should have send an orchestra and a choir to Spa to hear Beethoven tell them his and Schiller's wonderful views of fraternal relations between all nations" I said and a German replied: "If there were *Americans they* would have an understanding for such extraordinary means of reconciliation—they would certainly enjoy it—they *have* ideals."

This little remark may show that we feel that the American people is [sic] much better than the others are. The love of my country urges me to look out, all around, for improvements for our own people. I noticed—when I read your most interesting book: "Newer Ideals of Peace" that your patriotism does not blind you either as to the faults of your nation. And I took many informations about your people and I learned a good deal that might be a blessing for our people too. The great respect your men are showing towards women seems first of all a most important means of real

[26] The U.S. Senate rejected the Versailles Treaty and the League of Nations Covenant in November of 1919.
[27] After the Treaty of Versailles was signed in 1919, a number of conferences were held to deal with the question of German reparations in particular. The one at Spa in Belgium met from July 5 to 16, 1920; it was the first to allow representatives of the German government.
[28] Sister Maria is quoting Friedrich Schiller's "Ode to Joy": "Every man a brother plighted . . . Millions in our arms we gather / To the world a kiss be sent / Past the starry firmament / Brothers, dwells a loving Father."

culture and most worthy of imitation.—But I must not bother you with so long a letter, knowing that from every part of the world people claim to enjoy your kindness. It seems as if you were a good friend, dear Miss Addams. The money you gave us for our hungry orphan children has been very welcome and our little ones say "Vergelt's Gott" to thank you dear Miss Addams for your kind present.[29] I wish you could see them—perhaps there will be a day that brings you to the Boards [she means banks] of the Rhine again and then perhaps I might ask you to come and see our convent. I would enjoy a personal acquaintance with you. You are no stranger—I read so many of your books. . . . Most of your ideas find a very ready response in my mind. As for social institutions it seems that they have been founded in your country by the real sympathy and kindness of generous women, while in our country most social laws and organizations are due to the government and the state politics.

I wish, Dear Miss Addams, that you may be successful in all your efforts for humanity for many years to come. May God bless all your good works and may the gratitude of thousands of people be your comfort in all your toil.

Believe me yours very sincerely and grateful
Sister Maria.

3. A German Activist Appeals to Addams for Help

After the war, German women often called upon their prewar acquaintances in the American women's movement to appeal for support for their projects. In this letter,[30] Anna Lindemann reflects on the consequences of the war for the German population and especially the women. She asks Jane Addams to help sustain institutions that were devised under the National Women's Service during the war (see Part III, document 1, Mabel Harding, "German Women and the War"). Before the war, Lindemann had praised Addams as a more remote and abstract ideal of womanhood, serving her community in the Chicago slums. Now Addams had become a central figure in international relief work and embodied a possibility of pragmatic help for Germans.

Lindemann pointedly describes the pauperization of the middle class

[29]   "*Vergelt's Gott*": "God reward!" (i.e., "May God reward you!").
[30]   Anna Lindemann to Jane Addams, Stuttgart, April 16, 1921, Jane Addams Papers, SCPC (and *JAP*, reel 13).

caused by the postwar devaluation of the German currency. Her description is a good characterization of the early years of the Weimar Republic, when the welfare state was established by the constitution but many measures were not implemented because of a lack of funds. Welfare measures were also hampered by the fact that many middle-class women could not return to the volunteer work of the prewar years because they needed gainful employment. Other than a handwritten remark—"acknowledged"—on the letter, we do not know how Addams responded.

Anna Lindemann to Jane Addams

Stuttgart-Degerloch
Württemberg, Germany
April 16th 1921

Dear Miss Addams,

I hear from Mrs. Chapman Catt, that she has sent you a copy of an appeal I addressed to her for help in a matter I have very much at heart.[31] I had myself intended to write to you, but my time is so entirely taken up by my official work and my duties as housemother that at this time I was not able to do more than write to Mrs. Catt, whom I needed not tell much about the objects I wanted help for, as at the second Board meeting of the I.W.S.A. in London I had told her a good deal about them. Mrs. Catt's answer—full of kindness and affectionate interest—has been somewhat of a disappointment.

We women here who are fighting against hopeless odds, know of course that the greater part of the civilized world is economically in a difficult position at present and yet we cannot help feeling that what to a country like the U.S.A. is a passing inconvenience, means for our own country a constantly accelerated sliding into an abyss of whom nobody yet knows whether there will be a way out for future generations. When I wrote to Mrs. Catt, what I had at heart was something like the following: during the war we German women, especially those trained by the women's movement, took—as women in all belligerent countries have done—on our own initiative an active part in fighting the disastrous effects that the war from the beginning had exercised on the home, on the women wage-earners, on the children.

[31] Carrie Chapman Catt (1859–1947), American suffragist, president of the National American Woman Suffrage Association (1915–1920) and the prime mover within the IWSA, presiding over six of its congresses. Although she joined Jane Addams in founding the Woman's Peace Party, Catt felt that she could not promote peace during the war and at the same time pursue her main goal of woman suffrage. In 1925, however, she organized the Conference on the Cause and Cure of War, which met in Washington annually thereafter until 1939, Catt serving as its chair until 1932.

With the blockade and our more and more perfected isolation, the task grew heavier. The more it became difficult, the more we learned. I am glad to say, our "Women's National Service" has given its service only to home needs and distress, and has carefully avoided any participation in war propaganda and the like. When the catastrophical down-break after the war, called the revolution, suddenly brought us political rights, we did—and have ever since continued to do—our best to continue in the direction so successfully taken up in war-time.

Here in our Former Kingdom of Württemberg, amidst a serious, hardworking, intelligent population, the "Women's National Service" of which I had been the chief organizer, had started a number of undertakings that had proved a great blessing. We decided to try as hard as could be to carry some of them on into what is technically called the time of peace. So far we have succeeded. But now I am becoming rather hopeless. The terrible poverty which is our present lot, is only slowly working its way. Many things work together to veil and dissimilate it at first. But with a horrible rate of progression it is eating itself into the bones and the marrow of our people. Not alone that, with the exception of a comparatively very small section of the population, the whole nation is rapidly exhausting its entire resource in clothes, furniture, etc. and is sinking to a level left centuries ago,—the public funds—in spite of the quite incredible hard taxation and the almost unbelievable rise in all kinds of dues—are utterly unable to even keep up what we had in social welfare institutions before the war.

There can therefore be no hope whatever for us women to find financial assistance for our new work in our own country, it is new work, it is work not built on the basis of charity, we have never appealed to any special chauvinist or class or religious set of feelings. The work we are trying to keep going is entirely grounded on the desire to help the women who wish to help themselves. Its object is always to make them stronger for the fight with life, to enable them to do their work better and more efficiently. The institutions I am at present appealing for are three.

One of these I have started without any other financial help than what we in the Women's National Service earned by our business undertakings in which we employed the women whom the war had thrown out of work. That is our School for Mothers. I do not know if there is anywhere else something exactly like it. In Germany it is the first, and I hear that the English Schools for Mothers are not quite the same. Our school has been going on for more than 4 years now and has proved an enormous blessing. It consists of the School itself, in which official women doctors, trained nurses and excellent pedagogic teachers teach the women—women expecting their first child, newly married women, women who have lost babies etc. etc.—how to prepare for the coming child, how to nurse it, feed it, clothe it; the woman doctor teaches how to treat it in cases of illness, at what signs to call a doctor, what to do till the doctor arrives, how to carry out the doctor's precepts and so forth.

The women pedagogue teaches how to educate the child, from the first day of its life (and before!). The chief part of the teaching of course treats the small child, but the whole course follows the child till it leaves school; the dangers of the borderland between childhood and youth, physical and psychical, are specially usefully treated. The school possesses a museum lovingly brought together of everything you can think of to help its purpose, down to collection of good and bad toys, good and bad picture books and so forth. Every lesson is divided into a theoretical and practical part. The women learn all that is to be done to the child by practicing it first on a big doll and later on live babies. They learn to prepare the food, to make suitable clothes etc. They also learn how to occupy the growing child to its own advantage.

We have attached a Creche and a Kindergarten to the School, so that the women can see the practical application of all they have been taught. In the Kindergarten the Montessori method is applied (combined with elements from Fröbel) and it is wonderful to see how the women are interested in these ideas.[32] The school has also courses for elder sisters, for young nurse-maids, for unemployed women and so forth. The former pupils keep coming for advice, and as a system of Evenings for Mothers has developed, to which—at the earnest desire of the women—we have lately added evenings for parents, to which the husbands are brought, because the wives want them to learn more about education!—I can only give you a very feeble impression of what is being done. There is life in the School, earnest endeavour and much love for the work. We have *many* friends for it—but too little money!

My second great care is our Holiday Home for working mothers. I started it in the last year of the war. The Minister of War had called me as a councillor on women's questions and it was my and my colleagues' work to protect the women doing war-work as well as possible against the bad effects of that work. We soon found that the few existing holiday homes were either too expensive or took the women too late, when some definite disease had already been acquired. With the help of funds given at that time both by the Empress Auguste Victoria and by the Imperial Government we

---

[32] Maria Montessori (1870–1952) was an Italian educator and originator of an educational system that is based on the belief in children's creative potential, their motivation for learning, and their right to be treated as individuals. Friedrich Wilhelm August Fröbel (1782–1852), founder of the kindergarten, was an influential German educational reformer. The kindergarten movement found worldwide support despite being banned as subversive by the Prussian government between 1851 and 1860.

started a Home, very well situated and in every way suited for the purpose.[33] We have kept it going till now, but in a few months' time the available funds will be at an end. There we take women in all cases, where a stay of some weeks in the Home will enable the woman to go on with her work and where no other Holiday Home is available. We also take exhausted mothers of large families.

The price is as far as possible adapted to the economic position of the women. This home is as far as I know the only one of its kind. We lay great stress on the mental atmosphere of the place. The Matron is a kind of genius who knows how to bring gladness and joy to the most overworked and downtrodden creature. She has from the beginning established kindly relations between our Home "Little Switzerland" and a neighboring Deaf and Dumb Asylum as well as an Institution for the Blind. Our downhearted women workers, as they gradually gain heart in the peace and the homely atmosphere of the Home, begin to invent (gently led by the Matron) all sorts of amusements and pleasures for the inmates of those two homes. It is wonderful how this apparently very simple device helps to bring about the surprisingly good effects of the home.

We have kept it free from every tinge of officialdom—and we are very happy to see how much good can be worked in a comparatively simple way. Since the end of the war I have been taken over as councillor on questions of women's work by the Ministry of Labour, and the Holiday Home is now being carried on under supervision of the government, but we are given entirely free hand in its management. But though all the official places that have anything to do with the Home, value it quite as fully as we do, they are now and for the next few years, *utterly unable* to grant any means for it. These are heart-rending experiences; when one sees how much an institution is needed, how splendidly it works, and yet is forced to *agree* that the economic position of our country makes it impossible to get the necessary funds.

The third institution I am trying hard to keep up is also a child of the war. In order to be able to do the best we could for the women workers, we established in the chief industrial places of the country what we call: Hilfsstellen für Frauenarbeit; Welfare centers for women workers. They do not give charity, their one object is to assist the women workers in all difficulties that either arise out of her work or that her work prevents her from seeing to herself. They have at present a great deal to do with unemployed women, teaching them new professions, getting them special grants in cases of exceptional need and so forth. They assist the workers (of all classes of course) in getting a needed time of rest; it is they and the factory welfare workers who work hand in hand with them, who send the guests to

[33]   For Empress Auguste Victoria, see Part III, document 1.

our Holiday Home, provide for the children in the meantime and so forth. They also help in providing clothing etc. if it is needed for undertaking a new job of work. They help to get young girls good places as apprentices and if necessary they assist in fitting them out. I cannot enumerate all they do, the cases coming to them for advice are many and very various. The one common feature is that they are all women struggling through life with their own strength, who by the exceptionally hard conditions that women even more than men now have to reckon with in Germany, need a friendly hand to help them over particularly steep and stony places.

In the first years we have been able to do much work with comparatively little money, because we had honorary work nearly everywhere. But the altered circumstances make honorary work more and more impossible especially for women. Those women who used to devote their spare time to help work, belong nearly all of them to the categories that suffer most heavily from our present economical position. If we want to keep the work going, we must pay the workers at least in the 5 or 6 chief industrial places. It would be a sad pity indeed if it could not be kept going, for these sad times in our country are saddest for women; it is hard to know whether of these it is the women, who must work and want to work suffer most, or those who ought to work but are for some reason unable to.

We can in our Hilfsstellen only care for the first class. They need more assistance than in former periods of special economic distress. Circumstances at present are so very strong against the women workers. All the men who used to find work in the colonies, in the provinces now taken from us, . . . come pressing into our smaller and poorer country seeking for work to maintain their families.[34] That makes the competition in the labour market, which is bad enough owing to our lack of coal and raw material, very bitter indeed, and it is chiefly the women who have to suffer the consequences. On the other hand, it will take *years* before numberless men have found their equilibrium again after the war and its consequences. Our Hilfsstellen have very much to do with assisting women who must do paid work because their husbands simply *will* not sufficiently provide for the family. It is one of the symptoms of a great disease, but one falling very hard on many very valuable women and mothers.

I hope I have given you something of an adequate idea of the three purposes for which I need funds (and need them *soon!*). It may seem curious that I address myself to the women of a country quite likely still formally at war with us. But—apart from the fact that there are very many Americans of Suabian origin who will perhaps be glad to help their old country—I feel sure that the spirit of our work, the effort to help those who try hard to help themselves, must appeal specially to American women. The value of

---

[34] Under the terms of the Versailles Treaty, Germany had to give up its colonies.

American money is high at present, and it goes very far in our country.[35] I cannot see any hope to keep up the work I have spoken of beyond the end of the autumn, or next winter at the very utmost. That is why I appeal to you to help me. My letter has been unfinished for almost a month. You know—though nobody outside our country can really and fully know—how dark and sad these last weeks have been for us. It seemed impossible in those days to reach out one's hand for help. All strength was needed to bear up inwardly against the dark forces bearing down upon us. But time passes. I have waited too long already. I cannot tell you in words how thankful I shall be if you can be of help to me in the matter I have laid before you!

Yours very sincerely,
Anne Lindemann
Stuttgart - Degerloch
Panoramastr. 6

4. The Weimar President Praises Jane Addams

In 1921, Jane Addams presided over the third congress of WILPF at Vienna. While at the Summer School in Salzburg, she received letters of thanks for her work on behalf of international reconciliation and famine relief, from the German Red Cross and from Friedrich Ebert, the first president of the Weimar Republic and first SPD head of a German government.[36] Ebert shared Addams's vision of practical reform as well as her commitment to international reconciliation and to transcending the limits of nationhood.

Like the preceding letters from private German citizens, this recognition by the German head of state shows that in the 1920s Jane Addams probably enjoyed more popularity in Germany than in her own country. This time, however, the reaction in the American press had a much more conciliatory tone than after the visits she made to Germany during and immediately after the war, suggesting a change in American public opinion toward the former enemy.

[35] See Part IV, document 2.
[36] Friedrich Ebert to Jane Addams, July 21, 1921, Jane Addams Papers, SCPC, series 1 (and JAP, reel 13); translated by Sally Robertson. Clipping attached: "Ebert Calls Jane Addams Kindest Woman in the U.S."

Friedrich Ebert to Jane Addams

Office of the President

Berlin, July 21, 1921

Dear Miss Addams:

On the occasion of your visit to Europe, I would like to express deep gratitude to you in the name of the German government and the German people for everything that you have done for Germany and others in the spirit of loving international reconciliation and magnanimous humanitarianism.

Soon after the cessation of hostilities, you and a number of like-minded women visited Central Europe, which was suffering under the terrible consequences of the war and the great turmoil—Germany's situation was nearly unknown in your home country at that time. It is thanks primarily to your reports that the necessary enlightenment was created and the funds were mobilized for many generous aid campaigns, notably the children's aid fund of the American Quakers in Germany. You are still working untiringly, as always, as president of the Women's International League for Peace and Freedom, as director of new aid organizations, at public congresses, and in private circles in the service of alleviating human suffering. More than ever, the world needs minds that see past the current confusion of nations to the broad perspective and set to work solving the crises. We can emerge from our current predicament only if the hate generated by years of bloody world war is stopped and the people have the will to work together on rebuilding. May these principles, which you have always stood for, finally prevail, and may international peace and social peace crown your work.

In expression of my feelings of highest respect,
Yours very sincerely,
[signature]

5. Florence Kelley on the 1921 Vienna Congress

In her account of the third women's peace congress, held in Vienna in 1921, Florence Kelley did not pretend to be objective.[37] During her previ-

---

[37] Florence Kelley, "The Women's Congress at Vienna," *Survey*, September 1, 1921, pp. 627–29.

ous two decades as secretary of the National Consumers' League she had perfected a prose style of passionate commitment to social justice reforms. Here she brought that style to bear on her interpretation of the first meeting of the Women's International League for Peace and Freedom.

She orchestrated her report around five principal themes: the growth of women's political power; the call for peace education for children; universal disarmament; the recognition of many struggles for national autonomy; and the social justice prerequisites for a lasting peace.

Changes in women's political power were dramatized by the experience of Austrian women, who in 1913 were prohibited from attending political meetings, but by 1921 could vote and held office at all levels of government. This transformation among European women led Kelley to generalize about the political empowerment of "white women" throughout the world, her words consciously marking a racial divide that highlighted work remaining to be done, as well as the relatively privileged position of enfranchised women. The issue of racial justice was specifically addressed by a woman who brought African as well as African-American perspectives to the congress.

Conference resolutions expressed the delegates' hopes that future wars might be avoided through new forms of education. German delegates identified authoritarian education as a wellspring of militarism, and Kelley highlighted the prescient conference, warning that national chauvinism should be avoided in ethnic histories by teaching them from the perspective of world history.

While the earlier congresses had ruled specific considerations of national interest out of order, these were now discussed, and the right to national autonomy recognized for colonized peoples in Ireland, Armenia, Georgia, the Ukraine, India, and Egypt. Though powerless to take concrete action in this regard, women reformers now took a stand.

Their finely crafted resolution about social justice called for concrete action by members "to initiate and support laws looking to the graduate abolition of property privileges," and "to awaken and strengthen among members of the possessing classes the earnest will to alter the economic system in the direction of social justice." The revolutionary moment through which they were living, the logic of peace with justice, and the unity among this group of reformers, many of whom were now meeting now for the third time, led them to endorse social justice as one of their core principles.

The group's optimism about the future was nowhere better expressed than in Kelley's hope that universal disarmament might be achieved by the time of the next congress. So great had been the changes in women's public power in the space of a few years, so great was the contemporary revulsion against war, that they could envision themselves as part of a new era in human history.

The Women's Congress at Vienna
by Florence Kelley

Why Vienna? Why the city so recently decimated by starvation and the influenza plague? The city in all Europe of raging midsummer heat? Why should that city have been chosen for the meeting of the Third Congress of the Women's International League for Peace and Freedom in July? Three answers suffice among many possible ones. Vienna is accessible for members from the new nations who must be enlisted if the league is to consist of groups pledged to peace and freedom in all countries; many people from the impoverished nations could travel to Vienna and live throughout the congress because of the fabulous decline in the Austrian rate of exchange; and finally, and of great importance, the Austrian section pressed their invitation with a fervent plea that delegates from all the world should come and see how art and culture may survive not only prolonged war but a deadly peace. These three things make it a suitable place for an International Peace.

This wise decision brought people from twenty-eight countries as delegates, fraternal delegates, delegates at large, and visitors, according to the political conditions in the nations whence they came. From the Ukraine came women living under four ascertainable governments: the Bolsheviki in the East, the Poles in the West, and two in the area between. Twenty-one telegrams were received from Ukrainian groups who were unable to send delegates.

At a great public evening session, a daughter of Radich, the Croatian agrarian leader, described the non-resistant, or passive-resistant, movements of the peasants in her part of Jugo-Slavia.[38] In the sessions and on committees Germans, Poles, Hungarians, Bohemians, Greeks, women from nations still at war and others from the *disjecta membra* of the old Austrian empire, conferred and discussed in the honest (and sometimes painful) effort to serve the common cause of a new world.

From China, Japan, Australia and Mexico came young women, one a member of the Society for International Friendship recently formed among influential women in Tokyo.

[38]   The *Report of the Third International Congress of Women, Vienna, July 10–17, 1921,* listed Mlle. Milica Radic as a visitor (rather than a delegate) from Croatia. Stepjan Radic (1871–1928) was a peasant leader and advocate of Croatian autonomy. No biographical information was available on his daughter.

Among the fraternal delegates were Mrs. Henry Villard of New York, from the Women's Peace Society, Mrs. Curtis from the Pan-African Congress, and Mrs. Maud Swartz from the Women's International Labor Congress.[39] Mrs. Villard, whose sailing had been delayed by the coal strike, arrived toward the end of the congress, interested chiefly in non-resistance. As a fraternal delegate, giving a greeting from the Women's Peace Society, she made a noble address upon non-resistance. She was given the courtesy of the floor on two other occasions, one being the discussion and adoption of the following resolution:[40]

> Whereas we believe that wars will never cease until human life is held sacred and inviolable, it is hereby resolved that we adopt the principle of non-resistance under all circumstances.

A majority voted for this resolution, after the chair had ruled, in response to a point of order raised by the chairman of the British section, that such vote would change the basis of membership, that the vote was an expression of individual opinion and purpose, and that it could not be taken as binding the sections.

In general the resolutions introduced by the national sections and from the floor, by their number, variety, and by the tenacity with which several were advocated, registered growth in confidence keeping step with the growth of women's political power since the first Congress at The Hague in 1915.

From Holland, Dr. Aletta Jakobs [sic], one of the original organizers of the league, presented a resolution which binds the league to make revisions of the Treaties its principal aim.[41] This undertaking would obviously be an empty gesture without the vast spread of suffrage. The women of the white race having obtained political power everywhere except in the Latin countries (including in this exception South Africa), the Holland resolution becomes Number One in a World Program for which the foundations did not yet exist when the congress met at The Hague in 1915, or when the Treaties were still in the making in 1919.

Inextricably interrelated with the Holland resolution is the plan recom-

[39] Fanny Garrison Villard (1844–1928), American suffragist and pacifist. Daughter of abolitionist William Lloyd Garrison and wife of wealthy reformer Henry Villard, she was prominent in both suffrage and peace activities. She attended the Zurich congress in 1919.

Maud O'Farrell Swartz (1879–1937), American suffragist and labor leader. She became president of the Women's Trade Union League the year after the Vienna congress.

For Mrs. Curtis, see Part IV, document 8.

[40] The Women's Peace Society, founded in 1919 by Fannie Garrison Villard, was based on principles of total disarmament and total nonresistance.

[41] For Aletta Jacobs, see Part III, document 2, Heymann and Augspurg, "Women's Work," note 15.

mended jointly by the American and British sections, under which a cable message carried congratulations to President Harding on calling an International Conference for Disarmament. All sections were urged to devote the week preceding that conference to demonstrations on a national scale in favor of *immediate world-wide* disarmament. Those sections whose governments were invited to take part were recommended to stimulate them by deputations and in all other feasible ways. The international interchange of speakers was especially emphasized.

These immediate activities affecting world government shared the first place with the age-long work of education. The curse of past mis-education, and the threat for the whole human race that lurks in the present survivals thereof, found recognition on all possible occasions. Resolutions were adopted without discussion in favor of abolishing corporal punishment in all forms of education, including that in reformatories; and also for protecting children against misuse for political purposes—such, for instance, as having them take part in political parades.

Reform in Education

An extraordinarily illuminating divergence developed from the conflicting experience of Germany and Austria. Speakers from Germany attributed the World War largely to their own state monopoly of education which had, for fifty years, consistently fostered militarism. The Austrian women on the contrary, in whose country one of the most precious gains of the revolution is the transfer of the schools from ecclesiastical domination to the secularized state and the city, overflowed with untried confidence in their newly acquired power as citizens. The crux of the matter was stated by Madame Duchène, of Paris, in her question: "If the self-governing nations cannot control their schools, in the interest of the people, and of the future peace of the world, what is the basis of our hope that we can control any part of our governments?"[42] For this question no answer was forthcoming.

More than one American delegate was, however, moved to dwell in silence, with renewed anxiety, upon the proposed federal department of education in the United States, with its many opportunities for censorship and military propaganda of various sorts.

In Central Europe the use of school "readers" as a long established, traditional means of stupefying young children is a burning topic. The congress, therefore, referred to its new standing committee on education a suggestive resolution emanating from Vienna, as to the use in the schools

[42] For Gabrielle Duchène, see Part III, document 4, Chamberlain, "Women at The Hague," note 41.

of cheap, well printed editions of the classics of all peoples, as a common inheritance of the youth of the world. The congress recommended to the sections the appointment of committees to examine school texts, to strive to eliminate passages which tend toward war, and to promote the use of material adapted to stimulate respect for and understanding of the other nations.

The president of the congress said, at a public reception held in what is doubtless the most beautiful room in any city hall in the world, that she had attended a suffrage meeting presided over by the mother of the president of the Austrian Republic in 1913 when the Austrian women were prohibited by law from belonging to any organization having a political aim. She returned eight years later to find suffrage extended to all women over 21 years of age, with eleven women sitting in the lower House of Parliament, four in the upper House, and twenty-three as members of the city council of Vienna. In the face of these rapid changes, who would venture to say that Permanent Peace or any other unpopular cause was hopeless?

Even the basis for peace seemed not so far away when the large audience containing many Austrian officials listened with profound interest to a French woman, Mademoiselle Melin, who, although her devastated home was not yet rebuilt, held war itself as an institution responsible for the wretched world in which we are all living.[43] Mademoiselle Melin spoke superbly then as she did once more on the Thursday following the congress when, again in the city hall, she addressed an audience of wounded soldiers who applauded to the echo of this French woman telling them that there could be no victor in modern warfare. It was her magnanimity as well as her exquisite oratory that carried her message, although perhaps both were rivalled in a Belgian delegate, Mademoiselle Lucie Dujardin, who addressed the congress.[44] She had been carried to Germany in January, 1915, had remained there, in one prison camp after another, until, threatened with tuberculosis, she was invalided to Switzerland in July, 1918. Upon her return to Belgium, after the Armistice, she had organized an association of those who had been imprisoned in Germany, that they might feed German and Austrian children. She was able to report to the congress that this association had received 2,000 children as guests in Belgium; she made her speech, however, in order to thank the delegates for what the various sections had done for her compatriots.

Among twenty-eight resolutions adopted by a body composed of such varied elements, there was inevitable divergence as to timeliness and importance. The scope of the following appears to be well-nigh universal:

[43] For Jeanne Mélin, see the Introduction, note 150.
[44] The editors have been unable to identify Lucie Dujardin.

Since the Women's International League for Peace and Freedom aims at the peaceful solution of conflicts between social classes as between nations, it is the duty of its national sections and of its individual members to initiate and support laws looking to the gradual abolition of property privileges (for instance by taxation, death duties and land reform) and to the development of economic and individual freedom, and to work to awaken and strengthen among members of the possessing classes the earnest will to alter the economic system in the direction of social justice.

Self-Determination and Protection of Minorities

The resolution dealing with Ireland was introduced by the British section, in accordance with the rule of the league that oppressed peoples do not present their own grievances to be voted on, but they shall be presented by delegates from the dominant nation, all concerned having previously come to an agreement as to substance and form. The resolution reads:

> Resolved that this congress while welcoming with enthusiasm the truce arranged between Great Britain and Ireland upholds the claim of the Irish people to national self-determination, and recognizes Ireland's struggle for independence is of vital importance to the civilized world, inasmuch as peaceful international relations cannot be assured until the principles of self-determination and government by consent are universally accepted.

Following this the attention of the world was called to the position of Armenia, Georgia, the Ukraine, India and Egypt.

In international meetings on the Continent, besides resolutions of a binding character, there exists a useful and convenient device known as "Voeu," equivalent to the phrase "the sense of the meeting" as used by the Society of Friends. The foregoing paragraph is a case in point. The congress recorded its opinion though immediate concrete action could not be pledged.

Resolutions must, of course, be adopted. Without them an international congress is unthinkable. But sometimes precious treasures of thought, suggestion and warning appear which promise to outlast the fruits of all our faithful drudging. Such is the proposal of Dr. Ferrière, of the International Red Cross, that a series of histories should be prepared by men of the ripest scholarship, covering the new Succession States of the old Austrian empire, these histories to be prepared from the standpoint of world history and translated into the languages of all these states.[45] It is hoped thus to

---

[45] The editors have been unable to identify Dr. Ferrière.

save the children of these lands from the curse of being taught, each one, solely the traditions of his own people and those from the chauvinist point of view.

Warning solemn and nobly uttered came from the fraternal delegate from the Pan-African Congress, Mrs. Curtis, the widow of a former American minister to Liberia. Her message, beautifully given, and heard with the utmost respect, was summed up in the closing words: "There is no White Justice and no Black Justice. There is only Human Justice. Peace will never reign in the world until this truth becomes the guide to action of all peoples."

Overriding lively protest from the floor, Jane Addams declined reelection, insisting that the choice of the president be left to the executive committee of which she remains a member. Emily Green Balch, for twenty years on the faculty of Wellesley College, was unanimously reelected to the office of secretary of the league.

If, before the fourth congress meets at the call of the executive committee, universal disarmament becomes an accomplished fact, the Women's International League for Peace and Freedom will have had an honorable share in that achievement.

Seen in retrospect the characteristics of the congress were vitality, growth and determination. More delegations and larger ones, the reappearance of important members of the Hague and Zurich meetings, even the overcrowding of the program with unforeseen matters too important to be ignored or delayed, all demonstrated vigorous life and the will to continued effort.

Seen in prospect, the Women's International League for Peace and Freedom will continue its work with the League of Nations, striving for changes in the Treaties. It will back to the limit of its powers President Harding's Disarmament Conference. Through its national sections and new standing committee it will help to remodel education.

At the Hague meeting in 1915, woman suffrage in its present extent was still merely a hope, and the European press marvelled that women there gave their attention to a reform still remote. At Zurich in April, 1919, the League of Nations integrated with the Treaty was for some a hope, for others a dread, for all an imminent event. Today the fate of European civilization depends upon the re-writing of that Treaty in the shadow of horrible experience.

B. Racializing the Dialogue

6. Racist German Propaganda Addressed to American Women

Between April 1920 and the French occupation of the Ruhr in January of 1923, a number of organizations in Germany initiated a propaganda campaign against the deployment of French colonial troops for the occupation of the Rhineland, which had been provided for in the Versailles treaty. The initiators of the campaign realized the importance of generating international rather than national protest; they translated their writings into a variety of languages and distributed them in Europe, North and South America, and Australia, often secretly supported by the German Foreign Ministry. They especially targeted German immigrants in the United States and American women, who were well known for their political activism. The campaign counted on American racism and the American leverage in the postwar world to discredit and ultimately end the French occupation altogether.

Although there were relatively few sexual assaults under the French occupation and colonial soldiers by no means committed a disproportionally large share, an enormous body of propaganda emerged in Germany, sometimes resembling quasi-factual police reports, sometimes bordering on the pornographic. The writings were generated by a number of organizations, ranging from the relatively moderate Rhenish Women's League, which was connected with the German Ministry of the Interior, to the decidedly racist and anti-Semitic Fichte Bund (Fichte Society). Interestingly enough, few of these organizations employed women as spokespersons. By and large, the campaign ceased by 1922, because it had proved more harmful than helpful to the cause.

The following leaflet[46] is an example of the most blatantly racist propaganda. In an "appeal to the conscience of all white nations in the world," the Fichte Bund addressed American women for two reasons: they were supposedly familiar with the alleged problem and were thought to have enough political clout to plead Germany's cause with their legislators. The fact that the Fichte Society sent its material to Jane Addams and even to the NAACP points to their misconceptions about American reform groups. Its authors were also uninformed about the geography of American race relations, placing lynchings for alleged rape in the "Wild West" rather than in the South.[47]

Out against the Black Horror!
Urgent Appeal to Americans!

An awful crime against the white race, against our German Women, maidens and children is being perpetrated by the French in using black and coloured troops for the occupation of German territory in an ever increasing number without our being able to prevent it. We therefore resort to the only means at our disposal, viz.: to an urgent public appeal to the conscience of all the white nations in the world.

In the Wild West when a coloured man outrages a white woman, he is lynched without more ado. But what have our German women, girls and children to suffer from the African troops in the occupied districts? What says the world to hundred of thousands white people being enslaved by black and coloured savages? What says the world to the ever increasing assaults and crimes committed by these wild beasts on German women and children? Do the other white nations of the world know about this? It must really be doubted, for it can hardly be believed that they should have no fellow-feeling for the disgrace which is being perpetrated on us and thus on all white people. Therefore the crime committed by the French must be shouted all over the world and the other white nations must be made aware of that this disgrace hits them as well as us.

In front of us lies a pamphlet of about a hundred pages entitled: "Coloured Frenchmen on the Rhine," a cry of distress from German women (Published by H.R. Englemann, Berlin).[48] These represent the police records of a large number of crimes committed by black and coloured

---

[46] "Horror on the Rhine," flier in "Reference File," Jane Addams Papers, SCPC, series 14 (and *JAP*, reel 32).

[47] For more on black women's perspectives on black American troops in Europe, see Addie Hunton and Kathryn Johnson, *Two Colored Women with the American Expeditionary Forces.*

[48] To be obtained from the office of "Ideal and Life" at the price of Mk. 2.- plus increase and postage. [This footnote is in the original.]

THE LIMITATIONS OF NATIONHOOD

men. Anyone's blood must boil at the horrors committed on defenceless women and children reported in these pages in a cold matter-of-fact way.

In them special emphasis is laid on the fact that the cases not placed on record would be far more numerous than those officially reported, which seems but natural as the feeling of shame restrains in many cases the victim from denouncement, partly from fear of retaliation, for often denunciators have been punished for libeling black troops.

Many millions are being paid by the French to suppress publication of these crimes and to stifle German appeals for help. The newspapers published in the occupied districts have been forbidden by the French to report crimes committed on white women. In some places the papers were compelled to publish declarations according to which the black troops had committed no assaults: Nevertheless

It is a fact that black soldiers push white women from the footpaths assisting with the butt ends of their rifles;

It is a fact that the French have started compulsory brothels with white girls in them for the use of coloured soldiers;

It is a fact that the number of births (coloured bastards) is steadily increasing;

It is a fact that parents, teachers, clergymen have been punished because they had forbidden to the girls in their charge any intercourse with coloured soldiers;

It is a fact that a nigger took part for months at the sittings of the Police Court and Court of Appeal at Landau and expressed his scorn and contempt for the white accused;[49]

It is a fact that a French officer to whom an outraged young wife applied for help, bawled out to her: "These fellows have been away from home now for 2 1/2 years and must have it. And they are specially keen on fair hair." (Police Court Sitting of 10. April 1920);

It is a fact that black soldiers are outraging boys and infect them with venereal diseases;

It is a fact that girls are seized, tied on seats or held by the black soldiers and then violated until they expire;

It is a fact that mothers who run to help their ill-used children, have been simply shot down;

It is a fact that white women have been torn from their beds and that their fettered husbands had to look on whilst their wives were being outraged;

It is a fact that up to the beginning of 1921 the following cases have been put on record by the police:

40 cases of attempted rape

49   Landau, a city in Rhineland-Palatinate.

70 cases of accomplished rape

20 cases of sexual misdemeanour of various other kinds

7 cases of unnatural intercourse with boys.

The French chauvinists are trying to hide these facts. Abroad the news is spread that the Blacks have been withdrawn from the Rhine long ago. These lies are spread so persistently, that America has repeatedly enquired by cable whether the coloured troops had been withdrawn. All that has been done is that on approach of the cold season and owing to the many cases of illness amongst the soldiers, part of them has been transferred to more southerly districts, but with the warmer season coming round again, their number keeps on increasing. France does not dream of withdrawing the black troops. On the contrary France wishes to make the occupation of German territory by black troops a permanent institution by introducing compulsory military service in Africa and decreeing that out of the three years service two years have to be served in Europe, but of course not in France. The "Victor" Foch even called the blacks the strongest pillar of French power.[50]

No age, no bodily condition gives immunity from the Black Horror. Pregnant women and even aged matrons have been violated in bestial ways. "Could the walls of cells inhabited by raving maniacs speak of the psychic tortures endured by these victims," say the director of a lunatic asylum "even the hardest heart would break."

"We had been in hopes" many German women cry out in their distress, "that our misery would be known sufficiently to the world and that the world's conscience would bring forth assistance. But those in whose clutches we find ourselves announce scornfully that our press and government are lying and that not the white women have to be protected against the black and yellow soldiers of the French Republic, but vice versa, the niggers from the island of Madagascar had to be protected against the immoral influence of the white women on the Rhine!" The same nigger who in France is only considered as a third-rate man and is subjected there to the strictest discipline, is thus allowed to bear himself in the Rhineland as lord and victor. The French government is thus adding cynical contempt to insult.

In view of the barefaced scorn and compelled by the unspeakable disgrace heaped by the French on us and all white people, we are opening a campaign with intellectual weapons. Millions of fly-leaves must be sent out to England, Denmark, Sweden, Norway, Holland, Spain, Switzerland and

---

[50] Ferdinand Foch (1851–1929), supreme commander of the Allied armies in France in Worlds War I. Foch was central in drawing up the terms of the armistice with Germany at Compiègne. He visited the United States in a tour honoring his military achievements in 1921.

THE LIMITATIONS OF NATIONHOOD

Italy, across the ocean to North and South America, to Australia, in fact wherever white people live, but particularly to England and North America.

You members of the white race! help us to free our women, girls and children from the hell in the occupied district into which they have been cast by the black and colored hords [sic] of Africa. Read this appeal to your friends, don't throw it away, pass it along from hand to hand, ask for more fly-leaves if you have use for them.

Americans! Where would the French have been without your help in the world's war? Now that Germany has been overpowered, the French as "victors" distribute medals for bravoury [sic] for the occupation of German towns where no armed adversary has ever met them and scoff at their former helpmates.

Americans! We have sufficient pride in us, to bear stoically the distress inflicted on us as the vanquished, without crying for help, but outrages on the bodies of our white women and children we will not submit to. You have taken our weapons from us, give them back to us, or help us by the weight of your voices to put a stop to the darkest crime ever committed in the world's history: the Black Horror. Help us if you have any feeling for the awful disgrace which is being done to our white women on the Rhine by the eager lust of African savages.

[list of names appended: The Board of the Deutsche Fichte-Bund e.V.]

7. Mary Church Terrell Protests to Jane Addams

The propaganda campaign against the "Horror on the Rhine" provoked hardly any protests from American feminists. Jane Addams initially thought the reports credible and voiced her protest in a letter to Secretary of State Hughes. The State Department never replied, perhaps because it had already determined that most of the German claims were fabricated.

The campaign did, however, cause a heated, albeit short-lived, debate within the American branch of WILPF, when the Executive Committee asked its only African-American member to sign a petition seeking the removal of the colonial troops. Like Jane Addams, Mary Church Terrell was a charter member of both the NAACP and WILPF. She had been engaged in the international women's movement for over two decades, often the only black participant at international meetings, where she felt that she not

only represented the black women of the United States and Africa, but of all non-white countries in the world.

In the following letter to the president of WILPF,[51] Terrell aptly characterized the German propaganda as "another violent and plausible appeal to race prejudice." Although she expressed sympathy for the German victims of the alleged attacks, she pointed to atrocities committed by American soldiers in Haiti and to the fact that "black women have been the victims of assaults committed upon them by white men and men of all other races."

Most important, Terrell had access to information that convinced Addams that the appeals on behalf of German women and children constituted a racist campaign to end French occupation in Germany. The letter reflects the close relationship between the two women. Addams's change of mind was brought about by a combination of her trust in Terrell and Terrell's record of work for the national and international women's movement, as well as information that Carrie Chapman Catt received from German suffragists at an international meeting in Geneva.

After Terrell's intervention, the American branch of WILPF adopted the WILPF policy, which condemned the use of colonial troops outside their country but purposely avoided the question of rape because it "complicated the issue."

Mary Church Terrell to Jane Addams

1615 S St. N.W.
Washington, D.C.
March 18, 1921

My dear Miss Addams;
It is plainly my duty to write to you concerning a matter in which you are deeply interested, I know. I have been asked to sign a petition asking for the removal of the black troops from occupied German territory. The most terrible crimes are said to be committed by these black troops against the German women. I belong to a race whose women have been the victims of assaults committed upon them by white men and men of all other races. As a rule, these men have ruined and wrecked the women of my race with impunity. For that reason I sympathize deeply with the German women, if they are really the victims of the passions of black men. I pity them in their present peril as I pitied the French women, when the newspapers told us of the brutal treatment they received at the hands of the German soldiers

---

[51]   Mary Church Terrell to Jane Addams, Washington, D.C., March 18, 1921, Mary Church Terrell Papers, Library of Congress.

who were quartered in France.[52] Because the women of my race have suffered so long and so terribly from assaults committed upon them with impunity by men of all races, I am all the more pained at the brutal treatment to which German women are now said to be subjected by the black troops.

However, I am certain that the black soldiers are committing no more assaults upon the German women than the German men committed upon French women or that any race of soldiers would probably commit upon women in occupied territory. Our own American soldiers treated the Haitian women brutally. On good authority it is asserted that young Haitian girls were actually murdered by some of our soldiers. I can not vouch for the truth of that statement, but it is not at all difficult for me to believe that white Americans would treat colored women as brutally as our soldiers are said to have treated the Haitian women.[53]

I can not sign the petition asking for the removal of the black troops, because I believe it is a direct appeal to race prejudice. In all the statements concerning the matter, great emphasis is laid upon the fact that these troops are worse than white soldiers. That is a reflection upon them which I am sure they do not deserve. Charges are always preferred against soldiers of all races who are quartered in the land they have conquered. I can readily understand that if a German woman were to be outraged, she would prefer to suffer at the hands of a white man than at the hands of a black man. But, even though that be true, I can not sign a petition asking for the removal of these troops because they are black.

On good authority I have been informed that the charges preferred against the black troops are not all founded in fact. Mrs. Catt investigated the charges against the black troops when she was in Geneva and found, according to the testimony of reputable people living in the region where the atrocities were alleged to have been committed, that these black soldiers had conducted themselves with more courtesy and consideration than any white troops who had been stationed there.[54] Two German delegates told Mrs. Catt that there was no movement in Germany to ask France to remove these colored troops and that, so far as they knew, there was no complaint in Germany on that score. Mrs. Catt says that the three German women with whom she talked in Geneva promised to investigate the charges against the colored troops which were being circulated in this country and to let her know later.[55] "I saw all three of them in London

---

[52] During World War I.

[53] Terrell is referring to the U.S. military occupation of Haiti in 1915.

[54] For Carrie Chapman Catt, see Part IV, document 3, Anna Lindemann to Jane Addams, note 31.

[55] The "three German women" might have been Anna Lindemann, Marie Elisabeth Lüders, and SPD Reichstag deputy Adele Schreiber, who also attended the 1921 IWSA conference in Geneva.

early in December," says Mrs. Catt, "and again they reiterated the same statement made in Geneva, which was to the effect that atrocities such as are being described in the United States could not have been committed by the Army of Occupation without the masses of the people of Germany knowing about it, and that they had heard nothing which warranted such charges being made."

And there has recently been an indignant disclaimer of the propaganda campaign against the black troops which was made by some of the leading business men in the Rhineland. Director Ruetten declared that investigation by the Rhineland Traffic Association had shown that the stories of molestation of the population by the troops of occupation were untrue.[56]

I cannot sign the petition asking for the removal of the black troops with these facts staring me in the face. The propaganda against the black troops in this country is simply another violent and plausible appeal to race prejudice.

It is very painful to me not to do anything which you or the organization which I love would like to have me do. Knowing you as well as I do, however, I feel sure you do not want me to be untrue to myself or to the race with which I am identified simply to please my friends. I do not want to be a stumbling block or a nuisance as a member of the Executive Committee. If it will help matters any, I am willing to resign. You have always been such a true friend to me, my esteem and affection for you are so great. I do not want to do anything which will annoy or embarrass you as the head of the International League for Peace and Freedom.

I am not at all sure I can be present at the Annual Meeting next month. I shall try to be there.

Please speak frankly to me and if you can present any facts which seem to you to prove that the petition should be signed, do not hesitate to send them to me. I am not narrow. I want to know the truth and do right.

With gratitude to you for the many kindnesses to me in the past and with the highest esteem, I am sincerely yours,

Mary Church Terrell

8. The WILPF Vienna Congress Resolution on Colonial Troops

Resolutions do not normally make compelling reading. This one, however, passed at the Third International Women's Peace Congress in Vienna in

[56] One of the reasons why the propaganda campaign ended was that it was hurting the tourist trade.

1921, captured both the global breadth of WILPF's new postwar vision and the complexities that attended its entry onto the world stage of international relations.[57] Some resolutions printed in the Congress *Report* remained comfortably abstract. For example, the one on "Race Equality" reads: "We believe no human being should be deprived of an education, prevented from earning a living, debarred from any legitimate pursuit in which he wishes to engage, or be subjected to any humiliation on account of race or color. We recommend that members of this Congress should do everything in their power to abrogate laws and change customs which lead to discrimination against human beings on account of race or color." Similarly, a resolution on "The Jews" held "that no restriction should be placed on the civil or political rights of the Jews because of their race." The following resolution on the use of colonial troops proved more complicated, however, because it created a potential conflict with the WILPF goal of race equality.

As the secretary-treasurer of WILPF in Geneva, Emily Balch was on the front lines of a controversy that pitted French colonial troops occupying the Rhineland against racist appeals for their removal. The controversy educated her on the use of colonial troops in modern warfare, and thanks to Mary Church Terrell's intervention (see previous document), to the prejudicial basis for some of the opposition to their use.

As a result, Balch's proposed resolution had two parts. First and more extensive was a stirring pacifist critique of the use of colonial troops in modern warfare; second was a subtext about rape that both expressed and rejected racist attitudes toward African troops. That subtext noted that the soldiers were torn from their homes "and from all women of their own race," suggesting that they might constitute a threat to women not of their race. But in a "Subsequent Note" (the likes of which appeared for no other resolution), Balch stated that she "purposely avoided other questions involved in the use of coloured troops in occupied districts," not from "lack of sympathy with those that are suffering from this aftermath of war, but because these questions are of quite a different order and complicate the issue." Complicating the issue were racist misrepresentations about rape by black troops. Balch bowed in the direction of the occupied people, expressing sympathy for those who were "actually illtreated" as well as "for those whose feelings have been wounded by what they feel as a studied insult." But she deplored "this new stumbling block . . . in the path of friendship and mutual respect between the races."

By prior arrangement Jane Addams next called upon Helen Curtis, who had lived in Liberia. Curtis "spoke of the conditions under which the black

---

[57] Women's International League for Peace and Freedom, *Report of the Third International Congress of Women: Vienna, July 10–17, 1921* (Geneva, 1921), pp. 76–78. Italics indicate emphasis in the original.

troops went to war," although it was not apparent that she had visited black troops in Germany. While she expressed sympathy for the African troops, Curtis also reinforced the salience of sexual issues involved in their deployment in a white population.

Military Use of Native Populations of Colonies

Emily Balch, after moving the resolution

Resolved that this League make every possible effort to oppose the military use of "native" populations, said:

The use by the Great European Powers of troops drawn from their colonies is a menace to civilisation that is not fully realized. Especially do the working people fail, as yet, to grasp its significance.

We have seen in this war the old distinction between the army and the civilian population almost fade out before the tremendous fact of the conscription of entire peoples.

We have now before us the beginning of the military exploitation, for the purposes of those who hold the power in their hands, of the people of the continents where they control colonies and spheres of influence.

Such military use of so-called "native" populations has various aspects, all of them serious.

First, is the outrageous wrong done to the soldiers and their families. Conscription direct, or veiled as voluntary recruiting, tears them from their homes and from all women of their own race, and condemns them to unnatural and hideous life in foreign barracks when they are not in active service in trenches or on the "field of honour." We rejoice that slavery is dead, but is not forced military service as literally slavery as chattel slavery itself, and more horrible?

Secondly, the fact that colonies can be used as a source from which to draw troops—troops endless in numbers, cheap, docile, and recklessly courageous—makes such colonies enormously valuable to the imperialists. This greatly intensifies the struggle to secure control of colonial areas and of spheres of influence, and this struggle is a most potent cause of wars. Other reasons for securing such control—the wish for supplies of raw materials, for "native" markets and for territory for colonising surplus populations—are economic, and it is not in the nature of things impossible to secure their advantages by treaty and international agreement without securing political mastery of the territory in question. But in order to use territory as a source of troops it is necessary to have political and military control; and as long as one country has colonial troops others will seek to have the same and will fight to secure this territory from which to draw them.

Thirdly, the European is becoming, thank God, cynical as to war. It is not so easy any more to order him to march in any direction his superiors may choose and to fire at the word of command on his neighbours across the border or on his fellow workmen in case of civil conflicts or strikes. He has become an untrustworthy instrument for such uses because he has begun to think.

But the remoter peoples, standing outside of European quarrels, can be trusted, if they are drilled and trained to use weapons of precision, to use them as directed. If the population of Africa and Asia are once really militarised by European masters the end of this phase of civilization has come.

It is good to see that that great Frenchman, Charles Gide, is alive to this menace.[58] But it is curious that up to this time the masses who are seeking better and juster social conditions realize it so little. We can do no better service to them and to the cause of peace than to urge the matter on their attention. I have done and shall do so at every opportunity, and beg you to do the same.

Before I close I want to call your attention to a special point of immediate interest. As regards the restricted area, that is allotted under the Peace Treaty as Mandates of the B class we have the support of the text of the Covenant of the League of Nations which provides for "the prevention of the establishment of fortifications or military and naval bases and *of military training of the natives for other than police purposes and the defence of territory* . . ." (Art.22).

Yet this solemn undertaking is apparently to be violated, for France makes "reserves" on this point. I understand this to mean that she proposes to raise troops in these colonies for use in Europe (though without resorting, nominally, to conscription).

Get your gouvernment [*sic*] to protest against this breach of the Covenant. Write and protest to the Commission on Mandates: above all try to get labour leaders to understand the situation.

Our Geneva office, 6 rue du vieux College, will be glad to receive and forward such protests. It will also send on request the memorial on this subject presented by us to the first League of Nations Assembly.

The militarisation of the other continents for the purposes of European quarrels threatens the future of Europe, Asia, and Africa alike. It must be met promptly and while it is relatively small. European public opinion will be strengthened by the growing unwillingness of awakening peoples to be thus abused and exploited. But it is time for European public opinion to arouse and make itself overwhelmingly felt.

---

[58]   Charles Gide (1847–1936), French economist, social reformer, and pacifist.

Subsequent Note.

In making this very brief address on a great subject I purposely avoided other questions involved in the use of coloured troops in occupied districts. This was from no lack of sympathy with those that are suffering from this aftermath of war, but because these questions are of quite a different order and complicate the issue.

Every feeling person must experience a deep sense of pity not only for those of the resident population that have been actually illtreated, but for all those whose feelings have been wounded by what they feel as a studied insult. Furthermore it is a terrible misfortune that this new stumbling block should have been put in the path of friendship and mutual respect between the races.

The *Chair* introduced *Helen Curtis,* a resident of the United States for most of her life, whose husband was now a minister in Liberia, Africa, and who was therefore well informed about the Conditions in Africa . . .[59]

Helen Curtis spoke of the conditions under which the black troops went to war. She was present when they left their country, when they said good-bye to their wives, whom many of them never saw again. She saw how they were treated in the hospitals. One of their worst complaints was that they were not allowed to speak to a white woman. The only pleasure they were allowed was visiting public houses, where they acquired serious diseases, this sort of entertainment being permitted to them. She felt sure there would be no end to the conflict between different races until all use of force was stopped and until all nations disarmed.

The resolution on the Military Use of Native Populations of Colonies was then *voted.*

[59] Florence Kelley, "The Women's Congress at Vienna" (reprinted here in Part IV, document 5), was probably better informed when she called Curtis "the widow of a former American minister to Liberia."

C. German Women Return
to the Dialogue

9. Red Scare Tactics Used on German Activist Visiting the United States

Gertrud Baer's visit to the United States in 1922 was the first of many made by German women during the next decade as they returned to the dialogue after the traumatic events of the preceding years. The American branch of WILPF invited Baer to give joint lectures with women from Britain and France, urging recognition of the Soviet Union, the release of political prisoners, and the withdrawal of American troops from Central America. The plan to have Baer speak on the same platform with English and French women marked an important step toward reconciliation among former World War I enemies.

Baer's experience, however, turned out to be very different from women activists' prewar travels. In the 1920s, she and other German women came to a country where women reformers were coping with harassment arising from the Red Scare. Although immigration officials claimed that they prevented Baer from entering the country for lack of funds, it seems likely that, as the *New York Times* reported, she was detained pending a Department of Justice "investigation of alleged communism." Baer's detention also prevented her from keeping an appointment at the White House.

Baer's trip to the United States marked the beginning of a friendship with Jane Addams that lasted until Addams's death in 1935. Although Addams and her fellow women reformers had lost some of their prestige, they still had enough influence to succeed in their demand for Baer's release. German newspapers reported on the incident, prompting Lida

Gustava Heymann to inquire anxiously about Baer's detention in a letter to Addams.

German Teacher Here to Speak for Peace
Taken Off Ship as Suspected Communist

[*New York Times,* New York, May 1, 1922] Agents of the Department of Justice went on board the steamship George Washington on its arrival yesterday and took off Miss Gertrude [*sic*] Baer, a German teacher who was scheduled to address the Women's International League for Peace on Monday and to attend a reception at the residence of Mrs. Henry Villard.[60]

Miss Baer was detained because of information received by the Department of Justice that she belonged to the Communist Party, many of whose members have been deported and others imprisoned in this country.

Miss Baer was scheduled to speak on Tuesday in the Engineering Societies building on the subject, "Can Women Boycott War." Miss Jane Addams, it was announced, is to preside at this meeting. Other speakers were to be Mrs. Arnot Robinson of England and Mlle. Thérèse Pottecher of France, and it was stated that this was to have been the first time since the war when women of these three countries would have spoken in public from the same platform.[61]

A Special Board of Inquiry will be held on Ellis Island to decide whether Miss Baer will be permitted to land.

————

WASHINGTON, April 30.—The Women's International League for Peace brought its three-day session to a close today with a mass meeting here at which resolutions were adopted urging recognition of the Russian Soviet Government and the release of all prisoners held "for expressions of opinion." Withdrawal of American troops from Haiti and Santo Domingo also was demanded.

Mrs. Arnot Robinson, the British representative, and Mlle. Therese Pottecher, the French delegate, both condemned the Versailles Treaty in speeches at the mass meeting. Mrs. Robinson, who is Vice Chairman of the

[60]   For Fanny Garrison Villard, see Part IV, document 5, Florence Kelley, "The Women's Congress at Vienna," note 39.
[61]   The editors have not found biographical information about Mrs. Arnot Robinson or Mlle. Thérèse Pottecher.

THE LIMITATIONS OF NATIONHOOD

British Labor Party, said the present trade depression in Europe is "making for internationalism."

Miss Baer Released from Ellis Island

Jane Addams Intercedes for German Peace

Promoter Detained by Authorities

[*New York Times*, New York, May 2, 1922] Gertrude Baer, a German teacher who was taken off the steamer George Washington Sunday by agents of the Department of Justice and held at Ellis Island at their request, was released yesterday following a hearing before a special board of inquiry. Miss Baer, who came to the United States on invitation to speak before the Women's International League for Peace, went to the home of Mrs. Henry Villard at 525 Park Avenue.

Robert E. Todd, Commissioner of Immigration at Ellis island, said he understood the reason for detaining Miss Baer, who was a second cabin passenger, was because of lack of funds.

Jane Addams of Hull House, Chicago; Lillian B. Wald, and Mabel Kittredge met Miss Baer at Ellis Island and interceded in her behalf.[62] Miss Addams said that Miss Baer came here to promote international peace and had no intention of teaching communistic theories. Miss Baer is Secretary of the German section of the Women's International league.

WASHINGTON, May 1.—White House officials were informed today that one of those on President Harding's engagement list for the day, Gertrude Baer of Hamburg, Germany, a delegate to the meeting here of the Women's International League for Peace, would be unable to fill the engagement because of detention at Ellis island. The visit of Miss Baer to the White House, it was said by officials there, had been arranged by the State Department at the request of the German Embassy. Department of Justice officials said they had requested her detention upon arrival yesterday at New York, pending investigation of alleged communistic beliefs.

Delegates to the meeting of the International League for Peace had an

---

[62]   For Lillian Wald, see Part II, document 6, Alice Salomon, "Social Work in America," note 65. The daughter of a leading New York minister, Mabel Kittredge was a generous donor to the Henry Street settlement and a close friend of Lillian Wald.

engagement today with Secretary Hughes to present a plea for recognition of Russia.[63]

Woman to Bar War in Future, She Says

Fraulein Bauer [sic] Tells Peace Society

Replacing of "Man World" Will Do It

1,000 at Meeting of League

English, French and American Speakers on Same Platform with German

[*New York Times,* New York, May 3, 1922] Three women speakers imported from England, France and Germany under the auspices of the Women's International League and the Women's Peace Society for a pacifist campaign in this country made their first speeches in this city last night at a meeting in the Engineering Societies Building in West Thirty-ninth Street. An audience of about 1,000 persons, mostly women, greeted them.

One of the speakers was Fraulein Gertrude [sic] Baer of Germany, Secretary of the Youth Movement there and an officer of the Women's International league, who grasped the hand of Mlle. Therese Pottecher-Arnould [sic] of France and assured her that the women of Germany would do all in their power to avert war in the future. Both were replying in their speeches to the question: "Can Women Boycott War?"

The German woman received an enthusiastic greeting from her audience on this, her first appearance in this country, and she was praised by Miss Jane Addams the Chairman, and Mrs. Henry Villard, President of the Women's Peace Society. The French speaker and Mrs. Arnot Robinson, the English representative, had previously spoken at meetings in Washington and Baltimore, but Fraulein Bauer had not been able to join the campaign until last night.

She said that a "man system" controlled the world and that women must replace "the masculine principle with a feminine principle—our supreme principle should be the sacredness of life." She asserted that the fear developed under this "man system" prevented complete disarmament and negotiation with Russia. She pointed out the growing influence of women in German political life and said there were forty women in the Reichstag.

"There are two Germanies—the old Germany and the modern Ger-

[63] Charles Evans Hughes (1862–1948), American jurist and statesman who served as Associate Justice of the Supreme Court (1910–16), Secretary of State (1921–25), and Chief Justice of the Supreme Court (1930–41).

International group at the 1924 WILPF congress in Washington, D.C. From the left: Andrée Jouve, Gabrielle Duchène, Cornelia Ramondt-Hirschmann, Jane Addams, Gertrud Baer, and Marguerite Dumond. Swarthmore College Peace Collection.

many. You know enough about the old Germany, so that I will tell you only about the modern. This modern Germany is the outgrowth of defeat. New movements are springing up in all parts of Germany among persons who suffered much. The working people will never again enter another war."

Miss Addams and the other speakers also answered the evening's question affirmatively and told how they thought women could exert their power to avert wars.

The speakers will appear in several other cities as part of the movement to stir anti-war sentiment among women.

GERMAN WOMEN RETURN TO THE DIALOGUE

10. Jane Addams Plans for German Visitors

Madeleine Doty joined the dialogue between American and German social justice feminists at The Hague in 1915, Zurich in 1919, and Vienna in 1921. Trained as a lawyer, she traveled widely in Europe in 1915–1919, writing compelling accounts of her trips to Germany in 1915 and Russia during the Revolution of November 1917. After the war, she worked as the International Secretary of the Women's International League for Peace and Freedom, then as editor of *Pax International* for the League of Nations. In 1919 she married Roger Baldwin, head of the National Civil Liberties Bureau, which in 1920 became the American Civil Liberties Union. In 1924, Doty asked Addams to help organize speaking engagements for German friends attending the fourth WILPF Congress in Washington, D.C. Addams's reply is printed here.[64]

After the congress, a train called the "Pax Special" took the delegations to the special summer school that WILPF held at Hull House in Chicago, making numerous stops along the way. Despite accusations from the Daughters of the American Revolution and the American Legion that the German and Russian delegations were made up of spies, the summer school was quite successful.

Because of years of inflation, many middle- and upper-middle-class German women lacked the funds to attend. As the following letter shows, the American organizers tried to help them finance the trip. Addams believed that Americans would be interested in lectures on the present situation in Germany, and women like Lida Gustava Heymann and Gertrud Baer certainly had a sufficient command of the English language to attract a paying audience. Some German delegates stayed as long as half a year lecturing throughout the country (see the next document "Messages of Europe"). Their lectures were probably similar to the ones they gave at the WILPF Summer School.

Despite the currency problems, German participation at the congress was quite substantial. At the summer school, Anita Augspurg spoke on Goethe as an internationalist, Lida Gustava Heymann on democracy and reaction in Europe, and Auguste Kirchhoff on anti-Semitism as an after-

---

[64]   Jane Addams to Madeleine Doty, Chicago, February 8, 1924, Jane Addams Papers, SCPC (and *JAP*, reel 16).

math of war. Gertrud Baer, by far the youngest member, organized a symposium on student antiwar protest. The fact that Heymann and Augspurg were hosted during their stay in Chicago by Addams's life partner Mary Smith points to their close relationship with that preeminent "social politician."

Jane Addams to Madeleine Doty

February 8, 1924

My dear Madeline Doty:

Isn't it fine that our German friends will soon be here? I am very much interested in what you tell me of their plans. We hope to have them all, as you may have seen by the tentative program, to speak in our Summer School in May and if possible I think it would be better to have them speak in the Eastern cities, Boston, etc. up to the time of the Congress and be in this neighborhood after the Summer School in May.

Have you tried the Open Forum Speakers Bureau? I should be glad to write to them if you authorize it and see what they can do. The fees they usually pay are only about $50.00 but they have many connections through the East. I am inclosing [sic] a letter from them for the sake of giving you the address. I was a little annoyed by having them put me on their list of speakers without consulting me, but they are hustlers and very nice people. I think Fraulein Heymann with her good English could have a great many engagements, especially if she spoke on the present political and economic situation in Germany, or something of that sort. Mrs. Catt of New York and Miss Blackwell of Boston and others of the old time suffragists ought to be ready to help get engagements.[65]

We want them of course in Chicago and will begin as soon as we know their exact dates but I feel so strongly that it would be better for the Summer School if they made their first appearance then and also traveling about in Illinois and Wisconsin they would get quite as many engagements in May and June as they would in March and April and it would be much pleasanter for them. . . .

Faithfully yours,
Jane Addams

---

[65] For Carrie Chapman Catt, see Part IV, document 3, Anna Lindemann to Jane Addams, note 31. Alice Stone Blackwell (1857–1950), American feminist, was the daughter of woman suffrage leaders Lucy Stone and Henry Browne Blackwell. By 1924 she was active in a range of radical humanitarian causes.

11. Pages from a Keepsake

After they returned from the congress and the Summer School of the Women's International League for Peace and Freedom, many European delegates stayed on in the United States for a number of months, often to supplement their income by lecturing. The American dollars they hoped to earn would go far in their inflation-racked homelands. A number of European delegates wrote short reminiscences of their trips. The greetings, printed and bound, were presented to Jane Addams and probably to other members of the American branch. Booklets like this were common as thank-you gifts or for holidays and anniversaries. This one contained messages in English, German, and French, from twenty-eight women representing virtually all European countries from Ukraine to Ireland, from France to Norway.[66]

As the following excerpts from "Messages of Europe" show, the experience of the German delegates was quite diverse. Lida Gustava Heymann and Anita Augspurg were particularly fascinated by American architecture. Gertrud Baer, who had organized a symposium on students' protests against the war at the Summer School, was impressed by the rich cultural tradition she encountered when she lectured in Harlem. Another German delegate praised the American organizers for convening the congress despite a climate of stark isolationism, where pacifism was "unpopular and little understood."

Bremen pacifist Auguste Kirchhoff observed the effects of women's suffrage as well as new inventions that freed middle-class American women from household drudgery. The German delegates keenly observed the consequences of the enfranchisement of American women, especially its effect on the relationship between the sexes. Usually, they were pleased by what they saw, the "freedom and independence of the American women" and the "good fellowship between the sexes," even if economic equality—as in Germany—existed only on paper.

[66] From "Organizational File: Women's International League for Peace and Freedom," Jane Addams Papers, SCPC (and *JAP*, reel 44). Augspurg and Heymann message translated by the editors.

Messages of Europe, Christmas 1924
To Jane Addams, to Our American Friends

The year 1924 brought many European members of the International Women's League for Peace and Freedom to America for the first time. They saw the new world: its people, its institutions! The year is drawing to an end, we look back. Our thoughts wander across the ocean. Enormous lakes, streams, waterfalls, landscapes and cities pass by our mind's eye; what remains are the things that pleased us most. I cling to the architecture, which contributed the most to my stay, except for what I received from people.

I see the skyscrapers in New York, which stand out against the sky at sundown, bold and majestic. I see the magnificent building of the Lincoln Memorial in radiant moonlight, the Washington obelisk drenched by the sun, the dome of the Capitol in its glorious nightly illumination. Deeply moved, I stand in front of the Freemason's temple in Washington.[67] The allotment of space, the simple design, the exquisite material—solemnity grasps the soul. A people that creates such buildings will certainly have much to give to the world in the future.

Thoughts wander to American friends and my heart warms up. In loyal friendship, I shake the hands of all who enhanced our stay in America by their hospitality, a hospitality that made us feel at home wherever we went. In loyal companionship, I think of our American co-workers who, like us, fight for peace and freedom with the same perseverance and energy, against a world of brutal force and bondage.

I think with joyful pride of the small group of courageous women who wrote the fight for equal rights for men and women on their banner, fighting against an overwhelming majority of men and, unfortunately, women. They mobilize everything, their whole selves, to achieve their goal.

America—Europe! Beauty, friendship, here and there. Happiness and sorrow, wealth and poverty, struggle here and there, but every dimension is larger over there. The world is the same everywhere! It is what man makes it. The majority of mankind believes in mastering it with force, and has created chaos.

We women of the International League for Peace and Freedom condemn all violence and work in the spirit of conciliation and friendship, which is cement that never fails and which has created a wonderful community of women since 1915. Our American sisters whom we met in 1924,

---

[67] Augspurg and Heymann probably mean the Scottish Rite Temple on 16th St. NW, designed in 1911–15 by John Russell Pope (1874–1937), architect of the National Gallery of Art and the Jefferson Memorial.

first and foremost Jane Addams, newly strengthened our belief in the power that never fails and we thank them from the bottoms of our hearts.

Anita AUGSPURG and Lida Gustava HEYMANN
delegates from Germany

In the lectures on my 5 months' trip to the U.S.A. there are two points which again and again rouse the enthusiastic interest of our audiences in the big public meetings: the beginning intellectual and human Equality of your black fellow-men and women and the Emancipation of youth in your country.

I shall never forget an evening meeting in the Negro District of New York, where a wholly black audience interviewed me on the economic and political situation in Europe with questions so clever and so much to the point that one felt: here is the deep and passionate sympathy and understanding for the oppressed, from the part of those who are still bound to suffer. For the roots of the material and psychic needs of the oppressed are the same wherever they are to be found in the world, as their hopes and wishes and longings are the same. But these colored men and women are much richer than our race. That showed in their art, their music, pieces of which are on my writing table ever since I left your continent, that showed in the concert which the students of Washington University: boys and girls gave for us in May. To lay bare the productive artistic and intellectual sources of this race, overlaid by false conceptions and the thoughtlessness of their more powerful white brethren, and to achieve giving them full economic and social equality will be one of the greatest deeds of a great generation, of that generation which is joining hands with the high-spirited independent new Youth of all continents.

Your young people, specially your c.o.'s, those opposing military drill in Colleges and schools and those who aim at a world free from war and based on social, political and economic justice for all without distinction of sex, race, class and creed are an enormous stimulus to me and my comrades wherever I speak and write about them. Their failure is our failure, their success is our success. Thanks to them and all those in your country who understand and support them. For it is the autonomous, self-conscious and self-responsible Youth to whom a new future belongs.

Gertrud BAER Delegate of Germany

When one is looking back to time of splendid days, shining like a bright and wonderful light into the monotony of daily life, it seems quite a difficult task, to pick out one single impression as one of the most agreeable ones. What I felt most intensely like a warm flood of sympathy surrounding me everywhere, was the sublime and noble sort of American hospitality. Among all the fine and interesting arrangements made for us in the course of about seven weeks, I appreciated most our Chicago Summerschool and everything connected with it. And one of my deepest impressions and kindest remembrances is Hull House and the hours spent there.

Knowing, however, that many of my European comrades are feeling the same, and being afraid to repeat things, which others will say much better than I am able to do in a foreign language, I should like to point to an experience which deeply impressed me: to the excellent position of the American woman in family and social life.

I don't know much about the American woman in business life. Realising however the economic struggle to be very hard in America, I suppose there will be no overwhelming difference with European countries, where equal rights and equal payments up to this term, at best exist on the paper. But a remarkable matter of fact, striking every foreign traveller in the United States, is the very high standard of freedom and independence of the American woman and, corresponding with it, the exquisite politeness and respect on the side of the American man.

Surely these qualities have their roots in old times, where this land of colonisation had a lot of men and a great want of woman. Sex minorities, as history proves, don't suffer the fate of national minorities, on the contrary: They are not suppressed and persecuted, but highly estimated and appreciated. So from old times the American woman had a good chance, to be sure.

A Chicago professor, with whom I discussed these things and who agreed with me in the minority question, gave me another reason for the good position of the American woman: he told me that in his country generally the education of women is better than that of men, because the struggle of life claims all the forces of the man at an early age. He is to earn his living at a time when the woman can still learn and study. This explanation is not perhaps influenced by American politeness: it corresponds to the facts, and is confirmed by a German professor, living in America in his book on the United States published in Germany.[68]

Surely it is not a mere formality—as the superficial observer may be inclined to think—that the gentleman takes off his hat the moment a woman enters the elevator, that walking with a woman he always takes the traffic side, that he offers his seat to her in overcrowded trolleys and buses, and does all sorts of chivalrous courtesies to help her and make her feel at ease. According to my opinion all those manners and customs have a deeper root: they are the visible signs of good and noble sentiments. Isn't it a won-

[68] Kirchhoff is probably alluding to Hugo Münsterberg's *The Americans*. Münsterberg (1863–1916) was the brother of Berlin social reformer Emil Münsterberg and the uncle of Else Münsterberg, who translated Jane Addams' *Twenty Years at Hull House* into German. A German-American psychologist and philosopher, he taught at the University of Freiburg and at Harvard.

derful expression of respect and veneration when the son rises as soon as the mother enters the room and does not sit down again before he has helped her to get her seat?

When, years ago, in Europe, we were fighting for the vote, we often met with the peculiar idea, that all chivalrousness had to cease from the moment we should get equal rights: for, as comrades, we could not expect or claim any particular courtesies any longer. Surely we don't claim them, but we enjoy them as a free gift of that kindness which—if generally used in social life—would be the best condition for the new and peaceful order of human affairs we are struggling for. And we enjoy them twice more if they are connected with a fine standard of real good fellowship between the sexes.

We will not forget that some of the Western States were the first territories in the civilised world which gave the vote to women, and, in defending this measure which was scorned at and declared to be the ruin of all true womanhood and healthy politics, they proved their worth. Now we have the vote in a great many European countries and the prophetized catastrophes did not occur. Nevertheless the European women—exceptions always confirm the rule—have still to fight against traditions and old prejudices, that don't exist in America. In Europe the old commandment of the Bible, that the wife has to obey her husband still overshadows many homes and many women's lives. In America, however, plenty of freedom and independence, guaranteed to the women from the very beginning, has developed wonderful qualities of prudence, self-reliance and decision.

Surely this effect is not only due to ideal moments; it is also influenced by very practical circumstances: the simplifying of the American household and the emancipation of women from drudgery by the highly developed technical science. If there is one thing to raise my envy, it is the American "kitchenette" with all its electrical and technical wonders. And if I sometimes feel a little homesick, thinking of the United States, it is—beside the dear friends I left there—for the wonderful American homes, not defended by fences and hedges, but standing free and hospitable, overshadowed by wonderful old trees, on the green lawns of the blessed country.

Auguste KIRCHHOFF
Delegate of Germany

I was residing in the United States in the winter and spring 1924, and this gave me an opportunity, exceptional in the case of a foreign delegate, of seeing something of the work, which was undertaken by the American branch of the W.I.L. in preparation of the Congress at Washington. I doubt very much whether some of the European branches realized the difficulties of that task, when they decided to assemble at Washington. Did they realize the vastness of the country, which they hoped to move by their

WILPF booth at Christmas fair in Stuttgart, 1931. The sign reads, "Booth of the Women's International League for Peace and Freedom, German Branch." A poster with the silhouettes of children appeals to mothers and educators to teach pacifist principles and reject books and toys that glorify war. Swarthmore College Peace Collection.

appeal, and the difficulty of rousing interest in problems, which seem remote and complicated to a people, absorbed in their own affairs, and inclined to look upon European questions with suspicion and diffidence? Did they realize the great chasm which divides Europe from America, Europe, impoverished, suffering from unemployment, disappointed and embittered. America, prosperous, hard-working, pleasure-seeking and hopeful of a great future? What could a few women do, one might ask in despair. The American members of the W.I.L. were fully conscious of these difficulties. They had been fighting what seemed a losing battle when the call came to them from Europe, and yet they decided to accept the challenge. And the organisation, instead of breaking down under the increased weight, was infused with new life. Then when the time of the arrival of the foreign delegations came, it was gratifying to see women, who had stood up for peace in the various countries of Europe, step down the

GERMAN WOMEN RETURN TO THE DIALOGUE

landing bridge in New York Harbour, where they were met by their American comrades, and to hear them address crowded audiences within a stone's throw of the White House. It seemed as if under the chairmanship of Miss Jane Addams, Europe had been given an opportunity to speak freely. The more the foreign delegates realize how unpopular and little understood the Pacifist cause was in the United States, and how difficult it was to swim against the stream [we] felt constrained to admire the moral courage of [our] hostesses.

Irma A. RICHTER[69]
Delegate of Germany

My dear Miss Addams,

I am happy to be given the opportunity of offering you my heartfelt thanks for the time spent in Washington in May and to express at the same time my great admiration for your indefatigable work in favor of the understanding amongst nations which we all strive for.

I shall never forget the days spent at the Congress. The communion of thought, feeling and action which united all delegates from the five parts of the world and which was an expression of their fervent will and desire for understanding is the surest guarantee for the success of our work in future times.

In extending my thanks to all our American friends, it may be allowed to add the wish and entreaty to you, dear Miss Addams, to remain in the future as you have been in the past, our valuable leader in the just case which we defend.

Yours very sincerely,
Adele Schmitz[70]
Delegate of Germany

12. Alice Salomon on the Modern American Woman

Among the American reformers who visited Alice Salomon in postwar Berlin was Julia Lathrop, a former resident of Hull House and head of the United States Children's Bureau. In 1923, Lathrop invited Salomon to the convention of the National Conference of Social Work in Washington. As one of five honorary delegates from Europe, Salomon delivered a lecture entitled "The Relation of the Church to Social Workers."

69   The editors have found no biographical information on Irma Richter.
70   The editors have found no biographical information on Adele Schmitz.

The congress was an opportunity for Salomon to renew old acquaintances and make new friends. Since she had to return to her school to supervise final exams, she declined an offer for a lecture tour through the United States, but she returned in January of 1924 for several months. The tour, in which she was heralded as the "German Jane Addams," proved to be strenuous but rewarding. Salomon felt that she gained much deeper insight into everyday life and into social reform projects than on her 1909 trip. Her lectures focused on the republican government in Germany, of which she was a staunch defender. As she had fifteen years earlier, Salomon stayed at Hull House in Chicago.

After her return, Salomon published a number of articles on social reform in the United States as well as two books. *Kultur im Werden* (Culture in the Making) conveys her travel impressions, touching on gender and race relations as well as on geography, climate, and culture.[71] She was more enthusiastic about life in the United States and the opportunities it offered to women then ever before. "Should I ever be born again as a woman," she wrote in the introduction, "I would only wish to be born in the United States."

Salomon's travel writings contrasted with those of scores of German industrialists, engineers and labor leaders who traveled to the United States in the 1920s. They generally admired the country's high standard of living and praised such technological marvels as the assembly line, but they tended to view the United States as a spiritual wasteland and to characterize the power of women as representative of the nation's vulgarity. Salomon, on the other hand, echoed the writing of German women before the war, celebrating the power and autonomy that women enjoyed in America. Challenging her readers to expand their usual definition of culture, she refuted the conventional German opinion that the young American nation lacked cultural refinement. Sketching women's culture in terms that would appeal to German readers, she emphasized that women pursued "not material ideals but humanitarian and personal ones," guided not by reason but by the soul. She pointed to the achievements of a distinctly female culture that expressed itself chiefly and successfully in a commitment to social reform.

The Cultural Influence of Women

The intellectual life of American women is actually not intellectual activity at all, but rather social activity. The realm of culture, which is left almost

71   The selection reprinted here is from Alice Salomon, *Kultur im Werden: Amerikanische Reiseeindrücke* (Culture in the making: Travel impressions from the United States) (Berlin: Ullstein, 1924), chap. 11, pp. 100–111. Translated by Sally Robertson. Italics indicate emphasis in the original.

completely to them, exhibits negative features in science and art. If one does not count as culture the special character impressed upon social life by women, if one interprets culture in the unambiguous sense attributed to the word in Germany, then there is actually hardly any American culture. One would then also deny the possibility of there being a specifically female culture.

Observation of American life, however, actually seems to prove the opposite, that feminine culture and feminine values are different from those brought forth previously under male dominance or autocracy. All doors were opened for American women much earlier than for women in the European countries. They could develop and present themselves with no restrictions. With their talents and powers unrestricted and unfettered, they did not need to wear themselves out with protests and battles, nor strive for equality with men, in order to get equal rights. The women therefore traveled the path prescribed by their natures. They gave external form to that which lay innermost and demanded expression, and these were not things to be perceived with reason, but with the soul. These were not material ideals, but humanitarian and personal ones. They saw the same thing that had been the living ideal in the spirit of the pilgrims, a domain of justice, fraternity, and mutual assistance, and they set about moving harsh, bitter reality closer to this ideal. The best of them, the most talented, most intelligent, wisest, and greatest became social and moral reformers.

Have they achieved anything that deserves to be called culture? Or have they simply chased after phantoms? Does America simply bear the stamp of the naked battle for existence pursued by men, softened neither by beauty nor by spirit, or have the women placed something else next to this, brought something new into the world, created institutions consistent with their ideals, designed human relationships as symbols of their convictions and feelings?

To answer this question would be to judge whether Americans are better, more moral, healthier, happier, than people in other countries. Who has the necessary objectivity to do that, and where would we find the standards to be applied?! Therefore, one can explore the cultural influence of American women only by referring to individual, distinctive phenomena of American life.

Ruskin once said: "There is no wealth like life; life with all its power of love and joy. That country is richest which has the greatest number of healthy, happy people. And that man is richest who, in addition to fulfilling his own most personal life goals, uses his person and his possessions to achieve the greatest helpful influence on his fellow man." These words could have been written as a motto for the life of American women. Nowhere does one find such energetic efforts on behalf of morality and the common good as in America. The wealth of the nation, which *consists of healthy and happy people,* appears to be an ever-present goal.

Certainly, *the business world is exceptionally brutal.* It does not even throw a veil over its motives. It tolerates only things that pay. There are companies with signs over their doors stating "Persons over 40 are not accepted." And there are elderly workers who dye their hair to get a job. The economic principle has naked and unrestricted dominion over large areas of life.

European industrial nations have also gone through periods, however, when small children were whipped to keep them at work and their lives were sacrificed mercilessly to the profits of the employer. In the old countries, too, moral culture has not kept pace with technological development. In Germany, as well, the realm of the spirit has had no power over life. And it was the Moloch of mammonism which brought the youth of Europe to the battlefields of world war and threatened to bring about the demise of Western culture.

Truly, despite all our tradition of art and science, we have reason to wonder whether new standards are being created somewhere, standards of a moral culture, a social order which could cause a brighter morning to dawn for humanity.

Perhaps this new way is coming in America. At any rate, along with the traditional way of life, another sphere of life exists there. America remains the land of contrasts. Alongside the crass self-interest (or more accurately, the unchecked power drive) exists a *passion* for service, the extent and depth of which is found hardly anywhere else. This certainly requires the background of this virginal land of unlimited opportunity, which is reflected in a gaiety, an openness, an exceptional freedom of human relations. This very widespread attitude brings forth a generosity, a nobility which has much more to do with the availability of opportunity than with the actual greater wealth of Americans. The day laborer, the office worker has it just as much, indeed often more, than the millionaire. But he, too, parts with his riches for good causes to a degree which cannot be explained simply by the different proportions of America, but may be due more to the fact that the man who gets rich quick has stronger instincts of acquisition than of possession, that his passion is not really for things and material values but for personal fame and power. It may also be related to the fact that the instinct toward helpfulness became well-developed in the pioneers because they could not have existed at all without mutual assistance, just as the immigrants showed an indescribable willingness to make sacrifices for their families and neighbors, perhaps arising from the feeling of isolation in a strange land. . . .

In women, however, the passion for service has a different character. It is more personal, oriented toward *devotion and involvement of their own being.* For them, the second part of Ruskin's claim applies above all: "That man is richest who uses his person and his possessions to have the greatest helpful influence on his fellow man." The idea that one's own life is only worth as much as one can give, not as much as one can receive, is commonly held by large numbers of educated women. In the women leaders, this idea has found a power of accomplishment which can spring only from the gifts of the heart, not of the intellect.

There is hardly a task of social or moral reform for which this willingness to serve cannot be obtained. In this regard, all social circles, parties, churches, and professions are one. An appeal to service always finds fertile ground, and if the object of service is comprehensibly portrayed, the impulse will soon be followed by action.

This generosity arising from within, this drive—which sometimes expands into visions and prophecies—this attribute is the *pinnacle of American culture.* It is what kindles in many Europeans, consciously or not, such a strong love for the far-off land.

It is this American character trait which also explains the diverse *plans for saving the world* which so often arise. From this trait derive the moralizing attitude in art and science, and the efforts toward moral reform with which the land is so rich. The enthusiasm for the war also could not have been unleashed had the idea of a war of liberation from militarism not been suggested to the masses. Wilson's Fourteen Points would have been impossible without the idea that America had a calling to be the protector of justice in the world. It was disappointment at the failure of this world mission, and the feeling that the Europeans speak a different language in political matters, that caused the turn-about in the attitude of the American people, the turning away from their own leader and the rejection of the politics of intervention.[72] But the clearest, most unambiguous demonstration of this quality of helpfulness and service was the campaign organized by America during and after the end of the war to aid the destitute countries.[73] All of us share a deep debt of gratitude to America—France and Belgium, Germany and Russia, Serbia and Austria—gratitude for aid which was given from pure humanitarianism, from a sense of empathy for all who are oppressed and burdened.

This selfless dedication of men and women who came here like missionaries bringing not only material aid, but conquering the European continent, like the missionaries, with their teachings, their *active faith,* all this is only a reflection of what goes on continually in America.

The *neighborhood aid,* which found its best expression in the settlements, would not be possible if women and men of the propertied and educated classes did not voluntarily become neighbors of the poor. This form of service, which ultimately requires surrender of one's private life or any kind of

---

[72]   The U.S. Senate rejected the Versailles Treaty and the League of Nations Covenant in November of 1919.

[73]   Salomon herself had taken part in administering the Save the Children Fund and other public and private American relief efforts. See Part IV, document 1, Alice Hamilton and Jane Addams, "After the Lean Years."

leisure time outside of one's work, seems possible to us only in the form of a Franciscan ideal of asceticism. It does not have this basis for the Americans. It is "help where help is needed." It is development of all the good forces which slumber inside of people. It is Americanization, and that is an inviting project which attracts the best powers to it. It is often the wives and daughters of the rich who seek such projects. All of this, however—this proximity of acquisitiveness and dedication, materialism and idealism—only shows how quickly single-minded life goals change once they are fulfilled. Where acquisition becomes an end in itself, instead of a means, the machine soon runs empty, and the demand for the true substance of life seeks fulfillment in extremes, in social work.

Women predominate in this work and are its leaders. It attracts the strongest female personalities, a type of woman whose intellectual and social talents often exceed those of the men involved in the work.

America has *broken new ground in many areas of social work:* in creating juvenile courts, in redesigning reformatory education, in building public playgrounds, and in improving prison methods, although in this latter area, darkness and dread still rule in some states. Recently, a radicalism has developed in the fight against common illnesses and public health risks which can almost be called a hygiene crusade, and which is an example to European nations. Particularly when one sees America again after a long absence, one notices with what determination the slums have been removed, street cleaning has been improved, and sources of infection have been battled.

All of this is further encouraged by the characteristically American conviction that anything can be achieved with knowledge and skill. The power of the mind is judged like a mechanism for implementing practical plans to achieve ideal purposes. Americans therefore attack with a fiery enthusiasm tasks that other countries would consider solvable only by decades-long development.

Yet all social work relies on *private initiative and private funding,* just as nearly all municipal political reforms can be traced to the intervention of the social workers. In general, every government regulation is opposed. This is not just because the Constitution of the United States severely complicates the passing of uniform legislation—all protective laws for workers and children lie within the jurisdiction of the individual states—but also because the people fundamentally resist all coercive measures, because they are convinced of the value of voluntary action. Proposals for compulsory insurance legislation encounter the strongest opposition. American democracy is much more the embodiment of the ideal of freedom than that of equality.

It is impossible to judge whether the wonderfully developed private welfare work was produced by the absence of public institutions, whether the absence of state welfare intensified the conscience of the citizens and made them more conscious of social responsibility, or whether conversely the government machine was made superfluous by the spontaneous helpfulness, this national character trait.

In any case, this passion for service which is apparent in all areas of social life is a grand attempt *to devise a culture of personal life, to produce a humane, moral culture*. It comes closer to being a synthesis of thought and action, of spirit and life, than the cultures of nations whose image has so far been created almost exclusively by men. Perhaps this is the form of *a feminine culture*, that it places the humane above the material, life above property, morality above technology. Perhaps humanity needs this new touch in order to save the cultures of the past from ruin.

What differentiates and distinguishes America from other countries is *the myth of the promised land*. This is what produces the special brand of American idealism, the power and courage of which cannot be overcome, even by defeat and disappointment, and which is full of self-confidence and energy, youth and hopefulness. It is an idealism that ignores everything learned by the European nations through centuries of hard-won experience, ignores the imperfection of all human activity. It is an idealism which believes that matters can be put in order in such a way that the ideal law, once conceived and embraced, will become the law of reality for all eternity.

That is the essence of American culture.

13. A Young German Reformer on American Welfare Laws

During the second half of the 1920s, a younger generation of German women entered the dialogue with American reformers. Elisabet von Harnack came from a prominent Berlin family that was well established in social reform and feminist circles. Her father, Adolf von Harnack, taught at Berlin University and was one of Alice Salomon's religious mentors. Her older sister, Agnes von Zahn-Harnack (1884–1950), was a friend of Salomon and Marie-Elisabeth Lüders and the last president of the League of German Women's Associations (BDF).

After receiving her Ph.D. from the University of Berlin in 1919, Elisabet von Harnack worked at Friedrich Siegmund-Schultze's settlement on Berlin's East Side, where she was in charge of the Boys' Clubs. Her contact with American settlement workers might have originated there. The assis-

THE LIMITATIONS OF NATIONHOOD

tant headworker, Alix Westerkamp, had worked at Chicago's University Settlement during the early years of World War I; Lillie Peck (1888–1957), later to become president of the National Federation of Settlements, lived at the Berlin settlement for a few months in 1921.

Elisabet von Harnack's letter to Jane Addams conveys the ongoing exchange among settlement workers on both sides of the Atlantic.[74] The work of Hull House continued to have a central position in the international settlement community. Many of Harnack's friends and family had met Jane Addams, and one of them had arranged for Harnack to stay in Chicago. Harnack's visit strengthened both personal and professional ties, which she would carry over into the post–World War II period. Her enthusiasm about educating her fellow citizens about American social work and the reform activities of the settlements resembled Salomon's after her first visit in 1909; however, Harnack's letter also reflects how isolated German reformers still felt in the international community even nine years after the war.

After her return, Harnack reported on methods of American social work and the successes of the mothers' pension programs that had been enacted since 1911, in a professional periodical founded in the mid-twenties, the *Deutsche Zeitschrift für Wohlfahrtspflege* (German Journal for Welfare Work).[75] Like many German women reformers, Harnack considered these programs exemplary, because they preferred family care to institutions, because they depended on the supervision of skilled women social workers like themselves, and because they saved money, always an important consideration for social workers whose efforts were constantly impeded by the fiscal crises of the Weimar Republic. In the 1920s, German social workers increasingly looked to America for new methods, especially the family case and budget studies that Harnack cites in her article. Harnack considered it "worthwhile to provide German women social workers with such practical and clearly arranged schedules." Harnack's evaluation of the "truly preventive and constructive" work of American social workers and her comparison of their workload to that of their German counterparts showed her readers that the Weimar welfare state could profit from programs pioneered on the other side of the Atlantic.

[74] Elisabet von Harnack to Jane Addams, Berlin, January 5, 1927, Jane Addams Papers, SCPC (and *JAP*, reel 18).
[75] The selection reprinted here is from Elisabet von Harnack, "Renten für alleinstehende Mütter mit unmündigen Kindern in den Vereinigten Staaten von Amerika." *Deutsche Zeitschrift für Wohlfahrtspflege* 3 (1927/28), pp. 348–50; translated by the editors.

Elisabet von Harnack to Jane Addams

Berlin-Grunewald
[...] Buntschuhstr. 2
1-5-27

My dear Miss Addams,

I am now back in Berlin after a very smooth and comfortable passage; only it was somewhat lengthy (12 days) and the very few passengers were either dull and uninteresting or frightfully chauvinistic and conservative. So I felt very lonely, much more so than I ever did in Chicago, and I became very impatient to get home.

Here I found my parents very well and very happy to have me back, looking so well too; they are very grateful, that apparently I was so excellently cared for. We had some fine Christmas holidays together. Of course I have to tell and to report everywhere about Hull House and Chicago. My friends and my family are specially anxious to hear how you are faring. I do hope your health is improving.

I have to thank you so very much, dear Miss Addams, for all your kindness and for giving me the privilege to be your guest at Hull House for such a long time. More than ever I regret that my English is so very poor that I can't find the adequate words to express my gratitude and veneration. I can only say: Thank you ever so much.

As I was for the first time after the war in a foreign country, I had of course a very strong feeling of the terrible isolation in which we in Germany have lived during the last 12 years. It is not only the want of money—which of course counts much—but as well the lack of international intercourse and touch, that handicapped us in our many fields. At the same time I met so much understanding for our troubles, so much good will, so much faith in our recovering, that I have come back with much more hope and courage for our country than when I left. I would [wish], a good many more Germans could have so wonderful and stimulating experiences as I had!

I am sorry, I could not add so much to social life in Hull House; but here I am trying to destroy prejudices and to make people acquainted with social work and settlement life in America. It is the only way to prove something of my everlasting gratitude.

With all good wishes for a happy New Year
Yours very faithfully
Elisabet von Harnack

Elisabet von Harnack
Pensions for Single Mothers with Dependent Minor Children in the United States of America

In 1909, President Roosevelt convened a welfare conference at the White House which chiefly studied questions of accommodation, education, and support for dependent children. There were representatives of the State Boards of Charities as well as of the large private child welfare organizations at the conference, and they came to the conclusion that needy children should remain with their families whenever possible. In those cases where it was not feasible, a suitable foster family should be found. The idea of a permanent stay in a large institution was rejected for normal cases, and institutions were only deemed acceptable for special cases. The family was not only preferred as the cheaper option, but it was explained in great subtlety and detail that upbringing at home developed a person more fully and enabled him better to fulfill his duties as a human being and a citizen. As Americans say it in their brief and vivid style: "home made children" [English in the original] are preferred. This view of the great importance of family life as the "highest product of civilization," as the location of the "most important formation of spirit and character," meant a fundamental rejection of the customary practice of accommodating children in orphanages, reform institutions, and unfamiliar foster families without considering their own family situations. Surely this new approach was at first a rather theoretical idea on the part of a few leaders of child welfare work. The practical sense of Americans, however, ensured that ways and means were found to put it into practice. Many conventions, conferences, and lectures in the ensuing years spread the idea of bringing up children in their own families.

Without new laws it would not have been possible, for example, to give single mothers the opportunity to raise their dependent minor children in their own homes. The old practice of charity would of course have necessitated "indoor relief" [English in the original], that is, the children would have been put in institutions or foster families and the mother required to find gainful employment if she could. In 1911, Illinois and Missouri led the way for a new kind of law, which created a framework for the support of needy children in their own homes. In the following years, most of the states have followed the examples of Missouri and Illinois, creating "Aid to Mothers Laws" or "Mothers' Pensions" [English in the original] of various forms and sizes. In 1926, forty-two of the forty-eight states of the Union had such laws.[76]

---

[76]   See Bulletin no. 162 of the Children's Bureau in Washington, 1926: "Public Aid to Mothers with Dependent Children." [This footnote is in the original.]

The essence of these laws is the following: Single mothers with needy children can receive monthly support from public funds, enabling them to maintain a modest household and to retain control over the upbringing of their children. This support is not poor relief that has to be paid back later, but rather something like a state pension; usually its nature and amount are adapted to the individual needs of the family. The management of the household is under constant surveillance by social workers. The pensions are granted until the children can support themselves. The implementation of these laws and the administration of the designated funds often lie with the "Juvenile Courts." Because of these educational tasks, the character of the Juvenile Courts becomes similar to that of the German youth welfare office. Usually there is some surveillance by the state to ensure equal benefits and utilization of the experiences made in the individual cases.

The particulars differ enormously in the forty-two states, and therefore the effect and success of the legislation differs enormously. First of all, some states allow only widows to apply for mothers' pensions. As a consequence, only a very small segment of needy children are included. The majority of the states, however, grant pensions to widowed, deserted, and divorced mothers as well as to those with husbands who are completely incapable of gainful employment, in a state hospital, an institution for epileptics, or in jail. Only a few states explicitly include unmarried mothers, but often deserted women are included in this category. Some states give pensions to persons who have assumed maternal duties, e.g., to grandmothers, stepmothers, or second-degree relatives. All of the states require a certain affiliation with the community. The minimum requirement is a two-year residence in the respective district. The maximum requirement is American citizenship (which, as everybody knows, can only be acquired after five years of residence), a minimum five-year residence in the respective state, and a two-year residence in the district where the need for help occurred. Of course, regulations like the latter render the meaning of mothers' pensions illusory, since the majority of single mothers with needy children are found in newly arrived immigrants' families. These families earn very little income in the beginning and are not yet able to save for sudden emergencies (death of the breadwinner, incurable illness, and the like). In the many states where only American citizens are entitled to such a pension, all these cases are excluded. They fall under the provisions of the general public charities, which are often insufficient and backward, or they have to rely on private charity, which, however, usually is provided generously and sympathetically.

Of course, indigence as defined by the poor law is the prerequisite for receiving a pension. The granting of a pension is preceded by very detailed investigations, for example whether there are assets that could be utilized, or claims to insurance companies, employers, or other agencies, and finally whether there are family members who could be liable and are able to help. In some states, the women are allowed to keep a small savings or property, like a homestead with interest [a mortgage] no higher than the rent for a comparable apartment.

In the majority of the states, the mothers receive the pensions until their children turn sixteen. For every child who reaches this age, the total payment is cut by a certain amount. If children are permanently disabled, the pension is often granted beyond their sixteenth birthday.

About the amount of the pensions I can only say the following: In some states, the maximum amounts are set mechanically, and they are totally insufficient. The purpose of the legislation—the maintenance of the household and in turn a good upbringing of the children—can hardly be achieved this way. In other states, the amounts are quite adequate. For example, the support for a mother with three children ranges between twenty and seventy dollars a month. In general, the laws that leave full scope for the individual case have proven to be much more practical. In these cases, the pension is adapted to the individual needs of the family and their respective living conditions. Usually, a standard budget drawn up for the city, district, or state by one of the large charity organizations or a research institute is the basis for a family budget.[77] These standard budgets are drawn up with great circumspection and elaboration. They are the indispensable tools for example, of Chicago social workers. It would be worthwhile to compare these budgets to German estimates of the cost of living and to provide German women social workers with such practical and clearly arranged schedules.

After about six months, the family budgets are checked and, if necessary, adjusted. If the children are grown and do not demand the entire time of their mother any longer, part-time employment of the mother or any gainful activity inside or outside of the home is entirely endorsed.

The two excellent case studies[78] available on the administration and handling[79] of mothers' pensions conclude that the success of the measure stands and falls with sympathetic and appropriate surveillance by social workers. The entire enterprise is educational welfare work for the benefit of the children. The single mother not only has to be "suitable and able to properly bring up her children," as stated in the law. She also has to be will-

[77] The best known are: Estimates on Family Budgets, New York Charity Organization Society, Home Economics Committee, 105 East 22nd St., New York City, and Standard Budget for Dependent Families, Chicago Council of Social Agencies, 17 North State St. Chicago, Illinois, 1925. [This footnote is in the original.]
[78] The Administration of the Aid to Mothers Law in Illinois by Edith Abbott and Sophonisba P. Breckinridge, Publications of the Children's Bureau, Washington 1921. [This footnote is in the original.]
[79] Standards of Public Aid to Children in their own Homes by Florence Nesbitt, Publication of the Children's Bureau in Washington 1923. [This footnote is in the original.]

ing to work hand in hand with the social worker. On the other hand, the family social worker has to be tactful and let the mother run her household independently. She should merely advise her on a sensible way of life and support her like a friend. One of the studies is based entirely on the case files of Chicago. Once one has realized the wealth of detailed and exact facts that were obtained from more than 200 family files, one can only admire how accurately and completely these files were maintained. Of course we have to remind ourselves at the same time that a family social worker over there is in charge of about fifty such cases at a time, while here a social worker often has several hundred "cases!" There, the family social worker visits the family once or twice a month, her supervisor once or twice a year. It is amazing to observe from these files the social climbing of the families. They are by no means better off than the average workers' family, they by no means have a particularly advantageous background or show a particular mental mobility. This improvement of the situation of these families, real *constructive work* [English in the original] was achieved solely by the security of a fixed, if modest income, solely by the gradual and systematic elimination of certain ills (for example, wretched housing, poor hygiene, bad nutrition, and the like), solely by counseling and bringing up the children individually and methodically, according to their talents and capacities. Of course, such individual long-term care cannot be achieved everywhere but it is the goal of all social work and only this type of social work is truly preventive and constructive.

So far, Germany has tried to support needy children within the framework of the poor law and of general welfare work. This is by no means a fully satisfactory and successful solution. The creators of the Federal Youth Welfare Law were fully aware of the fact that it was very necessary to insure that children considered needy by definition of the poor law be brought up in their families.[80] The troubles of the present have so far prevented them from realizing their ideas. Let us hope that the day is not too far when all German children benefit from the educational laws and all needy mothers find enough competent and kind-hearted advisers on education.

---

[80] Initiated in 1920 by thirty female members of the Reichstag, the *Reichsjugendwohlfahrtsgesetz* (Federal Law for the Welfare of Youth) of 1922 standardized measures for youth welfare that had been created in some German municipalities before the war. In particular, the law regulated education, guardianship, and the treatment of juvenile offenders.

14. A German Politician Writes
for American Reformers

In 1929, ten years after the founding of the Weimar Republic, *Survey*—still the leading American reform periodical—dedicated a special issue to "The New Germany." The contributions included greetings from Chancellor Hermann Müller, an article by Foreign Minister Gustav Stresemann, a drawing by the renowned artist Käthe Kollwitz, an assessment of German social work, and articles discussing economics, youth, culture, and the arts. On the whole, both German and American contributors painted a very positive picture of a society that had genuinely accepted the Republic, and the response to the issue in both countries was enthusiastic. Marie Elisabeth Lüders, one of the most distinguished German women politicians before and after World War II, wrote on the position of women.[81]

Professional women like Lüders made the most of the changes that the Republic brought. For them, the 1920s represented the culmination of the German women's movement's efforts. An American audience might well perceive her as a person who had achieved a goal projected by women's movements on both sides of the Atlantic—a strong voice in the legislative process.

Although many liberal middle-class feminists like Marie Elisabeth Lüders and Gertrud Bäumer saw the Deutsche Demokratische Partei (German Democratic Party) as their political home, the party actually did little to advance women's rights after 1919, except for Lüders's campaign for a reform of the divorce laws, which was also supported by the Social Democrats. In the article, Lüders did not conceal her dissatisfaction with political parties across the board. With many members still opposed to women's political participation, she wrote, parties neither realized the "interests and needs of women" nor appreciated "the general political and cultural importance of women's work." But by the end of the decade the impact of women's work on parliamentary politics as well as on the general political culture was discernible and Lüders was convinced that the process of women's emancipation could not be reversed.

---

[81] Marie Elisabeth Lüders, "The German Woman's Place," *Survey*, February 1, 1929, p. 557. Italics indicate emphasis in the original.

The German Woman's Place
by Dr. Marie Elisabeth Lüders
Member of the Reichstag

Consequences of the War have profoundly changed the status of women in Germany. They had no vote, no right to participate in parliament or local legislatures, though in some especially progressive cities they were permitted "advisory" functions with regard to certain charity and "welfare" matters. All efforts of women's organizations to open the way for women in public life were thwarted by the opposition of the men and the indifference of the women themselves. Women demanding "equal rights" were largely of the self-supporting class—those who knew by experience the disadvantages and injustices ensuing from exclusively male control of legislation and administration. Even in those days many women of the "housewife" class realized that changed conditions necessitated reform of the marriage system, with regard especially to property rights and the mother's control of education and child-welfare. But the great mass of the women, overburdened with household cares, had no time, strength or money to participate in their own emancipation.

As for the men, only those of the Left or the Middle parties, and the Socialists, supported the women—and that mostly on paper.[82] The others, and the government, totally rejected these ideas, and the conservatives beheld them with a kind of terror; regarding the whole movement as inappropriate, even contrary to divine order. The influence of the churches is to this day adverse, and that deters many women.

During the War, however, millions of women found themselves suddenly and for years *alone,* confronted by unwonted responsibilities. They had not only to continue their domestic duties and cares, but to earn the means of bare living. Often they had to assume the command of offices and farms, taking the place of the absent husband or other man or men. For years women had to bear not only the grief and loneliness but the heaviest burdens of circumstances.

So, after the War, such women were no longer objects for the protection and domination of men; no longer were they disposed to obey the will of the male partner; no longer were they mystified by the wonders of his employment.

This total revolution in the position of women, not only in the political but in the economic field, and in the human intimate personal relations, is

---

[82] By "middle parties," Lüders means the German liberal parties, traditionally the center of the political spectrum, like the Deutsche Demokratische Partei (German Democratic Party) and the Deutsche Volkspartei (German People's Party). The Sozialdemokratische Partei (Social Democratic Party) made woman suffrage part of its party platform in 1891.

not realized by many to this day. But I believe it is one of the most important factors leading toward acknowledgment of the right of women to equality in all fields, everywhere, unconditionally.

It is now quite impossible for the German woman that man shall rule the economic and political life; that only he shall determine the content of the laws, the rights and duties of women. Many men, too, are now quite reconciled to the fact that their sole dominance is past, formally and practically; *that henceforth woman stands and will stand, both in professional and in personal life; no longer behind, but beside the man.*

Many who look at the development of German conditions only as outsiders, and others within Germany, will say that woman's coming within the great circle of our political responsibilities has not greatly changed things; especially that her influence in political life upon the parties and on parliamentary work is very small. True until today it is, that her influence on the parties is much smaller than it should be in the interest of the political life of Germany. Strange as it may seem, the political parties are almost the only great organizational form in Germany which, in the general alteration of condition, has suffered little change. They sit unaltered on their patched-up programs, together with persons burdened by their thousand inherited limitations. These hinder the parties in their political development and in their indispensable reorganization. And they hinder them too often in the realization of the interests and needs of women; in their appreciation of the general political and cultural importance of woman's work. Here lies the conflict between the influence of women upon the parties and the effects of party limitations upon women's interests.

Despite the party political limitations, the influence of women on parliamentary politics as well as upon social and cultural progress has brought very clear recognition of woman's understanding of affairs; still more of the *human* aspects—real *living* as contrasted with mechanical aspects—of things; has been the real cause of the enactment of several new laws and of the important modification of others. Still more, it has changed profoundly the whole atmosphere of approach to problems of German politics, economics and culture. Especially strongly has it effected those subjects which naturally are nearest to the life and interests of women—such as education and teaching, welfare of mothers and children, dwellings and housekeeping, professional and vocational training, marriage, citizenship, etc. The women are especially eager to keep the rights the new Constitution has given to them, and they are very eager too that these rights shall be exercised in the most loyal sense.[83] Also in self-

[83] Article 109 of the Weimar Constitution stated that in principle men and women had the same civic rights and duties; Article 119 based marriage "on the equality of the sexes"; and Article 128 removed all gender discrimination for public office and civil service. But the more

defense, because in some matters—such for instance as questions of equal conditions for women in the public service—men still try to evict or exclude them. So also in matters of wages and salaries.

In spite of the fact that many things rightly demanded by women have not been gained; that many are indifferent and unappreciative, many others afraid; it would be an error to suppose that German women on the whole do not know their political position and powers, or that they would go backward one step in the field that they have gained. They are determined to keep what they have gained; to conquer what they do not yet possess, with the great will to keep their rights and to do their duty to the whole people.

15. Alice Salomon Salutes Jane Addams

One of Alice Salomon's last contributions to *Die Frau* was a tribute to Jane Addams;[84] Addams's portrait appeared on the cover of the magazine. Addams's popularity in Germany had waned somewhat after the relief campaigns of the early 1920s, as it had in the United States after 1915. The Nobel Peace Prize in 1931 finally brought recognition in both countries for her life's work. For Salomon, the award of the Peace Prize to the woman who had inspired much of her work was an affirmation of her own efforts for social reform. In the eyes of Salomon and other German and American social reformers, the woman once considered Chicago's "first and most important citizen" was now honored as a "wise statesman."

Like Addams, Salomon saw the settlement work of the 1890s as one basis for the creation of international organizations in the 1920s. Like Addams, she made a direct connection between social work and work for international peace, for according to Salomon, "an uncompromisingly embraced social sentiment knows no national boundaries." More than any other woman of her time, Addams embodied this ability to transcend the limitations of nationhood.

The publication of this article marked the end of fifty years of dialogue between German and American women reformers. The bourgeois German women's movement and its primary periodical had undergone extensive

---

conservative Civil Code, dating from the turn of the century, was still the law of the land, leaving all decisions in marriage and family matters to the husband and maintaining strict divorce laws.

[84]   Alice Salomon, "Jane Addams," *Die Frau* 39 (1931/32): 227 ; translated by Tammy Huck.

changes since 1896, the year Salomon first contributed to *Die Frau*. After Helene Lange's death in 1929, Gertrud Bäumer had become the sole editor. Salomon contributed more than sixty articles to the journal during her lifetime. In August of 1932, *Die Frau* dedicated an entire issue to Salomon's work on the occasion of her sixtieth birthday. But early in 1933, the laws of the National Socialist regime prohibited Jews from contributing to German publications. Salomon published her last article in *Die Frau*, an essay on the beginning of women's social work in Germany, in September 1933. Although the League of German Women's Associations dissolved in the spring of 1933, *Die Frau* continued publication until 1944.

Jane Addams

When I saw Jane Addams for the first time at a banquet in 1909 in Chicago, the mayor celebrated her as "the city's first and most important citizen." Now she has been honored as a "wise statesman" with the Nobel Peace Prize.

Jane Addams found her way into social work in her youth. She was thirty years old in 1891 when she founded Hull House, a settlement in one of Chicago's poorest districts.[85] There she created a center for social assistance among neighbors who had immigrated from every nation. Her work was directed to the most primitive needs and wants of the Irish, Germans, Italians, Greeks, and Negroes. She grew from social worker to social and municipal politician. No social measure or legislation has come into being in America which she did not propose or guide.

From the neighborhood she extended her view over ever wider horizons, onto the entire world. When the war broke out she tried to keep America out of it. She participated in the convening of the women's congress at The Hague in 1915, which aimed to bring about peace and out of which then grew the Women's International League for Peace and Freedom. She traveled by order of the congress to the responsible statesmen of all the warring nations to negotiate for peace. After the war, she led the hunger relief effort in all countries, especially in Germany. No animosities held her back.

No living woman has spoken up for peace more courageously and more bravely and more effectively.

She proceeded from social work to working for peace, for an uncompromisingly embraced social sentiment knows no national boundaries. In this

---

[85]   Hull House was founded in 1889, when Addams was twenty-nine.

view, anyone who needs help is one's neighbor. Peace and bread are complementary concepts. Jane Addams works for peace because war causes not only hunger and misery, but also because it appears to her as an expression of hatred and hostility, of the attitude that forms the basis of all social ills.

She wants to bring about a new world conscience as the basis of true Realpolitik. To her, the interdependency of peoples is the most powerful truth of our time.

THE LIMITATIONS OF NATIONHOOD

EPILOGUE

THE DIALOGUE DESTROYED

Social Democratic Party flier warning women about the Nazi Party, 1930. "Women," it reads, "This is how you will be treated in the Third Reich. 'Woman must become handmaid and servant again,' says Nazi leader Feder. This is why *no woman* is represented in the party of the swastika. Your answer: Fight the Nazis—for Social Democracy." Bildarchiv Preußischer Kulturbesitz, Berlin.

Alice Hamilton in Nazi Germany

When Alice Hamilton visited Nazi Germany in 1933, she reported her impressions of life under a dictatorship to Addams in the two letters reprinted here.[1] These letters, as well as the three articles that she published in *Survey Graphic* after her return, offer a remarkably lucid analysis of the effects of Nazi rule. Her first contribution conveyed the general atmosphere of suspicion—the fear of spies and denunciation—that kept her acquaintances from discussing the political situation where they could be overheard. Private discussions, however, gave her a unique chance to "get below the surface," and she noted that the "change was not universal, . . . many Germans . . . regard what is happening in that distracted land with dismay, with shame, sometimes with despair." Even in the first months of the regime, long before the Nuremberg Race Laws or the pogroms of 1938, Hamilton keenly observed that Jews had become "victims of specially relentless persecution," not only facing physical privation but robbed of all respect. She gave a detailed account of the myths the "ignorant men" of the regime employed to justify the "cold pogroms" and pointed out that the wholesale dismissal of Jews from public service created positions for the Nazi clientele.

"Sound and Fury in Germany," Hamilton's account of the status of trade unions and social workers, provides a frightening inventory of the achievements of the Nazi "revolution." Trade unions had been dissolved, their property seized; social workers were fired if they were Jews, social democrats, or liberals, leading to "a very serious crippling of the services, for the majority of the workers came in under one of the above heads." Protecting her associates by not mentioning their names, Hamilton quoted an unnamed Alice Salomon, saying that most labor leaders were gone—"They have disappeared or they are known to be in concentration camps, or they have escaped over the border." Hamilton rightfully remained doubtful about the fate of the needy who were not affiliated with the party that now ruled the country.

---

[1] Alice Hamilton to Jane Addams, Hotel Kaiserhof, Berlin, April 22, 1933, Esther Loeb Kohn Papers, University of Illinois at Chicago Circle (and *JAP*, reel 24); Alice Hamilton to Jane Addams, on board the *Deutschland*, July 1, 1933, Jane Addams Papers, SCPC (and *JAP*, reel 24); also printed in Barbara Sicherman, *Alice Hamilton*, pp. 343–45.

Hamilton's third article, reprinted here,[2] assessed the position of women in Nazi society. Many of her observations remain valuable today. Whereas the German women's movement has been criticized for bowing to the Nazi pressure, Hamilton pointed out that "no woman of any prominence in the woman's movement is connected with the Nazi regime." She considered the dissolution of the BDF as "really a proud record" and sang the praise of its leaders, especially when compared to the "appalling silliness" that characterized the writings of prominent Nazi women.

In the Third Reich, women were assigned a new role in the building of a nation that had redefined itself as an ethnic community, brutally excluding all whom it considered undesirable. Women participated in the execution of Nazi policies in a variety of positions, from the party apparatus to the concentration camps, and most visibly in the Nazi mass organizations, but their role, as Hamilton correctly observed, centered around the goal of "healthy motherhood." Generous benefits for those considered racially fit were to assure the supply of farmers and soldiers Hitler needed to realize his expansionist designs. Hamilton pointed out that the dismissal of women from public service made room for Nazi sympathizers, and she correctly predicted that policies to return working-class women to their homes (which she considered beneficial) would fail in the long run. Indeed, by 1938, labor shortages prompted a campaign to get women back to the work benches and assembly lines.

Girls' education in the Third Reich centered on their future roles as "mothers of the race." Young girls joined Hitler's youth organization in large numbers even before membership became mandatory in 1939. The half-year stay in voluntary labor camps that Hamilton described became obligatory for college-bound high school graduates in 1934 and for all high school graduates in 1939. Practical work in the household of a large family in the city or a farm family in the country was to prepare "working maidens" ("Arbeitsmädchen") for their own future duties and was combined with theoretical instruction in home economics and party doctrine in the afternoons. Alice Hamilton could not anticipate these developments in 1933, but her account of woman's place in Nazi Germany certainly made clear that the days when women participated in the building of German democracy had passed.

---

[2] Alice Hamilton, "Woman's Place in Germany," *Survey Graphic*, January 1934, pp. 26–29, 46. Italics indicate emphasis in the original.

Woman's Place in Germany
by Alice Hamilton, M.D.

There is a group of women in Germany who are well known to progressive women the world over, who are familiar faces at the international meetings of the great women's organizations, where the German group have stood out for their ability. These women were leaders in the suffrage movement before Germany had woman suffrage, and the old organizations persisted as the General German Women's Union (Allgemeiner Deutscher Frauenverein). They also had their General Federation of Women's Clubs, they had an important branch of the International Association of University Women, and of Women's Physicians, and the Union of Women Teachers of Germany was an extensive and influential organization. Inside these groups were women members of the Reichstag, for Germany had many of them during the years when an American congresswoman was a rare and conspicuous figure, and women were government officials, school councillors, university teachers, judges. I met in Geneva at the first international economic congress in 1927 a German woman delegate, the only one sent as a fully accredited delegate of her government, though others were there as alternates.[3]

German women had a long and hard fight but they had won a fair measure of equality under the Republic. Now it all seems to be lost and suddenly they are set back, perhaps as much as a hundred years.

It would be very wrong for me to quote any woman by name. I can only tell you that I talked to many of the leaders of these organizations, wise, experienced women, who saw their impending fate—the program of the Nazis against women did not move so rapidly as the one directed against the Jews—and saw no possibility of averting it. They were courageous; they told me that rather than to submit, which meant expelling all members with Jewish blood and declaring themselves in sympathy with National Socialism, they would see their organizations dissolved. And it did come to that. For weeks we could not find out what was happening after we left Berlin, only that the Königin Luise Bund, which corresponds to our Colonial Dames and DAR, had bowed to the command from above and been absorbed in the new organization of Nazi women. The fate of the others was not published, but we saw the announcement that from then on there would be but one organization in Germany, composed of Nazi women, Aryans all, with a leader appointed by Hitler. There was no delegation this year to the International Council, for there was no organization left to send one.

Now at last comes an authoritative statement concerning the women's clubs, which is issued in English by a propaganda society in Berlin

[3]   Probably Marie-Elisabeth Lüders.

(Wirtschaftspolitische Gesellschaft E.V. Berlin NO. 10 Margarethenstr. 1).
Here we learn that the two large organizations which head the list above,
together with the teachers' union, voluntarily dissolved early in the year.
All the other organizations declared themselves ready to cooperate in the
new state and have been combined with the Nazi women's associations into
one organization, the Deutsches Frauenwerk, or German Women's Work.

So the liberal women's organizations kept their word and did not yield.
This is really a proud record. No woman of any prominence in the
woman's movement is connected with the Nazi regime. I was told of spirited young woman who said to her brother, an ardent Nazi, "How can you
ask me to join your party when you are turning the finest women in Germany out of the teaching profession?" And he answered, "But what can we
do? They will not join us and we cannot let them build up an opposition."

The new Nazi women's association has a man at its head, appointed by
the government, State Councillor Krummacher, with a woman as an assistant, Dr. Paula Siber, who is also consultant for women's affairs in the Department of the Interior.[4] An irreverent young woman sends me from
Germany Dr. Siber's recent pamphlet on the woman question, plentifully
adorned with exclamation points, which, however, are not needed to make
me see the really appalling silliness of this influential lady. It is a piece of
flowery sentimentality such as might have been written in the early part of
the last century, without a touch of realism. Woman is a mythical figure, a
throbbing heart, while man, equally mythical, is embodied intellect. "To be
a woman means to be a mother. . . . All womanly knowledge springs from
the deep roots of the woman's soul, while the special mental power of man
arises in the colder atmosphere of the absolutely intellectual. The coldness
and hardness of the man longs for the softness and warmth of the woman."

This pamphlet cannot be dismissed as merely silly, for it bears the impri-
matur of a powerful man, Frick, minister of the interior, who, indeed, contributes the preface.[5] We are obliged to treat it as the authoritative
expression of the Nazi leaders and so we must delve through the syrupy
sentimentality for the hard core that lies inside.

Dr. Siber declares at the outset an absolute break with "liberalistic-Marx-
istic democracy" and all its works, and repudiates the *Frauenbewegung* as a
movement among middle-class women for intellectual emancipation and
among working women for material comforts, both of them contrary to
woman's true nature, and in accordance with Jewish doctrines of sex equal-

[4]   Paula Siber (1890–?), a district leader in Düsseldorf, developed pragmatic programs like
cooking and sewing classes, day-care and fundraising activities to draw mothers, housewives,
and teachers into party activities. Successful in the early days of the regime, she soon had to
yield the leadership of the Nazi women's organization to Gertud Scholtz-Klink.
[5]   Wilhelm Frick (1877–1946), as minister of the interior (1933–1943), Frick held one of
the most influential positions in the Third Reich.

ity and sex freedom, which render woman rootless. There are pages and pages on motherhood and its glories, on child-bearing and its joys, and we are told that the motives for limiting the number of children in a family are all materialistic, liberalistic, Marxistic, and egoistic. The state is all-important, not the individual child, not the mother; the state needs children, therefore the refusal to bear children is treason to the state. "To awaken and renew the will in men and women for large families is the pressing task of the new woman's movement."

It follows that the education of girls is to be for motherhood and is to be quite different from that for boys, nor are the two sexes allowed to become accustomed to each other—decidedly not, for this [would] lead to the loss of the finest womanliness. Girls must have the best of physical training, sports and play, but always with duty in mind, and sacrifice, "yes, with so much joy in their hearts that they will be able to make sacrifices all their lives in the service of duties gladly accepted." Such sacrifices are not required of men and therefore in this, as in all things, the two sexes are different and their training must be different. The higher school are to be open to women and they may engage in all studies and may become teachers and doctors, for who would forbid women to be doctors when the woman's heart is needed at the bedside, as much as the man's scientific knowledge? The last year of school is to be passed in a compulsory labor camp, but the provision for these camps has not yet been made and for the present the voluntary camps must be used. The inference is that the latter are Nazi institutions, but this is far from true. They grew up under the Republic and were founded by Eugen Rosenstock of Breslau, now an exile in this country.[6]

Dr. Siber recognizes the problem of the superfluous women—of whom there are said to be 1,900,000; indeed, she says that "the large disproportion of women and the bitterness of the lot of the unmarried is at the bottom of women's restlessness and it drove them under the liberalistic regime to strive for equality with men." But she offers no solution for those who under the Nazi regime are being ousted in favor of men except to say that under National Socialism everything is woman's work that concerns womanhood and motherhood, and goes on to enumerate the wonderful callings open to them, the care of all the helpless, sick in mind and body, of the old and the delinquent, and the education of little boys and of all girls. But surely this was true under the Republic and it is hard to see why it should be called the "real liberation of woman from the prison of self and family into the glorious freedom of work for the nation." This is her concluding paragraph:

[6] Eugen Rosenstock-Huessey (1888–1973), German-American historian and sociologist who founded voluntary labor camps for workers, farmers, and students in 1926. He emigrated to the United States in 1933.

The woman's movement of National Socialism claims for itself the honor of being the most advanced expression of the movement for the renewal of womanhood. Its foundation and its driving power are in the heart of woman; its determination is to recognize pure womanhood; its aim is the highest development of woman's nature and her incorporation in the service of the National Socialistic Commonwealth.

Now the plan to remove women from industrial work and return them to home and family would spell no hardship for the majority of German women, if it were possible. It is true that there are women of the educated class who would much rather do professional work than housework and who wish to be self-supporting even if they are married, or at least to supplement their husband's earnings, but I very much doubt that this is true of women of the working class. I believe that the vast majority of working women would be thankful to have only their homes to manage, not to do the double-task of factory-work and housework. Hitler's program for women would doubtless be hailed with joy and relief by millions of them if it could be carried out, but they know it cannot be, and apparently the leaders are discovering this, too.

It was quite evident during the first six months or so of the Nazi regime that the relegation of woman to her position of a century ago was carried on with vigor and with German thoroughness. Not that the newspapers carried much about it, but rumors came of wholesale discharges, first of married women, then of women in whose families there were male money-earners. Sometimes we were told that employers were objecting to the substitution of young men for experienced typists and secretaries and that the telephone exchanges were in a sad way after the girls were turned out. The brochure from Berlin which I mentioned above gives interesting sidelights on this phase of the Nazi regime, not by telling what happened, but by assuring foreigners that certain things were not permitted any longer. Thus we read that although the Nazi ideal is to place women in the family it has been found that this ideal cannot always be realized. A woman of mature years who is not yet married probably will not be able to marry and she must not be crowded out of her job, for that simply means that she will swell the number of unemployed. So a woman who cannot marry has the right to a job. To be sure it has been laid down as a principle by the Nazis that in case of competition between a man and a woman for a job the man is to have the preference if he is equally suited to it, but women are not to be pushed out of work for which they are better qualified than men, e.g. teachers, welfare workers, saleswomen, clerks, and secretaries. Wherever, in the excessive zeal of the first months, women have been dismissed from such posts, failure has resulted and the government has now issued orders that the ousted clerks and stenographers must be reinstated because the men that replaced them were so inexperienced as to considerably affect the smooth conduct of business.

The same thing was true of the dismissal of women officials and teachers, and the Reich minister of the Interior forbids such dismissals, even of married women, unless there is a qualified man to take the place. He also recognizes the fact that many women work because they must and he decrees that no woman is to be discharged unless her economic future is assured. However, the Nazi government hopes to bring it about that women shall be employed only in womanly work, domestic service—which is to be increased by making it cheaper—and welfare work, including nursing, playground and gymnastic work, and of course young women are encouraged to marry.

Women are entirely excluded from parliament. The National Socialist party has never had a woman on its list of candidates and when Hitler dissolved all the other parties and the question arouse as to which of their members were eligible to join the Nazi party, it was decided that no woman and no clergyman was eligible. Still, as the brochure naively says, since the parliaments of the various states have been dissolved, and in the Reichstag only one party exists, the elimination of women is of no practical importance.

The attitude of the Nazis toward women is, therefore, frankly and avowedly a reversion to the past. Hitler sees but one task for them, healthy and abundant motherhood, and in his book he has made his reasons clear. In the Germany of his dream he needs strong peasants to provide food so that German will never again starve under a blockade by her enemies, and strong soldiers to restore her prestige and bring under one Reich all the Germans in Europe. Girls, therefore, are to be trained with healthy motherhood as the goal, which means that a strong physique comes first in importance, then character-building, last intellectual training. No more is stress to be laid on the individual, that fatal error of progressive education. The state is all, the individual counts only as he serves the state, and the girl is to be taught that the state requires of her child-bearing and child-rearing, not work which man can do as well as she or better. Competition between the sexes is to be abolished by the elimination of the women. Along with this relegation of women to their earlier status goes an attempt to bring back old-time chivalry, lost during the age of equality. I am sure I have never been given a seat in a crowded streetcar as often as I was in Germany, certainly not in my own country.

The urge to raise the birthrate, so important a part of Hitler's program, was seen in several measures which were passed in the first three months of his rule. There is a tax on the unmarried, which applies also to the widowed and divorced, but not those over fifty-five years of age or if they are supporting children or helping support relatives. It is made easy for overburdened mothers to employ more domestic servants by abrogating unemployment insurance for those servants and by permitting the head of the family to claim exemption from his income tax for as many as three servants, just as if they were his children.

Young couples are loaned 1000 marks to buy furniture and cooking utensils, and this can be repaid in monthly installments of 1 percent (no interest is charged) and on the birth of each living child 25 percent of the debt is written off. Large families are encouraged in every way. The new head of the organization of women doctors—the old was dissolved and all officers were asked to resign—who was of course appointed by the government, urged in her inauguration speech the necessity for doing everything to increase the population of the country and condemned all measures of birth control as Marxist, liberalistic and unpatriotic. Yet one of the best sellers in Germany this year was a book entitled *A Nation Without Space*.

Women doctors, lawyers, teachers, all expressed grave apprehensions at the impending outlook for them in the Germany of today. More than one told me that in a few years not only would they have been driven out of the professions but even excluded from the universities and from all but a very rudimentary intellectual training. It is true that the Nazis promise new professions for women, assistant heads of girls's schools—apparently the head is always to be a man—leaders of the compulsory labor camps for girls, heads of the motherhood schools, mothers' helpers, "spiritual advisers" and so on, but the women who have not been trained under the new system may find it hard to substitute such work for their independent professional life.

The truth is that here, as in so much of the Nazi program, the decisive factor is unemployment and the imperative demand for jobs on the part of adherents who have been promised work when there is no increase in work and who must be satisfied at the expense of people who can be trusted to submit in silence. That all Nazi women will so submit may be doubted. We were told that there were some stirrings of revolt among them, that at one of the first meetings of the new Nazi "Women's Work" they were bold enough to announce their adherence to all the Nazi program except the part which deals with women. American journalists reported that there was considerable resentment among the women who came in thousands to the great Nazi rally in Nüremberg this summer when they found that they were being completely ignored. One of the former leaders of the Woman's Movement (*Frauenbewegung*) told me that all the work for sex equality in Germany must be begun all over again, but she did not despair, though she felt that her group could do nothing. The Nazi girls, she said, would no longer submit to a program which would mean hopeless drudgery and poverty for the great majority, and there would come a new revolt for women under new leaders.

In Russia in 1924 it was the children, and young people, the Pioneers, and the Young Communists, who interested me most—and in Germany the same thing was true. The two experiences were very similar. In both countries the revolution has caught the enthusiasm of youth and in both the response has been the same. It was the girls especially who gave us an impression of devotion to a great vision. Hitler's girls have little of the pomp and circumstance that makes life so exciting for the Brown Shirts; for them his cause is really one of effort and sacrifice. I asked a girl student what her plans for the future were. She was in Königsburg University, specializing in history and economics and hoping to teach in the university.[7] "But," I said, "what if the National Socialists carry out their plans to put women out of the professions and back into the home?" She faced me with flashing eyes. "Very well!" she said. "If the fatherland asks that sacrifice of me, I am ready." . . .

We visited some of the voluntary labor camps for girls (founded by Rosenstock under the Republic) where high-school graduates who have passed their college entrance examinations join with peasant girls in a life of hard physical work and total lack of the ordinary comforts of life. I think of a camp near Stettin, a bleak, unheated house, large dormitories with springless cots, straw sacks for mattresses, rough army blankets.[8] The girls had to go from the second story to the basement to wash and the basins and showers had warm water only twice a week. They worked in the vegetable gardens, they milked the cows, fed the pigs and geese and fowl, they even cleaned the stalls and pigpens, and of course they washed the clothes and scrubbed the floors and did the cooking. Many of them were gently bred, but you could not pick them out, for all were in rough clothes, all rosy and energetic and full of vigor. When their six months training is over they were to go to the country, to the new settlements, where they would relieve the settlers' wives, taking charge of the house and barnyard while the wife was working in the field.

I thought of William James' vision of each youth and maiden giving a year of service to the country and though I could not possibly imagine American girls doing work such as these German girls are capable of, it would still be a beautiful thing to see the same spirit over here.[9] But James' vision was of a moral substitute for war, the voluntary labor of the young men and women alike was to be for creative productive ends, not for war. Hitler's vision is just the reverse. He will have the education and sports directed toward the production of soldiers who are to liberate Germany, while the training of girls is to be directed toward fruitful motherhood so that the supply of Germany's soldiers shall not fail.

I cannot close this third paper on Hitler's Germany without saying some-

[7]   Königsburg, town in the former East Prussia, now Kaliningrad, Russia.
[8]   Stettin, in 1933 a town in the German province of Pomerania, now Szczecin, Poland.
[9]   William James (1842–1910), American psychologist and philosopher.

thing about the causes that underlay the amazing upheaval. To foreigners it seems like a madness, a mass hysteria, breaking out suddenly and unexpectedly and probably destined to subside as soon as leaders and followers come to realize the effect it has had on the outside world. But this is a very superficial view. There are deep-lying causes for Hitlerism, some of which at least, call for sympathetic understanding. First comes hopelessness. "Hitler is the leader of the hopeless," I was told, "of the ex-officers who had no future any more, of the jobless youths, of the small shopkeepers crushed by the economic depression, of the hordes of unemployed with their scanty, starvation doles." Hitler promised them work and bread.

If one talks with Germans about their own experience one gets a cumulative impression of what these people have lived through since 1914, almost twenty years. . . . Of course all this was made harder to bear by the belief that the miseries were mostly forced on Germany by her enemies.

And then the long-drawn out civil war between radicals and Nazis, with almost daily battles in the streets. Tourists came and went without guessing what was really happening, for it all went on in obscure parts of the city. Among ordinary people the fear of Communism grew and the government was felt to be a feeble thing, always torn between right and left and not daring to use strong measures with the extreme left. Our country has lived through several Communist scares and we look back on them with some amusement and no little shame—for we know there was so little to justify the ugly panic. But imagine our discovering after the last presidential election that one sixth of the votes had been cast for Foster![10] I think we would have had a first-class exhibition of national hysteria, judging from our past history. Therefore we have no right to be scornful of Germany's panic after the Reichstag fire. Russia is much closer to Germany than it is to us, and if Communism is a thing to dreaded, as most Communists sincerely believe, Germany has far greater cause to dread it than we. . . .

Of the injured national pride, the resentment over Germany's loss of power and prestige, I cannot speak; that is a subject in itself. It may be that those are right who say this is the chief cause of the success of Hitler. But there is a third contributory cause which should not be forgotten—Hitler's cleverness in providing the Germans with scapegoats for all their ills. We know that our deplorable financial condition cannot be blamed justly on any one class.

But suppose we had a scapegoat, suppose there were those whom we believed to be absolutely responsible, would not there be a growing resentment in this country which might at any time break forth into violence?

---

[10] William Z. Foster (1881–1961), American trade union organizer and leader of the American Communist Party who ran for the presidency several times during the 1920s, receiving an unprecedented 103,000 votes in 1932.

The Germans have only too many scapegoats. The Versailles treaty, which means the Polish Corridor, the cession of German Poland and Upper Silesia, of Alsace and Lorraine to France, the seizing of Germany's colonies, the fantastic reparations—this is the scapegoat of educated Germans, while the masses have the Jews who are responsible for everything—the War, the defeat, the peace terms, the revolution of 1918, Communism, government extravagance, unemployment and low prices. This they really believe. . . .

Somebody has said that the Germans have been spiritually isolated from the world so long that they have ceased to see things as the rest of us do. And now they are shutting themselves off as never before. What is to be the end?

Alice Hamilton to Jane Addams

Hotel Kaiserhof, Berlin
April 22, 1933

Dearest J.A.

What would I not give to be able to talk to you for a bit and to tell you all the things I cannot write about the people I am seeing here whom we both know and a lot of others whom you know and I did not. It is not a cheerful time in Berlin, dark and bleak with a bitter wind that is much colder than an American wind with the thermometer way down. As for the mental atmosphere it is what you might imagine only far more so. We have met very lovely women, all of whom you know, and I have never felt so full of admiration for my own sex. They are steady, courageous, clear-minded and sweet and when I compare my life with what they have been through I feel like a child that has always been shielded and safe. For of course I have never faced real danger in my life nor known what suspense and fear mean. We have just come from a quiet little lunch with your gentle friend who told me to remind you that you were her first guest in that flat when you and I came in 1915.[11] Your photograph is there. She will be leaving it soon for a very small one. Just now it is as if the Ku Klux Klan had taken possession of Chicago and you were waiting to see what would happen to H.H. [Hull House] We read the papers very carefully, for each day there is a new pronouncement, especially by the minister of education. The movement then is all back toward the time of Germany's greatness, the ideals of discipline and obedience and rational consciousness. Corporal punishment has already been re-introduced. The papers say there are 10,000 political prisoners in Prussia, 5000 in Bavaria. So far as I can discover, the important

[11] Hamilton probably means Alice Salomon.

ones of the W.I.L. are outside the country, certainly one is in prison.[12] Women are not of any importance in the Nazi movement, rather the program includes the return of women to the home and to womanliness.

I have the same feeling as in 1915 and 1919 of being very welcome to a little group of very lonely people for whom I can do nothing really but who find it a relief to be able to talk. Our friend who was in America last year is not yet back in Berlin but we shall see him Tuesday.[13] So far he has not been molested.

We leave here the first of May and go to a little village east of here where we shall have an introduction. Then we are to be in charge of an organization which undertakes to show foreigners around the Polish Corridor and East Prussia. It is most clearly a propaganda affair but as everyone says, much the most practical way of seeing that remote part of the country.

Young Alvin Cope and his wife are here—you remember Mrs. Walter Cope, Leila Cope of the Quakers of Germantown?[14] They are the nicest sort of young people and we love to visit them. He is working in the University but has decided to go over to England instead. They are the only Americans we have seen except the Consul, Messersmith who is very nice.[15] I have an appointment with Dolly [?] Swope Monday.[16]

With love to you all,
Alice

Alice Hamilton to Jane Addams

On Board the *Deutschland*
July 1, 1933

Dearest lady—We are in a dense fog, crawling into port where we hoped to be at ten this morning. Now we may have to lie outside for hours and perhaps miss the last train for Saybrook.

I am coming back in a mood of passionate patriotism worthy of a D.A.R. The Statue of Liberty will give me a real thrill for the first time. I don't care what faults a democracy has, it is a safe and human and liveable system and

12   At the time of Hamilton's visit, Lida Gustava Heymann and Anita Augspurg were living in Switzerland. Gertrud Baer probably was also outside the country.
13   Hamilton probably means Friedrich Siegmund-Schultze.
14   The editors were unable to identify Alvin, Walter, or Leila Cope.
15   George Strausser Messersmith (1883–1960), American diplomat who served as consul in Berlin from 1930 to 1933 and opposed the Nazi regime.
16   Hamilton could be alluding to social worker Mary (Hill) Swope (no dates available), the wife of former Hull House resident Gerard Swope (1872–1957), whom Addams knew. As president of General Electric, Swope and chairman of the board Owen D. Young took a keen interest in European reconciliation after World War I. It could not be verified whether Swope or his wife were in Germany at the time of Hamilton's visit.

nothing else is. As the days go on, Germany gets more and more unreal, nightmarish, and it is hard to believe that eight days ago I was really in Hamburg, talking with people who were living in fear, an increasing fear, who woke every morning with dread of what they might see in the papers, who would buy nothing and could make no plans because any day they might have to fly. You see, it has been growing worse instead of more lenient. About the middle of June there was a Conference of Leaders in Berlin behind closed doors, and immediately after that the program was stiffened, the great organization of the Steel Helmets—former soldiers and officers, aristocrats, conservatives—was dissolved, the party of Hugenberg and Papen was forbidden, and four violent speeches were made by Hitler and others, proclaiming that what has happened is only a curtain-raiser, the Revolution will sweep on.[17]

We found Frankfurt and Hamburg more terrorized than any cities we were in. Frankfurt is very tragic. Do you remember Tilly Edinger, a spirited young thing we met there in 1919? Her Mother was the one who founded the "Air Baths" in the parks, where we saw those pitiful starved children. Tilly's father was a famous neurologist and founded the Neurological Institute of the University.[18] Her mother and her mother's family were known for generosity and there was a street named for her father, while her mother's bust stood in the city's center for social work. Tilly is a gifted young scientist and worked in the Neurological Institute and of course she grew up with the consciousness of belonging to one of Frankfurt's best families and of being the daughter and granddaughter of highly honored people. When we saw her she had been requested to leave the Institute and formally expelled from the City Hospital where she did scientific work. The city's authorities telephoned her to come and get her mother's bust or they would throw it out. The night before, a beloved old couple, her mother's uncle and his wife, had killed themselves. They had seen everything go, their grandchildren forced out of school, their sons deciding to go to Belgium where life would be possible for them and they could educate their children. They themselves were told that they were not Germans but foreigners and a curse to the country and they decided death was better. He was a great benefactor to Frankfurt and founded the astronomical department in recognition of which a little planet was named for him "Mauritius."

All the people we met in Frankfurt were Jews and all waiting—to see

[17] "Party of Hugenberg and Papen": The German National People's Party (Deutschnationale Volkspartei). Franz von Papen (1879–1969), another nationalist politician, was a key figure in Hitler's rise to power and served as vice chancellor in his first cabinet.
[18] For Anna and Ludwig Edinger, see Part III, document 6, Hamilton, "At the War Capitals," note 67. Tilly Edinger, a paleontologist, later emigrated to the United States where she worked at Harvard's Museum for Comparative Zoology.

when the blow would fall—or left suddenly without positions or income and with no possible chance of any employment. If only we could open our doors to these people, they are so fine, but of course we cannot.

We went to Amsterdam for two blessed days, for I wanted to see Professor Ripley's wife who is staying there while he recovers from a mental breakdown.[19] She told me she had been in Geneva and saw Heymann and Augsburg [*sic*] and Gertrude Baer. The two first made a deep impression on her, as of course they would. They are not planning to return to Germany and seem to have grown much interested in astrology. Gertrude Baer was very restless and insisting she must go back but it would be useless. She would simply be sent to a concentration camp for an indefinite time. Just before we left Munich a young Hindu girl who was on the eve of taking her doctor's degree was arrested because she made a speech on Gandhi to a small group. The British Embassy will doubtless get her out but only on condition that she leave Germany at once—without her degree.

It is much worse than Russia. There the Whites were such a poor lot, one could be terribly sorry for them but nobody could wish them back in power. But in Germany the down-and-outs are the best people they have. So far, Siegmund-Schultze has not been touched personally, but his work is hampered in every way. The women of the old suffrage and reform groups, whom you met in Berlin told us they would never consent to turn Nazi and now they have been dissolved and no German woman will go to the meeting in Stockholm.[20]

Do write to me, you or Mary. I have had no sign of a letter in so long. We hear of sickening heat in Chicago and I am worried. I still count on seeing you in Hadlyme.

Clara[21] sends lots of love. It has been a rather dreadful experience for her but she has been endlessly plucky.

Yours always,
Alice

[19] Ida Ripley's husband William (1897–1941), an expert on transportation and labor economics, taught political economy at Harvard.
[20] Hamilton probably means the executive meeting of the ICW, held in Stockholm in 1933.
[21] Clara Landsberg (1873–1966), Hamilton's Bryn Mawr College classmate and a close friend of her sister, Margaret Hamilton, was the daughter of a reform rabbi from Rochester, New York. Landsberg lived at Hull House from 1899 to 1920.

Glossary of German Organizations

ASSOCIATION FOR SOCIAL POLICY (Verein für Sozialpolitik). Founded in 1872, this association brought together economists and progressive industrial leaders. Among its members were many renowned political economists and sociologists, among them prominent "academic socialists." At conferences and in their extensive publications, they addressed social and economic questions like protective labor legislation, factory inspection, and homework in a national as well as an international context. The association was dissolved in 1936 and newly founded in 1948.

ASSOCIATION OF GERMAN HOUSEWIVES (Deutscher Hausfrauen-verein). Founded in Berlin by Lina Morgenstern (1831–1909) in 1873, this organization acted as a lobby for housewives, offered advice on practical matters, and operated a cooking school as well as a labor exchange for servants. Morgenstern also edited its periodical, the *Deutsche Hausfrauenzeitung*. Eventually, the organization worked to improve housewives' rights and gain recognition of housewifery as a profession. Local associations united in the NATIONAL FEDERATION OF GERMAN HOUSEWIVES' ASSOCIATIONS (Reichsverband Deutscher Hausfrauenvereine, RDH) at the beginning of World War I, facilitating food distribution and mediating information on price control. After World War I, it was among the most conservative member associations of the BDF.

ASSOCIATION OF PROGRESSIVE WOMEN'S CLUBS (Verband Fortschrittlicher Frauenvereine). Founded in 1899, this was the umbrella organization of the women's clubs comprising the radical bourgeois German women's movement, such as the Verein Frauenwohl. Minna Cauer served as its president from 1899 until the organization joined the BDF in 1907. The Association represented 1500 members in 1913.

GENERAL GERMAN WOMEN'S ASSOCIATION (Allgemeiner Deutscher Frauen-verein, ADF). The oldest organization of the German bourgeois women's movement, founded in Leipzig in 1865. Its longtime president, Louise Otto (1819–1895), had led the women's movement during the short-lived revolution of 1848. Otto and Auguste Schmidt (1833–1902) edited the ADF publication *Neue Bahnen* (New Paths). ADF members worked for women's access to higher education and the professions, raising stipends for women who studied abroad and supporting private institutions for higher learning; they further demanded legal reforms as well as protective legislation for working women. Representing 14,000 members in 1913, the ADF was one of the more important member organizations of the BDF.

GENERAL ASSOCIATION OF GERMAN WOMEN TEACHERS (Allgemeiner Deutscher Lehrerinnenverein, ADLV). Founded in 1890 by Helene Lange and Clara Zetkin's teacher Auguste Schmidt (1833–1902), the ADLV became one of the largest professional associations for women. Representing 16,000 women teachers around the turn of the century and about 32,000 in 1913, it was the largest member association of the BDF. Its leaders petitioned for women's access to secondary schools and universities as well as for their own employment in these institutions. Many of the most prominent leaders of the bourgeois German women's movement—including Anita Augspurg, Gertrud Bäumer, Minna Cauer, and Helene Lange—were recruited from the teaching profession.

GERMAN ASSOCIATION FOR WOMAN SUFFRAGE (Deutscher Verein für Frauenstimmrecht). A number of German women activists, among them Anita Augspurg, Minna Cauer, Lida Gustava Heymann, and Käthe Schirmacher, founded this first German women's suffrage organization in 1902 in Hamburg, where they could circumvent the association laws that prohibited women's participation in politics. Its members played a key role in the founding of the International Woman Suffrage Alliance in Berlin in 1904. The German suffrage movement gained strength after the association laws were abolished in 1908.

GERMAN CATHOLIC WOMEN'S FEDERATION (Katholischer Frauenbund Deutschlands, KFD). The KFD was founded in 1904 in Cologne. Unlike the DEF, the KFD never cooperated with the BDF, because of the BDF's alleged "religious indifference." However, under its longtime leader Hedwig Dransfeld (1871–1925), the KFD cooperated with various women's organizations, especially in educational and legal work. In 1918, the KFD had some 112,000 members, organized in about 400 local branches and 600 associated organizations. Sticking to its firmly declared "political neutrality," the KFD never officially supported women's suffrage before 1918.

GERMAN FEDERATION FOR WOMAN SUFFRAGE (Deutsche Vereinigung für Frauenstimmrecht). Conservative women suffragists in Germany united in 1911 in the German Federation for Woman Suffrage under the leadership of Li Fischer-Eckert. They demanded the vote "under the same conditions that apply and will apply to men," not challenging the property qualifications that more than two-thirds of the German male electorate were subject to.

GERMAN PROTESTANT WOMEN'S FEDERATION (Deutsch-Evangelischer Frauenbund, DEF). The DEF was founded in 1899 in Kassel, five years after social reformer Elisabeth Gnauck-Kühne (1850–1917) initiated a "Protestant Social Women's Group" ("Evangelisch-Soziale Frauengruppe"). Under longtime president Paula Müller-Ottfried (1865–1946), members of the DEF volunteered in projects of the church charity Inner Mission; they waged battles for moral reform and against prostitution, alcoholism, and child labor. DEF women demanded the right to vote in church elections but explicitly rejected general voting rights for women because they feared that woman suffrage would strengthen socialist parties. In 1908, the DEF joined the League of German Women's Associations to support its conservative member associations in the fight against a reform of the abortion laws. It left the BDF in 1918 after the larger organization started to support women's suffrage. Representing 14,000 members before World War I, the DEF was one of the largest member associations of the BDF; it grew after the war, claiming 200,000 members at the end of the 1920s. Its strength contributed significantly to the increasingly conservative orientation of the bourgeois German women's movement after 1908.

GERMAN SOCIAL DEMOCRATIC PARTY (Sozialdemokratische Partei Deutschlands, SPD). The SPD was founded as the Socialist Workers' Party (Sozialistische Arbeiterpartei) in 1875, when the General German Workers' Association (Allgemeiner Deutscher Arbeiterverein, founded in 1863) and the Socialist German Workers Party (Sozialistische Deutsche Arbeiterpartei, founded in 1869) merged. The anti-socialist laws (Sozialistengesetze) outlawed the party and its publications in Germany between 1878 and 1890 and forced many of its leaders into exile. After 1890, the socialists consistently gained ground in elections to the national parliament. Demanding women's suffrage in its 1891 platform, the SPD remained the only German party to do so for almost twenty years.

GERMAN UNION FOR WOMAN SUFFRAGE (Deutscher Bund für Frauenstimm-recht). Anita Augspurg and Lida Gustava Heymann founded this organization after the 1913 congress of the German Association for Woman Suffrage failed to pass a resolution demanding a general reform of the electoral system. Members of the radical German Union for Woman Suffrage demanded equal voting rights for men and women without property qualifications.

GIRLS' AND WOMEN'S GROUPS FOR SOCIAL ASSISTANCE WORK (Mädchen-und Frauengruppen für soziale Hilfsarbeit). Founded in 1893 by Berlin councillor Emil Münsterberg together with Minna Cauer, Jeanette Schwerin (1852–1899), and other prominent social reformers, the "groups" wanted to draw women into organized charity work by providing them with a theoretical as well as a systematic practical education. Their lecture classes evolved into a more structured year-long course in 1899, supervised by its most prominent member, Alice Salomon, who founded the WOMEN'S SCHOOL FOR SOCIAL WORK in 1908. A number of women activists emerged from the ranks of the "groups," among them Marie-Elisabeth Lüders.

INTERNATIONAL CONGRESS OF WOMEN'S WORK AND WOMEN'S ENDEAVORS (Internationaler Kongress für Frauenwerke und Frauenbestrebungen). Not affiliated with any particular national or international women's organization, this congress met in Berlin in 1896 under the presidency of Minna Cauer. Seventeen hundred delegates from Europe and America exchanged information on the progress of women's emancipation and on their work in social reform and the professions in their respective countries.

LEAGUE FOR THE PROTECTION OF MOTHERHOOD AND SEXUAL REFORM (Bund für Mutterschutz und Sexualreform, BfMS). Founded in 1905, the BfMS drew its membership from among radical feminists and social reformers like BDF president Marie Stritt (1855–1928) as well as from promoters of eugenics and "racial hygiene." One of the most controversial reform organizations of its time, it advocated "free love" and a "new ethic," demanding welfare measures for single mothers, legal recognition of unmarried couples, and the reform of a criminal law that severely punished homosexuality and abortion. Compared with many member organizations of the BDF, the BfMS had a relatively small membership, about 4,000 in 1909. Its leader, Helene Stöcker, helped to initiate a worldwide network of sexual reformers, who met for an international congress in 1911 and founded the "International Association for the Protection of Motherhood and Sexual Reform."

LEAGUE OF GERMAN WOMEN'S ASSOCIATIONS (Bund Deutscher Frauen-vereine, BDF). Founded in 1894, the BDF was the umbrella organization of the mainstream bourgeois German women's movement. By 1895, 65 clubs had joined; by 1901, 137; and by 1913, when it cautiously campaigned for women's suffrage, the BDF represented 2,200 clubs, bringing its membership to about 150–200,000. Arguing that it wanted to "stay away from politics," the BDF did not admit socialist women's organizations.

PATRIOTIC WOMEN'S ASSOCIATIONS (Vaterländische Frauenvereine). Founded in 1866 during the German war against Denmark, to coordinate the work of nurses and women volunteers who provided clothing, food, and medical supplies for the army, 291 associations united into a central agency under the Red Cross in 1869. By far the strongest women's organization in Germany, it claimed to have half a million dues-paying members before World War I.

SOCIETY FOR WOMAN'S WELFARE (Verein Frauenwohl). Founded in 1888 in Berlin by Minna Cauer, this society quickly established branches in several German cities. Part of the radical wing of the bourgeois German women's movement, it especially promoted women's right to higher education and later fought against prostitution and the white slave trade.

WOMEN'S SCHOOL FOR SOCIAL WORK (Soziale Frauenschule). Founded by Alice Salomon in 1908, the Women's School for Social Work evolved from attempts to educate Berlin women systematically for charity work. The first secular school of its kind, it became the model for the education of social workers throughout Germany. In 1925 Salomon founded the German Academy for Women's Social and Pedagogic Work (Deutsche Akademie für soziale und pädagogische Frauenarbeit), which offered graduate work to social workers. Honoring the sixtieth birthday of its founder, the Prussian government named the "Soziale Frauenschule" in Alice Salomon's honor in 1932, but the name was revoked the following year. Until 1998 its buildings housed the College for Social Work, Fachhochschule Alice Salomon.

Biographical Notes

Biographical notes include authors of documents and other important contributors to the dialogue. Italicized names are of persons with their own entries.

ADDAMS, JANE (1860–1935), American social reformer and pacifist. Born in Cedarville, Illinois, to an elite family, Addams identified closely with her politically active father, a vigorous abolitionist who was a friend of Abraham Lincoln. A graduate of Rockford Female Seminary, she sought work commensurate with her talents. A brief enrollment at the Woman's Medical College of Pennsylvania proved unsatisfying, and she traveled and studied in Europe from 1883 to 1885. She returned to Europe in 1887–88, now traveling with her friend Ellen Gates Starr. After visiting Toynbee Hall in London's East End, the prototype for the social settlement movement, Addams and Starr launched their own social settlement, Hull House, in Chicago in 1889. There a community of women reformers emerged to become a vital force in American public life and in the international settlement movement. By 1900, Addams was the undisputed leader of a flourishing women's political culture and a well-known social reformer abroad.

Jane Addams's interest in peace arose naturally from her commitment to social democracy and the internationalism she experienced in Chicago's immigrant neighborhoods. In 1909 she became a founding member of the National Association for the Advancement of Colored People. With the outbreak of World War I in 1914, Addams was the clear choice to lead women's peace efforts both as chair of the Women's Peace Party and president of the International Congress of Women at The Hague. In 1919 she was elected first president of the Women's International League for Peace and Freedom, a position she held until her death, presiding over the league's conferences in Zurich, Vienna, Dublin, Prague, and elsewhere.

During the 1920s Addams struggled against conservative views that pilloried her for lack of patriotism. Internationally, however, she was adored by multitudes of women. In 1931 her work for peace was rewarded with a Nobel Peace Prize. She donated her prize money to the Women's International League for Peace and Freedom.

AUGSPURG, ANITA (1857–1943), German women's rights activist and pacifist. After a brief career as an actress, Augspurg started her fight for equal rights for women in 1890, demanding particularly their right to higher education and an end to state-regulated prostitution. In 1897, she was the first German woman to receive a law doctorate (in Zurich). With *Minna Cauer* and *Lida Gustava Heymann*, Augspurg founded the German Association for Woman Suffrage (Deutscher Verein für Frauenstimmrecht) in 1902. As a representative of the radicals within the German bourgeois women's movement, Augspurg attended the Women's Congresses at The Hague and in Zurich and was one of the leading members of the German branch of WILPF until it was dissolved in 1933. After editing a variety of pre-war suffrage periodicals, she and Heymann published *Die Frau im Staat* (Woman in the State), the leading publication of radical German woman pacifists in the Weimar Republic. Throughout the 1920s, Augspurg worked continuously and at great personal risk for international reconciliation. During the revolution in Bavaria, Augspurg, Heymann, and *Gertrud Baer* tried to mediate in order to prevent civil war. Augspurg represented the women's movement in Bavaria's short-lived provisional parliament. In 1923, she demanded Adolf Hitler's expulsion from her state after his unsuccessful coup d'etat. Augspurg was on vacation in Switzerland when Hitler came to power in January of 1933 and never returned to Germany.

BAER, GERTRUD (1890–1981), German feminist, pacifist, journalist, and teacher. Early in her life, Baer became a friend of *Anita Augspurg* and *Lida Gustava Heymann*. In 1914, she joined them in Munich to support their antiwar efforts. She served a short term as head of the women's division in the ministry for social welfare of the Bavarian republic in 1919. From 1919 to 1933, Baer worked for the liberal feminist periodical *Die Frau im Staat* (Woman in the State) and the pacifist periodical *Die Friedenswarte* (Peace Watch). In 1921, she became the executive secretary of the German branch of WILPF. With Heymann and *Frida Perlen*, Baer led the effort of German women pacifists to reconcile with French women after World War I and organized a "Tree Donation" in northern France in 1926. The following year, Baer became vice president of the German Peace Cartel (Deutsches Friedenskartell). A cofounder of the World Youth League, she traveled widely in Europe and the United States, most notably to the 1924 congress of the WILPF in Washington, D.C., forging close friendships with

Jane Addams and *Emily Greene Balch.* In 1929, Baer became joint chair-woman of the WILPF headquarters in Geneva. As a Jewish woman, Baer left the country in 1933. She continued her work for WILPF in Geneva and New York and eventually became an American citizen.

BALCH, EMILY GREENE (1867–1961), American educator and pacifist. After an education at Bryn Mawr College and travel and study in Europe, she met *Jane Addams* in 1892, and they developed a deep and enduring friendship. She then worked at Denison House, a social settlement in Boston, and pursued further study at Radcliffe College, the University of Chicago, and the University of Berlin, where she studied with Gustav Schmoller in 1895–96. There she renewed her friendship with Mary Kingsbury (Simkovitch), who was in Berlin studying with a fellowship from the Women's Educational and Industrial Union of Boston. At the year's end Balch and Kingsbury attended the last major International Socialist Trade Union Congress in London.

For twenty-three years Balch taught at Wellesley College, offering courses on socialism and Karl Marx, immigration, the theory of consumption, and women's labor force participation. By 1913 she was professor and chair of the department of economics. On various visits to Europe, she studied public assistance in France and Eastern European immigrants from the point of view of their origins. In 1913 she chaired the Massachusetts Minimum Wage Commission.

Balch's pacifism began during the Spanish-American War in 1898. In 1915 she took an active part in shaping the women's conference at The Hague. With *Jane Addams* and *Alice Hamilton,* she coauthored *Women at The Hague* (1915), which reported on the conference and subsequent talks with government leaders. From 1919 to 1922, she served as paid international secretary-treasurer of the Women's International League for Peace and Freedom, setting up the office in Geneva, and organizing the third women's congress at Vienna in 1921. On a voluntary basis she served in a variety of WILPF capacities, including president of the American section in 1931, and international president in 1937. In 1926 with five other American women, including two African-Americans, she investigated conditions in Haiti, which had been occupied by the U.S. Marines since 1915. Their resulting study, *Occupied Haiti* (1927), written primarily by Balch, recommended the restoration of self-government by the native black population. In *Refugees as Assets* (1939) she appealed to American readers to welcome refugees from Nazi Germany.

Balch received the Nobel Peace Prize in 1946 for her lifelong dedication to peace and social justice.

BÄUMER, GERTRUD (1873–1954), teacher and leader of the bourgeois German women's movement. After teaching school for a few years, Bäumer met *Helene Lange* in 1896. When Bäumer moved to Berlin in 1898 to attend the university, Lange quickly realized her potential and became her mentor and supporter in every respect. They lived and worked closely together for more than thirty years. In 1900, the two women edited the *Handbuch der Frauenbewegung* (Handbook of the Women's Movement), still a useful reference. From 1907 to 1910, Bäumer edited the publication of the General German Women's Association, *Neue Bahnen* (New Paths).

From 1910 to 1919 she was the president of the League of German Women's Associations (BDF), the largest women's organization in the country. Together with Helene Lange, Bäumer edited *Die Frau* (Woman) from 1916 to 1929; after Lange's death that year, she served as sole editor until 1944. From 1912 to 1944 she was coeditor of *Die Hilfe* (Help) with the liberal social reformer Friedrich Naumann (1860–1919). Like Naumann, Bäumer became a member of the German Progressive Party (Deutsche Fortschrittspartei), later the German Democratic Party (Deutsche Demokratische Partei). She was a delegate to the National Assembly and member of the Reichstag throughout the 1920s. She was a Ministerialrat (councillor in the ministry) in the Ministry of the Interior, the first woman in Germany to hold such a high government position, but was removed from it after the Nazis came to power. She continued to edit *Die Frau* under Nazi rule, for which she was heavily criticized after the war, and wrote a number of historical works. In 1949, she was one of the cofounders of the conservative Christian Social Party (Christlich-Soziale Partei).

Always skeptical of the values of international organizations, Bäumer vehemently opposed the international women's peace movement at the outbreak of World War I.

BIEBER-BÖHM, HANNA (1851–1910), German moral reformer. In 1889, Bieber-Böhm founded the Association for the Protection of Juveniles (Verein für Jugendschutz), fighting the double standard and state regulation of prostitution. As a member of the General German Women's Association, she was among the German delegates to the World's Congress of Representative Women in Chicago in 1893 and afterward one of the cofounders of the League of German Women's Associations (BDF). Bieber-Böhm's politics of moral reform represented the conservative wing of the German women's movement, advocating rigid prosecution of prostitutes, which put them into opposition to the Association of Progressive Women's Clubs (Verband Fortschrittlicher Frauenvereine).

CAUER, MINNA (née Wilhelmine Schelle, 1841–1920), German feminist leader. After the death of her husband Eduard Cauer, a well-known advocate of higher education for women, Minna Cauer became active in the German women's movement. In 1888 she founded the progressive Society for Woman's Welfare (Verein Frauenwohl). In 1893 she cofounded the

Girls' and Women's Groups for Social Assistance Work. Cauer served as president of several professional organizations for women and of the International Congress of Women's Work and Women's Endeavors (Internationaler Kongress für Frauenwerke und Frauenbestrebungen) in 1896. She was president of the Association of Progressive Women's Clubs until it joined the BDF in 1907. An early advocate for woman suffrage, she served on the board of the German Association for Women's Suffrage, which she founded in 1902 with *Anita Augspurg* and *Lida Gustava Heymann*. Her most important work, however, was for the periodical *Die Frauenbewegung* (The Women's Movement), which she edited at great personal financial expense from 1895 to 1919.

CHAMBERLAIN, MARY (1889–1939), American writer and reformer. Upon graduating from Vassar in 1909, Chamberlain received a fellowship that enabled her to complete study for a master's degree in sociology and economics at Columbia, and spend a year at the Sorbonne. She launched her reform career in 1911 by working for the New York State Factory Commission on an investigation of upstate canneries. Between 1913 and 1920 she worked for *Survey* both as a writer and as circulation manager. In 1920 she married Oscar Graeve, a novelist and editor, and had two children. She returned to work as associate editor and circulation manager of the *Woman's Journal,* a New York periodical addressed to new women voters in the late 1920s and early 1930s. In the 1930s Chamberlain enjoyed great success in a new career directing women's publicity for the presidential campaigns of Franklin D. Roosevelt in 1932 and 1936. For the 1939 election she invented the Rainbow Flyers, which did much to popularize the New Deal. Between elections she wrote the *Know Your Government* series that formed the backbone of the *Women's Digest* of the Democratic party.

CONRAD, ELSE (1873– ?), German writer and student of economics. The daughter of a university professor of economics in Halle, Conrad studied at the girls' school there. After traveling abroad, Conrad began studying economics at the universities in Halle, Heidelberg, and Zurich in 1899. In 1906 she received her Ph.D. for a dissertation on the Association for Social Policy and its efforts to secure protective legislation. The next year, she visited the United States. In 1917, Conrad edited the memoirs of her father, Johannes Conrad.

DOTY, MADELEINE ZABRISKIE (1879–1963), American lawyer and social reformer. Doty graduated from Smith College and New York University Law School. Her career began in 1913 when she was appointed to the Prison Reform Committee of New York. With the outbreak of World War I, Doty shifted her energies to peace, joining the Woman's Peace Party, and traveling to The Hague in 1915 for the Women's International Congress. She spent the next five years traveling through Europe writing articles for American and British newspapers and magazines about the effects of the war. Her books, *Short Rations: An American Woman in Germany* (1917) and *Behind the Battle Line: Around the World in 1918* (1918), built on her affiliation with the women's peace movement. In 1917–18 she toured Russia at the height of the Revolution while on a world tour sponsored by *Good Housekeeping* magazine. She attended the Zurich and Vienna congresses of the Women's International League for Peace and Freedom in 1919 and 1921. After the war Doty worked as the international secretary of WILPF, then as editor of *Pax International* for the League of Nations. In 1919 she married Roger Baldwin (1884–1981), head of the American Civil Liberties Union. She helped *Jane Addams* organize speaking engagements for German women attending the 1924 WILPF congress in Washington, D.C. Her unpublished autobiography and 1945 doctoral dissertation from the University of Geneva are available at The Sophia Smith Collection at Smith College.

EBERT, FRIEDRICH (1871–1925), leader of the German Social Democratic Party and president of the Weimar Republic from 1919 to 1925. Within the German Social Democratic Party, Ebert represented so-called revisionist, "trade union" socialism. He was primarily interested in the practical improvement of the living conditions of the working class and in its moral and social betterment.

Ebert became secretary general of the SPD in 1905 and succeeded August Bebel as party chairman in 1913. Under Ebert's leadership, the Social Democrats gained increased influence in national politics. Ebert was a staunch supporter of the war appropriations in August of 1914. Already part of the so-called Weimar coalition of the Catholic Center Party, the Democratic Party, and the Social Democrats established during the war, Ebert set up a socialist government after the armistice. The Weimar coalition, which regained power after the election for the constitutional assembly in January of 1919, elected Ebert as the first president of the Republic. The next year, the coalition—and with it, Ebert—lost its majority. Ebert steered the young republic through its first troublesome years. A major controversy over his appointing Gustav Stresemann of the right-of-center People's Party as chancellor, which had the unintended consequence of eliminating the Social Democrats from national politics for many years to come. Even after the country's economy was somewhat stabilized in 1924, the right continued its defamation of Ebert, who died an early death.

HAMILTON, ALICE (1869–1970), American physician, pioneer in industrial toxicology, and social reformer. After receiving her M.D. from the University of Michigan in 1892, Hamilton and her older sister Edith (1867–1963) spent a year in Germany, where Alice studied bacteriology and pathology at the universities of Leipzig and Munich. She benefited little from her studies and brought back impressions of German society as militaristic, anti-Semitic, and "women-despising," especially in academia. After spending a year at Johns Hopkins, she was appointed professor of pathology at the Woman's Medical School of Northwestern University in 1897. Hamilton became a resident of Hull House, where she soon made her way into the inner circle. For years she struggled to reconcile her scientific work with the needs of her immigrant neighbors and finally turned to the study of industrial diseases. She was appointed to the Illinois Commission on Industrial Diseases in 1908 and as a special investigator for the U.S. Bureau of Labor in 1911. Hamilton's studies on lead poisoning quickly made her the leading authority on this field, an investigator as well as a crusader for public health.

Hamilton continued her investigations during World War I and beyond, even when she was appointed assistant professor of industrial medicine at Harvard, the first woman ever to hold a faculty position at that school. She also immersed herself in international relations, accompanying *Jane Addams* to Europe in 1915 and 1919, serving as a member of the Health Committee of the League of Nations from 1924, and visiting the Soviet Union in 1924 and Nazi Germany in 1933. After her retirement from Harvard in 1935, Hamilton became a consultant to the Department of Labor, wrote textbooks and her autobiography, and stayed politically involved, deploring anticommunism and eventually protesting American involvement in Vietnam.

HARNACK, ELISABET VON (1892–?). Born in Berlin, Harnack was the daughter of the prominent theologian Adolf von Harnack (1851–1930). Beginning in 1914, she worked in Friedrich Siegmund-Schultze's East Side settlement in Berlin, Soziale Arbeitsgemeinschaft Berlin-Ost (SAG). She received her Ph.D. from Berlin University in 1919 with a dissertation on the day care of school children. She led several boys' clubs at the SAG settlement during the 1920s. Her contacts with American settlement workers probably originated here, since the assistant head worker, Alix Westerkamp (dates not available), had spent some time in Chicago's University Settlement in 1914. After World War II, Harnack worked as the principal official in Berlin's State Bureau for Labor and Social work and helped to revive *Alice Salomon*'s Women's School for Social Work.

HEYMANN, LIDA GUSTAVA (1868–1943), German feminist and pacifist, leader of the radical wing within the bourgeois German women's movement. Heymann started to work for social reform in Hamburg after her father's death made her financially independent in 1896. Her initial work was similar to American settlement work. She founded educational clubs and classes, organized female clerks, propagated dress reform, and fought against prostitution. In 1897 she joined a pacifist organization in Munich, where she met *Anita Augspurg,* her life partner. They shared many of their public activities, most notably in the radical wing of the bourgeois women's movement and the German peace movement as well as their private lives. They supported the short-lived Bavarian Republic after World War I. Heymann was a candidate on the Independent Socialists' ticket for the Weimar national assembly. For many years, Augspurg and Heymann lived on a farm outside of Munich, which they ran exclusively with female farmhands; they also traveled extensively. They were on vacation abroad when the Nazis came to power in 1933 and their property as well as most of their papers were confiscated. They never returned to Germany.

KELLEY, FLORENCE (1859–1932), American reformer. Born into a reform-minded Quaker family in Philadelphia, Kelley graduated from Cornell in 1882 and founded a school for working women in Philadelphia. Between 1884 and 1886 she studied and lived in Zurich, Switzerland, where she met exiled German and Russian socialists. In 1885 she married Lazare Wischnewetzky, and bore three children in the next three years. In a letter-writing campaign to American suffrage periodicals she urged the adoption of aspects of German socialist political culture. Kelley returned to New York in 1886; late in 1891 when her husband became violent she fled with her children to Chicago, where she joined *Jane Addams* and other women reformers at Hull House. There her leadership in an anti-sweatshop movement resulted in her appointment as Chief Factory Inspector of the State of Illinois, 1893–1897. From this position she resumed her dialogue with German social democrats, writing for two journals founded by Heinrich Braun (1854–1927), *Sozialpolitisches Centralblatt* (Central Paper for Social Politics) and *Archiv für Soziale Gesetzgebung und Statistik* (Archive for Social Legislation and Statistics). After her term as factory inspector ended in 1896, Braun hired her to write regularly for *Archiv.* In 1899 Kelley returned to New York as general secretary of the National Consumers' League, a position she held until her death. As a leading figure in the political culture of middle-class American women, she participated in international congresses organized by the Women's International League for Peace and Freedom at Zurich in 1919 and Vienna in 1921.

KIRCHHOFF, AUGUSTE (1867–1940), German women's rights activist and pacifist. Kirchoff joined the radical wing of the bourgeois women's movement after the turn of the century. In 1905 she founded the local branch of the German Association for Woman Suffrage in Bremen, where her husband served as a senator. She also founded the Bremen branch of the League for the Protection of Motherhood and Sexual Reform in 1909 and of the Association of German Housewives (Deutsche Hausfrauenverein) in 1915. Kirchhoff was among the German delegates to the Hague Congress as well as to the WILPF congresses in Zurich, Vienna, and The Hague in 1922. A prominent member of the German WILPF, she raised her five children on pacifist principles. In the 1920s, Kirchhoff published several articles on WILPF and its members, particularly *Jane Addams,* in German dailies. Although she was an ardent opponent of nationalism and anti-Semitism, she remained unharmed during the Nazi regime.

LANGE, HELENE (1848–1930), German teacher and feminist. Lange was one of the leaders in the first generation of German feminists. Famous for the "Yellow Brochure," a petition to the Prussian ministry of education demanding more scholarly curricula in girls' schools and an adequate education for women teachers, Lange throughout her life fought for equal educational opportunities. Herself a talented teacher, she did much to realize this goal, cofounding the General Association of German Women Teachers in 1890. Lange was a member of the board of the General German Women's Association from 1893 to 1921 and the board of the League of German Women's Associations (BDF) from 1894 to 1906, which made her a key member of the bourgeois women's movement for nearly three decades. She founded the periodical *Die Frau* (Woman) in 1893 and, with *Gertrud Bäumer,* edited it until 1929. Until it ceased publication in 1944, it was the most widely read publication of the bourgeois German women's movement, with regular articles on the American suffrage movement and its leaders, and on American women's subsequent political activities.

LINDEMANN, ANNA (died before 1949), German women's rights activist. Her husband Hugo Lindemann, an SPD politician, served as a member of the German Reichstag from 1903 to 1906 and as a member of the Württemberg state parliament until 1920. He published widely on German and English municipal socialism and English labor unions and, with Albert Südekum (1871–1943) and Rudolf Schwander (1868–?), put together a municipal yearbook before the First World War and again in the late 1920s. Anna Lindemann worked on this yearbook, as well as for the revisionist wing of the SPD. She raised two daughters and was active in local politics and community affairs as well as in the state, national, and international suffrage movements. She was president of the German Association for Woman Suffrage and an officer of that organization in the state of Württemberg. In 1915, she became third vice president of the International Woman Suffrage Association. Lindemann also held a leading position in the National Women's Service during World War I.

LÜDERS, MARIE ELISABETH (1878–1966), German social reformer and politician. Lüders started her career as a social worker in *Alice Salomon*'s Girls' and Women's Groups for Social Assistance Work, from 1901 to 1906. In 1910 she was one of the first women in Germany to graduate from college preparatory classes with an "Abitur," which entitled her to enter the university. She received a Ph.D. in economics from Berlin University in 1912, with a thesis on vocational training of working women. From 1912 to 1914, she was the first woman tenement inspector appointed in the Berlin suburb of Charlottenburg; she engaged in social work in Charlottenburg and later in Belgium during the war. From 1919 to 1932, Lüders represented the liberal German Democratic Party (Deutsche Demokratische Partei) in the National Assembly and the Reichstag. She worked especially hard for the new youth welfare legislation. With Agnes von Zahn-Harnack (1884–1950, sister of *Elisabet von Harnack*), Lüders founded the German Association of University Women (Deutscher Akademikerinnenbund) in 1926. In 1936 she published a nationalist memoir of her work in World War I, *Das unbekannte Heer* (The Unknown Army). In 1937 she was held by the Gestapo for three months and, after her release, was prohibited from publishing. From 1948 to 1950 she served as a Berlin city council member for the new liberal party, the Free Democratic Party (Freie Demokratische Partei), which she represented in the Bundestag from 1953 to 1961.

LINA MORGENSTERN (1830–1909) grew up in a wealthy Jewish family in Breslau in which the tradition of charity was highly respected. She exemplified the strong presence of Jewish women among German social justice feminists; in many ways her work created a precedent for that of Alice Salomon. After marrying in 1854, she moved to Berlin. The mother of five children, she founded the Society for the Promotion of Fröbel Kindergartens in 1859, although the Prussian government had once banned Fröbel Kindergartens as centers of socialism and atheism. She became best known for founding the Society of Berlin Soup Kitchens. She served on the board of the General German Women's Association (Allgemeiner Deutscher Frauenverein) from 1871 to 1885, organized the Berlin Housewives' Association (1873), and edited its newsletter, the *Deutsche Hausfrauen-Zeitung*, for thirty years. She became a leading women's rights advocate, founding a club to educate working women, which she headed from 1871 to 1874. At the founding of the League of German Women's Associations (Bund Deutscher Frauenvereine) in 1894, she tried to include working-class women in the organization.

PERLEN, FRIDA (1870–1933), German pacifist and women's rights activist. A member of the Stuttgart branch of the Deutscher Verein fur Frauenstimmrecht, where she almost certainly worked with *Anna Lindemann*. In August of 1914, Perlen sent a telegram to the kaiser, asking him to do everything possible to avoid the war; later she pleaded with the chancellor for an end to the fighting. Frida Perlen was a member of the group that organized the Women's Peace Congress at The Hague in 1915, but was denied a passport to leave Germany and could not attend the meetings. Despite harassment by the authorities, Perlen remained an active member of the German Committee of Women for a Permanent Peace, continuing her work in WILPF after the war. In 1933 she emigrated to Switzerland.

ROTTEN, ELIZABETH (1882–1964), German pacifist, educator, and journalist. Early in World War I, Rotten and Friedrich Siegmund-Schultze founded an organization to assist foreigners, mainly British citizens, who had been detained in Germany by the war. This laid the ground for her continuing work for peace and international understanding. In 1918, she was elected to the board of the New Fatherland League (Bund Neues Vaterland). She was also a member of the German Association for the Promotion of the League of Nations (Deutsche Liga für den Völkerbund). Rotten founded organizations for educational reform and international cooperation in education and taught at the Women's School for Social Work in Hellerau. In 1934, she emigrated to Switzerland.

SALOMON, ALICE (1872–1948), German feminist and social work innovator. A prominent figure in the German and the international women's movements, Salomon originated social work education for women in Germany. Bored by sitting at home after receiving the meager education then thought proper for the daughter of a middle-class family, she joined the Girls' and Women's Groups for Social Assistance Work in 1893 and was put in charge of their first courses for social workers in 1899. With special permission, Salomon studied at the University of Berlin from 1902 to 1906, receiving a Ph.D. in economics with a dissertation entitled "Reasons for Unequal Wages for Women and Men." In 1908 Salomon founded the Women's School for Social Work. In 1900 she became the youngest member on the board of the League of German Woman Organizations (BDF), acting first as secretary, then as one of the vice presidents of the organization until 1920. She resigned when it became clear that the organization would not elect a woman from a Jewish family as its president.

During the same period, Salomon also became an active member of the international women's movement under the auspices of her mentor and the longtime president of the International Council of Women, Lady Aberdeen. She helped to organize the 1904 International Women's Congress in Berlin. In 1909, Salomon was elected corresponding secretary of the ICW and traveled widely on behalf of the organization and of international social work in the following twenty years, including visits to the United States in 1909, 1923, 1924, and 1936. She was expelled from Germany the following year and emigrated to New York. The deaths of Lillian Wald and *Jane Addams* had severed her most important ties to American social workers, and it was impossible for Salomon to find employment in the post-Depression job market. She spent the remaining years of her life writing her autobiography, *Charakter ist Schicksal* (Character is Destiny, 1983).

SCHIRMACHER, KÄTHE (1858–1930), German feminist and journalist. A delegate to the Congress of Representative Women at the 1893 Columbian Exposition, Schirmacher traveled widely in Europe and America. She received her Ph.D. from the University of Zurich in 1895 and afterward lived in Paris until 1900. Her fluency in several languages made her a much-sought-after interpreter at many congresses of the international women's movement. Schirmacher's writings on the World's Fair were widely publicized.

She also wrote on general political questions and on the history of the German women's movement. In 1899 she cofounded the Association of Progressive Women's Clubs, the progressive wing of the German bourgeois women's movement, in 1902 the German Association for Woman Suffrage, and in 1904 the International Woman Suffrage Association (Internationaler Verein für Frauenstimmrecht). After 1904 she became a staunch political conservative, supporting German rearmament and its expansionist war aims during World War I. After the war, she represented the nationalist German National People's Party (Deutschnationale Volkspartei) in the Weimar national assembly in 1919. Her continued support of women's emancipation reveals the compatibility of radical feminism and right-wing nationalism in that era.

SIEGMUND-SCHULTZE, FRIEDRICH (1885–1969), German theologian, social worker, and pacifist. A proponent of internationalism, pacifism, social justice, and ethical reform through the churches, Siegmund-Schultze founded the sole German settlement house in Berlin in 1911 after visits to Toynbee Hall in London and Hull House in Chicago. Through the World Alliance, he tried to foster friendly relations between the English and Germans during and after the war. He edited *Die Eiche* (The Oak), one of the most prominent journals of the German peace movement, from 1913 to 1933. He also held several offices in Berlin's municipal offices for youth welfare and was appointed Honorary Professor at Berlin University in 1925. Siegmund-Schultze emigrated to Switzerland after 1933 and did not return to Germany until 1947. He was a staunch defender of the rights to conscientious objection after World War II.

SMITH, MARY ROZET (1870–1934), *Jane Addams*'s life partner. The daughter of a leading Chicago manufacturer, Smith became Addams's chief financial adviser and helpmeet in 1892. In 1895 she contributed to Hull House a building for children's programs. For the rest of her life Smith devoted herself to taking care of Jane Addams, often managing her correspondence, her schedule, and her health. Although they traveled extensively together, Mary Smith did not accompany Jane Addams to the Hague or Zurich meetings. Yet even when Addams traveled without her, Smith's money often paid for the trips, thereby contributing substantially to Addams's international contacts and her peace work. Smith formed independent relationships with *Florence Kelley*, Lillian Wald, and others among Addams's close associates. She contributed funds to the education of Addams's nieces and nephews and to Florence Kelley's children.

STÖCKER, HELENE (1869–1943), German feminist, pacifist and sex reformer. Stöcker's social activism began in the radical wing of the bourgeois suffrage movement, but she quickly turned to working for the benefit of unwed mothers and their children. The League for the Protection of Motherhood and Sexual Reform (Bund für Mutterschutz und Sexualreform), which she cofounded in 1905, aimed to reform sexual ethics and fight the double standard. Stöcker also asserted women's right to control their reproductive functions. She edited the organization's periodical, *Mutterschutz* and later *Die neue Generation* (The New Generation) from 1905 to 1933. Stöcker belonged to several German pacifist organizations, among them the WILPF, the New Fatherland League (Bund Neues Vaterland), German Peace Cartel (Deutsches Friedenskartell), and the German Peace Society (Deutsche Friedensgesellschaft) and cofounded War Resisters' International in 1921. She was one of the most distinguished critical left-wing intellectuals outside Weimar party politics. After the Reichstag fire in 1933, Stöcker fled Germany and lived in Switzerland, England, and the Soviet Union before arriving in the United States in 1941. Her papers are at Swarthmore College.

TERRELL, MARY CHURCH (1863–1954), American suffragist and pacifist. Mary Church's mother was a newly emancipated slave; her father, who was to become very wealthy, was the son of a slave and her white owner. When her parents divorced, she went north for schooling, graduating from Oberlin College in 1884. In the late 1880s she toured Western Europe, perfecting her already considerable knowledge of French, German, and Italian. In 1891 she married Robert Terrell, one of the first blacks to graduate from Harvard, and for many years a judge of the Washington, D.C., municipal court. They had two daughters. She became president of the newly organized National Association of Colored Women in 1896, and after serving three terms was voted honorary president for life. Around 1900 she began to speak more widely and at the 1898 convention of the National American Woman Suffrage Association delivered the address reprinted here, "The Progress of Colored Women." In fluent German and French, she spoke in Berlin in 1904 at the International Council of Women about the same topic. By then she had become a professional lecturer and writer about black history and life. A founding member of the National Association for the Advancement of Colored People, she often led protest delegations in Washington, D.C., and urged the passage of corrective legislation. In 1919 she traveled to Zurich to address the Congress of the Women's International League for Peace and Freedom. *Jane Addams* knew her as a member of the League's executive committee. After the passage of the woman suffrage amendment in 1920, she directed work among colored women for the Republican National Committee. After the publication of her autobiography, *A Colored Woman in a White World* (1940), she became even more active in protesting against racial discrimination.

Selected Bibliography

With the exception of biographies and autobiographies of major participants in the dialogue, this bibliography is limited to recent historical writings and other works cited in the Introduction.

Manuscript Collections

Jane Addams Memorial Collection, University of Illinois at Chicago Circle.

Jane Addams Papers, Swarthmore College Peace Collection.

American Relief Association Papers, Hoover Institution on War, Revolution, and Peace, Stanford University.

Carrie Chapman Catt Papers, Library of Congress.

Madeline Zabriskie Doty Papers, Sophia Smith Collection, Smith College.

Archives, Fachhochschule Alice Salomon, Berlin.

Survey Associates, Social Welfare History Archives, University of Minnesota, Minneapolis.

Mary Church Terrell Papers, Library of Congress.

Woodrow Wilson Papers, Library of Congress.

Women's Peace Party Correspondence, Women's International League for Peace and Freedom Papers, Swarthmore College Peace Collection.

Published Sources

Abbott, Edith. "Grace Abbott: A Sister's Memories." *Social Service Review* 13 (1939): 351–407.

Addams, Jane. *My Friend Julia Lathrop.* New York: Macmillan, 1935.

——. *Peace and Bread in Time of War.* New York: Macmillan, 1922.

——. *The Second Twenty Years at Hull House.* New York: Macmillan, 1929.

——. *Twenty Years at Hull House.* New York: Macmillan, 1910.

——. *Zwanzig Jahre Soziale Frauenarbeit in Chicago.* Translated by Else Münsterberg. Munich: C. H. Beck, 1913.

Addams, Jane, Emily G. Balch, and Alice Hamilton. *Women at The Hague: The International Congress of Women and its Results*. New York: Macmillan, 1916.

Albisetti, James C. *Schooling German Girls and Women: Secondary and Higher Education in the Nineteenth Century*. Princeton, N.J.: Princeton University Press, 1988.

Allen, Ann Taylor. *Feminism and Motherhood in Germany, 1800–1914*. New Brunswick, N.J.: Rutgers University Press, 1991.

——. "Mothers of a New Generation: Adele Schreiber, Helene Stöcker, and the Evolution of a German Ideal of Motherhood." *Signs* 10 (1985): 418–39.

Alonso, Harriet Hyman. "Nobel Peace Laureates Jane Addams and Emily Greene Balch: Two Women of WILPF." *Journal of Women's History* 7 (Summer 1995): 6–26.

——. *Peace as a Women's Issue: A History of the U.S. Movement for World Peace and Women's Rights*. Syracuse, N.Y.: Syracuse University Press, 1993.

——. *The Women's Peace Union and the Outlawry of War, 1921–1942*. Knoxville: University of Tennessee Press, 1989.

Alonso, Harriet Hyman, and Melanie Gustafson. "Bibliography on the History of U.S. Women in Movements for Peace." *Women's Studies Quarterly* 12 (Summer 1984): 46–50.

Annan, Noel. "The Intellectual Aristocracy." In John Harold Plumb, ed., *Studies in Social History: A Tribute to G. M. Trevelyan*, pp. 241–87. London: Longmans, Green, 1955.

Anthony, Katherine. *Feminism in Germany and Scandinavia*. New York: Henry Holt, 1915.

Athey, Louis L. "From Social Conscience to Social Action: The Consumers' Leagues in Europe, 1900–1914." *Social Service Review* 52 (September 1978): 362–82.

Backhaus-Lautenschläger, Christine. *. . . und standen ihre Frau: Deutschsprachige Emigrantinnen in den USA nach 1933*. Pfaffenweiler: Centaurus Verlagsgesellschaft, 1991.

Bane, Suda Lorena, and Ralph Haswell Lutz, eds. *The Blockade of Germany After the Armistice, 1918–1919*. Stanford, Calif.: Stanford University Press, 1942.

Bäumer, Gertrud. *Im Licht der Erinnerung*. Tübingen: R. Wunderlich Verlag, 1953.

Beck, Hermann. *The Origins of the Authoritarian Welfare State in Prussia: Conservatives, Bureaucracy, and the Social Question, 1815–1870*. Ann Arbor: University of Michigan Press, 1995.

Benker, Gitta, and Senta Störmer. *Grenzüberschreitungen: Studentinnen in der Weimarer Republik*. Pfaffenweiler: Centaurus Verlagsgesellschaft, 1991.

Benz, Ute, ed. *Frauen im Nationalsozialismus: Dokumente und Zeugnisse*. Munich: C. H. Beck, 1993.

Berger, Stefan. *The British Labour Party and the German Social Democrats, 1900–1931*. Oxford: Oxford University Press, 1994.

Berghahn, V. R. *Germany and the Approach of War in 1914*. New York: St. Martin's Press, 1973.

Bergman, Helena. "That Noble Band?: Male and Female Factory Inspectors in the Turn of the Century United States." Master's thesis, State University of New York, Binghamton, 1995.

Bessel, Richard. *Germany After the First World War*. Oxford: Clarendon Press, 1993.

Blackbourn, David, and Geoff Eley. *The Peculiarities of German History: Bourgeois Society and Politics in Nineteenth-Century Germany*. Oxford: Oxford University Press, 1984.

SELECTED BIBLIOGRAPHY

Boak, Helen L. "Women in Weimar Germany: The 'Frauenfrage' and the Female Vote." In Richard Bessel and E. J. Feuchtwanger, eds., *Social Change and Political Development in Weimar Germany,* pp. 155–73. London: Croom Helm, 1981.

Bock, Gisela. "Die Frauen und der Nationalsozialismus: Bemerkungen zu einem Buch von Claudia Koonz." *Geschichte und Gesellschaft* 15 (1989): 563–79.

Bock, Gisela, and Pat Thane, eds. *Maternity and Gender Politics: Women and the Rise of European Welfare States, 1880s–1950s.* London: Routledge, 1991.

Boris, Eileen. *Home to Work: Motherhood and the Political of Industrial Homework in the United States.* New York: Cambridge University Press, 1994.

Bosch, Mineke, with Annemarie Kloosterman. *Politics and Friendship: Letters from the International Woman Suffrage Alliance, 1902–1942.* Columbus: Ohio State University Press, 1990.

Boyd, Catherine. "Nationaler Frauendienst: German Middle-Class Women in Service to the Fatherland." Ph.D. dissertation, University of Georgia, 1979.

Bracher, Karl-Dietrich. *Die deutsche Diktatur: Entstehung, Struktur, Folgen des Nationalsozialismus.* Cologne: Kiepenheuer & Witsch, 1969. Published in English under the title *The German Dictatorship* (New York: Praeger, 1970).

Breckman, Warren G. "Disciplining Consumption: The Debate about Luxury in Wilhemine Germany, 1890–1914." *Journal of Social History* 24 (Spring 1991): 485–506.

Breen, William J. "Black Women and the Great War: Mobilization and Reform in the South." *Journal of Southern History* 44 (August 1978): 421–40.

Bridenthal, Renate, Atina Grossmann, and Marion Kaplan, ed. *When Biology Became Destiny: Women in Weimar and Nazi Germany.* New York: Monthly Review Press, 1984.

Brinker-Gabler, Gisela. "The Women's Movement in the German Empire: The Revolution Dismisses her Children." In Ingeborg Drewitz, ed., *The German Women's Movement: The Social Role of Women in the Nineteenth Century and the Emancipation Movement in Germany,* pp. 53–81. Bonn: Hohwacht, 1983.

——, ed. *Frauen gegen den Krieg.* Frankfurt: Fischer Taschenbuchverlag, 1980.

——, ed. *Frauenarbeit und Beruf.* Frankfurt: Fischer Taschenbuchverlag, 1979.

Broszat, Martin. *Der Staat Hitlers: Grundlagen und Entwicklung seiner inneren Verfassung.* Berlin: Deutscher Taschenbuchverlag, 1970. Published in English under the title *The Hitler State: The Foundation and Development of the Internal Structure of the Third Reich* (New York: Longman, 1981).

Bulmer, Martin, Kevin Bales, and Kathryn Kish Sklar, eds. *The Social Survey in Historical Perspective, 1880–1940.* Cambridge: Cambridge University Press, 1992.

Bussey, Gertrude Carman, and Margaret Tims. *Pioneers for Peace: Women's International League for Peace and Freedom.* London: Allen & Unwin, 1965.

Camhi, Jane Jerome. *Women Against Women: American Anti-Suffragism, 1880–1920.* Brooklyn: Carlson, 1994.

Canning, Kathleen. "Social Policy, Body Politics: Recasting the Social Question in Germany, 1875–1900." In Laura L. Frader and Sonya Rose, *Gender and Class in Modern Europe,* pp. 213–37. Ithaca: Cornell University Press, 1996.

Carpenter, Edward M., and Jaqueline Parker. "Julia Lathrop and the Children's Bureau: The Emergence of an Institution." *Social Service Review* 55 (1981): 60–75.

Carson, Mina. *Settlement Folk: Social Thought and the American Settlement Movement, 1885–1930.* Chicago: University of Chicago Press, 1990.

Carsten, Francis L. *August Bebel und die Organisation der Massen.* Berlin: Siedler Verlag, 1991.

Chambers, Clarke. "Women in the Creation of the Profession of Social Work." *Social Service Review* 60 (1986): 23–46.

Chambers, John Whiteclay II. *The Eagle and the Dove: The American Peace Movement and United States Foreign Policy, 1900–1922*. Syracuse, N.Y.: Syracuse University Press, 1991.

Chickering, Roger. " 'Casting Their Gaze More Broadly': Women's Patriotic Activism in Germany." *Past and Present* 118 (1988): 156–85.

———. *Imperial Germany and a World Without War: The Peace Movement and German Society, 1892–1914*. Princeton, N.J.: Princeton University Press, 1975.

Clark, Christopher M. *The Politics of Conversion: Missionary Protestantism and the Jews in Prussia, 1728–1941*. Oxford: Oxford University Press, 1995.

Clemens, Bärbel. *Menschenrechte haben keine Geschlecht: Zum Politikverständnis der bürgerliche Frauenbewegung*. Pfaffenweiler: Centaurus Verlagsgesellschaft, 1988.

Conzen, Kathleen. "Germans." In *Harvard Encyclopedia of American Ethnic Groups*, s.v. Cambridge, Mass.: Harvard University Press, 1980.

Coogan, John W. *The End of Neutrality: The United States, Britain, and Maritime Rights, 1899–1915*. Ithaca: Cornell University Press, 1981.

Costin, Leila B. "Feminism, Pacifism, Internationalism and the 1915 International Congress of Women." *Women's Studies International Forum* 5 (1982): 301–15.

———. *Two Sisters for Social Justice: A Biography of Edith and Grace Abbott*. Urbana: University of Illinois Press, 1983.

Cott, Nancy. *The Grounding of Modern Feminism*. New Haven, Conn.: Yale University Press, 1987.

———. "What's in a Name? The Limits of 'Social Feminism'; or, Expanding the Vocabulary of Women's History." *Journal of American History* 76 (1989): 809–29.

Craig, John M. "Lucia True Ames Mead: American Publicist for Peace and Internationalism." In Edward P. Crapol, ed., *Women and American Foreign Policy*, pp. 67–90. Westport, Conn.: Greenwood Press, 1987.

Crangle, John V., and Joseph O. Baylen. "Emily Hobhouse's Peace Mission, 1916." *Journal of Contemporary History* 14 (1979): 731–44.

Daley, Caroline, and Melanie Nolan, eds. *Suffrage and Beyond: International Feminist Perspectives*. New York: New York University Press, 1994.

Daniel, Ute. *Arbeiterfrauen in der Kriegsgesellschaft: Beruf, Familie und Politik im Ersten Weltkrieg*. Göttingen: Vandenhoek & Ruprecht, 1989.

———. "Der Krieg der Frauen 1914–1918: Zur Innenansicht des Ersten Weltkriegs in Deutschland." In Gerhard Hirschfeld and Gerd Krumeich, eds., *Keiner fühlt sich hier mehr als Mensch*, pp. 131–49. Essen: Klartext, 1993.

———. "Women's Work in Industry and Family: Germany, 1914–18." In Richard Wall and Jay Winter, eds., *The Upheaval of War: Family, Work and Welfare in Europe, 1914–1918*, pp. 267–96. Cambridge: Cambridge University Press, 1988.

Daniels, Doris Groshen. *Always a Sister: The Feminism of Lillian D. Wald*. New York: Feminist Press, 1989.

Dasey, Robyn. "Women's Work and the Family: Women Garment Workers in Berlin and Hamburg before the First World War." In Richard Evans and W. R. Lee, *The German Family: Essays on the Social History of the Family in 19th and 20th Century Germany*. London: Croom Helm, 1981.

Davis, Allen F. *American Heroine: The Life and Legend of Jane Addams*. New York: Oxford University Press, 1973.

Davis, Belinda. "Food Scarcity and the Empowerment of the Female Consumer in World War I Germany." In Victoria de Grazia and Ellen Furlough, eds., *The Sex of*

Things: Gender and Consumption in Historical Perspective, pp. 287–310. Berkeley: University of California Press, 1996.

Degen, Louise. *The History of the Woman's Peace Party*. Baltimore, Md.: Johns Hopkins University Press, 1939.

Doerries, Reinhard R. "Promoting *Kaiser* and *Reich:* Imperial German Propaganda in the United States during World War I." In Hans-Jürgen Schröder, ed., *Confrontation and Cooperation: Germany and the United States in the Era of World War I, 1900–1924*, pp. 135–66. Providence, R.I.: Berg, 1993.

Donat, Helmut, and Karl Holl, eds. *Die Friedensbewegung: Organisierter Pazifismus in Deutschland, Österreich und in der Schweiz*. Düsseldorf: Econ, 1983.

Doty, Madeleine Zabriskie. *Behind the Battle Line: Around the World in 1918*. New York: Macmillan, 1918.

——. *Short Rations: Experiences of an American Woman in Germany*. New York: Century, 1917.

Drewitz, Ingeborg. *The German Women's Movement: The Social Role of Women in the Nineteenth Century and the Emancipation Movement in Germany*. Bonn: Hohwacht, 1983.

Edwards, Maud L., Inga Elgquist-Saltzman, Eva Lundgren, et al., eds. *Rethinking Change: Current Swedish Feminist Research*. Uppsala: HSFR, 1992.

Einsele, Gabi. " 'Kein Vaterland': Deutsche Studentinnen im Züricher Exil (1870–1908)." In Anne Schlüter, ed., *Pionierinnen, Feministinnen, Karrierefrauen: Zur Geschichte des Frauenstudiums in Deutschland*, pp. 9–34. Pfaffenweiler: Centaurus Verlagsgesellschaft, 1992.

Evans, Richard J. "Bourgeois Feminists and Women Socialists in Germany, 1894–1914: Lost Opportunity of Inevitable Conflict?" *Women's Studies International Quarterly* 3 (1980): 355–76.

——. *Comrades and Sisters: Feminism, Socialism and Pacifism in Europe, 1870–1945*. New York: St. Martin's Press, 1987.

——. "The Concept of Feminism: Notes for Practicing Historians." In Ruth-Ellen B. Joeres and Mary Jo Maynes, eds., *German Women in the Eighteenth and Nineteenth Centuries: A Social and Literary History*, pp. 247–58. Bloomington: Indiana University Press, 1986.

——. *The Feminist Movement in Germany, 1894–1933*. London: Sage Publications, 1976.

——. "Theory and Practice in German Social Democracy, 1880–1914: Clara Zetkin and the Socialist Theory of Women's Emancipation." *History of Political Thought* 3 (Summer 1982): 285–303.

Farrell, John C. *Beloved Lady: A History of Jane Addams' Ideas on Reform and Peace*. Baltimore, Md.: Johns Hopkins University Press, 1967.

Ferguson, Niall. *Paper and Iron: Hamburg Business and German Politics in the Era of Inflation, 1897–1927*. Cambridge: Cambridge University Press, 1995.

Fischer, Conan. *The Rise of the Nazis*. Manchester: Manchester University Press, 1995.

Fitzpatrick, Ellen. *Endless Crusade: Women Social Scientists and Progressive Reform*. New York: Oxford University Press, 1990.

Foster, Carrie A. *The Women and the Warriors: The U.S. Section of the Women's International League for Peace and Freedom, 1915–1946*. Syracuse, N.Y.: Syracuse University Press, 1995.

Foster, Catherine. *Women for All Seasons. The Story of the International Women's League for Peace and Freedom*. Athens: University of Georgia Press, 1989.

Foster-Hayes, Carrie A. "The Women and the Warriors: Dorothy Detzer and the Women's International League for Peace and Freedom." Ph.D. dissertation, University of Denver, 1984.

Frandsen, Dorothea. *Helene Lange: Ein Leben für das volle Bürgerrecht der Frau.* Freiburg im Breisgau: Herder, 1980.

Franzen, Trisha. *Spinsters and Lesbians: Independent Womanhood in the United States.* New York: New York University Press, 1996.

Franzoi, Barbara. *At the Very Least She Pays the Rent: Women and German Industrialization, 1871–1914.* Contributions in Women's Studies, vol. 57. Westport, Conn.: Greenwood Press, 1985.

Frevert, Ute. *Frauen-Geschichte: Zwischen bürgerlicher Verbesserung und Neuer Weiblichkeit.* Frankfurt: Suhrkamp, 1986. Published in English under the title *Women in German History: From Bourgeois Emancipation to Sexual Liberation* (Oxford: Berg, 1988).

Gay, George. *Public Relations of the Commission for Relief in Belgium.* Stanford, Calif.: Stanford University Press, 1929.

Gerhard, Ute. " 'National oder International?' Frauengeschichte im Spiegel der internationalen Beziehungen der deutschen Frauenbewegung." *Ariadne* 24 (1993): 50–59.

——. *Unerhört: Die Geschichte der deutschen Frauenbewegung.* Hamburg: Rowohlt, 1991.

——. *Verhältnisse und Verhinderungen: Frauenarbeit, Familie und Rechte der Frauen im 19. Jahrhundert.* Frankfurt: Suhrkamp, 1978.

Geyer, Martin H. "Munich in Turmoil: Social Protest and the Revolutionary Movement, 1918–19." In Chris Wrigley, ed., *Challenges of Labour: Central and Western Europe, 1917–1920,* pp. 51–71. London: Routledge, 1993.

Gifford, Carolyn De Swarte, ed. *Writing Out My Heart: Selections from the Journal of Frances E. Willard, 1855–96.* Urbana: University of Illinois Press, 1995.

Gompers, Samuel. *Seventy Years of Life and Labor: An Autobiography.* 2 vols. New York: E. P. Dutton, 1925.

Gordon, Linda. "Black and White Visions of Welfare: Women's Welfare Activism, 1890–1945." *Journal of American History* 78 (1991): 559–90.

——. "The Peaceful Sex? On Feminism and the Peace Movement." *National Women's Studies Association Journal* 2 (Autumn 1990): 624–34.

——. *Pitied But not Entitled: Single Mothers and the History of Welfare.* New York: Free Press, 1994.

——. "Social Insurance and Public Assistance: The Influence of Gender in Welfare Thought in the United States, 1890–1935." *American Historical Review* 97 (1992): 19–54.

——. "What's New in Women's History." In Teresa de Lauretis, ed., *Feminist Studies /Critical Studies.* Bloomington: University of Indiana Press, 1986.

——, ed. *Women, the State and Welfare.* Madison: University of Wisconsin Press, 1990.

Green, Maurguerite. *The National Civic Federation and the American Labor Movement, 1900–1925.* Washington, D.C.: The Catholic University of America Press, 1956.

Greven-Aschoff, Barbara. *Die bürgerliche Frauenbewegung in Deutschland, 1894–1933.* Göttingen: Vandenhoeck & Ruprecht, 1981.

Grossman, Atina. "Gender and Rationalization: Questions about the German/American Comparison." *Social Politics: International Studies in Gender, State, and Society* 4 (Spring 1997): 6–18.

——. *Reforming Sex: The German Movement for Birth Control and Abortion Reform, 1920–1950.* New York: Oxford University Press, 1995.

Guarneri, Carl J. *America Compared.* 2 vols. New York: Houghton Mifflin, 1997.

Gustafson, Melanie. "Lola Maverick Lloyd." Master's thesis, Sarah Lawrence College, 1983.

Guttman, W. L. *The German Social Democratic Party, 1875–1933: From Ghetto to Government.* London: Allen & Unwin, 1981.

Hackett, Amy. "Feminism and Liberalism in Wilhelmine Germany, 1890–1918." In Bernice Carroll, ed., *Liberating Women's History: Theoretical and Critical Essays,* pp. 127–36. Urbana: University of Illinois Press, 1976.

Hagemann, Karen. "Men's Demonstrations and Women's Protest: Gender in Collective Action in the Urban Working-Class Milieu during the Weimar Republic." *Gender and History* 5 (Spring 1993): 101–19.

——. "Rationalizing Family Work: Municipal Family Welfare and Urban Working Class Mothers in Germany." *Social Politics: International Studies in Gender, State, and Society* 4 (Spring 1997): 19–48.

Hallgarten, Constanze. *Als Pazifistin in Deutschland: biographische Skizze.* Stuttgart: Conseil-Verlag, 1956.

Hamilton, Alice. *Exploring the Dangerous Trades: The Autobiography of Alice Hamilton, M.D.* Boston: Little, Brown, 1943.

Harrison, Patricia Greenwood. "Interaction between the British and American Woman Suffrage Movements, 1900–1914." Ph.D. dissertation, Tulane University, 1994.

Harzig, Christiane. *Familie, Arbeit und weibliche Öffentlichkeit in einer Einwanderungsstadt: Deutschamerikanerinnen in Chicago um die Jahrhundertwende.* St. Katharinen: Scripta Mercatuae Verlag, 1991.

Hause, Steven C., and Anne R. Kenney. *Women's Suffrage and Social Politics in the French Third Republic.* Princeton, N.J.: Princeton University Press, 1984.

Heidenheimer, Arnold J., and Peter Flora. *The Development of Welfare States in Europe and America.* New Brunswick, N.J.: Transactions Books, 1986.

Herrman, Ursula. *August und Julie Bebel: Briefe einer Ehe.* Bonn: Verlag J.H.W. Dietz Nachfolger, 1997.

Heymann, Lida Gustava, and Anita Augspurg. *Erlebtes, Erschautes: Deutsche Frauen kämpfen für Freiheit, Recht und Frieden, 1850–1940.* Edited by Margit Twellmann. Frankfurt: Helmer Verlag, 1992.

Hildebrandt, Irma. *Zwischen Suppenküche und Salon: Achtzehn Berlinerinnen.* Cologne: E. Diedrichs, 1987.

Holl, Karl. "German Pacifist Women in Exile, 1933–1945." *Peace and Change* 20 (October 1995): 491–500.

Holton, Sandra Stanley. " 'To Educate Women into Rebellion': Elizabeth Cady Stanton and the Creation of a Transatlantic Network of Radical Suffragists." *American Historical Review* 99 (October 1994): 1112–36.

Honegger, Claudia, and Theresa Wobbe, eds. *Klassikerinnen des soziologischen Denkens.* Munich: C. H. Beck, 1997.

Honeycutt, Karen. "Clara Zetkin: A Left-Wing Socialist and Feminist in Willhemian Germany." Ph.D. dissertation, Columbia University, 1975.

——. "Socialism and Feminism in Imperial Germany." *Signs* 5 (Autumn 1979): 30–41.

Hoogenboom, Ari. *Outlawing the Spoils: A History of the Civil Service Reform Movement, 1865–1883.* Urbana: University of Illinois Press, 1961.

Horne, John, and Alan Kramer. "German 'Atrocities' and Franco-German Opinion, 1914: The Evidence of German Soldiers' Diaries." *Journal of Modern History* 66, no. 7 (1994): 1–33.

Horowitz, Helen Lefkowitz. *Culture and the City: Cultural Philanthropy in Chicago from the 1880s to 1917*. Lexington: University of Kentucky Press, 1976.

Howard, N. P. "The Social and Political Consequences of the Allied Food Blockade of Germany." *German History* 2 (1993): 161–88.

Hunt, James C. "The Bourgeois Middle in German Politics, 1871–1933: Recent Literature." *Central European History* 11 (March 1978): 83–106.

Hunton, Addie W., and Kathryn M. Johnson. *Two Colored Women with the American Expeditionary Forces*. Brooklyn: Brooklyn Eagle Press, n.d.

Hurwitz, Edith F. "The International Sisterhood." In Renate Bridenthal and Claudia Koonz, eds., *Becoming Visible: Women in European History*, pp. 325–45. Boston: Houghton Mifflin, 1977.

International Council of Women. *Report of the International Council of Women, Assembled by the National Woman Suffrage Association, Washington, D.C., U. S. of America, March 25 to April 1, 1888*. Washington, D.C.: R. H. Darby, printer, 1888.

——. *Women in a Changing World: The Dynamic Story of the International Council of Women*. London: Routledge & Kegan Paul, 1966.

Jablonsky, Thomas J. *The Home, Heaven, and Mother Party: Female Anti-suffragists in the United States, 1868–1920*. Brooklyn: Carlson, 1994.

Jacobs, Aletta H. *Herinneringen*. Amsterdam: Van Holkema & Warendorf, 1924.

——. *Memories: My Life as an International Leader in Health, Suffrage, and Peace*. Edited by Harriet Feinberg, translated by Annie Wright. New York: Feminist Press, 1996.

James, Edward T., Janet Wilson James, and Paul S. Boyer. *Notable American Women, 1607–1950: A Biographical Dictionary*. 3 vols. Cambridge, Mass.: Harvard University Press, 1971.

Jensen, Joan M. "All Pink Sisters: The War Department and the Feminist Movement in the 1920s." In Lois Scharf and Joan M. Jensen, eds., *Decades of Discontent: The Women's Movement, 1920–1940*. Westport, Conn.: Greenwood Press, 1983.

Johnson, Robert David. *The Peace Progressives and American Foreign Relations*. Cambridge, Mass.: Harvard University Press, 1995.

Jonas, Manfred. *The United States and Germany: A Diplomatic History*. Ithaca, N.Y.: Cornell University Press, 1984.

Jones, Beverly Washington. *Quest for Equality: The Life and Writings of Mary Church Terrell, 1863–1954*. Brooklyn: Carlton Publishers, 1990.

Josephson, Harold, ed. *Biographical Dictionary of Modern Peace Leaders*. Connecticut: Greenwood Press, 1985.

Kaes, Anton, Martin Jay, and Edward Dimendberg, eds. *The Weimar Republic Sourcebook*. Berkeley: University of California Press, 1994.

Kaplan, Marion A. *The Jewish Feminist Movement in Germany: The Campaigns of the Jüdischer Frauenbund, 1904–1938*. Westport, Conn.: Greenwood, 1979.

——. *The Making of the Jewish Middle Class: Women, Family and Identity in Imperial Germany*. New York: Oxford University Press, 1991.

——. *When Biology Became Destiny: Women in Weimar and Nazi Germany*. New York: Monthly Review Press, 1984.

Kapp, Yvonne. *Eleanor Marx*, Vol. 1. New York: Pantheon Books, 1972.

Kater, Michael. *Doctors under Hitler*. Chapel Hill: University of North Carolina Press, 1989.

Katz, Michael B. *In the Shadow of the Poorhouse: A Social History of Welfare in America.* New York: Basic Books, 1986.

Kaufmann, Doris. *Frauen zwischen Aufbruch und Reaktion: Protestantische Frauenbewegung in der ersten Hälfte des 20. Jahrhunderts.* Munich: Piper, 1988.

Keegan, John. *The Face of Battle: A Study of Agincourt, Waterloo and the Somme.* New York: Viking, 1976.

Kelley, Florence. *The Autobiography of Florence Kelley: Notes of Sixty Years.* Edited by Kathryn Kish Sklar. Chicago: Charles Kerr, 1985.

———. *Our Toiling Children.* Chicago: Women's Temperance Publication Association, 1889. Published in German under the title "Die Lohnsklaverei der amerikanischen Kinder," *Die Neue Zeit* 7 (1889): 168–75.

[Kelley, Florence]. "Die Sozialdemokratie und die Frage der Frauenarbeit: Ein Beitrag zur Programmfrage." *Der Sozialdemokrat: Zentral-Organ der deutschen Sozialdemokratie* (Zurich), August 11, 18, and 25, 1886.

Kellogg, Paul. "Mary Chamberlain, 1909." *Vassar Alumnae Magazine,* June 1939, p. 15.

Kennedy, Kathleen. "Declaring War on War: Gender and the Americal Socialist Attack on Militarism, 1914–1918." *Journal of Women's History* 7 (Summer 1995): 27–51.

Kloppenberg, James T. *Uncertain Victory: Social Democracy and Progressivism in European and American Thought, 1870–1920.* New York: Oxford University Press, 1986.

Knock, Thomas J. *To End All Wars: Woodrow Wilson and the Quest for a New World Order.* New York: Oxford University Press, 1992.

Kocka, Jürgen. *Facing Total War: German Society, 1914–1918.* Cambridge, Mass.: Harvard University Press, 1984.

Koonz, Claudia. "Conflicting Allegiances: Political Ideologies and Women Legislators in Weimar Germany." *Signs* 1 (1976).

———. *Mothers in the Fatherland: Women, the Family and Nazi Politics.* New York: St. Martin's Press, 1987.

Kouri, E. I. *Der deutsche Protestantismus und die Soziale Frage.* Berlin: de Gruyter, 1984.

Koven, Seth, and Sonya Michel, eds. *Mothers of a New World: Maternalist Politics and the Origins of Welfare States.* New York: Routledge, 1993.

Kraft, Barbara S. *The Peace Ship: Henry Ford's Pacifist Adventure in the First World War.* New York: Macmillan, 1978.

Lacey, Kate. *Feminine Frequencies: Gender, German Radio, and the Public Sphere, 1923–1945.* Ann Arbor: University of Michigan Press, 1996.

Ladd-Taylor, Molly. *Mother-Work: Women, Child Welfare and the State, 1890–1930.* Urbana: University of Illinois Press, 1994.

Lange, Helene. *Lebenserinnerungen.* Berlin: F. A. Herbig, 1921.

Lebzelter, Gisela. "Die 'Schwarze Schmach': Vorurteile-Propaganda-Mythos." *Geschichte und Gesellschaft* 11 (1985): 37–58.

Lemons, Stanley. *The Woman Citizen: Social Feminism in the 1920's.* Urbana: University of Illinois Press, 1973.

Lewis, Arnold. *An Early Encounter with Tomorrow: Europeans, Chicago's Loop, and the World's Columbian Exposition.* Urbana: University of Illinois Press, 1997.

Levine, Daniel. *Poverty and Society: The Growth of the American Welfare State in International Comparison.* New Brunswick, N.J.: Rutgers University Press, 1988.

Lidtke, Vernon L. *The Outlawed Party: Social Democracy in Germany, 1878–1890.* Princeton, N.J.: Princeton University Press, 1966.

Lindenfeld, David F. *The Practical Imagination: The German Sciences of State in the Nineteenth Century.* Chicago: University of Chicago Press, 1997.

Linn, James Weber. *Jane Addams: A Biography.* New York: D. Appleton-Century, 1935.

Lipschultz, Sybil. "Social Feminism and Legal Discourse: 1908–1923." *Yale Journal of Law and Feminism* 2 (Fall 1989): 131–60.

Lowe, John. *The Great Powers, Imperialism and the German Problem, 1865–1925.* London: Routledge, 1994.

Lüders, Else. *Minna Cauer, ihr Leben und Werk: Dargestellt an Hand ihrer Tagebücher und nachgelassenen Schriften.* Gotha: L. Klotz, 1925.

Lüders, Marie-Elisabeth. *Fürchte Dich nicht: Persönliches und Politisches aus mehr als 80 Jahren.* Cologne: Westdeutscher Verlag, 1963.

Lutz, Ralph Haswell. *The Causes of the German Collapse in 1918.* Stanford, Calif.: Stanford University Press, 1934.

Lutzker, Michael A. "Jane Addams: Peacetime Heroine, Wartime Heretic." In Charles DeBenedetti, ed., *Peace Heroes in Twentieth-Century America*, pp. 28–55. Bloomington: Indiana University Press, 1986.

Macdonald, Lyn. *1914: The First Months of Fighting.* New York: Atheneum, 1988.

Mair, Craig. *Britain at War, 1914–1919.* London: Murray, 1982.

Maisel, L. Sandy, ed. *Political Parties and Elections in the United States: An Encyclopedia.* New York: Garland, 1991.

Marchand, Roland C. *The American Peace Movement and Social Reform, 1898–1918.* Princeton, N.J.: Princeton University Press, 1972.

Marcus, Jane. "Transatlantic Sisterhood: Labor and Suffrage Links in the Letters of Elizabeth Robins and Emmeline Pankhurst." *Signs* 3 (1978): 744–55.

McCarthy, Kathleen, ed. *Lady Bountiful Revisited: Women, Philanthropy and Power.* New Brunswick, N.J.: Rutgers University Press, 1990.

McLeod, Hugh. *Piety and Poverty: Working Class Religion in Berlin, London, and New York, 1870–1914.* New York: Holmes & Meier, 1996.

Meyer, Alfred G. *The Feminism and Socialism of Lily Braun.* Bloomington: Indiana University Press, 1985.

Meyer-Renschhausen, Elisabeth. *Weibliche Kultur und soziale Arbeit: Eine Geschichte der Frauenbewegung am Beispiel Bremens, 1810–1927.* Cologne: Böhlau-Verlag, 1989.

Michel, Sonya, and Seth Koven. "Womanly Duties: Maternalist Policies and the Origins of Welfare States in France, Germany, Great Britain and the United States, 1880–1920." *American Historical Review* 95 (1990): 1076–1108.

Miller, Carol. " 'Geneva—the Key to Equality': Inter-war Feminists and the League of Nations." *Women's History Review* 3 (1994): 219–45.

Miller, Francesca. "The International Relations of Women of the Americas, 1890–1928." *Americas* 43 (October 1986): 171–82.

Mommsen, Wolfgang J. *Imperial Germany, 1867–1918: Politics, Culture, and Society in an Authoritarian State.* London: Arnold, 1990.

———. *The Rise and Fall of Weimar Democracy.* Translated by Elborg Forster and Larry Eugene Jones. Chapel Hill: University of North Carolina Press, 1989.

Morgenstern, Lina. *Die Frauen des neunzehnten Jahrhunderts: Biographische und kulturhistorische Zeit- und Charaktergemälde.* 3 vols. Berlin: Verlag der Hausfrauenzeitung, 1888–1891.

Muller, Steven. "Nach dreihundert Jahren." In Frank Trommler, ed., *Amerika und die Deutschen: Bestandsaufnahme einer 300 jährigen Geschichte*, pp. 21–22. Opladen: Westdeutscher Verlag, 1986.

Muncy, Robyn. *Creating a Female Dominion in American Reform, 1890–1935.* New York: Oxford University Press, 1991.

Münsterberg, Emil. *Das amerikanische Armenwesen.* Leipzig: Duncker & Humblot, 1906.

Münsterberg, Hugo. *Die Amerikaner.* Berlin: E. S. Mittler und Sohn, 1904. Translated by Edwin B. Holt under the title *The Americans* (New York: McClure, Phillips, 1904).

Naumann, Gerlinde. *Minna Cauer: Eine Kämpferin für Frieden, Demokratie und Emanzipation.* Berlin: Buchverlag Der Morgen, 1988.

Newberry, Jo Vellacott. "Anti-War Suffragists." *History: The Journal of the Historical Association* 62 (October 1977): 411–25.

Nicolson, Harold. *Peacemaking 1919: Being Reminiscences of the Paris Peace Conference.* Boston: Houghton Mifflin, 1933.

Niggemann, Heinz. *Emanzipation zwischen Sozialismus und Feminismus: Die sozialdemokratische Frauenbewegung im Kaiserreich.* Wuppertal: Hammer, 1981.

———, ed. *Frauenemanzipation und Sozialdemokratie: Mit Beiträgen von Ottilie Baader, Lily Braun, Käthe Duncker, Clara Zetkin, Luise Zietz u.a.* Frankfurt: Fischer, 1981.

Nolan, Mary. *Social Democracy and Society: Working-Class Radicalism in Düsseldorf, 1890–1920.* Cambridge: Cambridge University Press, 1981.

———. *Visions of Modernity: American Business and the Modernization of Germany.* New York: Oxford University Press, 1994.

Norwood, Stephen H. *Labor's Flaming Youth: Telephone Operators and Worker Militancy, 1878–1923.* Urbana: University of Illinois Press, 1990.

Offen, Karen. "Defining Feminism: A Comparative Historical Approach." *Signs* 14 (1988): 119–57.

———. "Reflections on National Specificities in Continental European Feminisms." *U.C.G. Women's Studies Centre Review* (Galway, Eire) 3 (1995): 53–61.

Peterson, H. C., and Gilbert C. Fite. *Opponents of War, 1917–1918.* Madison: University of Wisconsin Press, 1957.

Peyser, Dora. "Alice Salomon: Ein Lebensbild." In Hans Muthesius, ed., *Alice Salomon: Die Begründerin des sozialen Berufs in Deutschland,* pp. 9–121. Cologne: Carl Heymanns, 1958.

Pickle, Linda Schelbitzki. *Contented Among Strangers: Rural German-Speaking Women and Their Families in the Nineteenth Century Midwest.* Urbana: University of Illinois Press, 1996.

Pierson, Ruth Roach, ed. *Women and Peace: Theoretical, Historical and Practical Perspectives.* London: Croom Helm, 1987.

Pierson, Stanley. *Marxist Intellectuals and the Working-Class Mentality in Germany, 1887–1912.* Cambridge, Mass.: Harvard University Press, 1993.

Pois, Anne Marie. "The Politics and Process of Organizing for Peace: The United States Section of the Women's International League for Peace and Freedom." Ph.D. dissertation, University of Colorado, 1988.

Pore, Renate. *A Conflict of Interest: Women in German Social Democracy, 1919–1933.* Westport, Conn.: Greenwood Press, 1981.

Quataert, Jean H. *Reluctant Feminists in German Social Democracy, 1885–1917.* Princeton, N.J.: Princeton University Press, 1979.

———. "A Source Analysis in German Women's History: Factory Inspectors' Reports and the Shaping of Working Class Lives, 1878–1914." *Journal of Central European History* 16 (1983): 99–121.

———. "Unequal Partners in an Uneasy Alliance: Women and the Working Class in

Imperial Germany." In Marilyn J. Boxer and Jean H. Quataert, eds., *Socialist Women: European Socialist Feminism in the Nineteenth and Early Twentieth Centuries*, pp. 112–45. New York: Elsevier North-Holland, 1978.

Randall, Mercedes M. *Improper Bostonian: Emily Greene Balch*. New York: Twayne, 1964.

——, ed. *Beyond Nationalism: The Social Thought of Emily Greene Balch*. New York: Twayne, 1972.

Read, James Morgan. *Atrocity Propaganda, 1914–1919*. New Haven, Conn.: Yale University Press, 1941.

Reagin, Nancy R. *A German Women's Movement: Class and Gender in Hanover, 1880–1933*. Chapel Hill: University of North Carolina Press, 1995.

Report of the International Congress of Women, Zurich, May 12 to 17, 1919. Geneva: Women's International League for Peace and Freedom, 1919.

Report of the Third International Congress of Women: Vienna, July 10 17, 1921. Geneva: Women's International League for Peace and Freedom, 1921.

Richebächer, Sabine. *Uns fehlt nur eine Kleinigkeit: Deutsche proletarische Frauenbewegung 1890–1914*. Frankfurt: Fischer Taschenbuchverlag, 1982.

Roerkohl, Anne. *Hungerblockade und Heimatfront: Die kommunale Lebensmittelversorgung in Westfalen während des Ersten Weltkrieges*. Stuttgart: Franz Steiner, 1991.

Rupp, Leila. "Constructing Internationalism: The Case of Transnational Women's Organizations, 1888–1945." *American Historical Review* 99 (1994): 1571–1600.

——. "Sexuality and Politics in the Early Twentieth Century: The Case of the International Women's Movement." *Feminist Studies* 23 (Fall 1997): 577–605.

——. *Worlds of Women: The Making of an International Women's Movement*. Princeton, N.J.: Princeton University Press, 1997.

Sachße, Carola. *Industrial Housewives: Women's Social Work in the Factories of Nazi Germany*. New York: Haworth, 1987.

Sachße, Christoph. *Mütterlichkeit als Beruf: Sozialarbeit, Sozialreform und Frauenbewegung, 1871–1929*. Frankfurt: Suhrkamp, 1986.

Salomon, Alice. *Charakter ist Schicksal: Lebenserinnerungen*. Basel: Beltz, 1983.

Salomon, Alice, et. al., eds. *Heimarbeit and Lohnfrage*. Jena: Gustav Fischer, 1909.

Sandmann-Bremme, Gabriele. *Die politische Rolle der Frau in Deutschland: Eine Untersuchung über den Einfluß der Frauen bei Wahlen und ihre Teilnahme in Partei und Parlament*. Göttingen: Vandenhoeck & Ruprecht, 1956.

Sarvasy, Wendy. "From Man and Philanthropic Service to Feminist Social Citizenship." *Social Politics* 1 (Fall 1994): 306–25.

Schirmacher, Käthe. *The Modern Women's Rights Movement: A Historical Survey*. Translated by Carl Conrad Eckardt. New York: Macmillan, 1912.

Schmitt, Sabine. " 'All These Forms of Women's Work Which Endanger Public Health and Public Welfare': Protective Labor Legislation for Women in Germany, 1878–1914." In Ulla Wikander, Alice Kessler-Harris, and Jane Lewis, eds., *Protecting Women: Labor Legislation in Europe, the United States and Australia, 1880–1920*, pp. 125–149. Urbana: University of Illinois Press, 1995.

——. *Der Arbeiterinnenschutz im deutschen Kaiserreich: Zur Konstruktion der schutzbedürftigen Arbeiterin*. Stuttgart: J. B. Metzler, 1995.

Schneider, Michael. *A Brief History of the German Trade Unions*. Bonn: Dietz, 1989.

Schnetzler, Barbara. *Die frühe amerikanische Frauenbewegung und ihre Kontakte mit Europa (1836–1869)*. Bern: Herbert Lang, 1971.

Schorske, Carl. *German Social Democracy, 1905–1917: The Development of the Great Schism*. New York: Russell & Russell, 1955.

Schröder, Hans-Jürgen. *Confrontation and Cooperation: Germany and the United States in the Era of World War I, 1900–1924.* Providence: Berg, 1993.

Schüler, Anja. "Die internationale Settlementbewegung: Interkulturelle Dimensionen städtischer Sozialarbeit in England, den Vereinigten Staaten von Amerika und Deutschland, 1884–1933." Master's thesis, Freie Universität Berlin, 1991.

Schulte, Regina. "The Sick Warrior's Sister: Nursing during the First World War." In Lynn Abrams and Elizabeth Harvey, eds., *Gender Relations in German History: Power, Agency and Experience from the Sixteenth to the Twentieth Century.* Durham: Duke University Press, 1997.

Schwabe, Klaus. "Die USA, Deutschland und der Ausgang des Ersten Weltkrieges." In Manfred Knapp, Werner Link, Hans-Jürgen Schröder, and Klaus Schwabe, eds., *Die USA und Deutschland, 1918–1975,* pp. 11–61. Munich: C. H. Beck, 1978.

———. *Woodrow Wilson, Revolutionary Germany, and Peacemaking, 1918–1919: Missionary Diplomacy and the Realities of Power.* Translated by Rita and Robert Kimber. Chapel Hill: University of North Carolina Press, 1985.

Scott, Anne Firor. *Natural Allies: Women's Associations in American History.* Urbana: University of Illinois Press, 1991.

Sewall, May Wright, ed. *The World's Congress of Representative Women.* Chicago: Rand McNally, 1894.

Sicherman, Barbara. *Alice Hamilton: A Life in Letters.* Cambridge, Mass.: Harvard University Press, 1984.

Simmel, Monika. "Alice Salomon: Vom Dienst der bürgerlichen Tochter am Volksganzen." In Christoph Sachße and Florian Tennstedt, eds., *Jahrbuch der Sozialarbeit,* pp. 369–402. Reinbek: Rowohlt, 1983.

Sklar, Kathryn Kish. *Florence Kelley and the Nation's Work: The Rise of Women's Political Culture.* New Haven, Conn.: Yale University Press, 1995.

———. "Hull House in the 1890s: A Community of Women Reformers." *Signs* 10 (1985): 658–77.

———. "Jane Addams's Peace Activism, 1914–1922: A Model for Women Today?" *Women's Studies Quarterly* 23 (Fall/Winter, 1995, Special Issue on Rethinking Women's Peace Studies): 32–47.

———. "Two Political Cultures in the Progressive Era: The National Consumers' League and the American Association for Labor Legislation." In Linda Kerber, Alice Kessler-Harris, and Kathryn Kish Sklar, eds., *U.S. History as Women's History,* pp. 35–62. Chapel Hill: University of North Carolina Press, 1995.

———. "Why Did Most Politically Active Women Oppose the ERA in the 1920s?" In Joan Hoff-Wilson, ed., *Rights of Passage: The Past and Future of the ERA,* pp. 25–38. Bloomington: Indiana University Press, 1987.

Skowronek, Stephen. *Building a New American State: The Expansion of National Administrative Capacities, 1877–1920.* Cambridge: Cambridge University Press, 1982.

Snowden, Mrs. Philip [Ethel]. *A Political Pilgrim in Europe.* London: Cassell, 1921.

Solomon, Barbara Miller. *In the Company of Educated Women: A History of Women and Higher Education in America.* New Haven, Conn.: Yale University Press, 1985.

Solomon, Hannah. *Fabric of My Life.* Chicago: Bloch Publishing Company, 1946.

Sperber, Jonathan. *The Kaiser's Voters: Electors and Elections in Imperial Germany.* New York: Cambridge University Press, 1997.

Stanton, Theodore. *The Woman Question in Europe.* New York: Putnam's, 1884.

Steenson, Gary P. *"Not One Man! Not One Penny!" German Social Democracy, 1863–1914.* Pittsburgh: University of Pittsburgh Press, 1981.

Steiner, Linda C. "The Women's Suffrage Press, 1850–1900: A Cultural Analysis." Ph.D. dissertation, University of Illinois Press, 1979.

Steinmetz, George. *Regulating the Social: The Welfare State and Local Politics in Imperial Germany.* Princeton, N.J.: Princeton University Press, 1993.

Steinson, Barbara J. "Sisters and Soldiers: American Women and the National Service Schools, 1916–1917." *The Historian: A Journal of History* 43 (February 1981): 225–39.

Stephenson, Jill. *Women in Nazi Society.* New York: Barnes & Noble, 1975.

Stoehr, Irene. "Housework and Motherhood: Debates and Policies in the Women's Movement in Imperial Germany and the Weimar Republic." In Gisela Bock and Pat Thane, eds., *Maternity and Gender Policies: Women and the Rise of the European Welfare States, 1880s–1950s,* pp. 213–55. New York: Routledge, 1991.

———. " 'Organisierte Mütterlichkeit': Zur Politik der deutschen Frauenbewegung um 1900." In Karin Hausen, ed., *Frauen suchen ihre Geschichte,* pp. 221–49. Munich: C. H. Beck, 1983.

Stromberg, Roland N. "La patrie en danger: Socialism and War in 1914." *The Midwest Quarterly* 18 (Spring 1977): 268–86.

Swanwick, Helena. *I Have Been Young.* London: Gollancz, 1935.

Szepansky, Gerda. *Frauen leisten Widerstand: 1933–1945.* Frankfurt: Fischer Taschenbuch, 1983.

Tennstedt, Florian, and Christoph Sachße. *Geschichte der Armenfürsorge in Deutschland: Vom Spätmittelalter bis zum Ersten Weltkrieg.* Stuttgart: W. Kohlhammer, 1980.

Terrell, Mary Church. *A Colored Woman in a White World.* Washington, D.C.: Ransdell, 1940; reprint, 1986.

Thönnessen, Werner. *The Emancipation of Women: The Rise and Decline of the Women's Movement in German Social Democracy, 1863–1933.* Frankfurt: Pluto Press, 1973.

Trask, David. *The American Expeditionary Force and Coalition Warmaking, 1917–1918.* Lawrence: University of Kansas Press, 1993.

Trommler, Frank, ed. *Amerika und die Deutschen: Bestandsaufnahme einer 300 jährigen Geschichte.* Opladen: Westdeutscher Verlag, 1986.

Twellmann-Schepp, Margrit. *Die deutsche Frauenbewegung im Spiegel repräsentativer Frauenzeitschriften: Ihre Anfänge und erste Entwicklung, 1843–1889.* Meisenheim a.G.: A. Hain, 1972.

Vellacott, Jo. "A Place for Pacifism and Transnationalism in Feminist Theory: The Early Work of the Women's International League for Peace and Freedom." *Women's History Review* 2 (1993): 23–56.

———. "Women, Peace and Internationalism, 1914–1920: 'Finding New Words and Creating New Methods.' " In Charles Chatfield and Peter Van Den Dungen, eds., *Peace Movements and Political Cultures,* pp. 106–24. Knoxville: University of Tennessee Press, 1988.

Vincent, Charles Paul. *The Politics of Hunger: The Allied Blockade of Germany, 1915–1919.* Athens: Ohio University Press, 1985.

von Ankum, Katharina, ed. *Women in the Metropolis: Gender and Modernity in Weimar Culture.* Berkeley: University of California Press, 1997.

von Bruch, Rüdiger, ed. *"Weder Kommunismus noch Kapitalismus": Bürgerliche Sozialreform in Deutschland vom Vormärz bis zur Ära Adenauer.* Munich: C. H. Beck, 1985.

von Liszt, Elsa. *Soziale Fürsorgetätigkeit in den Vereinigten Staaten.* Berlin: J. Guttenberg, 1910.

von Meding, Dorothee. *Mit dem Mut des Herzens: Die Frauen des 20. Juli.* Berlin: Siedler, 1992.

von Zahn-Harnack, Agnes. *Die Frauenbewegung: Geschichte, Probleme, Ziele.* Berlin: Deutsche Buchgemeinschaft, 1928.

Wall, Richard, and Jay Winter, eds. *The Upheaval of War: Family, Work and Welfare in Europe, 1914–1918.* Cambridge: Cambridge University Press, 1988.

Walworth, Arthur. *Wilson and His Peacemakers: American Diplomacy at the Paris Peace Conference, 1919.* New York: Norton, 1986.

Walzer, Anke. *Käthe Schirmacher: Eine deutsche Frauenrechtlerin auf dem Wege vom Liberalismus zum konservativen Nationalismus.* Pfaffenweiler: Centaurus Verlagsgesellschaft, 1991.

Weber, Marianne. *Max Weber: A Biography.* Translated and edited by Harry Zohn. New York: Wiley, 1975.

Weiland, Daniela, ed. *Geschichte der Frauenemanzipation in Deutschland und Österreich.* Düsseldorf: Econ, 1983.

Wenger, Beth. "Radical Politics in a Reactionary Age: The Unmaking of Rosika Schwimmer, 1914–1930." *Journal of Women's History* 2 (Fall 1990): 66–99.

White, Ronald C., Jr., and C. Howard Hopkins, *The Social Gospel: Religion and Reform in Changing America.* Philadelphia: Temple University Press, 1976.

Wickert, Christl. *Helene Stöcker, 1869–1943: Frauenrechtlerin, Sexualreformerin und Pazifistin: Eine Biographie.* Bonn: Dietz, 1991.

Wieler, Joachim. *Er-innerung eines zerstörten Lebensabends: Alice Salomon während der NS-Zeit (1933–1937) und im Exil (1937–1948).* Darmstadt: Lingbach, 1987.

Wikander, Ulla, Alice Kessler-Harris, and Jane Lewis. *Protecting Women: Labor Legislation in Europe, the United States, and Australia, 1880–1920.* Urbana: University of Illinois Press, 1995.

Williams, John. *The Other Battleground: The Home Fronts—Britain, France and Germany, 1914–18.* Chicago: Henry Regnery, 1972.

Wiltsher, Anne. *Most Dangerous Women: Feminist Peace Campaigners of the Great War.* London: Pandora, 1985.

Wobbe, Theresa. *Gleichheit und Differenz: Politische Strategien von Frauenrechtlerinnen um die Jahrhundertwende.* Frankfurt: Campus, 1989.

——. *Wahlverwandtschaften: Die Soziologie und die Frauen auf dem Weg zur Wissenschaft.* Frankfurt: Campus, 1997.

Zeller, Susanne. *Volksmütter-mit staatlicher Anerkennung: Frauen im Wohlfahrtswesen der zwanziger Jahre.* Düsseldorf: Schwann, 1987.

Index

The names of persons who appear in the Biographical Notes are printed below in boldface type. Bold page numbers refer to illustrations.

Hamilton, Alice, 28, 46, 59, 68, 71, 345–46
  delegate to Hague congress, 182
  delegate to Zurich congress, 232n
  travel in Germany, 245, 321–34
  writings of, 213, 218–26, 321–31
Hansson, Laura Mohr, 150n
Harden, Maximilian, 224n
Harding, Mabel, 183–89
Harnack, Adolf von, 223n
Harnack, Elisabet von, 28, 65, 66, 306, 308, 346
Harper, Ida Husted, 118n, 130
Heymann, Lida Gustava
  biographical information, 28, 346–47
  delegate to Hague congress, 47, 50, 54–55, 57, 204, 233, 235
  delegate to Zurich congress, 237, 241, 292
  in exile, 72–73, 334
  visit to United States, 294–95
  and Weimar Republic, 54–55
  and woman suffrage movement in Germany, 39, 207, 338
  writings of, 189–96
Die Hilfe (Help), 343
Hobhouse, Emily, 49, 193
Hoover, Herbert
  and British blockade of Germany, 56, 58
  and food relief after World War I, 245, 247, 255
Housewives' League, 186–87
Hull House, 17, 65
  financing of, 57n, 166
  programs of, 164–65
  reputation in Germany, 258
  residents of, 162–63
  and wage-earning women, 19, 98
  and WILPF summer school, 292–94, 297
  as a women's settlement, 17

Illinois Manufacturers' Association, 94n
immigrants. See social conditions: United States
imperialism, 192, 282–86
International Congress for Women's Work and Endeavors, 130–32, 338, 344
International Congress of Women for a Permanent Peace. See Women's Peace Congresses
International Conference for Disarmament, 271
International Conference of Socialist Women (ICSW), 45, 193, 195
International Council of Women (ICW), 26, 27, 118n, 169, 200, 350

and African American women, 13, 64–66
German members repressed by Nazi Party, 323
International Congress for Women's Work and Endeavor, 128, 130
response to Hague congress, 225
and Women's International League for Peace and Freedom (WILPF), 64
International Red Cross, 184–85, 266, 273, 339
  Patriotic Women's Association of the Red Cross, 40n, 185n
international relief efforts in Europe after World War I, 246, 272. See also American Friends Service Committee; Hoover, Herbert; International Red Cross; Quaker relief efforts in Europe
International Woman Suffrage Alliance (IWSA), 27, 86, 175, 205, 207, 261, 336, 351
  and rejection of pacifism, 45

Jacobs, Aletta, 191, 212, 219, 230, 241, 245–46, 270
Jagow, Gottlieb von, 221
Jewish women
  and anti-Semitism, 69
  as reformers in Germany, 66, 69
Jewish Women's League, 69
Jouve, Andree, 291
Jüdischer Frauenbund. See Jewish Women's League

Katholischer Frauenbund Deutschlands (KFD). See German Catholic Women's Federation
Kelley, Florence, 3, 60, 63, 202
  attacked by right-wing groups, 63
  biographical information, 12–22, 347
  delegate to Vienna congress, 267–74
  delegate to Zurich congress, 232n
  education of, 12, 14, 16
  employment of
    as factory inspector, 17, 90–95
    translation work of, 15, 18
  and Engels, 15, 18
  and gender-specific legislation, 21, 63, 103
  marriage, 15, 17, 28
  and National Consumers' League (NCL), 105
  organizer of Women's Joint Congressional Committee, 62
  and settlement movement, 17
  and socialism, 18

political culture (*continued*)
  United States
    class relations and, 32, 37
    effect of Red Scare. *See* Red Scare,
      United States
    internationalism. *See* Conference on the
      Cause and Cure of War;
      Women's International League
      for Peace and Freedom
      (WILPF); Women's Peace
      Congresses; women's peace
      movement; Women's Peace Party
    political parties
      Communist Party, 330n
      National Women's Party (NWP),
        62–63, 114
      Socialist Labor Party (U.S.), 15, 79,
        84
    right-wing groups, 63–65
      American Legion, 65
      Daughters of the American
        Revolution (DAR), 64–65, 292
      U.S. Department of War, 63–64
Post, Alice Thatcher, 232n, 240
Preussische Jahrbücher (Prussian Annals)
Progressive Liberal Party, 38
prostitution, 9, 84, 160
protective labor legislation
  Germany, 88–89, 120–23
    compulsory education laws, 122,
      162
    health insurance, 178
    hours legislation, 122
    workers' compensation, 122
  United States, 17–18, 81
    anti-child labor legislation, 19. *See also*
      National Child Labor Committee
    anti-sweatshop legislation, 109, 113
    anti-tenement house legislation, 19
    and civil service, 95, 158
    defeated in courts, 91, 113
    difficulties passing, 305
    hours legislation, 21, 91–93, 120, 122,
      157
      defeated in courts, 63
    gender-specific, 21, 103
    minimum wage laws, 7
    need for, 80, 95, 104–13, 122, 156

Quaker relief efforts in Europe after World
    War I, 245–46, 267, 273. *See also*
    American Friends Service
    Committee; Wood, Carolena
Queen Louise League, 323

racism
  in Germany, 275–79. *See also* Fichte
    Society
  international, 60–61
  in the United States, 29
Radic, Stepjan, 269n
Rankin, Jeanette, 232n
red scare, United States
  and intimidation of social justice
    feminists, 64n, 287
reform Darwinism, 11
Reichsjugendwohlfahrtsgesetz. See Federal Law
    for the Welfare of Youth
Reichstag, 132, 190, 194
  male suffrage and, 87
  women and, 85, 290, 312, 323
Reichsverband Deutscher
    Hausfrauenvereine (RDH). *See*
    National Federation of German
    Housewives' Associations
Rosenstock-Heussey, Eugen, 325n
Rotten, Elisabeth, 207, 246, 254, 350

Salomon, Alice, 4, 38, 188, 255, 338
  and anti-Semitism, 66–67
  biographical information, 350–51
  delegate to Zurich congress, 230n
  dissolves German Academy for Women's
    Social and Pedagogic Work,
    74
  education of, 32
  emigration to the United States, 29,
    73–74
  founder of Women's School for Social
    Work, 339
  and Hull House, 301
  impact of World War I on career, 43, 183,
    227
  and International Council of Women
    (ICW), 27–28, **126**
  role in international women's reform
    organizations, 41
  and socialism, 38, 40–41
  visit to United States, 64–66, 159–67,
    300–301
  and Women's School for Social Work,
    218
  writings of, 62, 159–75, 301–6, 316–18
Schepel, Annette Hamminck, 26
Schepeler-Lette, Anna, 25
Schirmacher, Käthe, 24, 26, 39, 160, 351
  writings of, 140–47
Schmidt, Auguste, 336
Schneiderman, Rose, 232n

Stritt, Marie, 218, 338
Südekum, Albert, 220, 348
suffrage, male, 27, 32, 87
suffrage, female. *See* Woman suffrage
    movement
Survey, 48, 59–60, 62, 66, 71, 74, 202, 213,
    218, 227, 229, 245, 313
Swanwick, Helena, 55–57, 241n
Swartz, Maud O'Farrell, 270n
Swift, Mary Wood, 118n

Taylor, Harriet, 150n
Terrell, Mary Church, 12–13, 22, 61, 65–66,
    114–19, 130, 283, 352–53
    delegate to Zurich congress, 232n
    response to racist propaganda, 279–82
Thomas, M. Carey, 130
transatlantic dialogue
    international organizations. *See*
        International Council of
        Women; International Woman
        Suffrage Alliance; Women's
        International League for Peace
        and Freedom
    opportunities for cultural exchange,
        23
        Chicago World's Fair, 24, 26, 130, 131,
            139
        Columbian Exposition, Chicago, 26,
            139n, 140–47
        higher education, 11–12
        Philadelphia Centennial Exhibition, 25
    participants
        African-American women, 28
        Jewish women, 28–29, 40
        marital status, 28
        social origins, 3
Treaty of Versailles, 245, 274–75
    German response to, 331
        impact on German social conditions,
            265
    U.S. refusal to ratify, 259

Union of Democratic Control, 222n

Vaterländische Frauenvereine. *See*
    International Red Cross:
    Patriotic Women's Association of
    the Red Cross
Verband Fortschrittlicher Frauenvereine. *See*
    Association of Progressive
    Women's Clubs
Verein Frauenwohl. *See* Society for Woman's
    Welfare
Verein für Jugendschutz. *See* Association for
    the Protection of Juveniles

Verein für Sozialpolitik. *See* Association for
    Social Policy
Vereinsgesetze (association laws), 33–34, 36,
    90
Verein zur Vertretung der Interessen der
    Arbeiterinnen. *See* Association to
    Promote the Interests of
    Working Women
Versailles, Treaty of. *See* Treaty of
    Versailles
Villard, Fanny Garrison, 270n, 288–90
Volkswohl (People's Weal), 128
Volkszeitung (People's Paper), 79, 84

wage-earning women
    Germany
        during World War I, 186–88
    United States. *See* Century Working
        Women's Guild; Women's Trade
        Union League; Working
        Women's Society, New York
Wald, Lillian, 163n, 232n
Weimar coalition, 345
Weimar Republic, 59–66, 261
    divisions among women in, 62
    economic crises of, 62, 207, 262
    social welfare policies of, 66
    and women, 315
Willard, Emma, 134n
Wilson, Woodrow, 51–52
Wolff, Frida, 195
Woman's Christian Temperance Union
    (WCTU), 8–9, 36, 64, 137–
    38
    and social welfare legislation, 36–37
Woman Citizen, 183–84
Woman's Committee for a Permanent
    Peace. *See* women's peace
    congresses
Woman's Journal, 80, 344
Woman's League of Canada, 200
Woman's League of the German Peace
    Society, 199
Woman's Tribune, 81
woman suffrage movement
    Austria, 268, 272
    Belgium. *See* La Fontaine, Léonie
    Denmark, 230
    England, 84, 241n
    Germany, 34, 39, 86, 241
        class and, 34, 40, 86
        organizations
            German Association for Woman
            Suffrage (Deutscher Verband für
            Frauenstimmrecht), 9, 39, 198,
            336, 341, 347–48

woman suffrage movement (*continued*)
>German Federation for Woman Suffrage (Deutscher Vereinigung für Frauenstimmrecht), 39, 218, 337
>German Union for Woman Suffrage (Deutscher Bund für Frauenstimmrecht), 40, 338
>passage of suffrage legislation, 35, 59, 262, 314
>and sick funds, 178n
>SPD and, 87
>and wage-earning women, 88
>writings about, 183–89

Holland, 205

International. *See* International Woman Suffrage Alliance (IWSA)

United States, 26n, 79, 144, 152, 240n, 261. *See also* American Woman Suffrage Association (AWSA), National American Woman Suffrage Association (NAWSA), National Woman Suffrage Association (NWSA)
>goals of, 80
>and Lyceum Bureau, 152
>and motherhood, 79
>and newspapers, 79. *See also New Era; Woman Citizen; Woman's Journal; Woman's Tribune*
>passage of suffrage legislation 1919, 63
>and wage-earning women, 79

Women's International Labor Congress, 270. *See also* Swartz, Maud O'Farrell

Women's International League for Peace and Freedom (WILPF), 27, 65
>and African-American women, 29
>and British blockade of Germany, 56
>delivery of peace message to world leaders, 53
>exiled German feminists and, 73
>first meeting of, 267–74
>German members and aftermath of World War I, 54
>and human rights, 283–86
>and League of Nations, 274, 285
>members of, 46
>principles of, 46, 60
>response to racist propaganda, 279
>support of German social justice feminists after World War I, 287, 292
>and racial conflict, 60–61
>resignation of American branch from the ICW, 64
>vilified by U.S. Department of War, 64

Women's Joint Congressional Committee (WJCC), 62

women's movement
>Austria, 207. *See also* Frölich, Bertha; Golinska, Darynska; Kulka, Leopoldine; Misar, Olga
>Belgium, 209n. *See also* La Fontaine, Léonie
>Denmark. *See* Daugaard, Thora
>England, 204
>>reaction to blockade of Germany, 240
>France, 232n. *See* Duchène, Gabrielle Laforcade; Siegfried, Julie Paux
>>declaration of French delegates to Hague congress, 200, 208n, 209
>Germany, 196
>>appeals for aid after World War I, 227–28
>>goals of, 189
>>impact of Nazi Party on, 328
>>nineteenth-century, 140
>>role during World War I, 261–62
>>and wage-earning women, 264–65
>Hungary, 207. *See also* Glücklich, Vilma; Pógany, Paula; Zipernowsky, Anna
>Sweden. *See* Lindhagen, Anna
>United States
>>and African-American women, 114–19
>>cross-class alliances, 97–98, 104, 110, 120. *See also* Century Working Women's Guild
>>cross-race alliances, 118
>>nineteenth-century, 136

Women's National Service League, 185n

Women's Peace Congresses, 45, 191
>Hague congress of 1915, 43, 47–48, 51–53, 191–96, 203–12
>>delivery of peace message to world leaders, 53, 212
>>and Fourteen Points, 51–52
>>German delegates to, 47
>>goals of, 223
>>opposition of women's groups to, 43
>>participation of wage-earning women, 47
>>response of BDF to, 191–202
>>resolutions of, 51, 211–17
>>role of Jane Addams, 48
>>U.S. delegates to, 46
>origins in Hague congress of 1899, 43n
>as precursors to WILPF, 237, 237n
>Vienna congress of 1921, 267–74
>>and human rights, 274
>>and racial justice, 268
>>resolutions of, 270–71, 273, 282–84